MW00528772

A Community Transplanted

Social Demography

Series Editors
Doris P. Slesinger
James A. Sweet
Karl E. Taeuber
Center for Demography and Ecology
University of Wisconsin-Madison

A
Community
Transplanted

*The Trans-Atlantic Experience
of a Swedish Immigrant Settlement
in the Upper Middle West,
1835–1915*

ROBERT C. OSTERGREN

The University of Wisconsin Press

The University of Wisconsin Press
114 North Murray Street
Madison, Wisconsin 53715

The University of Wisconsin Press, Ltd.
1 Gower Street
London WC1E 6HA, England

Copyright © 1988
The Board of Regents of the University of Wisconsin System
All rights reserved

Printed in the United States of America

5   4   3   2   1

Library of Congress Cataloging-in-Publication Data

Ostergren, Robert Clifford
A community transplanted: the trans-Atlantic experience of a
Swedish immigrant settlement in the Upper Middle West, 1835-1915
Robert C. Ostergren.
416pp..   cm.—(Social demography)
Revision of thesis.
Bibliography: pp. 365-391.
Includes index.
ISBN 0-299-11320-5   ISBN 0-299-11324-8 (pbk.)
1. Isanti County (Minn.)—Emigration and immigration.
2. Rättvik (Sweden)—Emigration and immigration.
3. Swedes—Minnesota—Isanti County.
4. Swedish Americans—Minnesota—Isanti County.
I. Title. II. Series.
JV6749.I83088   1988   88-211
325′.2485′097766—dc19   CIP

Contents

v

Illustrations

Figures

Plates

Tables

xi

Preface

AN APPROACH TO the study of the American immigrant experience that
has only begun to pay dividends in recent years is the reconstruction of
trans-Atlantic chain migrations. The idea behind this approach is to
trace a migrant population from its source area in Europe to the place or
places where it settled in America as a means of appreciating the total-
ity of the immigrant experience. The approach has two major benefits.
By paying detailed attention to the changing relationship between
migrant households and their immediate milieu at each stage, it sets the
migrant experience in spatial and temporal contexts that were most
meaningful to the actual participants. In other words, it allows us to
view the migrant experience from within rather than from without. Sec-
ondly, it breaks away from the long-standing tendency to view emigration and immigration as separate phenomena set within particular
national contexts. Scholars have often been overly preoccupied with the
effects of trans-Atlantic migration on sending or receiving societies,
when in fact it may also be viewed as an important link between changing conditions on both sides of the ocean.

While the idea for such studies has been around for a long time, relatively few have been completed, mainly because it is such a formidable
task to assemble the kind of individual data necessary to support longitudinal study of significant numbers of migrants over such extended
dimensions of space and time in both Europe and America. In addition,
the fact that emigrants from particular European source areas often
dispersed quickly in America tends to compound the data problem and
to make it all the more difficult to draw comparisons between the situations in which emigrants found themselves before and after migration.
For this reason, most attempts at this kind of study have been based
on chain migrations that took large numbers of people from small districts and placed them, at least for a time, in homogeneous immigrant
settlements.

This study is intended as a contribution to what appears to be a small
but growing genre of trans-Atlantic chain migration studies. The study
first took form in the middle 1970s as a dissertation. Over the years,

however, the early corpus of material has been systematically enlarged. "Attics, basements, new wings and additions" have expanded the original structure, as new lines of inquiry and new source materials have presented themselves and been pursued. In all, the present study represents roughly a decade's research. The investment has been rewarding in innumerable ways, but there has been one benefit that deserves special mention here. This is the intimate acquaintance I have made through the historical record with the more than one hundred migrants and migrant families that left their homes in the Swedish parish of Rättvik to seek a new life on the raw frontiers of Isanti County, Minnesota and Clay County, South Dakota. Although much of the data that I collected on these people eventually found their way into computer files, they were originally collected as bundles of index cards and loose pages stapled together under the name of each migrant household. Poring over these notes yielded many insights into the lives of these people, as well as a profound sense that I had come to know them all intimately. I can think of no better thing than to dedicate this book to them.

I am indebted to a great many individuals and institutions who have helped me along the way. In Sweden I owe a special debt of gratitude to Margareta Hedblom of Leksand, who arranged many valuable contacts for me in the Siljan district of Upper Dalarna and gave so much of her own time in support of my project. I am similarly indebted to Mats Peres of Rättvik's Övre Gärdsjö village, for his interest and assistance, and to Christer Bergin of Boda for his expert help in obtaining old photographs. I am also grateful to Dalarnas Museum in Falun for granting me permission to use photographs from the museum's excellent photo archive. My research in Isanti County would have suffered incalculably were it not for the assistance of Marilyn McGriff, who so ably directs the Isanti County Historical Society. I am grateful to her for her advice and unflagging interest in my project and to the Society for the unfettered use of its archival and photo collections. A special thanks also goes to Randolph Johnson, who heads the archive committee of the Cambridge Lutheran Church. His enthusiasm has always been an inspiration.

In crafting the many maps and graphs included in this book, the design expertise of David DiBiase of the University of Wisconsin Cartographic Laboratory was invaluable. Earlier versions of some of the maps and graphs were published elsewhere. The maps of midwestern settlement patterns in Chapter 1 (Figures 1.1 through 1.6) are adaptations of maps first published in my article, "Geographic Perspectives on the History of Settlement in the Upper Middle West," *Upper Midwest History* 1 (1981): 27–39, copyright 1981 by the University of Minnesota.

Figures 4.4–4.7 appeared in "Kinship Networks and Migration: A Nineteenth Century Swedish Example," *Social Science History* 6 (1982): 292–320, copyright 1982 by the Social Science History Association. Figures 7.4 and 7.5 were published in "Land and Family in Rural Immigrant Communities," *Annals of the Association of American Geographers* 71 (1981): 400–11, copyright 1981 by the Association of American Geographers.

Finally, I wish to thank John Rice, Kathleen Neils Conzen, and Harald Runblom for their insightful comments on the original manuscript. I am also most grateful to the American-Scandinavian Foundation, the Fulbright Hays Committee, and the Graduate School of the University of Wisconsin-Madison for the financial support they have rendered to various phases of this project. And I would be remiss were I not to express my appreciation to my wife, Carol, for her patience and understanding.

A Community Transplanted

1
Introduction

Immigration, Community, and the Agricultural Settlement of the Upper Middle West

ON A WARM midsummer day in 1880, a Minnesota farmer of Swedish origin, known as Hans Ersson Dahlsten, paused in his labors. He gazed on his holdings with an air of satisfaction. Hans Ersson had many reasons to be proud. The 120 acres of brush prairie he had homesteaded fourteen years earlier had been transformed into a neat and prosperous farm. Indeed, it ranked among the best in Athens township. Just the other day, when the census taker had paid a visit, Hans Ersson had been able to report a farm value of $800. A fine new house with a number of store-bought furnishings now stood where the first rustic shelter had been. Outbuildings scattered about the farmyard housed over $100 worth of implements, five horses, eight cows, three pigs, and poultry. The surplus production of this farm had brought him over $350 the previous year, more cash than he had ever earned before and further evidence of his prosperity. He knew, of course, that one should be wary of feeling too smug, for the Lord both gives and takes, but thankfully good fortune had smiled upon him for the most part during his years in America.

It had not come without hard work. The first years had been difficult, especially the first desolate winter. Much time had been lost away from home working in timber camps and foraging for food. Although these activities had kept the family clothed and fed, they left little time to improve the farm. But Hans Ersson and his sons had eventually cleared and tilled fifty acres, a figure that almost no one in the district could match. The twenty-five acres planted in wheat were looking good after a moist spring. Two other fields were devoted to corn and oats. There was no longer any need to work in the camps or forage. Instead, Hans Ersson had plans to clear more land next year and possibly purchase an additional forty acres so that his oldest son, Anders, would have land to support a new wife and family.

3

Now that he was in a reflective mood, Hans Ersson began to think about the momentous events that led to his present situation, not the least of which was the decision to emigrate from Sweden. That had been a difficult and exhilarating decision. Should he pursue an uncertain but, from all reports, promising future in America, or stay in the familiar, secure place where he was born and had spent the first forty years of his life? It was hard to turn away from the old parish, from friends and neighbors, from familiar sights and sounds, from the land he had worked for so many years to support his growing family. Yet he chose America. In part it was a matter of impulse; a fear of being left behind by the events that swirled about him in his home parish during the mid-1860s. A sober assessment of his prospects at home may have tipped the balance. There were undoubtedly other things as well. Somehow he and many others made the decision to leave in 1866 and started out on an adventure that had surely changed their lives.

What were his prospects in the old country when that fateful decision was made? He was born in 1827 on a farm in the village of Övre Gärdsjö in the parish of Rättvik. The name of the farm was "Perols." Back then he was known as Perols Hans Ersson. The name Dahlsten was something he acquired in America. The old farm was not one of the larger farms in the parish. It was relatively poor, although few farms in his home district would have been called rich. The Perols farm consisted of twenty-three *kappland* of arable and fourteen and one-half *kappland* of meadow—about three and one-half acres in America, a mere fraction of what Hans Ersson possessed now. Moreover, the farm was difficult to work efficiently. Even after the land reform of the 1830s, the arable was scattered over half a dozen locations around the village; some of them scarcely large enough to work.

By the time Hans Ersson was twenty years old and beginning to consider his prospects seriously, the Perols farm was supporting no fewer than twelve people. There were his father, a widower who had retired as the active head of the household; his two married brothers, their wives, and six children; and himself. At the time of his father's retirement, the farm had been divided between his two older brothers, both already married. While Hans Ersson received some compensation in this arrangement and had every right to remain on the farm with his brothers and their families, his chance of acquiring any appreciable portion of the farm seemed slim.

His outlook brightened measurably, however, when he married Björ Lisbet Carlsdotter late in the summer of 1850 and moved to the nearby village of Blecket to take up residence in her father's household. Björ, the ancestral farm of her family, was somewhat larger than his own. It had also been divided, as was the custom in the parish. The two parts were controlled by Lisbet's father and his brother and together supported sixteen people. Yet the marriage was advantageous because Lisbet's father was near retirement. Lisbet was the fourth of five daughters, but the first to marry. As a consequence, Hans Ersson was received on the farm as the *måg*, the son-in-law who would take control after the *head of the household retired. Lisbet's two brothers were young teenagers at that time and could play no immediate role in the transfer of property. Nor did her four sisters pose any immediate problem. In fact, they all proved to be marriageable and were removed from the picture, one by one, as they left to join spouses in neighboring villages.*

By the end of the 1850s, Lisbet's aged father stepped aside for Hans Ersson, who found himself in control of one-half of the farm, the other half belonging to Lisbet's uncle. While this outcome seemed better than could be hoped for, it was not without liabilities. There was the accumulated debt of marrying off Lisbet's four sisters and an obligation to care for Lisbet's father for the rest of his days. There was also a growing family to support. Lisbet had already borne him three sons who someday would require an inheritance of their own. The possibility of providing his children with land was further complicated by the fact that Hans Ersson was obligated to compensate Lisbet's two younger brothers, then in their twenties, who were beginning to think about their own futures. Yes, during the long winter of 1865–66, when he assessed his prospects at home against those of emigrating, the seemingly insoluble nature of the difficulties he faced ultimately persuaded Hans Ersson to take the chance.

But it was more than that. It was also the excitement that the notion of emigrating had raised in the parish. Everyone was talking about it. On Sundays after church, people had stood about in the churchyard and exchanged the latest news about America. Did you know that good land in America could be had for almost nothing? Had you heard that the first year's grain crop in America could make a poor farmer rich? There were still but a handful who had actually emigrated from Rättvik in 1865, but it was said that in the parishes to the north a great many had already been seized by "America fever" and emigrated. Now others from parishes all around were preparing to join them. It seemed unthinkable at first, but one continued to hear such remarkably good things about the new lands, there for the taking in a place called Minnesota. Much of the news came in letters from those who had gone, which gave it special credence. Excitement and speculation alone are not enough to send one packing. But when such things are combined with a feeling of camaraderie, that is when one resolves with family, friends, and neighbors to brave the unknown together; that is when one is carried far beyond the point one would ever go in a more reserved atmosphere.

As it turned out, Hans Ersson's decision to go to America was not made alone. His family was just one of sixteen Rättvik families that elected to emigrate together the following spring. After months of feverish preparation, Hans Ersson and his family set out with the other six families that were leaving their homes in the Gärdsjö district of Rättvik parish. It was the seventh of June, 1866. Together they proceeded down to the familiar parish church which stood so majestically on the shore of Lake Siljan. They had chosen the church grounds as the gathering place for everyone from the parish who was planning to emigrate, so that they might travel together. Several emigrant families from some of the lakeshore villages were waiting for them when they arrived, but they also had to wait a few days while families from the distant "high villages" around Boda made their way down to the lake.

There were few strangers among the Gärdsjö contingent of emigrants gathered on the church grounds. Hans Ersson had been joined in his decision to leave by Lisbet's two younger brothers. This group departure left the way open for a reunification of the farm in the hands of Lisbet's uncle. There would now be fewer demands on the meagre resources of that ancestral farm. Also joining the emigrant caravan was the family of Lisbet's sister Karin. They, too, were leaving a difficult situation in which the growing families of three married siblings had been eking an existence from the resources of a single impoverished farm. And then there was Hans Ersson's eldest brother, Erik, who had decided to follow Hans Ersson's lead and emigrate with his family. The departure of the two brothers left the Perols estate in the sole possession of the second brother, Anders Ersson. Kinship of a lesser order linked Hans Ersson with the other families in the group as well. Time had created elaborate patterns of kinship in the Gärdsjö district, from which few farm households were excluded. While the departure was in many ways a sad affair, the size and familiarity of the departing group helped buoy spirits as they set off on the long trek down to the coast and the voyage to the New World. Even as he stood in his field in far away Isanti County, Minnesota, Hans Ersson could still picture the scene of departure in front of the imposing structure of the old parish church. The image always played on his emotions, whenever he dwelt on it.

The journey to America had been long and tedious, filled with uncertainty. Despite the detailed instructions and cautionary advice the emigrant party had received from a Boda man who had made the trip two years earlier, no one could anticipate all of the situations that might arise in making such a long journey. The trip was far more arduous and took more time than anyone had anticipated. The heavy chests and packs of clothing, mattresses, kitchen utensils, tools, and other articles with which they set out proved too great a burden; many items had to be sold or discarded along the way. They traveled by foot and wagon to Arvika and by train to Christiania (Oslo), where they were forced to wait impatiently for three days before a steamer was ready to carry them across the North Sea to Hull, England. From there they traveled by train to Liverpool, where they encountered a maddening week-long delay waiting for the steamer that would take them to America.

The worst was yet to come, however. The trans-Atlantic crossing took a full two weeks, much of the time on rough seas. No one was prepared for the seasickness, nor was anyone prepared for the daily fare of rice and nearly inedible ship's bread available to those who felt well enough to eat. Everyone lost weight and weakened as the days passed. They could think only of getting off the ship. Eventually they reached New York City and disembarked at Castle Garden, where once again delays seemed interminable. Much to their dismay, the authorities confiscated and burned the mattresses they had carried all the way from home.

The last long leg of the journey took them by train from New York to Chicago, where they were met by confidence men eager to sell them tickets and advice on how to reach locations in the Midwest where they could obtain land. After much indecision, they purchased railroad tickets to LaCrosse, Wisconsin and steamboat tickets from LaCrosse to St. Paul, Minnesota from a friendly fellow Swede who presented himself as a land agent. On arrival in St. Paul they were non-plussed to find the same agent waiting for them, no longer a friend; he had seized their baggage and threatened to keep it until they paid him more money. Not knowing what else to do, they met his demands, fearing that they had no rights to do otherwise.

Hans Ersson was sure he would never want to undertake such a journey again. Nonetheless, they had made it safely and Hans Ersson found the bad memories faded after fourteen years. Now as he reflected on the journey, his thoughts passed impatiently to the more vivid memories of the final days in late summer when the party reached its destination at last. Those final days were filled with anticipation and excitement. After crossing the sea and half a continent, they found themselves walking the streets of the bustling Mississippi River town of St. Paul. The town was filled with a great many immigrant parties intent on taking land in the new Minnesota settlement districts, which lay some distance to the north and west of St. Paul. Their own destination was to the north, where Swedish immigrants were known to have established settlements in the St. Croix and Rum River valleys and where their contact, the man from Boda, had promised to meet them.

After several day's difficult journey, much of it through only sparsely settled territory, they reached a rolling and heavily forested area near a great bend in the sluggish Rum River. The immediate area had been occupied not more than two years earlier by Swedish immigrants, many of whom were from two neighboring parishes in their own province of Dalarna. The district had been organized for some time into a county with the strange-sounding Indian name of "Isanti." It was largely wild and unsettled, but it had been surveyed and was open to homesteading. True to his word, Hans Bäcklin, the man from Boda, was there to meet them. He had anticipated their arrival by arranging for them to settle in among their countrymen until they could select land and build homes for themselves. With a thin smile, Hans Ersson remembered what a relief it had been to be among familiar folk once again.

The next few weeks were spent exploring the district with a view to selecting the best possible land on which to file a homestead. On this there was much discussion and not much agreement. In the end, the immigrant party had split into three. The families from the high villages around Boda chose land near the farm of Hans Bäcklin, who, as a former resident of Boda, was particularly well known to them. A second group of families selected sites several miles to the west, along the narrow and winding course of the upper Rum. These were all families who hailed from the lakeshore villages of a district known as "Västbygge." Hans Ersson and his family were part of the third group, those who *came from the villages of the Gärdsjö district. This group moved downstream and to the south, passing through a settlement established by immigrants from the north Swedish coastal provinces of Hälsingland and Medelpad, and eventually laying claim to a good-sized brush prairie that stood roughly in the center of what would become known as Athens township.*

The fact that the emigrant party had split along the lines of traditional regional groups in the old parish was no surprise; folk from different parts of the parish had always done things their own special ways and probably always would. But there was also an advantage to their separation. Given the intention expressed by nearly everyone in the party to encourage as many friends and relatives as possible to join them here, it seemed only prudent that the party should disperse to separate settlement areas to allow plenty of space for the new arrivals.

And indeed, there was no lack of new arrivals. A good number of letters were sent home that first fall and by mid-summer of the next year word reached the settlers that new emigrant parties were forming back in the old parish. Hans Ersson's married nephew was among the party that arrived in the fall of 1867. Throughout the late sixties and early seventies, every fall was marked by the arrival of a new emigrant party from home. They brought stories of poor harvests and hard times at home and always the promise of more new arrivals yet to come. Before long all three of the areas colonized by the original party were filling with settlers. In many ways their new world began to sound and feel like home, even if it did not look like home. So many had come from Hans Ersson's native province that some had begun to call Isanti County "the Dalarna of America." Everywhere there were acquaintances and kin; the familiar dialect rang through the forest as folk gathered to help a newcomer get started; and on Sundays as well as all of the old holidays, people made their way to the new church to worship, to sing the old songs, and to visit after services as had always been the custom at home.

Without a doubt, the church was the center and the pride of the new community. It had been founded prior to the arrival of Hans Ersson's party by some of the early Swedish settlers, but the congregation was soon reorganized to include as charter members the growing number of parishioners who came from Rättvik. It was not long before the Rättvik people constituted an overwhelming majority, and the organizational structure of the new parish began to take on many of the features of the old one. In particular, the administrative apparatus of the old parish was carefully transferred to the new, including the old system of record keeping. The new parish was divided into four administrative districts, a common arrangement in Dalarna, with one for each of the three areas settled by the emigrants from Rättvik and a fourth for an area settled by people of more mixed origins. A parish council comprised of elected representatives from each of the districts was charged with the responsibility of overseeing the life of the community.

Hans Ersson was especially proud of his own service on the council. He had

taken an active role in most of the important decisions that shaped their commu-
nity, including the recent decision to establish a daughter church near his home
in Athens township. The new church would serve him and his neighbors more
efficiently than the mother church, which was more than nine miles away. From
the difficult decision to split the congregation, Hans Ersson understood, more
than ever before, the emotional value of the tightly knit community built by
people who had crossed the sea together. It made one feel secure in a new and
unfriendly world; in important ways it made life not so different from that he
had known in another place. Many of his neighbors were understandably fearful
of any action that might change or weaken the community. He had been lucky in
coming to America. His prospects had been much improved for having made the
move, but it was not his accomplishment alone. He must never forget that he had
done it in the company of others and by the grace of God.

Hans Errson Dahlsten awoke suddenly from his reverie. The sun had moved
a considerable distance across the sky. It was getting late. Somewhat guiltily he
realized that his daydream had gone on far longer than he intended and he re-
turned to his labors with a shrug, but also with the assurance of a man who felt at
peace with himself and his world.

Chain Migration and Immigrant Community Formation on the Agricultural Frontiers of the Upper Middle West

Nothing in the historical record tells us that Hans Ersson Dahlsten ever
spent part of a midsummer day in 1880 daydreaming in his fields. But he
did exist, and the events recounted in this fictitious day dream are all
real enough.[1] Indeed, variations on Dahlsten's reflections could well
have crossed the minds of hundreds of thousands of immigrant farmers
who settled the agricultural frontiers of the American Upper Middle
West between roughly 1830 and 1890. Hans Ersson Dahlsten's decision
to uproot himself and his family and travel to a new land in order to
better his "prospects" was a common one in many parts of northwestern Europe during those decades. Equally commonplace was the
manner in which he did it—following the advice of others who had gone
before; traveling in the company of others whom he knew and trusted;
encouraging others to follow him and build a society that offered new
opportunity and, at the same time, a measure of continuity with the
past.

The magnetic attraction for Dahlsten and many other emigrants
was a vast region of enormous agricultural potential. Its frontiers first
opened in the expansive decades before the Civil War and continued to
open until the limits of settlement were reached in the 1890s. Variously
known as the "Northwest" and the "Upper Middle West," the region

stretched westward and northwestward from the Grand Prairie of north central Illinois and the oak openings of southern Wisconsin to the Platte River valley of Nebraska and the line of the Missouri in the central Dakotas.[2] The territories and states that made up the region were, in large measure, peopled by immigrant settlers. That is not to say that the traditional opening of frontiers by the restless, westward-moving American was not important here; they shaped the region. They were the first on the land; the organizers of townships, towns and counties; the early entrepreneurs and political elite. But it was the immigrant settlers, most from the countries of northwestern Europe, who filled in the new frontiers and gave the region its lasting character.[3] By the end of the nineteenth century, no commonly recognized American region could claim such a high proportion of foreign born settled on the land as the Upper Middle West.

Although one often thinks of midwestern landscapes as being monotonous, there is a remarkable physical diversity within this region. Those who settled its successive frontiers encountered a whole gamut of landscapes, which together presented a wide range of environmental choice and opportunity (Figure 1.1).[4] At the time of settlement there was a broad base of hardwood forest and prairie openings in the southeast (Illinois, Iowa, and Southern Wisconsin), which extended in a north-westward-bearing arc along the Mississippi valley into Minnesota. This forest–prairie ecotone, with its rich soils and ready supply of wood and water, offered distinct advantages to the earliest settlers. To the north-east lay immense coniferous and mixed-hardwood forests, relatively inhospitable to agricultural settlement but rich in resources. To the south and west lay the vast expanse of humid, long-grass prairie, des-tined to become a cornucopia of midwestern agricultural wealth. And beyond that, the great semi-arid short-grass plains, whose changing and sometimes uncertain conditions would both reward and discourage agricultural settlement.

The advance of settlement across this region was not steady and relentless as one might be given to imagine. On the contrary, the advance was quite fitful, varying in efficiency and direction over time. In fact, the frontier was actually known to retreat at times. The advance of settlement appears to have been strongly influenced by physical fea-tures (Figures 1.2 and 1.3).[5] One can clearly see, for example, that the frontier made its deepest penetrations into new territory along river valleys. This was the case both before the Civil War and after, when the railroad might have freed the frontier from the influence of the drainage system. Settlement also advanced most rapidly, during the early dec-

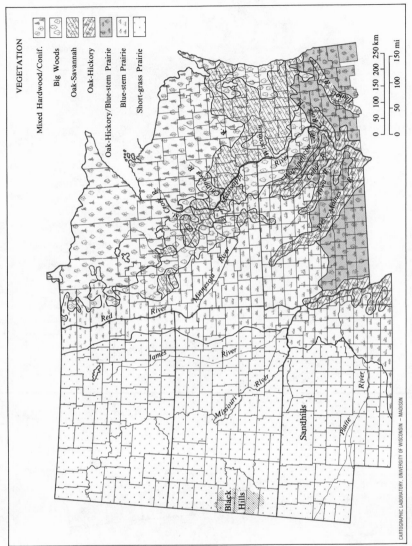

VEGETATION

Mixed Hardwood/Conif.

Big Woods

Oak-Savannah

Oak-Hickory

Oak-Hickory/Blue-stem Prairie

Blue-stem Prairie

Short-grass Prairie

CARTOGRAPHIC LABORATORY, UNIVERSITY OF WISCONSIN – MADISON

Figure 1.1 Drainage and Original Vegetation in the Upper Middle West

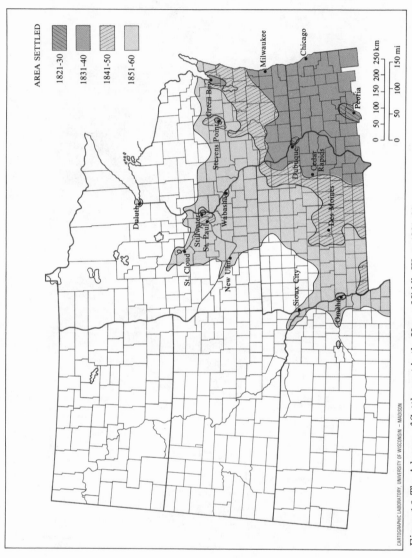

AREA SETTLED

- 1821-30
- 1831-40
- 1841-50
- 1851-60

CARTOGRAPHIC LABORATORY UNIVERSITY OF WISCONSIN – MADISON

Figure 1.2 The Advance of Settlement in the Upper Middle West, 1821–60

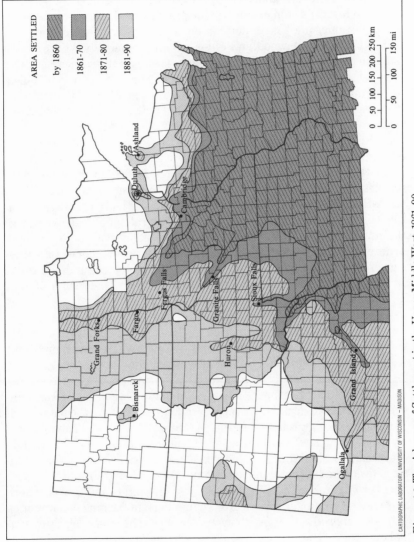

AREA SETTLED

- by 1860
- 1861-70
- 1871-80
- 1881-90

Ashland
Duluth
Cambridge
Fergus Falls
Grand Forks
Fargo
Granite Falls
Sioux Falls
Huron
Bismarck
Grand Island
Ogallala

0 50 100 150 200 250 km
0 50 100 150 mi

CARTOGRAPHIC LABORATORY, UNIVERSITY OF WISCONSIN – MADISON

Figure 1.3 The Advance of Settlement in the Upper Middle West, 1861-90

13

ades, across the oak and hickory savannahs of northern Illinois and southern Iowa and along the arc of the prairie–forest ecotone in Wisconsin and Minnesota. The American pioneers who led the advance preferred the familiar woodland environment, especially where it was found in combination with brushy openings and small prairies.[6] Settlers were reluctant at first to move out on the open prairie. A striking indication of this is the horseshoe-shaped configuration of the 1860 settlement frontier in southwestern Minnesota and northwestern Iowa, which left the broad zone of open and wet prairie between the Minnesota and Missouri Rivers outside the settled ecumene. It took over twenty years, as a matter of fact, to erase this reverse salient in the settlement line.[7]

Both timing and environment were key factors in the settlement process. They were important determinants of where people settled and the settlement experience they had. The frontier had a certain momentum of its own, driven by such factors as the rate of official surveying, the land promotions of railroads, the policies of land companies and government authorities, certain environmental preferences based on established American perceptions and technologies, and the great swings that characterized the nineteenth-century American economy. To a remarkable extent, the movement of settlers to new frontiers was as much a function of these forces as it was a matter of personal choice. Simple timing of arrival in America relative to the dynamics of the frontier was often crucial in determining not only where each immigrant would settle but, ultimately, the entire distribution of national groups.

The national groups that figured most importantly in the agricultural settlement of the region were predominantly from the German-speaking and the Scandinavian parts of Europe. Among the major non-English speaking groups were the Germans, Swedes, and Norwegians. By the 1890 census, when the agricultural frontier in the Upper Middle West had, for all practical purposes, begun to reach the limits of expansion, over one-half million German-born were living on the land plus another quarter million or so in the region's cities and towns. There were nearly a quarter million Norwegian-born in farming communities and one hundred and eighty thousand Swedes. There were also substantial numbers of Swedes and Norwegians living in urban places, although the Norwegians were less inclined towards urban settlement than the Swedes and Germans.[8] These three groups were followed in order by lesser but still significant numbers of Danes, Bohemians, Poles, and Dutch, and by a welter of other groups who were present in much smaller numbers.

The remarkable feature of the distribution of these groups is their high degree of segregation. Each group arrived in varying numbers at different times during the settlement history of the region. Yet they funneled towards certain frontiers depending upon timing, precedence, accident, and, in some instances, environmental choice. The result is evident even on distribution maps prepared at the relatively gross scale of county data (Figures 1.4, 1.5, and 1.6).[9] A quick comparison of the distributions of the three major groups in 1890—the Germans, Swedes, and Norwegians—reveals a remarkable exclusivity. To a large degree the settlement patterns of these national groups fit together like a large jigsaw puzzle. The Norwegian dominance of western Wisconsin and the counties on either side of the eastern half of the Minnesota–Iowa border, for example, dovetails nicely into the gaps between the major concentrations of German settlement in these three states. Similarly, the heavy Swedish concentration in the east-central counties of Minnesota fits easily into the discontinuous zone of Norwegian settlement that extends northwestward across the state and on into North Dakota.

At a closer scale, the settlement geography of the region may be likened to a vast cultural mosaic. In areas with the greatest clustering, whole counties were nearly filled by a single national group. This can be seen in the leapfrogging pattern of dense ethnic settlement in Wisconsin, parts of northern Illinois, eastern Iowa, and eastern Nebraska, and especially along the forest–prairie ecotone stretching northwestward along and above the Mississippi valley in Minnesota. On the open prairies, where settlement occurred later and at lower densities, clustering was also prevalent, albeit on a smaller scale. Wherever clustering occurred, the result was a patchwork-quilt pattern of residential segregation. The oft-repeated pattern is the spatial representation of a process basic to the settlement of the region; a process in which culturally homogeneous settlements formed through the establishment of strong axes of chain migration, the repeated movement over time of kin, neighbors, and friends between localities in Europe and the Upper Middle West (and often between settlements on successive midwestern frontiers). These communities were not only homogeneous at the national level, but often representative of certain provinces, districts, or even parishes—as was the case in Hans Ersson Dahlsten's community.[10] The clustering process worked best in areas where the settlement frontier moved slowly and quantities of land remained available for periods of time. In that situation, settlers from a particular region could manipulate the land system, recruit friends and relatives, and establish a

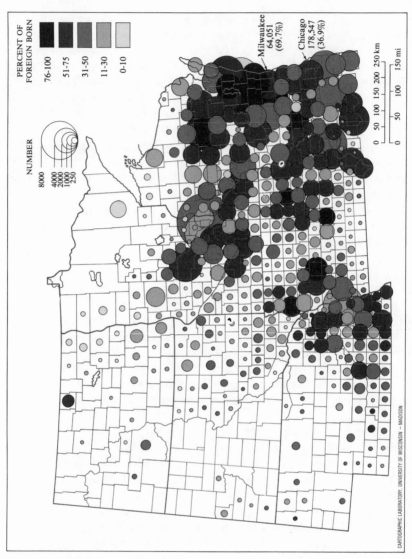

CARTOGRAPHIC LABORATORY, UNIVERSITY OF WISCONSIN – MADISON

Figure 1.4 German Settlement in the Upper Middle West, 1890

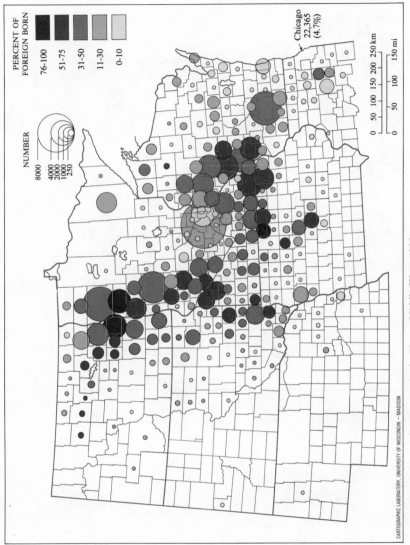

Figure 1.5 Norwegian Settlement in the Upper Middle West, 1890

CARTOGRAPHIC LABORATORY, UNIVERSITY OF WISCONSIN – MADISON

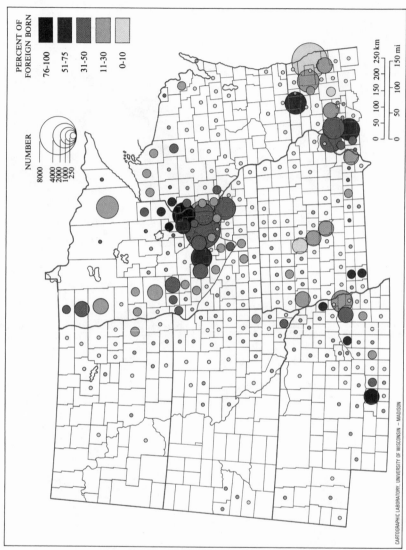

PERCENT OF
FOREIGN BORN

76-100
51-75
31-50
11-30
0-10

NUMBER

8000
4000
2000
1000
250

0 50 100 150 200 250 km
0 50 100 150 mi

CARTOGRAPHIC LABORATORY, UNIVERSITY OF WISCONSIN – MADISON

Figure 1.6 Swedish Settlement in the Upper Middle West, 1890

18

cohesive community. A web of kinship ties and personal relationships typically underlay the social fabric of the new communities. The immigrant rural church, which was often founded in a competitive and exclusive atmosphere, provided the institutional focus.

The process of rural ethnic community formation has not gone unnoticed in traditional American historical scholarship. Joseph Schafer's classic studies of Wisconsin settlement, for example, repeatedly demonstrated the immigrant's tendency to settle in culturally homogeneous colonies for the sake of mutual social support.[11] Historian of American immigration, Marcus Lee Hansen, detailed the step-by-step process by which the accretion of these kinship colonies occurred. He related how the farms of Yankee settlers were bought out by their immigrant neighbors so that they could be occupied by new arrivals from the homeland; how the social organism grew until it eventually reached the limits of expansion; and how it often divided to spawn new colonies that would receive the late arrivals and the offspring of the early settlers.[12] Countless other writers also observed the immigrants' efforts to recreate within an American context the social and cultural fabric they had left behind, but seldom has there been much of an attempt to explore the long-term trans-Atlantic implications of these observations. Instead, observations of this kind invariably seem to have been qualified or let drop, most apparently because they ran in direct contradiction to the perennial interpretive theme of American historiography, Turner's frontier thesis. As Kathleen Neils Conzen has pointed out, Schafer was curiously insistent on playing down the frequency and lasting importance of concentrated settlement, despite the evidence of his own work.[13]

Generations of historians grappled with and tried to reconcile themselves to the notion that the frontier was the crucible of American individualism and egalitarianism. That paradigm had no room for the notion of peasants reestablishing a communal past, rather than merging into an atomized or highly individualistic American society. As a consequence, historians tended to dwell as little as possible on the pre-migration experience of immigrants as an explanation for what happened to them in America. The "background" to emigration was treated as a factor of fleeting importance.[14] Most preferred to view immigrant behavior in an American context. By the middle of the twentieth century, Oscar Handlin's notion of the European immigrant had become more or less the general interpretation. Handlin's immigrants were uprooted from their peasant past and shocked by their initial encounter with a strange new world, with little hope of affecting more than a transitory transplantation of the old community in America. In short, efforts to reestablish the past were doomed to failure. Handlin's image stuck even though the immigrants he wrote about so sweepingly represented only one part of the American immigrant experience—that which originated in southern and central Europe and was largely confined to the immigrant quarters of eastern and industrial cities.[15]

In more recent decades, the notion of a persistent pluralism in American society has replaced the old concept of a melting pot. The historiography of American immigration and ethnic groups has taken on a new vigor, probing the roots of ethnic identity in a massive outpouring of detailed study. Historians have used hard data to explore immigrants' experiences of class, labor markets, family, and community in urban-industrial America.[16] But rarely have this work and the new interpretations it has raised been applied to the rural immigrant experience. While aspects of pre-migration experience and community have been significant variables in the multitude of recent urban studies, there has been relatively little parallel work in the rural context.[17] In fact, the idea of extending this kind of historical treatment to the millions of foreign-born who established themselves in rural America has only recently been raised.[18] The study of agricultural immigrants and their communities has all but laid in abeyance for decades. Early historical treatments did much to describe the settlement experience but drew back from an earnest appraisal of the effect of transplanted forms of social organization and behavior on American agricultural society.

Not only has the long-term significance of the rural immigrant community been poorly examined, the general historical conception of community itself has until recently been locked into a narrow mold. Historians, operating under the influence of ideas borrowed from sociology, have traditionally viewed the history of community in America as one of decline and replacement. The dichotomies of *Gemein-schaft–Gesellschaft,* rural–urban, traditional–modern, are necessarily sequential and therefore imply an inescapable movement from one condition to the other. Thomas Bender has argued that the "community breakdown model" has provided the basic structure for a whole series of influential monographs in American history that document the collapse of community in almost every historical time and setting.[19] Historians of colonial America in particular have engaged in a search for evidence of community decay. In one of the most sweeping and influential recent discussions of nineteenth century American society, Robert Wiebe created the image of a nation of "island communities" inexorably transformed into a highly specialized and impersonal national society.[20]

The immigrant community has not been exempted from this view. A recent book that reviews the historiography of community on the American frontier concludes that the failure of community for immigrants on the agricultural frontiers of the midwest was as inevitable as it was for all kinds of Americans:

In these colonies, except perhaps for those of the Hutterites, the frontier bolstered but little the forces working for community. True, it offered hardship and a reality for the metaphor of the wilderness. But it constantly tempered the ideal of stability. With its temptations to mobility, deeper attachments to place seldom lasted into another generation. The policy of establishing large, individualized farms in the West hindered the village ideal. The constant flow of new arrivals, both within and around the ethnic circle, injected heterogeneity and disunity. And the internal and external insistent pressures to assimilate into American society were drains, like slow hemorrages, on traditional community values.[21]

The general conclusion seems to be that, even if the frontier and the American land system failed to frustrate the inclination of the immigrant to settle among his own kind and to transplant old forms of social organization, the autonomy of any community structure the immigrant might have achieved was necessarily short-lived in the face of the general and inevitable American social trend towards mobility and distension.

At issue here is a basic conflict between "community" and "economic man." Most immigrants came to America to better their prospects. On this everyone agrees. Logically, they had to place pecuniary advantage above other things in order to realize that goal. Individual material success was the explicit justification for having made the move. Community existed only to the extent that it preserved the privacy of the individual and his family. While it was useful, community should not constrain the individual's personal freedom to exploit opportunity wherever or whenever it came.

For some historical geographers who have focused their studies on the European experience in settling colonial America, this theme has been an important synthesizing idea. James Lemon's fictitious character, Frederick Brown, the typical eighteenth-century Pennsylvanian of German descent, represented a segment of European society that actively "sought individual satisfaction." Brown and those like him imprinted Pennsylvanian society with a liberal individualism—an orientation to self more than to community—that became a model for much of the country.[22] R. Cole Harris has argued, on a broader scale, that the colonial American conditions of free land and poor markets were remarkably suited to nurturing the European nuclear family's aspirations for private control of land and freedom from the constraints of society. These conditions had the effect of making everyone equal for a time. Even when stratification eventually set in, it was based not on custom and inherited class distinctions, but on the independent farmer and his accumulated wealth in land. The encounter between nascent European ideals and the American environment resulted in a drastically simplified society.[23] For Harris, the same applies by extension to European immigrants on nineteenth-century frontiers: "Overall ethnicity tended to be locally and briefly decisive. The main patterns of regional development in nineteenth century America reflected the magnitude but not the particular pasts of a huge immigrant stream. The selective pressures of the seventeenth and eighteenth centuries continued, virtually in a continental receptacle."[24]

This view makes perfect sense to North Americans, nurtured as we are on ideals of personal freedom and achievement. In recounting his past, Hans Ersson Dahlsten quite naturally would have begun with his achievements and relative prosperity—a farm of his own, a comfortable dwelling, the capacity to provide a beginning for his offspring. But he would not have ended there. He would have gone on to recount other measures of his success that emphasized something quite different than individual achievement—attachment to community, place, custom, and faith. The drive for economic wealth and security was only a part of the immigrant experience. Newcomers also felt a need for the nonpecuniary security provided by the group and a sense of continuity with one's past. The achievement of the first did not necessarily diminish or surpass the second.

James Henretta, who has charged that scholars often fail to understand the consciousness or "mentalité" of people in preindustrial society, has suggested that the "calculus of advantage" was far more comprehensive than mere pecuniary gain.[25] Satisfaction and well-being were derived from the sphere of social and cultural activity as well as from the economic. Social interaction, belonging, and identity are all valuable human commodities. They can circumscribe everyone's activities to some extent, by imposing a social order that is comforting and desirable even in a situation where economic opportunity awaits the taker. Nor can one necessarily assume that the immigrants had been infused in Europe with "liberal" values and a preoccupation with the interests of the immediate family. While much evidence now suggests surprisingly little difference in household and family structure between pre-modern and modern European societies, the evidence is far from universal, nor does it tell us much about values or the power of restraint imposed on the household by relationships with kin, community, and institutions.[26] More reasonably, one must assume that, for all times in both Europe and America, a complex relationship exists between traditional social values and the marketplace in determining human behavior. Although often misinterpreted, Tönnies's conception of a *Gemeinschaft–Gesellschaft* distinction was never intended to mean that one must gain at the expense of the other. His models were forms of human interaction that coexisted in everyone's life.[27] Like everyone else, men and women in nineteenth-century immigrant communities had to shape that coexistence, simultaneously reconciling the forces of their personal ambitions and the social reality of their pre- and post-migration bonds to family, kin, and community.

This book is about people like Hans Ersson Dahlsten, the immigrant settlers who peopled the chain migrations and agricultural communities of the nineteenth-century American Upper Middle West. But it is more than a chronicle of what was undoubtedly the major experience of their lives. It is an attempt to assess what their experience meant to the future development of the communities they founded, as well as to the communities that they left behind. For Hans Ersson Dahlsten, the immigrant experience was a trans-Atlantic experience. Moving to America did not sever his ties with the old community. He was, in a sense, a part of both places. Many immigrants actually made the trip back and forth across the Atlantic more than once; some even intended to return for good some day. And what about those who remained behind? The axis of migration and communication that tied together places in Europe and America was a two-way street. Those in Europe maintained ties with the departed, often viewing the daughter settlements in America as exotic New World extensions of the old community. From America came new ideas that could be put to use in a European society experiencing rapid change. What happened in America was often as vitally important to the European relative of the American immigrant as nostalgia for the old community was for the immigrant.

This book is also historical geography. Like many works written by historical geographers, it begins with an historiographic issue but pursues that issue in a somewhat different manner than the approach an historian might apply to the same issue.[28] The study places the phenomenon of trans-Atlantic chain migration in an explicitly geographic context. The study is essentially an examination of the binding together of two places on opposite sides of the Atlantic. It seeks to understand how chain migration linked the fortunes of these two places over a finite period of time, in effect creating a unique, spatially constricted laboratory where one can observe the effects of a particular type of nineteenth-century migration simultaneously on both receiving and sending societies. Its basic thesis is that the discrete axes of migration and communication that were frequently established and maintained between places on either side of the Atlantic were the conduits for a prolonged series of back and forth impulses between places that both reflected and inspired change in each. The impact was perhaps first and foremost a matter of values and culture, but it ranged far beyond that to social and economic relationships, as well. Historians also set their empirical studies in place, but the effort is usually perfunctory. Geographic context rarely drives their analyses.[29]

The study also differs in the themes it emphasizes. It pays special attention to certain variables that are inherently geographic and that have often received less attention elsewhere. A persistent theme, for example, is the relationship between people and resources. This was an agrarian migration, whose people made their living from the soil both before and after having made the move. As a consequence, the changing relationships of people to the land embodied in tenure and inheritance patterns, proprietorship and wage labor, the seasonal round of agricultural work, the sexual division of labor, the influence of markets, and so on, take on special meaning. Similarly, there is special emphasis on the spatial aspects of community and on human identity with place. Given the exceptionally closed nature of migrations of this type, in which whole pieces of established communities broke away in order to establish facsimiles elsewhere, such territorial considerations loom larger than would be the case in other contexts. The highly agrarian character of both mother and daughter communities is especially significant here, because propinquity and attachment to place can be of greatest importance in the rural context.

But the study is also true to the ideals of a research program first proposed by historian Frank Thistlethwaite in 1960. Among other things, Thistlethwaite called for more studies that attempt to cover the entire migration experience, not just the European or American end of the story.[30] By taking the long view of the entire pre-migration, migration, settlement, and post-settlement experience for a particular group of migrants, this study hopes to provide a basis for better understanding the long-term impact of the trans-Atlantic linkage between agricultural communities in Europe and the American Upper Middle West. It reconstructs just one of these trans-Atlantic linkages, that which existed between the Swedish parish of Rättvik and the rather large daughter community established by Hans Ersson Dahlsten and his compatriots in Minnesota's Isanti County. There is also a limited exploration of the lesser link between this parish and a settlement in South Dakota, but the main focus is on the Rättvik–Isanti connection. The aim is to work within the spatial and temporal bounds of this trans-Atlantic laboratory, to view the transplanted community from within and, in so doing, see the evolving situation of both the migrants and those who remained behind as it may have seemed to them, as well as how it may have affected the world about them.

Design of the Study

Schematically, the study is set in a framework that places sending area and receiving area side by side, so that the old and the new community may be directly compared and related over time as they were affected by the migratory and informational axes operating between them (Figure 1.7). The scheme identifies a series of four temporal stages. The pre-migration stage sets the conditions that create a potential for emigration in the sending area. This stage is followed by one in which information from the receiving area stimulates migration potential, establishing a migration stream of selected individuals from the sending area. The third stage is a period of adjustment, in which the sending society continues to adjust to the conditions that stimulated the out-migration, the loss of the migrant population, and the flow of new information sent home by those who left. At the same time, the migrant population, carrying with them the memory of pre-migration experience, build a new community, adjust to the conditions of their new milieu, and react to new information about changing conditions at home. This stage may generate a renewed or secondary migration from the sending society and a return migration from the new community. The final stage is one of consolidation, equilibrium, and redefinition, in which both old and new communities reconcile themselves to the waning import of the trans-Atlantic connection and adjust to new challenges at home, although such adjustments may still reflect or even be highly dependent on the influence of the migratory experience.

In keeping with this generalized model of chain migration and community formation, the chapters in this book work forward in time and back and forth across the Atlantic. Chapters 2 and 3 deal with pre-migration conditions in Sweden as a whole and in the parish of Rättvik, in particular. Chapter 2 describes pre-migration social conditions in the parish at mid-century, while Chapter 3 analyses economic conditions.

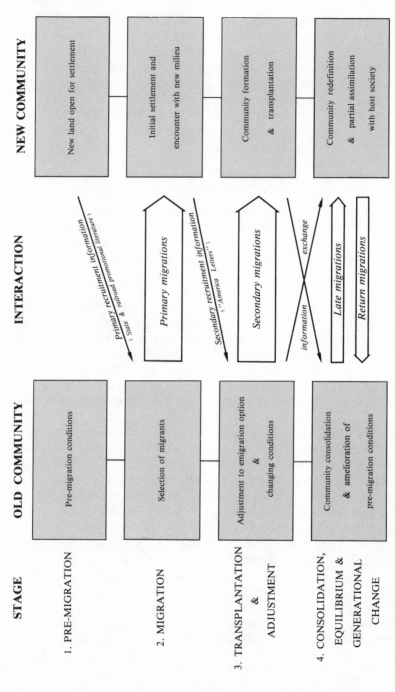

Figure 1.7 Generalized Model of Chain Migration and Community Transplantation

The process of migrant selection, the parameters of the trans-Atlantic migration axes, and the settlement processes that reestablished the bulk of the emigrants from this parish in two midwestern locations are the subjects of Chapters 4 and 5. The former describes the chain migration mechanism. The latter focuses on the initial encounter with a new and strange environment and with the unfamiliar American frontier economy. Chapter 6 is concerned with the formative first two decades of the transplanted community in America and with the trans-Atlantic relationship between mother and daughter communities during this period. It delves into the problems of adjustment to a new milieu and broaches the subject of potential conflict between communal and individualistic ideals. Chapters 7 and 8 examine the final stage, in which the migrant generation is replaced by a new generation and the communities on both sides of the Atlantic undergo important processes of redefinition. Chapter 7 is devoted to assimilation and change in the American community, while Chapter 8 assesses what happened to the society left behind. The last chapter is an epilogue that looks back on the entire trans-Atlantic experience.

The choice of a Swedish migration as a case study was, of course, deliberate. The most important consideration was the need to find the kind of extraordinarily complete data set that is absolutely essential to a study of this kind. Any study that seeks to trace the fortunes of hundreds of families and thousands of individuals in two different parts of the world and over a period of time sufficient to span generations, faces monumental problems of data collection. Of all the European countries, Sweden is unique for the quality and accessibility of its historical population records. It is probably the easiest country in which to develop a comprehensive historical data base for a particular population.[31] But finding good data for a sending area is only half the problem. The other half is creating comparable data sets for an American receiving area. Again, one of the best bets here is to work with a Swedish settlement, because Swedish Lutheran ministers in America often maintained detailed and continuous population records modeled after the ones their counterparts in Sweden were charged with keeping. This makes it possible to flesh out the rather discontinuous picture supplied by decennial U.S. censuses, and to create an American data base that is directly comparable to the Swedish.

Working with Swedish migration is fortuitous in another way. Migration research in Sweden has an especially long and distinguished record. The 1960s and 1970s have seen the most innovative use of Swedish data resources and the most systematic treatment of Swedish emigration. Much of this is due to the work of the Uppsala Migration Research Project, which consisted of as many as thirty scholars engaged over a ten-year period in a highly cooperative effort to advance understanding of the many facets of mass migration. The work of this group was highly coordinated and strongly attuned to theoretical models and methodologies in the social sciences. As such, it provides a background and context for the present study that would be difficult to duplicate for any other European country.[32]

The specific choice of the Rättvik–Isanti connection was the result of a search for a suitable example of community transplantation. The extensive area of Swedish settlement in the St. Croix and Rum River valley districts of east-central Minnesota was most likely to yield a good example and so was convassed to find a sizeable Swedish settlement with a specific place of origin in Sweden.[33] Quite a number of candidates were turned up, but the Rättvik community in Isanti county seemed particularly well suited. Over one hundred families from a single parish settled in the same district within a period of about twenty years. The American community which they dominated was focused on an Augustana Lutheran church that maintained a remarkably complete population register of the Swedish type. A survey of that register revealed that the migration of Rättvik people to Isanti was essentially a direct one without intervening stops in Sweden or America, which eliminated the data collection problems such stops entail. The fact that there was a smaller migration stream leading from this Swedish parish to a community in South Dakota was not discovered until later, but has served to enrich the example.[34]

The time period of the study was determined by two factors: the intent of the study and availability of source materials. Since the purpose here is to reconstruct the transplantation of community in its fullest trans-Atlantic dimension, the study must reach back far enough to assess pre-migration conditions in the source area. Conversely, it must extend sufficiently forward in time to observe the long-term implications of the migration on both source and receiving areas. The bulk of the chain migrations from Rättvik to Isanti took place during the twenty-year period from 1865 to 1885. The migrant generation of those years is therefore the focus of the study.

Ideally, the study should extend across the three generations that correspond to the pre-migration, migration, and post-migration eras. The data available for the Rättvik–Isanti connection fortunately span just enough time to take in all three generations. The Swedish population records for Rättvik actually extend well back into the eighteenth century, but the only time for which good data on land ownership and household wealth for the pre-migration era are available is the latter part of the 1830s and the early 1840s. These are precisely the years when the pre-migration generation was at its prime. Accordingly, the study begins around the year 1835. On the American side, the last available manuscript census is for the year 1910. However, a fairly complete atlas and farmer's directory for 1914, used in conjunction with church registers and a complete set of county records, makes it possible to extend the period for which a reasonably accurate accounting of the population may be assembled to roughly 1915. The study thus can follow the post-migration generation in America into their adult years. Comparable data exist for Sweden to 1915. The time period of the study, then, is the eighty years between 1835 and 1915, comprising the twenty years during which the migrations took place plus the thirty years before and after.

The data base on which the study relies is divided into two data sets. The first covers the population of the sending area from 1835 to 1915. It is based on the catechetical register *(husförhörslängd)*, a population register maintained by the parish clergy, which provides a continuous record of most of the significant events in the lives of each parishioner. It lists birth, baptism, death, marriage, place of residence, cathechismal knowledge and literacy, movements within and outside the parish, as well as occasional comments deemed appropriate by the parish priest. These registers are a continuous year-by-year accounting, which makes it possible to trace individuals over time without losing track of them—a peril one often faces when relying on censuses taken at regular intervals. This basic source is supplemented at regular intervals up to 1915 by the manuscript returns of the Swedish population and household tax register *(mantalslängd)*. In addition, property tax records *(taxeringlängder)* and land records are used from time to time to add economic information to the demographic and social information contained in the population registers. In sum, this study benefits from an exceedingly detailed data set for the parish of Rättvik, organized by household and extending more or less continuously over the entire study period.[35]

The second data set contains detailed demographic, social, and economic information on individuals in approximately 1,460 households resident in Minnesota's upper Rum River valley (nine contiguous townships in Isanti County) between 1865 and 1915. This set is based on the manuscripts of the decennial U.S. census and the manuscripts of the Minnesota state census, which was taken at mid-decade until 1905. The census manuscripts in themselves do not provide a continuous record of the population comparable to the Swedish material. (There are gaps of five years between each census, and a gap of ten years between 1885 and 1895 because the 1890 federal manuscripts were destroyed by fire.) A data set that is virtually as complete as its Swedish counterpart has been constructed by filling in data for the missing years from parallel sources. These include the catechetical registers of the Swedish Lutheran churches in the district, which were kept in the same fashion as in Sweden; the membership rolls of various nonconformist Swedish churches in the area, which provide some of the same kinds of information as the Lutheran registers; farmers' directories; county birth, death, marriage, and land records; and cemetery lists.[36] Information from these supporting sources and some extrapolation of census data allows a quite satisfactory, although imperfect, accounting of the population over fifty years. The data are organized by households and supplemented at five year intervals with economic information gleaned from county property tax rolls.

The combination of these Swedish and American data sets provide the data base that makes possible the reconstruction and the analysis of the trans-Atlantic experience of an immigrant community. It allows the essential linkage of immigrant households in America to the households from which they emigrated in Sweden—the first step towards a delimitation of the full range of their social and economic relationships with one another and with the households that surrounded them in both places.

2

The Old Community

Kinship, Village, and Church at Mid-Century

THE GREAT MASS of emigrants from Sweden to America left their homeland during the second half of the nineteenth century. Many of the first lived the formative early years of their lives during the 1830s and 1840s. They grew up and reached maturity in a world that differed significantly from the one they later decided to leave. Their expectations of adult life were based on the milieu of their parents' world. While pressing conditions in the early decades of the nineteenth century's second half may have prompted the decision to emigrate, deep-seated conditions from the past may actually have predetermined who would go and what they would hope to achieve. To understand the trans-Atlantic experience fully, it is first necessary to go back to the world of the emigrants' parents and ask what society was like in early nineteenth-century Sweden.

During the first half of the nineteenth century, Sweden was predominantly an agrarian society. That fact was strikingly underscored by the Swedish statistician Nils Wohlin in his celebrated 1909 report on the agricultural population of Sweden. He observed that over the ninety years from 1751 to 1840, the proportion of the population dependent upon agriculture for a livelihood scarcely deviated from an average of 80.59 percent.[1] The first significant deviation was recorded in 1850, with a figure of 77.94 percent. The relative importance of agriculture then eroded steadily under the impact of the Industrial Revolution. Sweden, in the first half of the century, was a society on the verge of momentous change. It was perhaps the last era in which working the land was the

31

primary and often the only means of subsistence for the vast majority of the population.

Of course, figures such as these often mask important changes already under way. It would be entirely misleading to suggest that early nineteenth-century Swedish society was static, placidly awaiting the Industrial Revolution. In fact, the structure of the Swedish agricultural economy had already begun to undergo significant changes in the previous century, changes that continued and accelerated in the early decades of the nineteenth century. The organization of traditional Swedish industries, such as the production of iron and timber, had also begun to show signs of transformation during this period. Even the towns were changing. Although towns held only about ten percent of the Swedish population up to 1850, many were growing beyond the customary upper limits of one or two thousand people for the first time.[2] Compared to many European nations, these developments were proceeding slowly. The industrial breakthrough in Sweden, and the rapid change in economic structure that accompanied it, was relatively late by European standards. As a consequence, the economic and social history of Sweden until mid-century is still the history of a premodern agricultural society.

A characteristic feature of society was that people's experiences were tightly circumscribed spatially. As in earlier centuries, travel was slow and difficult and few people wandered far from the place in which they were born. Recent studies have shown that mobility was far greater than previously thought, but the movement was predominantly over short distances and often circular—a shifting about as stages in the life cycle caused individuals to move from one location to another.[3] Most spent a lifetime within the boundaries of a particular province or county, often within a particular parish. As a consequence, an individual's range of experience was normally fairly limited. One knew well the immediate locality and perhaps the surrounding district, but firsthand familiarity with more distant places was rare and usually arose from special circumstances. Provincialism and localism were common traits among rural folk. Centuries of relative isolation had bred local idiosyncracies in dialect, custom, food, and dress, that set one area off from another. The regional consciousness based on these differences is embodied throughout Scandinavia in the term, *bygd,* which is used to denote the local culture region.[4]

Much of the social life of the Swedish countryside was associated territorially with the local unit of ecclesiastical and civil admininistration, the parish. Before 1860, everyone in Sweden was required to be a member of the State Church. Regular attendance in church and participation in communion were expected. The parish church was quite naturally the meeting place and focus of local life. One gathered at the church not only to worship, but to see friends and neighbors, to hear the latest news of marriages, births, and deaths, and occasionally to learn of important events outside the area. The parish clergyman, a graduate of one of the Swedish universities, was assigned to the parish as both the spiritual leader of the flock and the local representative of the state. He baptized children, taught them to read, and introduced them to adult life through confirmation at the age of fifteen. He married them; counseled them in their adult life; and kept a record of their cathechismal knowledge and beliefs, their comings and goings, the vital events of their lives, their literacy, and any unusual behavior. Burial on the grounds of the parish church was a necessary step towards the rewards of the afterlife. As servants of the crown, the parish clergy were also responsible for local civil administration. A clergyman headed the parish council, which was elected by the parishioners and saw to such local administrative matters as providing for the maintenance of roads and schools, relief for the poor, and lodging for travelers and soldiers.

While a certain identification with the church, and the community it served, was a mainstay of society, a deeper loyalty attached to kin and family. The head of the household commanded the respect and obedience of all family members. Sons and daughters gave freely of their labor while living in their parents' household. They were customarily sent off in their teens to work for neighboring landowners, where they lived as members of the family. As adults they often returned to work on their parents' farm until marriage or the eventual retirement of the household head. Marriages were commonly arranged with the good of the parental household and its future labor supply in mind. Throughout much of Sweden, only one son was chosen to inherit the farm. The other children received a portion of the estate as tenants to the father or brother or were left to hire themselves out to other farmers. Upon retirement, the old couple normally secured the right to be cared for until death by the son who inherited the estate. The ancestral home was a source of intense pride, worthy of substantial sacrifice in the cause of its preservation.

In the early eighteenth century, Swedish agriculture was governed by restrictive land policies and the dictates of an agricultural system rooted in the Middle Ages. Traditional land policy viewed a free and independent peasantry as the foundation of society. It was feared that the peasantry, if left to its own devices, would partition its land without restraint and eventually bring itself to ruin. To preserve the status quo and guard against an impoverishment of the peasantry, a complicated and restrictive system of laws and customs governed the expansion and subdivision of agricultural land.[5] In addition, the expansion of production in the small-holding farming economy was hindered by a common field agricultural system, which enforced a time-honored but inflexible pattern of production. Over most of the country, farm houses and outbuildings were grouped in compact villages, while the holdings of individual landowners were widely scattered about the village lands in numerous small strips. Pasture and woodland were usually held in common. The system necessitated a communal approach to the seasonal round. The peasant was obliged to sow and harvest his crops or graze his livestock when and where the village council decided it was appropriate for everyone to do so. While the system offered order and stability, it also was fraught with ineffiencies and barriers to improvement. Indeed, Swedish agricultural production barely kept pace with the population, necessitating grain imports, although in dwindling amounts, up until 1830.[6]

Despite the continuation of such restraints as a matter of tradition and continuity with the past, significant new developments were making themselves felt in the first half of the eighteenth century. A rapid expansion of the Swedish population began in the eighteenth century and continued unabated into the nineteenth. Sweden's population rose from approximately 1.8 million in 1750 to just over 2.3 million in 1800. By 1850, the population had risen to more than 3.5 million, an unprecedented 48.4 percent increase in the space of just fifty years. Remarkably, agriculture absorbed most of this rapid expansion despite a relatively limited resource base. But concomitant with the rising number of people living on the land were revolutionary changes in the organization of landed wealth and agricutural production, changes which were probably both cause and consequence of the population boom.

The Swedish government gradually began to loosen the restrictions of land policy in the eighteenth century. The impetus for change arose in part from the popular view that increased population and progressive agriculture were direct evidence of national prosperity. Another contributing factor was the slow rise of liberal doctrines about the value and independence of the individual.[7] By the late 1730s, these ideas began to be transformed into a sequence of progressively bolder laws that continued to be promulgated well into the nineteenth century. In 1739, for example, restrictions that held down the number of servants allowed on a farm were liberalized and in 1747 limitations on the division of farms were lowered for the first time. An act passed in 1749 required land surveyors to encourage the consolidation of holdings. The *storskifte* of 1772, the first compulsory enclosure law, required a substantial reduction in the number of strips held by landowners, but did not require that the village be disturbed. Later, the *enskifte* laws, first passed for the province of Skåne and then for the whole country in 1807, called for the breakup of the village and the consolidation of land holdings into large parcels. The *laga skifte* of 1827 went even further, requiring not only that lands be consolidated into as few parcels as possible, but that they also be contiguous wherever circumstances permit.

From the beginning there was opposition to these statutes, especially those that threatened to redistribute lands and break up old villages. The peasants, in particular, accepted these changes only grudgingly. As a result, the dates when laws were enacted frequently bear little relationship to the dates when their provisions were actually carried out. The redistribution and enclosure of property was a formidable task that required much preparation and planning, and the acquiescence of nearly everyone involved. By the end of the eighteenth century, surprisingly little land had been completely enclosed. Considerable progress was made in the early decades of the nineteenth century; by 1850 the greater part of Sweden south of Norrland and Dalarna had made the transition from communal village to individual farms. In some parts of the country, the process was never completed—even in the present century.

Especially important in balancing the demands of population against availability of land was the lifting of restrictions on the expansion and subdivision of existing farms. While no precise statistics tell us the expansion of cultivated area during the first half of the nineteenth century, it probably more than doubled.[8] The division of farms to accommodate sons and sons-in-law became more feasible because it was possible to enlarge holdings. Indeed, despite wholesale subdivision, the size of the average farm actually increased during this period. New households could also be created on the marginal extensions of existing farms through shareholding or rental arrangements. Finite land resources placed an ultimate limit to these developments, of course, but the freer subdivision of farms and the expansion of the arable did have two important social effects: a substantial increase in the size of the old smallholding proprietary class, and an even greater increase in the size of newer agricultural classes that came to enjoy a place on the land, if only a rather tenuous one.

At the beginning of the eighteenth century, the bulk of the peasantry could be divided into two major classes. The first was the small-holding class of peasant proprietors who formed the backbone of the Swedish agricultural population. The second was a regular servant class of unmarried domestics and farmhands who lived in the peasant household and served according to customary regulations regarding tenure and wages. This class was comprised primarily of the sons and daughters of peasants living at home or, as was often the custom, on neighboring farms.

In addition, two relatively new classes began to appear in this period. One was the *torpare* or "crofter" class. This term originally referred to new settlers of crown lands, who eventually joined the class of peasant proprietors once they had fulfilled certain requirements. By the middle of the eighteenth century, however, the term came to identify a class of tenants who settled on subdivisions of private land in return for supplying specified forms of labor and service to the proprietor. The emergence of this new class represented an accommodation whereby peasant proprietors could establish a reliable and cheap labor supply living on the most marginal part of their holdings. At the same time, the crofter gained the security of a long-term contract granting definite rights to a parcel of land and the possibility of adequate support for a family.

Living at a far lower level of security was another new class, made up of individuals who belonged to the sometimes indistinguishable categories of "cottager" *(backstugusittare)* and "live-in-laborer" *(inhyseshjon)*. Like the crofter, the cottager received a place on the land from a peasant proprietor, but it was normally a much smaller plot, often just a dwelling and a small potato garden. In return, the cottager paid for the land in some specified form. Unlike the crofter, cottagers received no guarantee that their labor or services would be regularly required by the owner, which meant that cottagers were often left to their own meagre resources in difficult times. The *inhyseshjon* was literally a person who had no place to live. Such individuals became live-in laborers who worked for the peasant proprietor or crofter in return for room and board, but without the regular arrangements afforded the servant class.

Over the century between 1750 and 1850, the size of Sweden's peasant proprietor class increased steadily, but its relative share of the productive agricultural population declined, especially during the early part of the nineteenth century. While the size of the peasant proprietor class increased by about a fifth between 1750 and 1850, the regular servant class more than doubled, the crofter class more than tripled, and the cottager and live-in laborer classes more than quadrupled. And in the early part of the nineteenth century, a totally new class of landless labor *(statare)* began to emerge on the larger estates.[9] As the relative importance of these new tenant and landless classes increased, a gradual but relentless proletarianization of the agricultural population began to take place.

Yet this process, which is so often cited as a key background variable for emigration, was not as sweeping as it might seem. In fact, the peasant proprietor class and the regular servant class still comprised four-fifths of the productive population in 1850, down just slightly from a century earlier.[10] The new classes had made impressive gains, but those gains must be measured against a base that was quite small to begin with. They were also partially offset by the growth of the old classes. The relative importance of these developments varied considerably across Sweden. In some areas, especially the rich lowlands of central Sweden and on the plains of Skåne where there were many estates, the proletarianization process was well advanced by roughly 1800. In other areas the impact was still exceedingly small. Nearly everywhere, however, the agricultural population was swollen with young people entering the years of family formation. While that demographic bulge had been characteristic for a long period of time, the agricultural system had reached a critical point by the middle of the nineteenth century. How these young people were absorbed into the system was a matter that varied enormously across Sweden. It became a key factor in the proclivity towards emigration in respective districts.

Increasingly apparent from the work of Scandinavian ethnologists and historians is the fact that the fundamental characteristics of Swedish peasant society and the speed with which it was being transformed in the eighteenth and nineteenth centuries varied greatly from one region to the next. These differences were a function of a complicated dialectic between the ecological setting, cultural tradition, and economic forces unique to each area.[11] One may generalize freely about the pre-emigration condition of Swedish society as a whole; but understanding at the macro scale is at best a synthesis of the range of experience everywhere. To understand the exact circumstances that led to emigration in a particular region or place, it is necessary to explore the structure and dynamics of society at far more intimate scales. For those who would emigrate from the parish of Rättvik, the portion of the world that was immediately relevant probably did not extend far beyond the boundaries of Dalarna.

The Regional Context: Swedish Dalarna

Of all Swedish provinces, none holds as special a place in the Swedish imagination as Dalarna. It has been the setting for some of the most dramatic episodes in Swedish history. In 1520, the future king of Sweden, Gustav Vasa, chose to mount his campaign for Swedish freedom in Dalarna, leading what became known as the Dalecarlian revolt against Danish domination. Dalarna also appeals to the imagination because it is an out of the way place where traditions and customs have faded slowly; a place where time seems to have stood still, where the romantic past lives on. But perhaps most importantly, it contains within its boundaries the full range of landscapes regarded as quintessentially Swedish—the barren *fjäll* of the Norwegian frontier zone, the "Norrland landscape" of vast forest tracts broken occasionally by clear lakes and powerful rivers, the open plains of central Sweden. It is, in many ways, a microcosm of the entire country; in the words of poet Erik Axel Karfeldt, "a Sweden on a reduced scale."[12]

But for all its variety, there are really only two major recognized sub-regions: Upper and Lower Dalarna (Figure 2.1).[13] Upper Dalarna comprises the northwesterly two-thirds of the province; a mostly forested, upland plateau which is cut through and drained by the two upper branches of the Dalälven (Västerdalälven and Österdalälven) and their tributaries. The intermittent and narrow plains that follow these two river valleys and surround some of the larger lakes of Upper Dalarna have historically supported a small-holding agricultural population, famous for its independence and self-reliance. Lower Dalarna, on the other hand, is more varied, both physically and economically. Its focus is the southeastward flowing Dalälven, along which are found a number of broad agricultural plains. These plains are outliers of the densely settled and highly productive central Swedish lowlands and together constitute the rich agricultural core of Lower Dalarna. Surrounding them is a vast region of irrgular hills and ridges, interspersed with small agricultural plains.

Lower Dalarna is most famous for its rich deposits of copper and iron, which became the basis of an extensive metal-working industry. Upper Dalarna is also known for its scattered iron deposits, which occur in the form of bog-ore on the marshes and lakes of the upland plateau. These deposits were exploited early in the Middle Ages, but the early Upper Dalarna iron industry was soon eclipsed by large-scale exploitation of the more concentrated mineral deposits of Lower Dalarna. By the end of the Middle Ages, the *bergslag* mining and metal working dis-

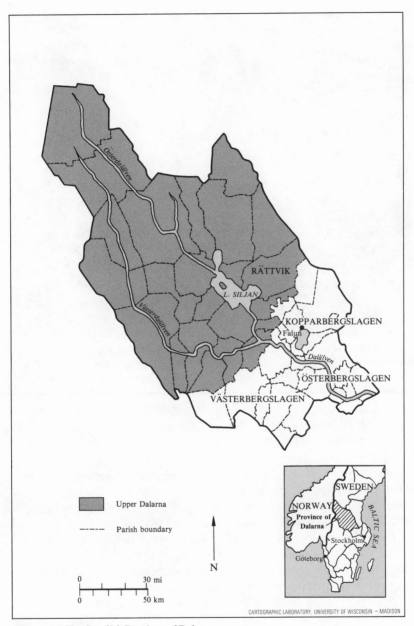

Upper Dalarna

----- Parish boundary

N

0   30 mi
0   50 km

CARTOGRAPHIC LABORATORY, UNIVERSITY OF WISCONSIN — MADISON

Figure 2.1 The Swedish Province of Dalarna

39

Plate 2.1 The core of Upper Dalarna. Lake Siljan is seen here from the heights
overlooking the island parish of Sollerön. With its many small agrarian settlements
separated by vast forest tracts, this region is often looked upon as the quintessentially
Swedish landscape.

tricts of Lower Dalarna (Kopparbergslagen, Österbergslagen, Väster-
bergslagen) were playing a major role in the early development of the
Swedish economy and state. Of the two sub-regions, Upper Dalarna is
clearly the backwater. Lower Dalarna, with richer resources, both agricultural and mineral, and a location more accessible to the rest of the
nation, has historically enjoyed a more productive economy and richer
contacts with the outside world.

   In addition to contrasts in physical geography, settlement, and economy, a significant cultural divide has long separated the two regions.
The gulf between them is perhaps best exemplified by linguistic differences. The local speech of Lower Dalarna is similar to that of the
neighboring central Swedish provinces of Västmanland, Uppland, and
Gästrikland, from which it was originally settled and with which it
always enjoyed much contact. It has also been highly influenced by the
foreign elements who settled there in association with the development

of the copper and iron districts. The local speech of Upper Dalarna, on the other hand, is a strikingly unique form of Swedish that developed over centuries of relative isolation. Not only is the speech of the entire region distinctive, but due to the remoteness and isolation of settlement within the region, dialects differ between settlement districts and even villages. The sharpest differences are between some of the larger settlement districts and are believed to be linked to the medieval division of the region into large ecclesiastical units.[14]

Upper Dalarna, then, has always been a unique region, and is what most have in mind when they speak of the "real Dalarna." It is a region of rather large parishes, with vast forest tracts that often separate the main settlements of one parish from the next. Because of their relative isolation, these parishes developed over the centuries into exceptionally cohesive communities, well known for their singularity of self expression in customs, dress, and folkways. The stubborn self-reliance and individualism of the Dalarna peasants, their resistance to outside forces and pressures on their way of life, are legendary traits. Indeed, the large parishes of Upper Dalarna have been referred to as "self-concious independent peasant republics".[15] But these parishes were also subject to the same forces of change that affected the rest of Sweden during the eighteenth and nineteenth centuries. To what extent were these forces significant in the region?

Like Sweden, the province of Dalarna experienced a dramatic increase in population between 1750 and 1850. Aggregate population figures for the entire province, however, show a rate of increase that was significantly below the national average. Between 1750 and 1800, the population increased by about twenty-six percent while the national population rose by more than thirty-one percent. The corresponding rates of increase for the first half of the nineteenth century were 23.6 percent and 48.4 percent, respectively. But these rather modest provincial rates are misleading. They are an average of the relatively low growth rates of Lower Dalarna and the much higher rates of Upper Dalarna. As in so many things, the two halves of the province were on independent courses. In fact, the rate of population growth in predominantly small-holding, agrarian Upper Dalarna roughly approximated that of Sweden as a whole from 1800 to 1850 and more than doubled that of the rest of the province. Here, as elsewhere, the increase was largely absorbed by agriculture, but in ways quite different than in other parts of the country.[16]

In Dalarna, the liberalization of land policy and customary restraints on production were slow to take hold. In 1850 the population of Upper

Dalarna still lived in more than 500 villages varying in size from a handful of people to over 800. The movement to enclose agricultural holdings never went so far in this region as to break up the old village form of settlement or to eliminate the need to regulate the use of resources communally. Land reform was introduced in 1803 under the *storskifte* and had been completed in many parishes by mid-century. The *storskifte* reorganization significantly reduced the number of parcels held by individual peasants, consolidated their holdings, and established a minimum farm size, but few of these accomplishments were lasting; the population simply reverted to old practices that led inexorably back to the prior condition of extreme land fragmentation. The breaking of new land during this period did increase the amount of arable, but farmers soon reached the limit of potential arable, which was no greater than perhaps three percent of the total area. Geographer Helge Nelson has observed that the total nineteenth-century increase in arable for the entire province of Dalarna was the lowest in central and southern Sweden and that, within the province, the increases were least for the parishes of Upper Dalarna.[17] The rising ratio of population to resources was not offset here by the liberalization of resource use and the expansion of resources to the degree that it was in other parts of Sweden.

Dalarna's development was also distinctive in that it did not experience the rise of a new landless proletariat. While the number of household heads in the small-holding peasant class increased by about one third between 1751 and 1850, the crofter class (which comprised an insignificant 2.5 percent of adult males engaged in agriculture in 1751) actually declined in both numbers and relative importance by 1850. In fact, there were only 339 crofters in the entire province in 1850, less than one percent of adult males engaged in agriculture.[18] On the other hand, the class comprised of cottagers and live-in laborers increased ten-fold over the same period, although from a relatively insignificant numerical base. Only a very small *statare* class was present in 1850, found mostly in Lower Dalarna, where larger estates had a greater demand for contract labor. What makes Dalarna unique is that much of its population increase was absorbed by the peasant class. The most significant increases were, in fact, among peasant's sons living at home or in service. Their numbers nearly doubled and their relative importance went from roughly one-quarter to nearly one-half of all males engaged in agriculture.[19]

That the bulk of the increase in population was absorbed within the peasant and farm servant classes rather than in the new semi-landed and landless classes was primarily due to the inheritance customs peculiar to this region. In most parts of Sweden, a single heir acquired the ancestral farm. In Dalarna, tradition subdivided holdings among all heirs. The result was a perpetual redivision of estates into ever smaller and more fragmented units. This process had gone on virtually unabated from early times, despite the imposition, from the end of the seventeenth century onwards, of various royal proclamations and schemes designed to arrest it. Even the *storskifte* provision setting a minimum farm size had little effect. This meant that the situation was not so automatically hopeless for the younger generation as it was in other systems. There was a strong incentive for young men to remain within the peasant class; to work on the farms of their fathers, relatives, and neighbors, and await the prospect of acquiring a share of the inheritance. It also meant, however, that the small farms of Upper Dalarna were in a constant state of subdivision and that the subdivisions were frequently too small to adequately support the peasant households that depended on them. Most of the population, as a consequence, was forced to turn to a variety of secondary and seasonal economic activities in order to earn a livelihood and still preserve an ancient and equal right to the land.

The parish of Rättvik, then, belonged to a large and historic region known for its exceptionally strong traditions. Deeply ingrained and foremost among these was a strong sense of community and place. Distinctive local differences in language, art, dress, and economy distinguished the many parish settlements of the region from one another. It was a region in which one's local origins were immediately apparent from one's appearance and manner. Unrestrained loyalty to and respect for the local community naturally fostered an independent and inward-looking social attitude. It was also a region without striking differences in wealth or class—a society that still seemed blessed, at mid-century, with a remarkable sense of its own equality and corporateness.

Spatial and Social Organization of Rättvik at Mid-Century

The parish of Rättvik is a part of what is often thought of as the core of Upper Dalarna. The core is a ring-like geologic depression known as the Siljan basin (also known as "Siljan Ring"). The geology of the basin is unique. It was formed primarily of soft limestone and slate bedrock quite unlike the plateaus surrounding the basin, which are underlaid by hard crystalline rock. In addition, the depression was covered in postglacial times by a vast extension of the sea that covered much of eastern and central Sweden. The combination of bedrock, marine deposition, and alluvium left by the rivers and streams that flow into the basin has blessed the Siljan area with fertile morainic and sedimentary soils. This relatively rich resource base has supported fairly dense settlement since early times. As a consequence, the large parishes of the basin are some of the most important in the region.

The parish of Rättvik is one of the largest and best known (Figure 2.2).[20] It is located on the eastern side of the basin and centered on the large northeastern bay of Lake Siljan, known as "Rättviken." Villages and cultivated fields cover the slopes and crests of the surrounding hills and look out over the wide bay below. The parish extends far inland, as well. In all, it measures roughly eighteen miles from north to south and about twenty-five miles from east to west. At the head of Rättviken, an ancient road leaves the lakeshore and winds its way up the broad and gentle valley drained by a small stream known as the Enån. The road follows the valley, climbing past a number of villages situated on scattered upland deposits of morainic clays and sands until it eventually reaches and crosses over a divide at Boda. From there it descends along the reverse valley cut by the Ändån, eventually passing out of the parish and ending up in Ore parish at the shore of Lake Ore. This well-traveled route marks the easternmost part of the Siljan Ring depression. The string of settlements it connects along the two valley floors constitutes the second zone of intensive settlement in the parish, the first being the beach ridges and hills surrouning the bay. High above the lake, and to either side of the Enån and Ändån valleys, are vast expanses of forest and waste stretching over remote sections of an immense plateau. These high sections of the parish were never permanently occupied, except for three small Finnish settlements located in the extreme eastern part of the parish and a small iron foundry, also located in the east, known as Dådransbruk.

The small and rather remote Finnish settlements of the plateau were established in the seventeenth century as part of a program initiated by Charles IX to encourage Finns to settle in certain unoccupied parts of Sweden. Charles hoped by extending settlement to secure additional tax revenues for the crown. The area set aside for Finnish settlements was referred to locally as the "finnmark." Rättvik's finnmark, like most such areas in Dalarna, was purposely set far from the center of parish life and on some of the poorest soils in the parish.[21] The population of the finnmark lived a separate existence, dependent on the meagre subsistence offered by infertile forest tracts and isolated (except in winter) by the difficult tracks leading down to the main settlements in the west. In fact, the finnmark had better communications in the nineteenth century

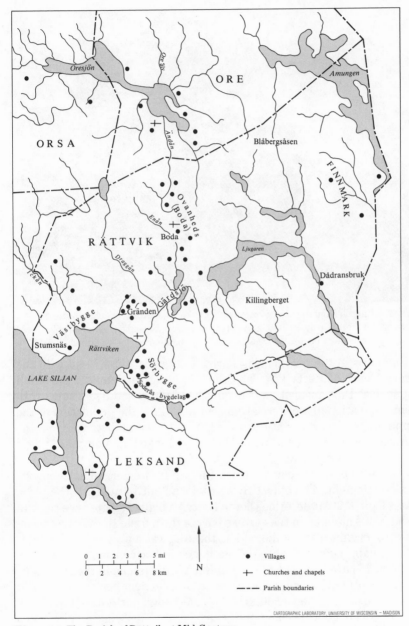

Figure 2.2 The Parish of Rättvik at Mid-Century

45

Plate 2.2 Rättvik from the heights overlooking Lake Siljan. Rättvik's church stands alone on the shore, easily accessible from land and water. Note the traditional pole fence along the roadside. (Courtesy of Dalarnas Museum, photograph by Axel Lindahl, 1893)

with places in the neighboring parish to the east than it did with the central part of Rättvik.[22] The other outlying settlement, the small foundry at Dådransbruk, was established in 1806 and had a small resident population of workers at mid-century. Like the population of the finnmark, the workers at this foundry kept a social distance from the agrarian population concentrated along the lake and along the valleys leading northward towards the parish of Ore.

No one knows for certain when Rättvik first emerged as an important settlement. The oldest Swedish document to mention the place dates from 1320. It describes how a Rättvik village acquired the right to fish Lake Amungen in the eastern part of the parish. In the early ecclesiastical organization of the region, the area was a part of Leksand parish. A chapel subservient to the mother church at Leksand, however, is thought to have been established in Rättvik sometime in the early thirteenth century. Rättvik appears as an independent ecclesiastical unit sometime during the period 1325–1442, although portions of the parish remained a part of Leksand until much later. In 1553, six small villages in the south, known as Söderås *bygdelag*, were officially transferred from the jurisdiction of Leksand to that of Rättvik. The last transfer of territory between the two parishes occurred in 1607, when the village of Stumsnäs, on the western shore of Rättviken, was transferred to Rätt-vik. The inhabitants of Stumsnäs themselves had applied for the trans-fer, mainly because of the difficulties of reaching the distant Leksand Church from their village in the spring and fall.[23]

The spiritual and administrative center of Rättvik was the church and parsonage, which stood on a small point of land jutting out into Lake Siljan. In the middle of the nineteenth century, this church served just under 8,000 people living in forty-one major villages and a score of minor settlements. Like many parish churches in Upper Dalarna, Rätt-vik's church was centrally located and accessible by the easiest mode of transportation—water. Large church boats were the traditional means of reaching the church from the "low villages" that clung to the slopes surrounding the bay. Parishioners from the inland "high villages" came down to the church on foot or in two-wheeled horse-drawn carts. Since the distance to church was considerable for most inhabitants of the inland villages, each household maintained a small structure *(kyrkstall)* on the grounds of the church, where one could tidy up, prepare meals, and find shelter in the course of the long Sundays that parishioners rou-tinely spent attending services and socializing on the grounds of the church. These structures lined the beach below the church and the road that approached the church from the north. The temporary settlement thus formed *(kyrkvallen)* was the social heart of the parish. There one met relatives and acquaintances from other villages, gossiped and debated about the issues of the day, made business deals, arranged mar-riages, and felt most keenly a general sense of belonging.[24] To those who gathered on the church grounds, there was ample evidence that the par-ish was a community. People all about them spoke in the same way, dressed in the same way, held the same interests, and together took a condescending view of the people in neighboring parishes.

From this place the parish was also governed. In its earliest form, the Swedish parish was a purely ecclesiastical organizational unit. But over time it increasingly took on the responsibilities of local civil admin-istration as well. The parish was governed by a parish council *(sock-enstämma)*. The council was an elected body, chaired by the parish priest, which had the authority to promulgate binding resolutions. In addition to the fiscal condition of the church, the council dealt with most civil matters of local importance, such as the running of parish schools, administration of the parish magazine, and provision of fire insurance, relief for the poor, and other collective measures undertaken by the par-ish community to protect and assist its members. There was also a

Plate 2.3 Church boat on Lake Siljan. The traditional means of reaching the church from the "low villages." (Courtesy of Dalarnas Museum, photograph by Anders Wicklund, 1890s)

Plate 2.4 Rättvik's church after services. The church yard, with its timbered stalls and shelters, was the social heart of the parish. The church structure dates from the Middle Ages. (Courtesy of Rättvik's Kommun Bildarkiv, photograph by Finn Lars Larsson, 1890s.)

church council *(kyrkoråd)* that dealt with purely ecclesiastical matters.[25] This marriage of ecclesiastical and civil functions remained the case until administrative reforms in 1862 introduced new civil organs to stand alongside the ecclesiastical. Local self-administration, a long tradition in Sweden, was instrumental in fostering a strong sense of local identity. In Rättvik, as in other parts of the country, an historically close relationship between local ecclesiastical and civil administration was part and parcel of that sense of identity.

During the first half of the nineteenth century, however, the close relationship between the institution of the church and local society in Sweden was strained over one issue: popular opposition to the formalism and barren theology of the state church. Early protest took the form of religious folk movements, which were most active in the sparsely settled far north of Sweden and in other areas where the population was poorly served by the state church. One of the earliest movements was the so-called "Reader movement" *(läsare)*. This pietistic group believed strongly in salvation by faith. Its believers saw too strong an emphasis on good works in the teachings of the state church. As early as the 1810s, small groups of Readers were established in Dalarna. They became particularly important in Orsa, a parish situated directly to the northwest of Rättvik. There they flourished for several decades, in spite of aggressively intolerant treatment on the part of the authorities in the 1840s and 1850s, before eventually merging with the Baptist movement around mid-century. Perhaps because of its close connections with regions in northern Sweden that were known for religious dissension, Orsa and some of its neighboring parishes in the upper Siljan basin maintained a well-earned reputation throughout the nineteenth century as a hotbed of religious dissension.

The situation in Rättvik, however, remained relatively quiet. Despite the close proximity of religious turmoil in neighboring parishes, there was remarkably little dissenting activity in Rättvik during this period. Church records merely mention the presence of Readers in the parish and their efforts to build their own church (apparently in the village of Blecket, but eventually abandoned). What little activity there was seems to have been deftly handled by the Rättvik clergy, who appear to have been adept at channeling dissension into positive activities within the existing framework of church and community.[26] As a consequence, Rättvik escaped the divisive early effects of the "awakening" experienced so painfully in other parishes. The leadership of the church and its identification with the community as a whole remained strong at mid-century, although the religious situation promised to become more complex and critical in the decades to follow.

While social community and ecclesiastical parish were in a large sense coincidental, there were important institutionalized internal divisions. With the exception of the finnmark, the villages and settlements of Rättvik were divided among four administrative districts, or *fjärdingar* (literally, "quarters"). This internal territorial organization of the parish dates from the early sixteenth century and is common to all of the large parishes of the Siljan basin. The division was originally carried out for taxation purposes, with the idea that each *fjärding* should be reponsible for one-quarter of the parish's total tax obligation. Later the *fjärding* assumed other administrative functions. In addition to the collection of taxes, the district functionary *(fjärdingsman)* was required, for instance, to transport criminals, to store reserves of perishable food, to establish civil obedience in instances of local physical violence or arson, to serve legal summons and arrest warrants, and to oversee the surveying of land. Although the functions of the *fjärding* gradually expanded over the centuries, the original territorial bounds of the four districts remained largely unchanged. Names changed on one or two occasions. There were also some minor boundary changes, but overall the *fjärding* system remained a remarkably stable and significant feature of the parish's internal spatial organization for more than three hundred years.[27]

In 1850 the westernmost of these administrative districts, known as Västbygge, comprised the villages situated on the south- and east-facing slopes of the hills to the west and north of Rättviken (Figure 2.3). Within Västbygge *fjärding* was a cluster of small villages (Sätra, Rovgärdet, Västberg, and Glisstjerna) that stood somewhat apart from the other villages. This cluster was known as "Gränden," a term that referred to the neighborly distinctiveness of these villages vis-à-vis those farther to the west. The southeastern district, known as Sörbygge, took in the villages strung out along the west-facing slopes on the opposite side of the bay. In earlier times, this *fjärding* extended up around the head of the bay to include the villages of Lerdal and Sjurberg, but these villages eventually were re-assigned to other districts. The other two *fjärding* districts, Gärdsjö and Ovanheds, comprised the "high villages" that occupied the shallow valleys that ran southward to the lake from the divide near the village of Boda and northward from the divide to the boundary with Ore parish, respectively. Gärdsjö *fjärding* originally centered on the villages of Övre Gärdsjö, Nedre Gärdsjö,

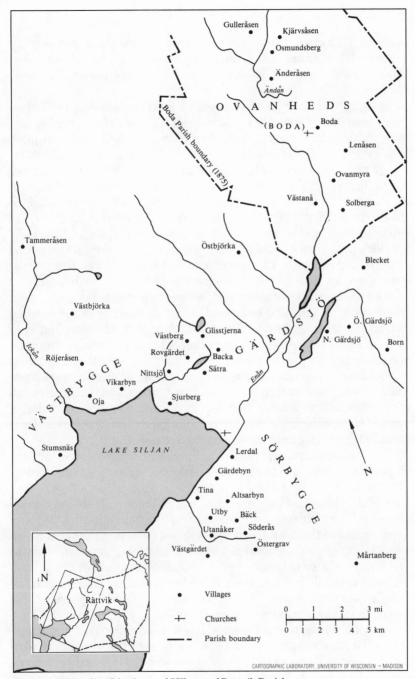

Figure 2.3 Fjärding Districts and Villages of Rättvik Parish

51

Born, and Blecket, but came to include several more peripherally located settlements as well. Ovanheds *fjärding* was originally known as Uppbygge. In the 1870s it became an independent parish, known as Boda.

In addition to their function as old administrative units, the *fjärding* districts were profoundly important socially because they served as sub-communities within the larger parish community. A striking indication of this may be seen in the pattern of intervillage marriage. While intra-village marriages were by far the most common, a substantial number of marriages each year joined individuals from different villages. Over-all, those who married outside the village were most likely to take a spouse from other villages in the same *fjärding*. This tendency is quite apparent from even a limited survey of marriage patterns. Of the 1,458 people who married outside their home village during the period 1858–67, for example, 72 percent married someone who lived in the same *fjärding* district.[28] The frequency with which marriage links crossed *fjärding* lines was highest, as one might expect, among new-lyweds who lived in villages located on the peripheries of the *fjärding* district. Distance and proximity inevitably play a role here. But resi-dents of such villages were still more likely to marry someone from one of the other villages in their own district than they were to marry across district lines, even where villages of an adjoining district were phys-ically closer. These patterns suggest that these old administrative dis-tricts were social isolates that had acquired, over the centuries, a marked sense of local identity which influenced the way their residents regarded themselves and those who lived outside the district.

Local identity was reinforced by linguistic differences within the parish, which coincided to a high degree with the *fjärding* organization. The traditional speech of Rättvik parish is regarded as a transitional form of the old *Dalmål*, the speech of Upper Dalarna. It shared charac-teristics of the more commonly understood Swedish dialects of the lower Siljan basin and the more specially developed dialects of the upper Siljan basin, although the similarities with the latter group are perhaps greater. In addition to the divergence of linguistic traditions along *fjärd-ing* boundaries, differences also existed between some villages, particu-larly in the central part of Gärdsjö *fjärding*. Gärdsjö proved to be especially distinctive in many ways, including its emigration behavior.[29]

One final illustration of the social importance of the *fjärding* commu-nity is the long and at times bitter struggle over the question of whe-ther Ovanheds *fjärding* should separate from Rättvik and become an independent parish. Secessionary sentiments among the people of

Ovanheds *fjärding* date back to the early seventeenth century, a period in which many Dalarna parishes were forced to grant independence to more remote areas. Rapid growth in population was a primary catalyst for independence, for it allowed remote areas to argue the need for their own church. The people of Ovanheds began their quest for independence in just that way. They petitioned for their own pastorate on the grounds that the *fjärding*'s population was sufficiently large, and that the distance and poor roads made it difficult to attend services regularly and to haul corpses down to the Rättvik church graveyard. In response, the *fjärding* was grudgingly granted its own chapel in 1618. The parish council blocked complete separation from the mother parish, partly out of suspicion that the seceding folk up in Ovanheds planned to seek a union with neighboring Ore parish.[30] Ovanheds had to be satisfied with winning the right to have its own chapel, to which Rättvik's parish priest was duty-bound to travel periodically for the purpose of holding services.

The struggle, however, did not end there. Relations between Ovanheds *fjärding* and the rest of the parish were marred for the next 250 years by intermittent petitioning, mistrust, and intrigue over the issue. In 1732, Ovanheds finally won the right to bury its dead on the chapel grounds, but even that concession failed to put an end to separatist feelings. Agitation continued, eventually going so far as to circumvent official channels and petition the royal authority directly. In the end, a royal letter dated June 27, 1856, officially separated the chapelry from its mother parish, recognizing it as the new parish of Boda. The separation did not become a reality, however, until nearly twenty years later, when in 1875 the new parish finally received its own clergyman.[31]

An incident during the separation underscores the strength of people's feelings of local identity and purpose associated with the *fjärding* unit. As part of the separation process, the northernmost villages in Gärdsjö *fjärding* were given the opportunity to join the new parish because they were physically closer to the new church at Boda than they were to the mother church. After due consideration, they categorically refused, preferring instead to maintain their ties with the other villages of their *fjärding* and with the mother church on the shore of Lake Siljan.[32] The time-honored bonds of church and community were not easily torn asunder, not even for the sake of convenience.

At its most intimate level, however, life in Rättvik revolved around village and kin. The village was an ancient organizational unit made up of ancestral farms. By the nineteenth century, most of the parish's villages had existed for centuries. Over the ages, many had been enlarged as population pressures and the availability of suitable land allowed.

This was especially common during the eighteenth century. But through it all, there was also a strong element of stability. The majority of farms that made up Rättvik's villages at mid-century could trace their lineage far into the past. Handed down from generation to generation, the ancestral farm was a venerable place that commanded respect and loyalty, as did the village of which the farm was a part. The inhabitants of these villages knew one another well regardless of whether the villages were large or small. Their families had dwelt among one another for as long as most could remember. Indeed, generations of marriage between farms made nearly all of them relatives, however distant. If a sense of community existed in conjunction with parish and church at the broadest level, and with the *fjärding* at a secondary level, it was strongest at the level of the village, where the bonds of kinship and personal loyalties were most intense.

The villages of Rättvik varied greatly in size, ranging from a few households to 500 or 600 souls in 1850. With rare exception, the entire village population was engaged in agrarian pursuits. Indeed, less than 1 percent of the economically active population in the parish derived their living from a nonagrarian pursuit. Those who did were principally the parish clergyman; a physician; a merchant or two; the operators of a few small hostelries, grist mills, and iron foundries; and a handful of military officers. At mid-century, this bourgeois element *(ståndskultur)* was extremely small and geographically concentrated in the lower part of Lerdal village, not far from the church. This small social group would someday expand to become the new center of the community, but in 1850 that development was still several decades away.[33] For the moment, life remained focused on the limited horizon of the agrarian village, just as it had for centuries before.

The agricultural villages, within which the day-to-day routine of work and leisure was largely confined, were of irregular form. They were composed of dwellings and outbuildings clustered along winding streets, the uneven terrain often dictating their haphazard layout *(terrängbyn)*. Surrounding these clustered settlements lay the fields and meadows to which they were symbiotically tied; and beyond them, the forest tracts that frequently marked the boundaries between village lands or the edge of the upland forest plateau, on which permanent agriculture was unfeasible. The dwellings and outbuildings of each farmstead were normally arranged around the perimeter of a rectangular area, forming a courtyard, as was the style throughout Dalarna. Structures were built of wood according to building traditions that had evolved over the centuries.[34] The fields and meadows outside the village

Plate 2.5 Village and field. Boda village, as seen from the tower of Boda church in the late 1880s, displays the typical, compact arrangement of farmstead buildings and open fields with their narrow holdings. The stacked poles in the fields are used for drying the harvest. (Courtesy of Boda Hembygdsförening)

were open and divided into many small strips individually owned by villagers.

Seen in the summertime from the heights overlooking Lake Siljan or from the divide up in Boda, the villages of Rättvik seemed to be set quite naturally in the landscape, with the grey-brown farm buildings nested in the folds of a patchwork quilt of striped golden fields, light green meadows, and dark forest. The villages also appeared orderly and self-contained. The very tightness of their form and the order of their surroundings could elicit a sense of the intimacy of life that went on within their bounds. That intimacy was important, for it introduced a high degree of social control in village life. The village was quite naturally a gossip mill; little that was of social interest could be hidden from view. The opinion of friends, neighbors, and family understandably both inhibited and supported village life. No one took unusual action without generating widespread discussion that ran along prescribed social networks.[35] Village economic life also demanded a high level of social conciousness and responsibility. While property was held individually, land holdings in the fields and meadows around the village were highly fragmented and complex. Centuries of partible inheritances on a small resource base had made them so. As a consequence, the conduct of agriculture necessitated a certain amount of cooperation between households. The time for plowing, sowing, haying, harvesting, grazing of stubble, and so on, had to be regulated in order to make maximum use of limited resources and to avoid getting in one another's way. Villagers therefore agreed to bylaws and collective responsibilities. Irresponsible disregard for bylaws and common agreements was punished with fines and ostracization. Conformity to the will of the majority was an unavoidable condition of village life. While the village was made up of individual households, each with its own property and freedom of action, in many ways it operated as a collective dedicated to the common good.

But ultimately, the most important social framework structured vil-

Plate 2.6 Interior of a Rättvik farm house (Sparvgården, Backa village). The woman wears traditional Rättvik dress, including the distinctive horizontally striped apron. The mistress exercised complete control over the household economy, in addition to being responsible for children, livestock, field work, and sundry duties. The walls of farm dwellings were brightly painted by local craftsmen, whose distinctive style *(dalmålning)* was handed down from generation to generation. (Courtesy of Dalarnas Museum, date unknown)

lagers' lives at a more intimate scale. The farm household was society's basic social unit. In its most common form, the household included all of the persons living on a single ancestral farm. It was hierarchially organized, with one individual in firm control of authority and property. All members had prescribed functions and responsibilities. Many a household was an extended family. In addition to the household head and his or her family, it might include retired parents, married siblings, unmarried siblings, and other assorted relations in residence or service. By tradition in Upper Dalarna, the inheritance of landed wealth required some form of compensation for all children, usually piecemeal as the children reached maturity. Married sons and daughters therefore commonly continued to reside, along with their families, on the farm of their parents and to share in the ownership of the estate. Similarly, retired couples remained members of the household after they ceased to be economically active; the new household head was required to maintain them in their old age.

The degree of household extension on any given farm varied enormously depending on the stage of the life cycle occupied by the household head.[36] At certain stages, the household could be quite extended and enormously complex. At other stages, it might be reduced to a single conjugal unit. The size and maturity of the household head's immediate family, the labor requirements of the farm, and obligations to retired parents, siblings, and relatives were all important factors that entered into the equation. In a farm headed by an aging farmer, with several married offspring to provide labor, the household might include several conjugal family units. A young household head with obligations to retired parents and siblings, and offspring too young to work, would be another example. On the other hand, a middle-aged farmer whose grown children were not yet married, whose parents were deceased, and whose siblings had established themselves elsewhere, might head a household comprised of just one conjugal family. Under the most extended conditions, it was not uncommon for the ancestral farm to be subdivided between two or more siblings or in-laws. The division sometimes became permanent and lasted for generations. Under changed conditions at a later time, the farm may have been reconsolidated.[37] In 1850 the average farm household size in Rättvik, regardless of type, was 8.1 persons. Sizes ranged considerably, however. Large households could reach a dozen or more persons and contain as many as three conjugal units. Other households were as small as two or three persons.

At mid-century, 61.6 percent of all Rättvik farm households extended to include others in addition to the nuclear family (Table 2.1).

Table 2.1 Nuclear and Extended Farm Households in Rättvik Parish, 1846

	Household type		Number of extended households including:			
	Nuclear	Extended	Parents	Married children	Siblings and in-laws	No relation
Husband–wife households	351 (36.0%)	625 (64.0%)	248 (39.7%)	145 (23.2%)	397 (63.5%)	57 (9.1%)
Wife aged:						
20–29	27 (15.3%)	149 (84.7%)	136 (91.3%)	0 (0.0%)	126 (84.6%)	0 (0.0%)
30–39	108 (40.0%)	162 (60.0%)	55 (40.0%)	0 (0.0%)	117 (72.2%)	27 (16.7%)
40–49	107 (53.0%)	95 (47.0%)	40 (42.1%)	4 (4.2%)	81 (85.3%)	0 (0.0%)
50–59	68 (29.3%)	164 (70.7%)	17 (10.4%)	89 (34.2%)	69 (42.0%)	10 (6.1%)
60+	41 (42.7%)	55 (57.3%)	0 (0.0%)	52 (94.5%)	4 (7.3%)	1 (1.8%)
Single male head	39 (32.2%)	82 (67.8%)	11 (13.4%)	28 (34.1%)	5 (6.1%)	2 (2.4%)
Single female head	96 (57.5%)	71 (42.5%)	10 (14.1%)	33 (46.5%)	29 (68.2%)	14 (19.7%)
All households	486 (38.4%)	778 (61.6%)	269 (34.6%)	206 (26.5%)	431 (55.3%)	73 (9.4%)

SOURCE: Catechetical registers (*husförhörslängder*) for Rättvik parish.

The proportion of extended households varied, as suggested above, by age and type of household head. The great majority were husband–wife households with both spouses present. Among this group, the percentage of extended households was highest among those headed by very young couples: nearly 85 percent of households in which the wife was aged 20–29 were extended. Over 90 percent of those extended households included retired parents, and over 80 percent included siblings and in-laws. Where the wife was in her middle years, households were slightly more likely to be nuclear than extended. Of those that were extended, the most important non-nuclear group were married siblings and in-laws. These were the households in which two or more married children shared control of the ancestral farm. Households with older heads were more commonly extended, often to include married children and their young families.

Households headed by a single male or female differed widely in composition, but all shared one characteristic. The head of the household lost his or her mate to accident or disease; divorce was uncommon. Roughly two-thirds of all households headed by a single male were extended households. If a widower chose to extend his household beyond his immediate family, by far the most likely additional members were a brother or sister, the sister often fulfilling the role of the absent wife and mother. Households headed by a single woman, in contrast, much more often remained nuclear, with older sons taking their father's place. In the extended households headed by women, married children and household members of no relation played a larger role than was the case in widower households. In other words, single women with household responsibilites were more likely to hold the farm for one of their children, even if that meant taking in people who were not kin in order to maintain an adequate labor force. Men seem to have been less independent, readily accepting the support and presence of siblings under their roof.

Nearly all extended households included kin. Household members with no direct blood relation to the household head were relatively rare; only 9.1 percent of husband–wife households contained outsiders. This was partly due to the fact that most adults in Rättvik held property. A strong tradition of partible inheritance assured most young families some kind of landed wealth. This was a society of smallholders who largely fulfilled the labor requirements of their farms with the labor of their own children and kin. The only two instances where non-kin household members reached any significant level were in households headed by widows and young but established households (heads aged 30–39) where the parents were too aged and the children too young to be of any use. In the latter case, the labor of brothers and sisters was often limited since most would have recently established their own farms. There was often little recourse in these situations but to seek help from someone outside the kin group.

While relative position within the household organization—household head and farmer, married son or in-law with rights to the estate, unmarried son or daughter in service, etc.—was certainly a determinant of social status, the simple fact of residence on one of these farms was also a source of one's identity. People were known in the parish, not by their Christian name alone, but by the use of their Christian name in combined form with the name of the farm (gårdsnamn) on which they resided. Christian names employed the patronymic form. Farm names were, of course, place names. Thus individuals were identified through both parentage and place. Take, for example, "Perols Hans Ersson." The Christian name incorporated a forename, "Hans," with a second name identifying him as the son of Erik, "Ersson." The prefix "Perols" indicates that this person was a member of the farm household that bore the name "Perols." In this way the farm name was a sort of surname as well as a place name. Among acquaintances in the community, people were simply known by the farm name plus the forename, dropping the patronymic suffix; in this case, Perols Hans.

In Rättvik, place was especially important in establishing one's identity. A farm name could be used only as long as one remained a member of a farm household. Changing one's residence to another farm by reason of marriage, for either males or females, normally meant adopting the farm name of the new household. The same might happen in the case of a widow who moves to another farm following her husband's death. In other Dalarna parishes, it was the custom to retain the farm name of one's birth, regardless of later residence.[38]

Farm names were derived, for the most part, from personal names, usually male (e.g., Bengts, Daniels), although sometimes women's names were used (e.g., Saras, Sofias). Most names were of Christian origin, with biblical and saints' names especially common among the women's names. Many farm names employed combinations (e.g., Mårthans = Mårten + Hans, Perols = Per + Olofs). Others were derived from the names of vegetation, animals, special occupations, and places of origin, such as Liljas (lily's), Elgs (elk's), Skräddars (tailor's), and Finn (Finn's). Yet another group of farm names were derived from soldier's names (i.e., Lustigs, Flink).[39] Whatever the derivation, the practice underscores the significance of the ancestral farm as a place in this society. People were closely tied to place and kin. With the exception of some seasonal migration in search of work, most people lived out their lives within the borders of the parish, usually on or within a short distance of the farm where they were born. The ancestral farm and its name figured large in defining their place in the world.

With the long tradition of partible inheritance in Upper Dalarna, nearly all households in the parish were landed in some sense. The number of completely landless households was exceedingly small. Indeed, virtually no crofter (torpare) class existed. Most household heads were smallholders, and many adult members of farm households held portions of an estate as well. Yet some households were relatively disadvantaged with respect to landed wealth. On some holdings lived a backstugusittare, or cottager, who occupied a small back lot. These people were usually poor relations of the estate owners, sometimes retired parents or their siblings. Their numbers were not great; they lived with less than 3 percent of all households. In addition, there was always a floating population of unattached people (löse personer), mostly poor and infirm who subsisted as wards of the community, but even here the numbers were not very high. The poor and unattached traditionally received a degree of care and support from the community. Old provincial laws as well as Christian ideal required that the parish maintain funds for poor relief as well as an active system by which the disadvantaged could be supported through local initiative. Care for orphans, for example, was traditionally handled by a member of the parish council, whose duty it was to secure foster parents—although this was often done by the rather entrepreneurial means of "letting them out" to whoever would provide child care at the least expense to the parish coffers.[40]

Lastly, this agrarian society included a relatively small number of soldier households. Rättvik belonged to the general mobilization region charged with the responsibility of supporting the Royal Dalarna Regiment. Its prime responsibility was to furnish the rank-and-file soldiery of "Rättvik's Company" (72 men in 1849, roughly one for every 100 inhabitants). Although Sweden began to introduce conscription in the middle of the nineteenth century, military formations were still filled largely through the old system, under which a certain number of farms were charged with the collective responsibility of recruiting and maintaining one soldier, who could be mobilized in time of war or called up periodically for training and maneuvers. The group of farms that supplied a single soldier was called a *rote*. The members of the *rote* obligated themselves to support the soldier and his family according to a negotiated contract. These contracts varied considerably, but in general the *rote* agreed to provide its soldier with clothing, equipment, and travel or pocket money while he performed his duties away from home. In addition, the *rote* helped support the soldier and his family at home with a small cash salary, some provisions, and enough labor to keep his small farm going when he was away on service. An important and traditional part of that support was the provision of a food subsidy—grain, meats, butter, and cheese—delivered to his home at Christmastime. The soldier was also entitled to "holiday hospitality" *(högtids gästning)* at Christmas, Easter, and Whitsuntide. On those occasions, he would visit each of the households in the *rote*, receiving traditional hospitality from each in the form of food and drink.

Most soldiers in Rättvik held some land. They supplemented their income by working for neighboring farmers or engaging in some artisanal trade, such as shoemaking or tailoring. Some acquired a certain education in military service, especially those who went through the "Corporal School" and therefore could be employed as teachers. Unlike soldiers in other parts of Sweden, where soldiers at best held roughly the same status as crofters *(torpare)*, the soldiers of Dalarna were often the social equal of the smallholder. In Rättvik, more than a few held important positions. But at the same time, one must keep in mind that they were maintained primarily for military service and, as such, were a distinctive and partially dependent element of society. They stood somewhat apart as a group; during Sunday services at Rättvik's church, they sat in their own section. Their dependency arose from the fact that they surrendered a certain economic freedom to fill one of society's needs. As long as they remained in service, they could demand a small but assured level of support from their neighbors. Once old age or some other circumstance led to their dismissal, their support became more problematical. Some cases had to draw upon the resources of the parish that were actually set aside for poor relief.[41]

The old social community of Rättvik, then, was a multilevel affair organized around kinship, village, *fjärding,* and church. Its organization was familiar and old—in a word, traditional. People identified themselves at the broadest level with the parish community and the church, its central institution. They identified more intimately with *fjärding* and village; ultimately, with kin and farm. They lived in the context of these hierarchial levels of spatial and social organization. Their behavior conformed to the mores of the old community and its institutions, which at mid-century had not yet begun to show significant signs of change.

Patterns of Marriage and Fertility

One of the most revealing measures of the relative stability of Rättvik society during the mid-nineteenth century is the pattern of marriage and fertility. Marriage was the most important step in life for all members of the peasant community, mainly because it marked so many key transitions in social status and function. This was true for men as well as women. Because it was simply not possible in a peasant society for males even to contemplate marriage without first securing the means to support a wife and family, marriage could rarely precede the initial inheritance or acquisition of landed wealth. Land and marriage were two closely linked goals that marked the seminal passage in life: advancement from the mass of landless young men who lived and worked on the farms of their parents or nearest kin, to the ranks of the independent peasant proprietor. The precise timing and nature of the process that linked inheritance and marriage will receive detailed attention in the next chapter, which deals more specifically with the peasant's relationship to the land. For now, let it suffice to say that possessing land and being responsible for a family were both indicators of status in a free peasant society. They conferred tangible position in both household and community, and a degree of control over one's own destiny.

For women, too, the state of matrimony was the condition to which all aspired, for marriage carried both economic and social benefits. Marriage meant a transfer of family wealth to a daughter and her chosen spouse in the form of a dowry. It made her the central figure in a new economic alliance between her own parental household and that of her suitor. Marriage also fulfilled her social and biological roles. She acquired real status in the community as the wife and household manager of an estate, and only under the sanction of Christian marriage could she bear children with the respect of her peers. The partnership of marriage raised the status of both men and women to full participants in society and in the necessary reproduction of society.

Young people in Rättvik enjoyed a certain degree of free will in the selection of a mate. During specific times of the year when farm labor and household chores were less onerous, such as the brief period of relaxation around midsummer, boys were supposed to visit and court similar-aged girls in the village.[42] Affections and preferences between the sexes formed naturally during the teen-aged years through a variety of contacts. But just as important as romantic love, and more often than not the deciding factor, were parental plans for the future of their offspring. Young people ultimately made choices that were either dictated by their parents or subject to their approval. Wealth and lineage became important variables that severely restricted freedom of choice. Most parents concerned themselves early with the identification of suitable mates for their children. Many decided before the prospective couple came of age. Prominent among these strategems was the preservation of economic position, for wealth was normally transferred through marriage.[43] Maintaining and reinforcing kinship networks were also important.

In *Jerusalem,* Selma Lagerlöf's novel set in nineteenth-century Dalarna, young Ingmar Ingmarsson daydreams about explaining his luckless attempt at marriage to his father, who sternly replies that things surely would have gone better had he chosen "one of our kind."[44] Foremost among the many considerations for a prospective marriage was whether any prior kinship linked the farms in question. It was always best to marry into a proven situation, to reestablish kinship ties that had been made sometime in the past. The villages and *fjärding* districts of Rättvik were literally crisscrossed with dozens of finite kinship networks that were the products of generation after generation of marriages arranged with this kind of social selectivity in mind. Such marriage alliances were an important feature of a traditional agrarian society in which crop failure and famine occurred periodically. The alliance and re-alliance of households through marriage insured cooperation in times of stress.

An average-size village typically had several of these kinship-based social webs, usually centered on one or more families that were particularly active in extending themselves through marriage. Two or even three children of one household might marry the children of another. Triangular or even quadrangular arrangements of this type also occurred, creating a dense core of multiply linked households anchoring a network that might extend over a dozen or more households. These networks were often nested; that is, the geographical proximity of households had little to do with the linkage of households. Indeed, kinship networks often extended beyond the bounds of the village, although seldom beyond the bounds of the *fjärding* district. In village affairs, some networks stand out as more central than others. Certain networks appear to have run things while others played a more peripheral role. Villagers elected by their peers to positions of local responsibility frequently came from the same families, and it was not uncommon to find those families in the same kinship network.[45]

Only when the principals and their families had agreed to the marriage and the complex arrangements for the young couple's future residence were the man and woman officially engaged. Marriage banns were announced and duly recorded in the church books. A wedding date was set, usually for some time during the next year. Most marriages were scheduled for one of the festive periods of the spring or early summer, when travel was easy and the seasonal work schedule accommodating. During the period of courtship following their engagement, the couple often resided on the same farm, a practice that allowed the new son or daughter-in-law to become accustomed to their adopted household as well as their intended mate.

This period of courtship frequently resulted in the conception of a first child, whose birth often followed the marriage ceremony by only the briefest period of time. Prenuptial conceptions were not thought to be unusual or immoral by local society; few engagements were ever broken and the marriage ceremony was always scheduled early enough to legitimize the child's birth. Women who bore children out of wedlock were the subject of moral condemnation and brought shame down upn themselves and their families. Because society placed great emphasis on legitimacy, families who suddenly found a daughter pregnant without engagement often hastened to arrange an engagement and wedding before the birth of the child. This occurred with some frequency, as attested to by the significant number of short engagements and weddings that fell outside the traditional wedding season of late spring and early summer.[46] Nonetheless, there were a substantial number of illegitimate offspring whose names carried a notation to that effect in the parish record books.

In mid-nineteenth-century Rättvik, most men and women did not marry for the first time until they were at least in their twenties (Table 2.2). The median age for men was twenty-five years of age, for women, twenty-four. Teen-age marriages were extremely rare. Only about 1 percent of all women aged fifteen to nineteen were married. Since marriage in a traditional peasant society depended on the inheritance or acquisition of land, which in turn depended on the willingness of parents to provide a partial inheritance or a gift of land, it is not surprising that young people were forced to wait until well beyond the age when they were physically ready. For some, marriage was delayed until well into their middle years. First marriages for people in their thirties were not at all uncommon, and could even occur among people in their forties. In the decades leading up to mid-century, first marriages beyond the age of thirty accounted for roughly 15–20 percent of all first marriages and were largely responsible for an average age at marriage of more than twenty-six for men and close to twenty-six for women.

On the other hand, marriage occurred at an earlier age in Rättvik than was often the case in peasant societies. For example, Jon Gjerde's study of marriage in the pre-migration society of the Norwegian fjord district of Balestrand documented average and median ages at first

Table 2.2   Age at First Marriage, Rättvik Parish, 1837–77

	Married 1837–46	Married 1847–57	Married 1858–67	Married 1868–77
		MEN		
Mean	25.9	26.1	26.9	27.6
Median	25	25	26	26
Total number	502	529	461	610
		WOMEN		
Mean	25.7	25.7	25.1	24.6
Median	25	24	24	24
Total number	502	529	461	610

SOURCE: Catechetical registers for Rättvik and Boda parishes, 1837–77.

marriage of nearly thirty years.[47] Differences may partly be explained by the fact that Rättvik lacked a landless class of shareholders and laborers, for whom a lack of economic opportunity could have severely constrained and delayed the decision to marry. Relatively good times in Rättvik during the 1840s and 1850s were also a strong influence. During that time the parish experienced relatively low population pressure on an expanding land base. More land was available in part because of the extensive land reform of the 1830s, and a period of new lands colonization that followed over the next few decades. (These developments are discussed at length in the following chapter.) The prosperity and optimism of the period did not last, however. Deteriorating conditions in the 1860s and 1870s led inevitably to a decline in opportunity and to higher ages at first marriage for men, although not necessarily for women.

Throughout the middle of the nineteenth century, women experienced a steadily declining marriage age. New brides in the 1830s were, on average, nearly the same age as their husbands. In subsequent decades, the age gap between the sexes widened. Indeed, by the 1870s the gap had reached the point where new brides averaged a full three years younger than their men (see Table 2.2). The steady decline in the age at which females first married may also have been tied to the relative optimism and prosperity of the mid-century decades. The number of marriages in the parish increased rapidly after the mid-1840s, bringing a far larger proportion of all eligible women into marriage than had ever been the case, possibly even creating a mild condition of scarcity. The percentage of women ever married rose steadily for all age groups from the mid-1830s into the 1850s and 1860s, before showing signs of decline in the 1870s (Table 2.3). Never to have married was a far more common condition for women in the first decades of the century than it was in the middle decades. The difference was most noticeable among the young and the old. As fewer and fewer older women were living out their lives

Table 2.3 Percentage of Women Ever Married, Rättvik Parish, 1836–77

			Age			
	15–19	20–29	30–39	40–49	50–59	60+
1836	1.1	37.6	84.8	83.9	81.2	85.3
1846	1.2	37.9	85.4	85.2	81.4	86.0
1857	1.5	39.7	86.4	93.8	83.3	87.9
1867	2.3	44.0	83.2	91.5	90.0	94.8
1877	2.4	38.9	89.8	90.0	94.8	92.1

SOURCE: Catechetical registers for Rättvik and Boda parishes; 20 percent sample of all households, N = 331 (1836), 345 (1846), 435 (1857), 437 (1867), 457 (1877).

as spinsters, higher proportions of younger women were marrying earlier.

The increased tempo of marriage and the broader age spectrum of female participants during the middle decades of the century led to a noticeable rise in fertility. In recent years, social historians have increasingly turned to constructing fertility indices from household data in the form of child/woman ratios. Fertility change in Rättvik during the middle decades of the nineteenth century is demonstrated here by periodically computing the number of children aged 0–4 per 1,000 married women aged 20–49 (Table 2.4).[48] According to this measure, fertility among married Rättvik women was on the rise from the 1830s through the end of the 1860s, although the rate of increase declined over time. An increase in the rate of fertility of roughly 6.5 percent was recorded over the thirty years from 1836 to 1867, as the standardized number of small children per 1,000 married females went from 899.8 to 958.2.

As in many peasant societies, delaying marriage until relatively late in a woman's childbearing years was a significant restraint on fertility in Rättvik. Earlier marriage ages for women lowered the efficacy of that check on fertility during the middle decades of the century. The fact that more and more women were bearing children throughout their twenties, rather than just in their late twenties, may be seen in the sharp increases in the number of small children per married women in this age group in 1846 and 1857. These changes had considerable effect. The average completed family size in Rättvik was just under four children in the 1830s and 1840s. With noticeably higher levels of fertility, it jumped to well over five in the 1850s and reached nearly six in the 1860s. Although fertility rates in Upper Dalarna had long been on the rise, the Rättvik generation that came of age around mid-century seems to have significantly raised its propensity to form new family units and bear children, a development that would generate stressful repercussions for the generations that married during this period, and for their children.

The trend towards higher levels of fertility ended rather abruptly in the late 1860s or early 1870s. The number of small children per 1,000 married women suddenly dropped by more than 160 in the single decade between 1867 and 1877, a decline of nearly 17 percent. That decade witnessed almost a complete reversal of the demographic events of the previous three decades.[49] The steady drop in the age at which women were married was suddenly arrested. The percentage of women ever married in the 20–29 age cohort dropped from an all-time high of 44 percent in 1867 to less than 39 percent in 1877, a level more comparable to that of

Table 2.4 Number of Children Aged 0-4 per 1,000 Married Women Aged 20-49, Rättvik Parish, 1836-77

Age group	1836	1846	1857	1867	1877
20-24	642.9	714.3	916.7	933.3	625.0
25-29	1031.3	1060.6	1394.7	1121.2	1153.8
30-34	1244.4	1270.8	1258.1	1084.7	1034.5
35-39	1105.3	1150.0	955.6	1127.3	923.1
40-44	805.5	812.5	608.7	824.6	520.0
45-49	142.9	162.2	288.9	450.0	227.3
20-49	871.8	902.0	911.5	934.4	779.9
20-49[a]	899.8	930.8	944.2	958.2	796.8

SOURCE: Catechetical registers for Rättvik parish; 20 percent sample of all households, N = 195 (1836), 204 (1846), 260 (1857), 259 (1867), 259 (1877).
[a] Standardized for the age distribution of the population.

the 1840s. With more and more women delaying marriage until at least their late twenties, there was a concomitant drop in the number of small children per married woman in the lower age cohorts.

These precipitous trend reversals coincide with the onset of difficult times in the late 1860s. The positive effects of land reform and colonization efforts had begun to wane. Diminished opportunity was further aggravated by natural disaster, as the region was beset by a period of severe crop failures and famine. The coming of age of an enlarged generation, born and raised during times of relative prosperity and heightened expectations in the 1840s and 1850s, made the depressed conditions of the late 1860s doubly stressful, for it placed an unprecedented demand on newly limited resources of farm and community.

One means of easing the burden of that increased demand was emigration. The decision to emigrate would never be a universal strategy for all households in the parish, nor would it be entirely an individual decision. It was an option that had to be carefully weighed by the members of entire households and even kinship networks. Families reached their decisions first and foremost, within the context of their society. The imperative to perpetuate the custody of ancestral farms, the varying demographic constitution of individual households, the flexibility and relative position of kinship networks within village, *fjärding,* and parish community were all considerations, as we shall see, that restrained or moved individuals to leave for America.

As always, the social organization of the old community was a major determinant of everything that happened. Those who left would take with them a remembrance of the social fabric of this community and their place therein. But the fabric of life in the old community was more than just social organization. It was also woven around people's relationship with the land—the manner and degree to which households were able to derive a living from the resources at hand. While this very economic aspect of life was also traditional and cannot be completely separated from the social, it may be seen as a second factor in the pre-migration experience of the emigrants and deserves a chapter of its own. For it was the changing and difficult economic conditions experienced in the 1850s and 1860s that set the special circumstances of emigration from this place.

3

The Land They Left

Economy in Rättvik at Mid-Century

THE PEASANT ECONOMY of mid-nineteenth-century Upper Dalarna was founded on the possibilities offered by a varied, but not particularly generous or forgiving, environment. Meagre agricultural resources made arable land precious to the majority of peasants who lived by small-hold farming.[1] No more than 3 percent of the land area of Upper Dalarna was potentially arable and little of it was concentrated. The multitude of small plains that could be farmed were scattered here and there along the major valleys and around the shores of some of the larger lakes. These small plains derived from the post-glacial floodings that drowned low-lying areas throughout much of Sweden. In Dalarna, the high coast line of the post-glacial Ancylus Sea reached altitudes approximately 210 meters above the present-day sea level. Where the ice waters stood for long periods of time, relatively rich deposits of fine-grained, sandy soils were left behind.[2] While such deposits were often extensive in Lower Dalarna, they were generally narrow and discontinuous in Upper Dalarna, confined to lower areas where the drainage system had cut down through the high plateau. With the exception of these small areas of good soil, the region offered little more to agriculturalists than an impoverished morainic landscape covered with forest and marsh that was, at best, grudgingly hospitable to agriculture.

The arable that did exist was never plentiful enough to sustain the local economy. Most of the population, as a consequence, was forced to turn to a variety of secondary and seasonal economic activities to support themselves and their families. Of course, most peasant populations are obliged to engage in multifarious work. But the severe limitations of the agricultural resource in Upper Dalarna, and the tradition of sharing it with as many as possible through the constant subdivision of ancestral farms, necessitated an especially wide-ranging array of subsidiary activities that sought to utilize the various resources of the parish. Since many resources were found at considerable distances from farms and villages, a seasonal movement of people and economic activity was a basic feature of the economy. The vast forest tracts that separated agricultural settlements were used extensively at all times of the year. In the summer, villagers cut the natural grasses of bogs and meadows in the forest and took their livestock there to graze. Forest tracts were also burned periodically to sow with rye and root plants for a few years until yields declined or to create new pasturage. Wood cutting and the making of charcoal were important wintertime activities. The carting of charcoal down to the forges of the *bergslag* metal-working regions of Lower Dalarna was a time-honored source of outside income for the Upper Dalarna peasant household. Various forms of handicraft made from local materials were also produced for trade. Some parishes were known for their itinerant peddlers. In short, few local resources escaped use by the peasant. Arable and good meadowland were by far the most prized resources, but the forests and wastes, rivers and streams also yielded a good part of what it took to subsist.

For many, the inadequacy of local resources meant looking for seasonal work outside the boundaries of the home parish or even the province. Both men and women from Dalarna were highly sought in other parts of Sweden as seasonal labor on large estates, foundries, and, late in the nineteenth century, in factories and sawmills. The men were valued for their skills in practical work of all kinds—timber cutting, ground clearing, ditch digging, masonry, and construction. The women, who were not at all unimportant in this phenomenon, were taken on to perform domestic work, gardening, threshing, and factory work. Men were engaged primarily in the fall and winter; women in late spring and summer. Their seasonal wanderings down to the central and coastal provinces and cities in Sweden in search of work were commonplace until late in the nineteenth century. Extant registers of labor migrants from the Upper Dalarna parishes of Leksand, Djura, and Siljansnäs suggest that perhaps as much as 8 to 10 percent of the population was involved in an average year, although the actual numbers fluctuated considerably from year to year depending on economic conditions in the home parishes and in the areas where seasonal work was normally found.[3] The records also show that most wanderers returned to their home parish within a short time. Remarkably few remained in the areas where they found work, most likely because of nearly universal land ownership among the Dalarna peasantry and a coincidental high degree of attachment to the home district.[4]

Upper Dalarna, then, was a region whose agrarian economy was shaped by a peculiar blend of traditions regarding the use of resources. The economy was able to absorb the steady increases in population in the early to mid-nineteenth century, but it remained, throughout the period, an economy dangerously close to the threshold of subsistence. Not only were the available resources barely sufficient; the vagaries of nature could easily upset the balance. High latitude and an interior location within the landmass of the Scandinavian peninsula put the region on the margins of the agricultural ecumene. Winters were long and relatively severe, with around 200 frost days the norm. The season was also prone to excesses. A late spring thaw or a killer frost before the growing season was over occurred with some frequency. Until late in the nineteenth century, when improvements in transportation made movement of surplus grain from other regions feasible, the loss of a crop due to such vagaries in the weather could spell disaster. In some of the worst recurrences of famine, the population was reduced to eating bread made from the bark of trees and suffered horribly.

The peasant economy of Upper Dalarna depended on the careful use of meagre resources and a high degree of human cooperation. It was one of the countless "peasant ecotypes" of preindustrial Sweden, unique in its resources and traditions, unique in its stage of development.[5] It probably conformed more to the general conception of a true peasant economy than did the economies of many other parts of Sweden,[6] due primarily to its relative isolation from the centers of developing trade and commercial activity. As a consequence, it was slow to adopt the telltale signs of modernization so frequently cited for agricultural economies; namely, rapidly increased inputs of labor, land, and capital.[7] In a word, the mid-nineteenth-century economy of Upper Dalarna was traditional.

People and Resources in Mid-Century Rättvik

In Upper Dalarna's Siljan basin, the arable resource that underlay the peasant economy was perhaps a bit more abundant than in many other parts of the region. Here the "high coast line" of post-glacial Lake

Ancylus stood at about 50 meters over the level of Lake Siljan, which meant that the waters of Lake Ancylus were sufficiently high to inundate much of the so-called Siljan Ring—the donut-shaped geologic depression that includes, moving clockwise, lakes Siljan, Orsa, Skattungen, and Ore (Figure 3.1). In the lower parts of the depression (up to 20–30 meters above the level of the lake), fine-grained marine deposits were fairly common and constituted the major attraction for agricultural settlement. Settlement was especially dense around the upper and lower ends of the lake, where these deposits were most extensive.

Settlement also occurred on some morainic soils found at higher elevations within the Siljan Ring. These soils, left by glacial action and generally coarse and stony, offered some agricultural potential primarily because they were formed from the limestone and shale bedrock that underlay the Siljan Ring formation. At higher levels lay the gravely old beach ridges of the post-glacial sea, stony soils left by old glacial spillways, and patches of sandy soils left by old ice lakes. These morainic and sandy soils were the basic resource for many of the "high villages" located on the margins of the ring and many of its higher areas, such as the divide in north central Rättvik parish. Little ground outside the ring held any agricultural potential. Rising above the Siljan depression on all sides, as well as in the middle, is a high plateau of hard crystalline rock. The plateau areas offered only thin and infertile soils, often too stony and coarse even to break for agricultural purposes. The plateaus were covered with extensive coniferous forests and scattered peat bogs and were generally devoid of permanent agricultural settlement.

Within the parish of Rättvik, the type and quality of the arable resource varied considerably.[8] Marine sediments are particularly extensive around Rättviken at the eastern end of Lake Siljan. Sediments from post-glacial times cover much of the slopes facing the bay and extend for a distance up the lower Enån and other stream valleys that empty into the lake. Most of the villages of Sörbygge *fjärding* were built upon this resource, as were many of the lower elevation villages of Västbygge *fjärding*. In contrast, the higher villages of Västbygge *fjärding*, as well as the villages in the *fjärding* districts of Gärdsjö and Ovanheds, were founded to take advantage of limy morainic soils or sandy lake bottoms left by glacial streams and lakes.

The differences in natural fertility between these two types of soil—the marine and the morainic—were considerable. Evidence appears in the soil surveys conducted in the 1830s in conjunction with the *storskifte* land reform.[9] Within the recognized administrative districts of the parish, the average quality of village soils were found by the *storskifte* sur-

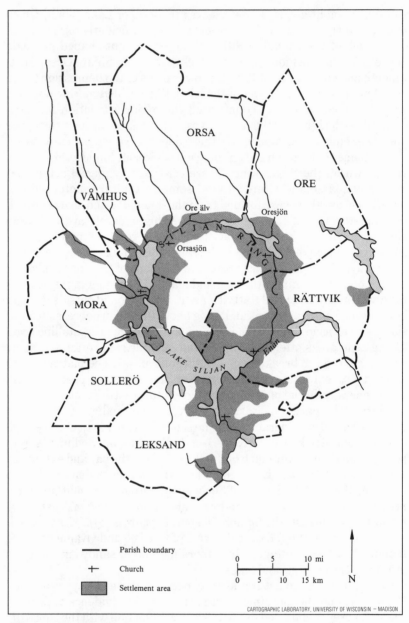

Figure 3.1 The Siljan Basin

74

veyors to vary by as much as 15 percent from the average for their respective districts. In addition, average soil quality for the districts as a whole varied from the parish average by a similar magnitude. In general, the parish's best soils lay in the Sörbygge villages of Tina, Bäck, Utby, Gärdebyn, and Lerdal, and in the Västbygge village of Vikarbyn. Some of the parish's least fertile soils were located in Gärdsjö *fjärding*, especially the sandy and stony soils of Nedre Gärdsjö, Övre Gärdsjö, and Blecket villages. Relatively infertile soils were by no means limited to the Gärdsjö villages, however. Stumsnäs village in Västbygge *fjärding*, Mårtanberg in Sörbygge, Västanå in Ovanheds, and some of the Gränden villages also ranked low in the *storskifte* evaluations.[10] Despite these internal variations, famous historical accounts of agricultural conditions in Upper Dalarna single out Rättvik for its superior soils and crop yields.[11] According to these observers, the parish as a whole was better off than any of its neighbors.

Soil fertility, however, is only one means of assessing the relative arable wealth of the parish's villages and districts. The quantity of arable and the pressure of population upon the resource are mitigating factors that must also be considered. The quantity of arable that had been cleared and cultivated by the middle of the nineteenth century was close to the maximum possible. In all, Rättvik's arable amounted to a mere 4,943 acres, just under 2.5 percent of the total land area of the parish.[12] The settlement of the parish had been a centuries' long process by which every small plot of ground suitable for cultivation was gradually colonized and brought into production. In the aftermath of the *storskifte* land reform of the 1830s, the pace of new land colonization was particularly rapid. Reliable statistics on the actual amount of new land brought under cultivation during individual decades in the nineteenth century are unfortunately lacking, but it is clear that a considerable amount was added during the 1840s and 1850s.[13] Nonetheless, some of the smallest villages in the parish existed in order to exploit no more than a dozen or so acres of cultivable land. Nowhere was the arable resource extensive enough to give the impression of anything approaching abundance. Even the largest villages cultivated no more than 300–400 acres, roughly equivalent to half a survey section in the midwestern United States. The pressure of population on this limited resource was heavy nearly everywhere. On the average, individual households in the parish possessed something over three acres of arable. Many possessed less than an acre (Figure 3.2). For a household to possess more than half a dozen acres was exceptional; to possess more than a dozen, virtually unknown.

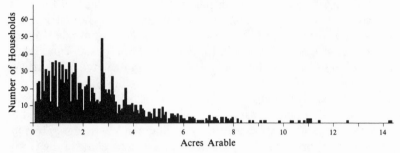

Figure 3.2 Distribution of Arable by Household, Rättvik Parish, ca. 1842

When the factors of soil fertility, quantity of arable, and population pressure are brought together at the village and *fjärding* level, a picture of the geographic distribution of landed wealth in arable emerges (Figure 3.3). Sörbygge *fjärding* stands out as the part of the parish with greatest per capita arable wealth. Blessed with good marine soils spread over sunny south- and westward-facing slopes and with relatively modest population pressure, the villages of Sörbygge had a natural advantage over much of the rest of the parish when it came to reaping benefits at harvest time. The other three *fjärding* districts were more or less equally less well-off. Of the three, Västbygge, which also had quantities of marine soils, was in a marginally better situation, although the differences between its villages was great. Variable population pressure on resources seems to have played some role in Västbygge. The village of Vikarbyn, for instance, which possessed some of the parish's most fertile soils, was also the most populous village. As a consequence, it ranked somewhat below middling in per capita arable wealth. The same can be said for the Gränden villages of Västberg, Rovgärdet, and Glisstjerna. On the other hand, the poor morainic soils of some of the high Västbygge villages, such as Stumsnäs and Nittsjö, were so impoverished as to ensure low levels of arable wealth despite relatively low population pressure. Gärdsjö *fjärding*, with some of the poorest soils in the parish, was able to show respectable levels of arable wealth vis-à-vis other districts only because the quantity of arable relative to population was fairly great. This was especially true in the core villages of Övre and Nedre Gärdsjö, where levels of per capita wealth in arable were close to the median values for the parish. In the north, the situation of Ovanheds *fjärding* was quite mixed. A few of the villages occupied some of the least fertile soils in the parish, while others (Boda, Lenåsen, Ovanmyra) enjoyed some remarkably rich morainic and lake

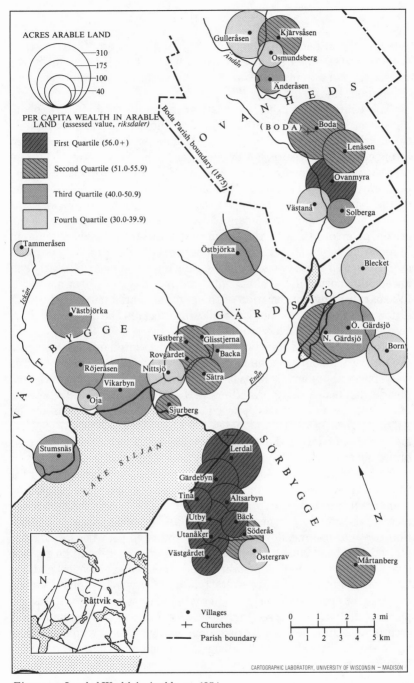

ACRES ARABLE LAND

─310
─175
─100
─40

PER CAPITA WEALTH IN ARABLE LAND (assessed value, *riksdaler*)

First Quartile (56.0+)

Second Quartile (51.0-55.9)

Third Quartile (40.0-50.9)

Fourth Quartile (30.0-39.9)

Tammeråsen

Gulleråsen
Kjärvsåsen
Osmundsberg
Änderåsen

O V A N H E D S

(BODA)   Boda
Lenåsen
Ovanmyra
Västanå   Solberga

Östbjörka

Blecket

G Ä R D S J Ö

Västbjörka

V Ä S T B Y G G E

Västberg   Glisstjerna
Rovgärdet   Backa
Röjeråsen   Nittsjö
Vikarbyn   Sätra
Oja
Sjurberg

Ö. Gärdsjö
N. Gärdsjö
Born

Enån

Stumsnäs

L A K E   S I L J A N

Lerdal

S Ö R B Y G G E

Gärdebyn
Tina   Altsarbyn
Utby   Bäck
Utanåker   Söderås
Västgärdet   Östergrav

Mårtanberg

N

Rättvik

N

• Villages
+ Churches
─ ─ Parish boundary

0   1   2   3 mi
0 1 2 3 4 5 km

CARTOGRAPHIC LABORATORY, UNIVERSITY OF WISCONSIN – MADISON

Figure 3.3 Landed Wealth in Arable, ca. 1854

77

bottom soils, situated on high ground where they caught the warmth of the sun and escaped the risk of frost that was always present in the valleys. Population pressure on the arable resource was relatively light throughout this *fjärding*.

These differences in arable wealth are a significant factor in explaining spatial patterns of wealth variation within the parish, most notably the marked deviation of the Sörbygge villages from the others. Differences in arable wealth, however, are only part of the picture. The general shortage of good arable necessitated a mixed crop and livestock economy. Since earliest times the Rättvik peasant household depended on the complementarity of these two activities. Animal husbandry was traditionally the more important of the two, especially in areas with relatively poor soils. Indeed, the size of a farm was traditionally thought of in terms of the number of animals it supported rather than its physical size. Although these two sides of the peasant economy more nearly balanced one another in the nineteenth century, they were always difficult to separate. Any appreciation of the general spatial pattern of wealth differentials in Rättvik must also take into account the degree to which resources were available to support livestock.

Most essential to the support of livestock were land that could be used to raise fodder crops and land that could be grazed. Such resources were fairly abundant in Rättvik in the form of natural meadowlands. Meadowlands were far more extensive than arable, covering 9.4 percent of the area of the parish as opposed to the 2.4 percent that was arable. Among the several different types of meadowland, the most extensive and most valued were the natural meadows *(slog)* found on the margins of the village arable. These were open areas that were naturally dry or ditched to drain off excessive moisture. They were highly valued for their low moisture levels and the richer grasses that were planted on them from about the sixteenth century onwards. Where farmers relied on animals more than crops, *slog* was valued more than arable. In addition, wet natural meadows *(svad)* and exhausted peat bogs *(myrslog)*, which both dried out sufficiently in the summer months to be cut and grazed, could be found deep in the forest lands. Forest meadow and bog lands were not as extensive in Rättvik as they were in some Dalarna parishes, but they were fairly abundant in the western and southeastern parts of the parish. Interestingly, the very best meadowland of all was created quite unintentionally by human action. These were the grassy right-of-way ditches *(slussar)* along the parish and village roads. The fertilization these areas received from passing horses and livestock and

Plate 3.1 The fields and village of Backa in late summer. The harvest is already drying on racks in the fields. The fence along the village road protects the luxuriant growth of grasses in right-of-way ditches—one of the most prized sources of animal fodder. (Courtesy of Dalarnas Museum, photograph by Carl Ståhlberg, Jr., ca. 1900)

the drainage from nearby fields produced a luxuriant grass that could be cut as many as three times in a single summer.[14]

According to land records from the 1850s, village lands in Rättvik parish included 20,212 acres of natural meadow. The average farm household could therefore lay claim to nearly fifteen acres of meadowland, or roughly four times the average amount of arable. The quality of meadowland varied across the parish in much the same manner as the arable (Figure 3.4). In general, the best meadows lay in the south among the Sörbygge villages, while poorer resources were found in the north and west. Villages in the north and west, however, compensated for the relative inferiority of their meadowland with much larger amounts. The ratio of per capita meadowland to arable was one and a half to two times greater in most villages of Västbygge, Gärdsjö, and Ovanheds than in the south. The greater amount of meadowland in these villages was usually more than enough to compensate for inferior land. The northern and western parts of the parish thereby offset the greater arable wealth

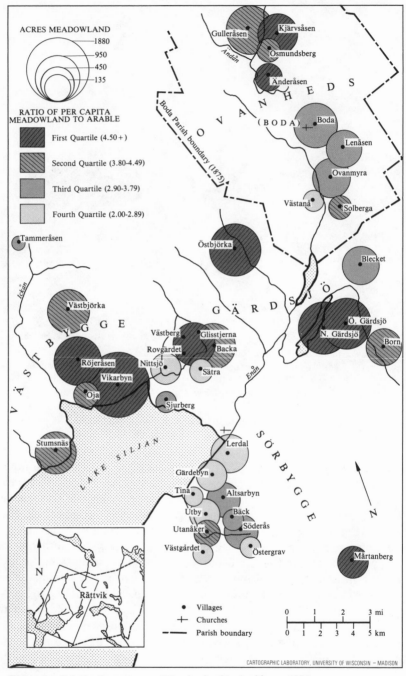

ACRES MEADOWLAND
1880
950
450
135

RATIO OF PER CAPITA
MEADOWLAND TO ARABLE

First Quartile (4.50+)

Second Quartile (3.80-4.49)

Third Quartile (2.90-3.79)

Fourth Quartile (2.00-2.89)

Tammeråsen

Gulleråsen   Kjärvsåsen
Osmundsberg
Anderåsen

OVANHEDS

(BODA)   Boda
Lenåsen
Ovanmyra
Västanå   Solberga

Östbjörka

Blecket

Västbjörka

VÄSTBYGGE

Västberg   Glisstjerna
Rovgärdet   Backa
Röjeråsen   Nittsjö
Vikarbyn   Sätra
Oja
Sjurberg

GÄRDSJÖ

Ö. Gärdsjö
N. Gärdsjö   Born

Enån

Stumsnäs

LAKE SILJAN

Lerdal
Gärdebyn
Tina   Altsarbyn
Utby   Bäck
Utanåker   Söderås
Västgärdet   Östergrav

SÖRBYGGE

N

Mårtanberg

N
Rättvik

• Villages
+ Churches
— — Parish boundary

0   1   2   3 mi
0   1   2   3   4   5 km

CARTOGRAPHIC LABORATORY, UNIVERSITY OF WISCONSIN – MADISON

Figure 3.4 Relative Importance of Meadowland to Arable, ca. 1854

80

of the south by placing more emphasis on meadowland resources and animal husbandry.

The other major land resource in Rättvik was forest land. Until the nineteenth century, forest land was held in common by the parish. As part of the *storskifte* land reform in the 1830s, however, forest lands were divided among the villages and then divided in turn among village households. Thus, by mid-century forest lands were individually owned, at least on paper, and their commonality was a thing of the past.[15] The forest resource was by far the most extensive, covering 88.8 percent of the parish. It was also no doubt a bit inhibiting in its wildness, despite the recent surveying and subdivision. Throughout much of the first half of the nineteenth century, parish records repeatedly report encounters with bears, wolves, fox, and lynx who stole out of the forest depths to wreak bloodthirsty havoc on peasant livestock.[16]

Although vast and sometimes forbidding, the forest lands offered much to the peasant economy. For one thing, they could be grazed. Most villages practiced a form of transhumant herding of livestock, taking animals long distances into the forest to graze the extensive forest lands that surrounded small summer settlements maintained expressly for the purpose of summer grazing. On a prescribed date each year (usually the tenth of June), most of the livestock were driven to the summer settlement *(fäbod)*, which was usually located on a natural meadow somewhere in the forested wastes of the northwestern or eastern parts of the parish. There they would remain for about three months, watched over by certain members of the household. In Rättvik the distance from the home village to the summer *fäbod* varied greatly, ranging from two to twenty-five miles. The livestock were taken to the same *fäbod* year after year, since most peasant households normally held land and had grazing rights at a particular site. Most of these seasonal settlements were associated with a particular village, although in quite a few cases households from more than one village may have shared it.[17]

The value of the transhumant husbandry of livestock in the summer, of course, was the relief it offered to the meadowlands around the home village. It removed the stress of sustaining livestock for a significant portion of the year. The summer's growth in hay and fodder material could therefore be dried and stored for the coming winter. Many Dalarna parishes had multi-tiered *fäbod* systems, whereby livestock were taken to more than one *fäbod* over the summer months. This was not the case in Rättvik, which had a "one *fäbod* system" because its forest lands were not sufficiently extensive to support a complex system.[18] Nor was the configuration of the parish particularly appropriate

Table 3.1   Population, Households, and Land Resources in Rättvik Parish, 1854

Village	Population[a]	Households[a]	Acres arable[b]	Acres meadow[b]	Acres forest[b]
	SÖRBYGGE FJÄRDING				
Mårtanberg	123	22	107.1	397.3	3,384.6
Söderås	193	34	133.1	476.3	5,289.4
Östergrav	126	23	67.6	163.3	2,530.2
Västergrav and Utanåker	98	19	118.6	271.4	4,175.6
Västgärdet	98	17	65.5	148.7	2,882.9
Utby	174	36	146.6	309.9	7,059.5
Bäck	71	13	51.0	183.0	2,327.5
Altsarbyn	202	38	141.4	457.6	6,741.3
Tina	91	18	55.1	136.2	2,585.4
Gärdebyn	249	45	137.3	377.5	5,079.4
	VÄSTBYGGE FJÄRDING				
Stumsnäs	227	42	162.2	702.0	4,996.0
Öja	94	14	34.3	250.6	1,268.8
Tammeråsen	34	5	14.6	67.6	436.8
Röjeråsen	300	54	182.0	949.5	7,467.2
Västbjörka	254	44	149.8	742.6	4,718.5
Vikarbyn	590	98˙	312.0	1,885.5	13,234.0
Sjurberg	93	18	44.7	182.0	1,508.0
Nittsjö	195	33	108.2	312.0	2,796.6
Västberg, Rovgärdet, and Glisstjerna	224	41	139.4	748.8	5,882.2
Sätra	107	20	91.5	203.8	2,995.2
	GÄRDSJÖ FJÄRDING				
Lerdal	310	59	265.2	577.2	8,788.0
Backa	413	73	233.0	832.0	7,939.4
Blecket	287	42	145.6	653.1	4,887.0
Born	196	32	119.6	541.8	4,978.5
Övre Gärdsjö	308	58	239.2	1,022.3	7,187.4
Nedre Gärdsjö	284	54	253.8	1,086.8	7,500.5
Östbjörka	278	47	185.1	1,104.5	5,868.7
	OVANHEDS (BODA) FJÄRDING				
Västanå	129	21	80.1	167.4	1,741.0
Solberga	80	14	57.2	205.9	1,869.9
Ovanmyra	247	47	195.5	621.9	6,717.4
Lenåsen	199	33	126.9	530.4	4,602.0
Boda	362	70	239.2	791.4	8,671.5
Änderåsen	89	16	62.4	283.9	2,257.8
Osmundsberg	90	15	46.8	212.2	1,684.8
Kjärvsåsen	191	35	138.3	637.5	6,148.5
Gulleråsen	337	54	162.2	923.5	5,888.5

(*continued on the following page*)

Table 3.1 Population, Households, and Land Resources in Rättvik Parish, 1854
(*continued*)

Village	Population[a]	Households[a]	Acres arable[b]	Acres meadow[b]	Acres forest[b]
		FINNMARK			
Finnbacka	98	16	42.6	384.8	1,644.2
Dalstuga	70	13	26.0	233.0	1,790.9
Bingsjö	167	27	62.4	436.8	3,467.4
Totals	7,678	1,356	4,943.1	20,212.0	174,844.0

SOURCE: 1854 description of Rättvik parish in the archives of *Lantmäteriet* in Stockholm.

[a] Excludes non-farming population.

[b] Excludes land occupied by farmsteads, waste land within the immediate village holdings, and land held by the parish in common.

to a multi-tiered system. According to an 1834 document that codified the organization of the Rättvik system, some forty-odd *fäbod* settlements were maintained within the parish boundaries. Most were used exclusively by Rättvik peasants, although in a few cases rights were also held by villagers from neighboring parishes. Eighty-nine percent of the parish households in 1834 had *fäbod* rights. The document groups the *fäbod* sites into five major geographic tracts, four serving the main settlements of the parish and one serving the settlements of Rättvik's finnmark. In the years after the 1834 codification, the system changed little. Some smaller sites were added, but these additions were balanced by the abandonment of marginal sites. The system flourished until late in the century when the introduction of new higher-yielding grasses and fodder plants, as well as the introduction of commercially available fodder products, made the system superfluous.[19]

Aside from the value of natural meadowlands, openings, and peat-bogs to help maintain livestock, the forest lands had one other major agricultural utility: they could be periodically burned to produce clearings on which crops could be sown. The practice, known as *svedjebruk,* is an ancient one in Sweden and an especially important one in the morainic, coniferous forest lands of Upper Dalarna. It was labor intensive work usually undertaken jointly by a number of households. They generally chose high ground to reduce the risk of frost and preferred sunny, south-facing slopes where good drainage and dry ground could be assured. In the first year, all the trees on the chosen site would be felled and trimmed to create a heavy layer of brushwood on the ground. In the following year, usually around late June, the site would be burned. Shortly thereafter, grain would be sown in the cool ashes. Rye was the

Plate 3.2 Forest peat bog. All forms of natural meadow were highly valued, including remote forest bogs. These bogs were normally dry enough in the summer to be cut once or twice and then grazed.

principal *svedjebruk* crop, although the best part of the clearing, where the ashes were thickest, was often reserved for turnips. While little could be expected of the rye crop in the first year, delayed as it was by the burning, the second year normally brought a bountiful crop. Clearings were expected to yield two or three grain harvests before the soil became impoverished. Then they were used to produce grass for hay-making. After another two or three years, the clearing was left to be grazed and eventually reverted to forest cover.[20]

This form of forest clearing was restricted by the authorities during much of the seventeenth and the eighteenth century, chiefly because mining and metallurgical interests in some parts of Sweden feared the eventual disappearance of forest lands from which charcoal could be cheaply obtained. The regulations, however, were not easily enforced in distant places such as Upper Dalarna. The practice was freed of all restraints in the nineteenth century, when the forest lands were divided up among peasant freeholders. *Svedjebruk* served as an important source of foodstuffs and fodder throughout much of the middle decades of the nineteenth century. In Rättvik, the practice was common through the 1850s and 1860s but declined in the latter part of the century as improved yields and the importation of commercial animal fodder made the practice of *svedjebruk* an increasingly arduous means of increasing production given the return.[21] There is some debate as to which side of *svedjebruk* was most important to the Dalarna peasant, the additional production of foodstuffs or the enlargement of the carrying capacity of peasant lands for livestock. The Finnish settlers of the resource-poor finnmark areas, who were perhaps the greatest practitioners, appear to have been most interested in the grains and root crops. The Swedish peasants, who possessed more arable, may have been more interested in expanding the potential to support livestock.

The forest lands also contributed wood for building and household use and raw material for a variety of wood and handicraft products that were sold outside the parish or used in the payment of taxes. Demand existed from fairly early times for both wood and charcoal for local mining and iron production. This local demand was replaced in the late Middle Ages by a prodigious demand for charcoal emanating from the *bergslag* mining and metallurgical districts. When the royal copper industry at Falun began to exhaust local resources of wood and charcoal in the sixteenth century, the crown imposed a "wood tax" on Rättvik and surrounding parishes, payable in the form of rough timber or charcoal. By the mid-seventeenth century, the growing demand for charcoal in the copper district precipitated a conversion of the wood tax to a new annual tax payable only in charcoal. It also created a market for all the charcoal that could be hauled down to the mines and forges around Falun.[22]

In this way, the forest lands became a considerable asset and the site of much economic activity in the winter time, when the menfolk spent long periods of time either in the forests cutting timber and manufacturing charcoal in crudely built charcoal ovens *(mila)* or on the frozen trails hauling sledges of charcoal down 30 miles to the copper district at Falun. According to an 1837 report, Rättvik produced more charcoal than any other Upper Dalarna parish.[23] Such activities made the division of the old common forest lands in the 1830s an important development, for it gave peasant proprietors the right to dispose of these resources independently. In the reorganization of forest lands, each village received an equal share, which was then divided among village households according to their landed wealth. Each household received a portion of its allotment in the form of "home forest" *(hemskog)*, "fäbod forest" *(fäbodskog)*, and "outlying forest" *(utskog)*. While the villages received their respective parcels in neatly defined blocks of substantial size, the parcels awarded to individual households were surveyed as narrow strips running across the entire village allotment—a somewhat less than ideal shape for efficient exploitation.[24] But exploitation was soon taken out of peasant hands in any case. With the first glimmerings of demand for saw timber around the middle of the nineteenth century, peasants began to have their first encounters with speculators who offered them contracts to purchase timber rights on their forest lands. According to an 1862 report on economic conditions in Rättvik, outside interests had already purchased rights to at least one-third of the parish forest.[25]

For many, the natural resources of the parish alone were not enough to satisfy all the demands of making a living. Most of what was produced was consumed at home. Before the latter part of the nineteenth century, there was little surplus production and no real market for it, both of which are hallmarks of a true peasant economy. Yet the need for essential wares that could not be produced at home meant the peasants required at least a modest cash income. In part this was provided through the sale of forest products and home handicrafts. Beyond that, the peasants relied heavily on the tradition of finding seasonal work outside the parish (herrarbete). The practice had its origins deep in the past, perhaps sometime in the Middle Ages, and has been studied exhaustively in Dalarna by quite a number of Swedish scholars.[26] For some Dalarna parishes there are detailed records of these wanderings that allow statistical analyses of their importance over time.[27] Such records do not exist for Rättvik, although we may assume that the pattern was similar. Essentially, the data show a fluctuating pattern of participation, with the numbers of seasonal wanderers rising and falling from year to year as conditions changed in the home parishes and in the areas where work was found. In general, participation was high throughout most of the 1840s and 1850s. Göran Rosander, in his exhaustive study of Swedish labor wanderings, cites sources from the 1830s that suggest participation in Rättvik may have amounted to six or seven hundred men, women, and children, about 8 percent of the population. There is also evidence that the heaviest wanderings from Rättvik took place in the winter and early spring.[28] The contribution made to the local economy by money earned from seasonal labor wanderings was substantial. According to an 1868 report, the parish earned 100,000 Riksdaler annually through herrarbete.[29]

Thus, at mid-century, the land resources of Rättvik supported a subsistence-oriented peasant economy. The peasant population made a living by garnering what they could from a number of resources, none of which was especially rich or in abundant supply, but which together were apparently adequate to meet the basic needs of the population. What the land could not supply was obtained through a number of subsidiary activities, the most important of which were the sale of charcoal and seasonal work outside the parish. These activities were important means of meeting tax obligations and securing the cash income necessary to purchase basic commodities that could not be produced at home. The sale of timberlands to outside interests was a harbinger of things to come. Working for wages was becoming more common, renewed land reclamation was under way, and new crops and animal feeds were already being experimented with on the parsonage lands. But, by and large, the agricultural economy of this place, in which the emigrants to America grew up, was still a traditional one, having far more in common with the past than the future.

The Seasonal Round

Perhaps nowhere is the traditional nature of the Rättvik peasant's economic life more apparent than in the seasonal round. Subsistence in an economy built on much multifarious activities required that the entire peasant household, as well as the community of which it was a part, be locked into a rigorous calendar of economic activity. Environment, tradition, and the collective decision of all involved set the timing and scope of work. Tradition divided the work among the sexes and among adults and children. It was not a society in which individuals found much time or opportunity to devise innovations or radical departures from the time-honored and accepted way of doing things. Instead, each step in the annual cycle led inexorably to the next, with short breaks of reduced activity or holiday observances in between. The rhythm of the cycle seemed to take on a life of its own. Descriptions of the calendar of work in premodern societies are common features of anthropological and ethnographic work and can provide considerable insight into the fabric of economic life. The annual cycle through which a mid-century household in Rättvik lived and worked is roughly as follows.[30]

The seasonal round began in the spring. Spring was the time of year when nature began its annual reproductive cycle. In many ways it was one of the busiest times. Spring came sometime in April, or at the latest by early May. Its arrival was marked by a multitude of small tasks, many of which inolved hauling materials and required the use of a horse. The portion of the previous summer's cutting of hay that had been left in the small hay barns that dotted the meadows had to be hauled home to replenish depleted winter stocks. Firewood for household use was also hauled home at this time and stacked. The manure that had accumulated over the winter had to be hauled out to the fields and spread. Early spring was also the time for the family's annual trip to a market town for needed goods and wares. The horse was, without doubt, the premier creature maintained by the peasant household. Not every farm possessed a horse, essential though they were. In fact, perhaps one out of four lacked them. These households were assisted by their horse-owning neighbors, who by tradition helped them haul fodder and wood on an agreed day, the expected payment being a good meal and drink. Such was the cooperative tradition by which the peasant economy functioned. The sharing of labor and equipment was commonplace in all seasons and activities. There was even a communal obligation to contribute to the maintenance of roads in the area, each household or group of households having been assigned to a particular section.

In all seasons, a well-developed sexual and age-specific division of labor was a salient feature of the system. Men, women, and children were expected to make particular contributions, out of doors as well as in. In the early spring, one of the tasks women attended to was the malting of grain. This was followed by smoking the meat butchered that spring. Women and the older children also helped with the spreading of manure. In the meantime, the menfolk set about making repairs on outbuildings, fences, and equipment. This was also the time when some of the young men and women set off for summer *herrarbete*.

The most important obligation for the women and children was the care of the livestock. As soon as the snow was gone, the small animals were released from their winter stalls and led into the forest near the village to browse the new green shoots that would be pushing up out of the soil. Small animals from the entire village were mixed together to form a single herd, which the young children encouraged to follow a prescribed grazing path each day. These animals, chiefly sheep and goats, were kept in roughly equal numbers in Rättvik. The sheep and goat population of the parish in the 1850s totaled around 10,000 animals. The sheep were kept for their wool and the goats for their milk. Swine and poultry were uncommon; both required specialized fodder or consumed grain better reserved for human consumption. Neither were suited to the transhumant grazing patterns that were so basic to animal husbandry in this region. The springtime grazing in the forest was a frivolous time for both animals and children, a time to shake off the lethargy of winter. Most of the animals bore affectionate names and could frequently be seen gamboling about with the children in the forest.

Later in the spring, near the middle of May, the serious business of planting began. The exact time for sowing was a matter of guesswork, experience, and tradition. The peasant watched for a variety of signs from nature, made familiar by common folk-sayings; for example, when the birch leaves are the size of mouse ears or when the patches of snow on a ridge reach a certain size, or, as they often said in Rättvik, when the earth turned to gray dust after it was harrowed.[31] Any of these conditions signaled that it was time to shoulder the seed bag and sow. The time for sowing grain was also tied to certain celebrated days of the church calendar. The best spring planting time, for instance, was said to occur sometime during the three days before and the three days after Eric's Mass (May 18th). Before sowing could begin, however, the ground had to be plowed and then worked over with a harrow. Spring plowing was not always necessary. If time had permitted and the onset of frosts had not been too early, the plowing may have been done in the autumn. Running a harrow across the fields against the grain of the plowing was always necessary, however, to break up the clumps. In fact, in Rättvik it was customary to use a hoe to break up clumps of earth even after harrowing.[32] Once the seed was sown, the fields were harrowed again to set the seeds in the soil and finally packed down with a wooden roller.

Spring planting was a critical task that had to be done efficiently, given the shortness of the growing season. The general rule was that it was best done in the space of about a week, once conditions were right. It was also something that had to be done cooperatively, since a four-course rotation system was standard throughout the parish. With the exception of some of the smaller villages, the arable belonging to a village was divided into four major fields, each of which received a particular use each year. All villagers were expected to conform to the agreed system; cooperative efforts to plow and sow the open fields were commonplace. The traditional rotation scheme for a field was to plant barley the first year, a blend of peas and barley (blandsäd) the second, barley again in the third, and to let the land lie fallow the fourth. After the grain was sown, it was necessary to put in and fertilize the potato patch and to plant a small garden for turnips, cabbage, onions, and hops. A small allotment was also set aside for flax and hemp. These tasks were largely carried out by the women and children. While they were so occupied, the men were in the forest, for popular wisdom had it that this was the best time to burn the forest for svedjebruk.

The cultivation of grain crops was always pursued somewhat differently in Rättvik than it was in neighboring parishes. Barley was the principal crop, partly by tradition and partly because of unique soils and

Plate 3.3 Spring planting. These men are harrowing the fields (against the grain of plowing) to set the seed in the soil. Most agricultural work was done cooperatively even though land was held individually. Note the use of horses, the traditional beast of burden in Dalarna. (Courtesy of Dalarnas Museum, photography by Bäck Anders Olsson, date unknown)

growing conditions at the eastern end of Lake Siljan. The oldest field crop in Dalarna was rye, but barley supplanted rye early in Rättvik's history—a development that occurred much more gradually in neighboring parishes. As early as the sixteenth century, the parish was known for its barley production. The quality of the crop received special mention in reports on agricultural conditions in Dalarna (Hülphurs, 1757).[33] Meanwhile the importance of rye steadily declined. By the early nineteenth century, the parish produced only one-sixth as much rye as barley. Most of that was produced on burned forest clearings rather than the village arable. Rättvik also diverged from its neighbors in that it was slow to adopt oats as an important crop. Oats emerged, in the first half of the nineteenth century, as the dominant crop for all of Dalarna, but the amount grown in Rättvik was curiously negligible and remained so until late in the century.[34]

The blending of seeds in at least one field was a common practice throughout Dalarna. It increased the chance of high yields since one or both of the planted crops were likely to do well. It also introduced a second crop into the rotation system, which played a role in renewing the fertility of the soil. The type of blend, however, was subject to local preferences. Most Dalarna parishes used a combination of barley and oats, but in Rättvik it was a combination of barley and gray peas *(pisum arvense).*[35] In fact, peas were the uniquely characteristic crop of Rättvik with respect to other Dalarna parishes and to Sweden as a whole. Peas became a specialty here as early as the latter part of the sixteenth century. In 1573, the pea harvest in the three parishes of Mora, Orsa, and Rättvik accounted for four-fifths of the entire Dalarna harvest, and most of that was produced in Rättvik. By the early decades of the nineteenth century, one-third of the planted arable in Rättvik was reported to be in peas (either exclusively or blended with barley), although a more accurate estimate may have been about one-sixth. The popularity of the crop varied between villages. Those with large amounts of arable and the best-developed rotational systems clearly favored the cultivation of peas, while smaller villages did not. In the middle of the 1850s, when the cultivation of peas reached its height of popularity among Rättvik peasant proprietors, the total share of the arable planted in peas may have been as high as one-third, although some villages may have planted as little as one-tenth.[36] Gärdsjö *fjärding* was the center of Rättvik pea production.[37]

The cultivation of potatoes was a relatively new but important activity at mid-century. The potato had been slow to catch on in Rättvik. Although it was introduced sometime late in the eighteenth century, it remained fairly unimportant in the first decades of the nineteenth century. In many villages at that time, potatoes were not grown at all. Its use spread rapidly, however, during the 1830s. In part, the sudden acceptance may have been related to the *storskifte* land reforms, which fostered greater freedom from customary restraints about what should be grown. In any case, the potato had become a well-integrated and indispensable part of the peasant diet by the 1840s. Indeed, when potato blight struck the parish in 1846, there was official concern that the supply of grain might not be sufficient to make up for the loss of potatoes in the food supply.[38]

With the onset of June, it was time to make preparations to take the livestock to the *fäbod.* Cattle and sheep were taken to the distant pastures for the summer and certain tasks needed to be tended to before they were ready for the journey. The cattle needed to be let out into the nearby forest tracts for several hours a day in the weeks before departure to gather the strength necessary for the long trip. Poor feed and several months' confinement in the dark animal barns during the long winter had left them weak and emaciated. At the same time, the sheep were herded in from the forests, shorn, and fitted with a cord around the

Plate 3.4 Summer grazing settlement. These *fäbod* buildings at Tyskberget were used in the summertime by herdsmaids from Övre Gärdsjö village. Herdsmaids divided their time between tending livestock foraging in nearby forest tracts and making butter, cheese, and soft whey cheese from cow's milk. A small piece of Lake Ljugaren is visible in the background. (Courtesy of Dalarnas Museum, photo by Axel Boëthius, 1890s)

neck, from which hung a wooden stick identifying the owner. They were often marked with a clip on the ear as well. The sheep, with the children attending, were then customarily released for one last run in the forest on the day before departure.

The day of departure was traditionally the tenth of June, except when the tenth fell on a Sunday, when it was delayed to the eleventh. According to village by-laws, nobody could set out before the agreed date. There were fines for doing so, since an early departure meant a head start on the resources of the forest meadows. The day of departure was a festive occasion. Entire households would accompany the animals to the *fäbod*. Everyone went for the enjoyment and also because there was much work to be done there making repairs and getting things in order for the summer. For many, the distance was long and the trip exhausting, but it was one of the major events of the year. At the *fäbod* settlement, each household, or sometimes two or more households in partnership, maintained a small cabin and an array of out-buildings. On the evening of arrival, the peasants held a council meeting of sorts, in which the general rules and procedures for the summer's grazing would be agreed upon by all participants. Normally they divided the forests into a number of grazing areas and devised a rotation system to exploit them systematically. Everyone remained at the *fäbod* for a day or two, after which most returned to the home village, leaving behind a few of the young girls to tend the livestock. The herdsmaids remained there alone for about three months, although other members of the household would return from time to time for haymaking and to haul provisions to and from the site. The livestock were usually taken from the *fäbod* to the home village at the end of August or in the first half of September, so that they might simultaneously graze the stubble and manure the newly harvested fields.[39]

The girls who spent their summer at the *fäbod* had two principal tasks. One was to watch over the animals. The other was to make butter, cheese, and soft whey-cheese from the cows' milk. The production and preservation of these products was an important activity, because they were a basic component of the peasant diet through the long winter and the cows' lean diet in winter produced no milk. Milk cows were an essential part of the livestock maintained by each household. At mid-century, the average household possessed two or three cows. At one time they had been far more numerous. The sixteenth century saw as many as six per household. Why the decline in numbers? A major reason was that the nineteenth-century cow was considerably larger than the cow of earlier times. At the end of the Middle Ages, cattle in Rättvik weighed between 250 and 300 pounds apiece. By the middle of the nineteenth century, their size had increased to perhaps 450 pounds. Nonetheless, they were still small and underfed by modern standards. While the quality and amount of fodder and pasturage had improved over the centuries, it was at best barely sufficient to maintain the beasts. The most a peasant could provide for a cow during the long winter months, when they were kept in the barn, was a few pounds of hay, straw, and leaves a day. With such poor sustenance, the animals were usually weakened by summer. Even with the improved summer diet, a healthy cow was expected to produce barely 500 liters of milk annually, only about one-tenth of what one might expect today.[40]

Back at the home village, the waning days of June were relatively peaceful. All of the livestock were absent except for the goats, who remained in order to supply milk while the cows were away. The grain in the fields could pretty much take care of itself, so the menfolk busied themselves with a number of other projects. Tools had to be readied for the haying season which was fast approaching. This included the repair and assembly of hay-drying racks. Roof repairs were often accomplished at this time and the remainder of the previous year's grain and potatoes were distilled to produce draff and spirits. The women meanwhile applied themselves to a variety of early summer chores, the most time-consuming of which was baking. Spring baking was one of two major bakes every year; the other was in the fall, after new flour milled from the grains and potatoes of the new harvest became available. The spring bake normally lasted three to four days, during which women baked a variety of breads and cakes in large numbers and hung them from the ceiling to dry. Women also took this opportunity to dye cloth and yarn and to sew garments. There was a major laundry and housecleaning effort (which was repeated during the winter).

The end of the summer activities was marked by the midsummer holiday. In Rättvik, midsummer was celebrated simply. A lack of "sweet milk" meant that the usual holiday breads were unavailable. According to custom, the children were sent out into the meadows to pick flowers to give the home the proper atmosphere. A maypole raising and attendance of services in the flower-bedecked church were the big events of the day. In the aftermath of midsummer a few quiet days marked the lull before the onset of the haymaking season.

Haymaking began around the first week in July and could last into early August. It began or ended at the *fäbod,* depending on village custom, but for most of its duration it took the entire village out into the meadows surrounding the village fields. Everyone worked together to bring in the hay—adults, women, and children. Entire households moved into the small hay barns that stood in the meadows. This eliminated time wasted traveling back and forth between farmstead and meadow and lengthened the work day to the maximum. Food was prepared in the meadows and even the goats were taken along to provide milk. The daily routine was to be out in the meadows to cut hay by four o'clock in the morning, while the dew was still on the ground. It was men's work to cut the hay using a long-handled scythe. The women raked the cut stalks into piles and the children gathered up by hand the stalks that may have been missed by the rake. A breakfast of herring and potatoes and perhaps some gruel left over from the last evening meal was served at seven and then everyone was back at work until the noon mealtime. After a lunch that consisted of porridge and bread, everyone paused to rest until mid-afternoon. For the remainder of the afternoon and most of the evening, with a short break for sandwiches, everyone helped bind the cut hay into bundles and stacked them on the drying racks. Around eight or nine in the evening there would be a dinner of gruel and sandwiches before retiring for the night. The next morning the work would begin anew.

The work was done by all able-bodied men, women, and children above the age of twelve. The long hours and the back-breaking labor made this the most physically demanding of all agricultural work. It was also the most feverish, because only a limited amount of time was set aside for haymaking and it was important to gather in as much as was humanly possible, because even that might not be enough to get the live-stock through the winter. Old people are said to have gone out of their way to stoop and pick up with their fingers a few stray straws that might have fallen between rocks or into bushes. The need for fodder was so great that even the trees could not be overlooked as a source. Women and children spent much time from middle to late summer harvesting branches and leaves from the deciduous trees and bushes that bordered the meadows. Birch, alder, and ash trees were the most common sources. The younger trees were cut down and the branches of older trees were removed, then the material was bound together into sheafs which were set against racks to dry. Later, the woody parts were cut away for kindling wood, leaving the leafy portions to be used as fodder for the goats and sheep. The bark of these trees was often cut away to use as fodder, too. When the gathering and drying of leaves and hay was completed, usually by the beginning of August, there was still the task of hauling it to the barns to be stored. Some was hauled to the small barns in the meadows, usually by hand, even though the distance might be several hundred yards. Most was hauled by hand or in carts to storage sheds in the farmyard.

The grain harvest began in August. Rye was the first crop to come in. The menfolk moved into the forests for several days to reap the rye that had been sown in the ash of burned forest plots. Rye was harvested with a hand sickle because the ground was usually too stony to use the long-handled scythe. One had to stoop down, gathering as much of the grain as one could in the left hand and cutting it off with the right, being care-ful not to drop any of the precious stalks.[41] The cut rye was bound in sheafs and left to dry on racks for several weeks. With the rye crop in, the village turned to the ripening fields of barley and peas. The barley harvest was associated with Bartholomew's Mass (August 24th) in most parts of the Siljan basin, but in practice it often occurred earlier, since no one wanted to risk a killing frost. Countless folk sayings reminded the peasant that it was better to take in a green crop than a frozen one.[42] Barley was cut in the fields with the long-handled scythe. Harvest teams customarily broke into working pairs, consisting of a man who would cut the grain and a woman who would bind it into a sheaf. The children were charged with gathering up the bound sheafs. Once the grain was cut, the men worked to stack the sheafs to dry in carefully designed piles *(snes)* supported on stakes stuck in the ground. Each parish had its own way of constructing these piles, replete with variations that could be used in the

Plate 3.5 Sexual division of labor in Rättvik. These women are grubbing potatoes while the man in the background looks on. Men, women, and children took part in the potato harvest, but it was often the women who did the actual potato grubbing. (Courtesy of Dalarnas Museum, date unknown)

case of threatening frost. Then peas were harvested, in much the same manner as the barley except that a shorter scythe was used and the sheafs were dried on racks rather than stacked in piles. After two or three weeks of drying in the field, the barley and peas were carried to barns in the village. The entire process was normally concluded by *Mickelsmäss* (St. Michael's Mass, September 29th).

Even then, the harvesting was not over. There were still the potatoes to bring in, not to mention some of the smaller garden crops, such as hops and flax. These tasks came around *Mickelsmäss* or shortly thereafter. The digging of potatoes, in particular, required much labor and a considerable amount of cooperation between households in the village. It was done by teams that went about the village grubbing potatoes in one plot after another. The teams consisted of ten to fifteen persons drawn from neighboring households, who would space themselves in a line along one end of the plot and then systematically work their way across it on their hands and knees, digging out potatoes as they moved along. The exhumed potatoes were then dumped in sacks or carts and taken to the potato cellars. Men, women, and older children all took part in the potato harvest, but it was often the women who actually grubbed for the tubers.

With the cool, crisp days of autumn came threshing time, the year's last major piece of agricultural work. Threshing began in Rättvik around the end of September or early in October, right after the harvest was in and the animals were brought home from the *fäbod* to graze the stubble in the fields. Threshing was laborious and time-consuming. It was accomplished by manually beating the grain. On every farm, from early morning to late in the evening during the autumn months, the air was filled with the rhythmic thumps of the threshing hammer. Sometimes two men would work in tandem, each pounding the grain as the other's hammer was in its back swing. At times, there were even four threshers to make the work go faster. In these combinations, Rättvik stood apart from some of the neighboring parishes, where it was customary to expand the number of threshers in multiples of three rather than multiples of two.[43] Once the grain had been beaten, the women undertook the work of separating the grain from the chaff. First they sifted the grain in a basket whose bottom of woven straw let the small bits of chaff fall through. Then they "tossed" the grain. This required a certain amount of skill. One knelt on the floor at one end of the barn and tossed grain with a small shovel out over the floor. The grain was tossed into a draft let in through a barn door, with the intention that the draft would blow aside the lighter chaff, separating it from the heavier grain kernels. The skill lay in properly positioning oneself with respect to the draft and in mastering the precise wrist action necessary to achieve the most satisfactory results. The grain was then cleaned, dried, and milled by hand or taken to a local water-driven gristmill. The number of weeks consumed by threshing varied with the size of the harvest and the quality of the grain, but it was quite common for the threshing to last until the Christmas holidays. It was not unknown for it to carry over into January or even February.

Threshing, of course, was not the only fall activity. Time had to be set aside for other work, as well. The men had fields to plow, time and weather permitting. Once the winter's supply of fodder had been taken in, its size and quality determined how many animals could be fed over the winter. The surplus had to be slaughtered. In addition, it was necessary to get the winter's charcoal production under way. As the autumn wore on, more and more time had to be spent in the forest making charcoal, for it often represented the household's most important source of cash income. The men were almost continuously in the forest making charcoal by early December and would remain there until Christmastime.

For the women, too, the autumn months were demanding. The autumn slaughter of animals brought with it a number of tasks reserved

Plate 3.6 Making charcoal on the forest lands of Nittsjö village. Charcoal was produced
by partially burning wood inside an earthen oven *(kolmila)* from which air could be
excluded. The charcoal was taken to market on sledges. (Courtesy of Dalarnas Museum,
photography by E. H. Kvist, 1890s)

exclusively for the women, such as boiling fat. In addition, the flax had
to be swingled, or beaten and cleaned, an enterprise undertaken jointly
by the women of the village. There was also much work connected with
the production of linens and woolens. And through it all was the unre-
lenting daily chore of feeding and caring for the animals, a chore left

entirely to the women, although the children were of some assistance. The animals, by now stabled in barns for the winter, required attention at least three times a day. Early every morning, one had to go out and shovel manure, milk the cows and goats, and feed all the animals. Two more feeding trips would be required later in the day.

As the Christmas holidays approached, the pace quickened. In addition to their regular chores, women were expected to prepare a variety of specialized food and drink and to engineer a thorough housecleaning to create the best impression for holiday visitors. Christmas was the major holiday of the year, a truly joyous occasion, and a time of all too brief relaxation before the long winter set in—for the men and children in the household. The toil of preparation must have required extra cheer from women.

The holidays came to a close with Epiphany, after which it was time for the men to return to the forests to haul loads of timber and charcoal to some of the local iron works or down to Falun. These activities kept them away from the farm intermittently for the remaining winter months. At the farm, the short, dark days of winter settled into a domestic routine broken only by the visits of peddlers from surrounding parishes, who passed through the village with their packs of homemade goods. The principal activities at this time were a variety of domestic crafts. During the long winter evenings after chores were done, the women settled in to bring to fruition the wool and linen work begun in the autumn. They would gather at one farm or another to card wool and spin woolen or linen yarns, while they discussed the season's marriage market and gossiped shamelessly. The long hours spent weaving were less frivolous. Once the yarns were ready, weaving took up much of the daytime, especially from late February into March when the daylight hours grew longer. Throughout the winter the task of keeping the animals continued, and as spring approached there was always the worry, borne primarily by the women, that the fodder would not last. If the situation looked grim, they had no recourse but to go into the forest and gather whatever could be found. Those that could not be fed had to be slaughtered, a loss of the fodder the beast had consumed and less meat than fall slaughter would have provided.

As winter waned and spring approached, the men came home from the winter's hauling and busied themselves with a number of late winter chores. With the household together once again, this was also a time for socializing. One of the great events of the season was, of course, Easter, the biggest holiday of the year after Christmas. Not only were there the traditional services at church and holiday fare at home, but the Saturday before and the day after Easter were ordinarily filled with well-attended auctions, meetings, and social gatherings. This was also the time of year for weddings, the peasants' finest family celebration. A wedding was an auspicious occasion, when it was tremendously important to showoff family and possessions most proudly. The house, spruced up to look its very best, was filled with guests, who were treated to a prodigious amount of food, drink, merrymaking, and dancing, all of which could last for two or three days. The time for such frivolity, however, was limited. By the end of April, good spring weather was fast approaching and the "social season" around Eastertime gave way to work.

Such was the annual cycle to which virtually every peasant household was tied. Tradition defined every activity. Knowing when and how to do things was in large part a matter of oral tradition passed down from generation to generation. Folk wisdom about the vagaries of the environment, the temperament of livestock, the quality of a crop, and a thousand other things were part of the peasants' inheritance. But the cycle was also a matter of social convention. In the peasants' minds, the activities that rounded out the year were temporally bound to the major celebrations of the religious calendar. Everyone, for instance, expected the harvest to be completed by St. Michael's Mass and saw their religious observances as the fitting conclusion to the harvest work. The organization of work was also an affirmation of social order and responsibility within the parish. It incorporated various arrangements between households and villages that had been in force for as long as anyone could remember. The custom of providing the work of one's horse on certain days to those who lacked the beasts, the cooperative teamwork between households at harvest time, the systematic organization that gave everyone a fair chance to exploit the summer meadows around the *fäbod,* are all examples of the high level of human cooperation customary in this system. The ways of doing work in the parish were also a measure of the power of local culture. In almost every public act, subtle differences in timing and technique set Rättvik off from its neighbors, just as their distinctive traditions set them off from one another.

The cycle of work was geared to meeting the demands of subsistence as efficiently as possible. There were busy periods that allowed no rest or relaxation; but these times were punctuated by days and even weeks, often marked by important holidays and observances, in which the pressure was not as great. Not that life was not hard at all times; that certainly was true. But the work cycle seems to have been designed to satisfy basic requirements rather than to produce surpluses. The peasants worked to reach an adequate level—bringing in enough hay to carry the livestock through the winter, preparing an adequate amount of charcoal to yield the cash required to purchase necessary goods, cultivating enough land to have an adequate supply of food for the current year and seed for the next. The fear was always of falling short. In this respect, the annual cycle of work in Rättvik seems a confirmation of A. V. Chayanov's conception of peasant society, which posits that peasants would accept the drudgery of labor only to the extent necessary to sustain their households. It is indeed remarkable that, even though the authorities had thought to establish grain magazines in each of the parish's *fjärding* districts, a survey of their contents in 1838 found that the reserves were surprisingly small.[44] The urge to accumulate beyond certain levels was not central to the local economy.

The annual cycle reveals much more about the fabric of economic life. It demonstrates a well-prescribed sexual division of labor. Each sex made its own specific labor contributions to the household economy. Decision-making was divided as well. Men decided the use of the arable, meadow, and forest, while women were responsible for the husbandry of the animals, the rearing of children, and the operation of the home. Despite the clear division of responsibility, the household economy depended on the complete integration of the contributions made by each sex. Haymaking and harvesting, for example, would have been impossible without both sexes working side by side. The family and the household may have been formally organized along patriarchal lines, but in practice the economic role of the female spouse was virtually indispensable. In addition to the male household head *(husbonde)* there had to be a "head woman" *(husmor)* for things to run as smoothly as they should. Male household heads who suddenly found themselves widowers were usually quick to remarry, often for economic reasons more than social or sexual. Those who did not found the household economy seriously impaired.

The annual cycle of work shows, too, that the cultivation of crops and the husbandry of animals were fully integrated activities. The best example of their symbiotic relationship was the practice of grazing animals on the arable after the harvest so that the animals might obtain nourishment from the stubble at the same time that their droppings nourished the soil. The animals also provided the draft power needed to plow and to haul loads. In turn, the animals could not survive the winter without fodder, much of which was cut from meadowland around the village and the *fäbod*. No peasant was in a position to entirely specialize production in either cultivation or husbandry.

Finally, it is important to note the relative absence of paid labor on

Rättvik farms. Peasant households met their labor requirements as much as possible through members of the household. Of course, the composition of the household could vary considerably. As we have seen, the degree to which the peasant family was extended varied according to the household head's stage in the life cycle. But regardless of whether the household consisted solely of a nuclear family or was extended over three generations, the labor it could put into the field remained remarkably stable. In other words, there was a natural equilibrium between the peasant household and its needs. This is not to say that help was not acquired from neighbors from time to time, or that young men and women from neighboring farms were not taken temporarily into service in exchange for room and board. These things were customary. It is to say, however, that there was no army of landless workers in Rättvik who were completely dependent for their livelihood on being hired to work in the peasants' fields or meadows during the busy times of the seasonal round. Rättvik at mid-century was still a society of independent peasant proprietors who subsisted on the resources of their holdings, the labor of their households, occasional help from their neighbors and friends, and some seasonal work outside the parish. It was also a society that expected its children to enjoy, once they reached adulthood, the same land and proprietary status as their parents.

Land and Family in Pre-Migration Rättvik

That most Rättvik children in the mid-nineteenth century could still expect to become landed proprietors someday, in spite of high population growth rates, is a phenomenon that may be explained by three factors. One was the *storskifte* land reorganization of the 1830s. The *storskifte* reconsolidated the holdings of Rättvik households, which after generations of subdivision had become too small and fragmented to support further subdivisions. The newly consolidated holdings restored household heads' capacity once again to subdivide their land for the benefit of their children. The *storskifte* also set off a land reclamation boom. The increased clearing of new arable in the 1840s and the 1850s made the establishment of at least a limited number of new farms possible. Another factor was the multifarious nature of the Rättvik economy. The combination of agriculture with animal husbandry, charcoal production, and a myriad of other minor activities made it possible for many more people to be "landed" than would have been the case if arable were the sole support of the peasant household. The fact that no one expected to derive a livelihood entirely from the cultivation of crops made a society of many small-holders viable. Finally, the inheritance system favored an equitable transfer of wealth from parents to all heirs and gave parents considerable control over the process of new household formation.

The disorganization and fragmentation of lands in Rättvik, which the *storskifte* attempted to redress, was a product of the land inheritance system. Since early times it had been the custom to divide land not only among heirs, but also to fragment each inheritance into a number of parcels. Under this system, an equitable distribution of all resources meant that each heir was entitled to a share of the best and the poorest land. Thus, land falling in all categories had to be fragmented into parcels so that each heir would receive a fair share. When the process was repeated for later generations, the parcels were fragmented again and again until conditions became extreme. As early as the seventeenth century, the government decreed that only one heir should inherit land, hoping thereby to ease its increasing difficulties in determining property taxes. The decree was generally ignored throughout the province. By late in the eighteenth century, the division and scattering of property in Upper Dalarna had reached alarming proportions. A Royal Commission, sent to the region in 1787, reported that "the lawless manner in which farms in Dalarna have been divided into small pieces during this century has overstepped all bounds."[45] In addition to ignoring the earlier decree on inheritance, the Dalarna peasantry had ignored a royal proclamation that forbade dividing property to less than one-sixteenth of what was considered the minimum needed to support a farm. The commission went on to say that disregard for this principle was most flagrant in the parishes of Rättvik, Ore, Leksand, Bjursås, and Ål.

Some understanding of what this process meant to the pattern of land tenure in the parish may be obtained from an extant 1735 land register. In that year, the average holding in arable for a peasant household was roughly three and one-half acres. On average, those three and one-half acres were divided into roughly fifty parcels, which means each peasant household was cultivating crops in as many as fifty different places. Fragmentation was so advanced that some of the parcels were as little as one-tenth of a square meter in size.[46] When the *storskifte* did its work in the 1830s, the situation was scarcely any better. The average size of farms increased somewhat, due primarily to the clearing of new land, but the land might be divided into the same number of pieces as existed a century earlier. The average peasant worked holdings that were scattered all about the village arable and, not uncommonly, on the arable of neighboring villages as well. The exchange of parcels through marriage, in particular, led in many cases to holdings outside the home village. Meadowlands were similarly divided, often into even more fragments than the arable. It is hardly surprising that the authorities pressed again for land reform in the early part of the nineteenth century.

The *storskifte* land reform got underway in Rättvik on June 1, 1828, and took roughly a decade to complete. The land reform process involved six major steps: *(1)* surveying and grading all land, *(2)* mapping, *(3)* distribution of land to the villages, *(4)* establishment of a minimum property size that can support a household, *(5)* regulation of the *fäbod* system, and *(6)* division of village lands among households.

Its primary aim was to encourage villages and farms to barter for land parcels in the interest of creating larger and more viable units. Key to the process was the careful evaluation of property. The lands were therefore surveyed and graded by a surveyor with the assistance of two trusted representatives of the local peasantry. Each parcel was assigned a grade ranging from zero to ten indicating its relative quality. The area of each parcel was then multiplied by its grade and divided by ten to produce a weighted measure of its value *(reducerade jordarealen)*. The process was designed to make the redistribution of land between villages and individuals, which came at a later stage and was potentially contentious, a relatively straightforward process since everyone would receive lands proportional to what they had before. In fact, the *storskifte* introduced a whole new nomenclature by which land could be discussed. For a long time afterwards, people in Rättvik spoke not of a farm's actual size, but of its "grades."[47]

Above all else, the *storskifte* reduced the severe fragmentation of property and generally improved the efficiency of agriculture. The average property owner came to possess four or five parcels instead of forty or fifty. The new parcels were all located within a reasonable distance of the homestead. Because they were so much larger, they were far easier to work. Meadowland parcels were also reduced in number and made more accessible. In order to achieve these consolidations, however, much property had to be exchanged and many owners found themselves with quite different land than they had previously possessed. In a very few cases, property owners actually had to move their homestead to another village. But the official grading of land made the exchanges palatable in many cases. If one's new properties turned out to be of poorer quality, there was consolation in the fact that they were at least more extensive. Conversely, smaller holdings usually contained better land. Not everyone was happy. The surveyor and his peasant assistants, however trustworthy, were unable to accomplish their work without strife, but differences were resolved and the redistribution was eventually finalized.

In addition to the redistribution of property, the *storskifte* accomplished one other major objective. In the fall of 1833, representatives of the parish agreed to establish a minimum property holding *(besuttenhet)*, or limit of self-sufficiency. The smallest size to which a farm could be subdivided was set at the amount of land necessary to support three people in an average year, or just under three acres after reduction by grading.[48] This included both arable and meadowland. It was also based, in part, on a royal determination that a farm ought to be able to support the equivalent of one horse, three cows, six goats, and three sheep. By this definition, the parish was thought to be capable of supporting 1,322 landed households. To this was added a "twenty-year rule," which stated that any property owner whose possessions fell below this size had twenty years to enlarge his property to the minimum standard. Failure to do so would result in the property being forcibly put up for sale. Thus, the *storskifte* in large measure undid the extreme fragmentation of land over the prior two centuries and established a mechanism that might keep the process from reaching extreme proportions again in the future. Neither accomplishment lasted, however. The practice of dividing property among heirs continued unabated in the years after the completion of the *storskifte,* leading to a gradual refragmentation of property; the twenty-year rule was never enforced.[49] Nonetheless, land tenure in Rättvik was somewhat more orderly and less complex in the middle decades of the nineteenth century than it had been previously or would be in the future. This rejuvenated land base allowed peasant proprietors to view with some confidence the prospects of transferring landed wealth to their offspring.

The orderly transfer of land from the old generation to the new was one of the most weighty responsibilities borne by the Rättvik peasant. It had to be planned with extreme care, for land was the essence of the peasant's existence—the lifeblood of all previous and future generations. The system of land inheritance practiced in Rättvik was based, as in all parts of Sweden, on provincial law. The provincial laws of Dalarna favored the division of property among all heirs. All males had customary rights to their parents' property. Females had rights through marriage dowries, but not as strong as their male siblings' rights. Custom also gave tremendous emphasis to family lineage. Farms were hereditary, remaining within the same family for generations. Thus, if husband and wife died without children, the land automatically reverted to parents or other older relatives. In the event that land had to be sold, relatives had the first right of purchase. According to Dalarna law, land with no direct heirs had to be officially offered for purchase three times before it could be sold, and only if no relative stepped forward to purchase the property could it be sold to someone else. In short, landed wealth belonged to the family and was expected to remain a part of the family heritage. It could be partitioned within the limits of customary practice, but the ultimate goal and responsibility of the peasant proprietor was to see that landed wealth passed on within a prescribed lineage.[50]

While the manner of partitioning landed wealth among heirs was well defined by customary law, the timing of inheritances and land transfers remained at the discretion of the peasant proprietor. The decisions as to when heirs should receive their shares in the hereditary farm, and when the household head should give up his or her control of the estate, were crucial decisions because they controlled the processes of family formation and reproduction. The timing of these decisions was in itself a regulating mechanism on the number of people a farm must support. In earlier centuries, the transfer of wealth most often occurred near the time of the head of household's death. Lower adult life expectancies in the seventeenth and eighteenth centuries and higher infant mortality rates meant that the transfer ordinarily took place before the parents' surviving offspring were very old—and that there were not too many of them. These conditions helped restrain the pressure of population on land resources. But as life expectancy increased and mortality rates began to decline at the end of the eighteenth and during the nineteenth centuries, the circumstances surrounding the transfer of wealth began to change. The passing of the older generation and young adulthood of the new no longer coincided with any great frequency. There were also many more heirs as larger numbers of children reached adulthood. Given the limited land resources available, it became increasingly important for the older generation to employ strategies that extended the period of its proprietorship beyond the early adult years of its children, that made some provision for its old age, and, at the same time, extended to its children the sure prospect of an inheritance— one that would come early enough in life for them to marry and form families.

Two events were central to the intergenerational transfer of wealth: the marriage of children and the retirement of their parents. Landed wealth was a necessary precondition of marriage because without it the possibilities of earning a livelihood were poor. Therefore, receiving at least a portion of one's inheritance and entering into marriage were fully intertwined events that together constituted the major rite of passage for young adults. For most parents, however, it was a matter of prudent strategy to delay the occasion for as long as possible, to stagger the timing of each child's accession to this position, and to withhold a portion of each child's eventual inheritance until the parents' retirement. These plans ideally produced the most equitable division of lands and maintained the supply of labor on the farm. In other words, the transfer of landed wealth was a piecemeal process, carefully orchestrated to balance demands against the resources of the farm. Most adult children waited until their late twenties or early thirties to receive the wherewithal to marry. They ordinarily received a small parcel of arable and some meadowland, not enough in itself to support a new household. The new landowner, then, was a shareholder in an existing farm unit and was expected to bring his or her spouse into the parents' household, where they would remain until the old couple retired.

Of course, not all children could be accommodated immediately. Depending on circumstances, some were forced to wait longer. Parents also alleviated pressure on resources by arranging multiple unions between the offspring of two or more households. For example, the marriage of a daughter onto one farm might be bound by agreement to a compensating marriage that would take a son or daughter of the second household onto the first. Bilateral exchanges of this type were quite common. Triangular exchanges between three households or even more complex exchanges could also occur. Such alliances eased the inevitable problem of overextension as household heads accepted the spouses of newly married sons and daughters into the household. Alliances were also important because the marriage of sons and daughters in their twenties and thirties represented a substantial loss of labor if they left the farm. It was in the immediate interest of the household to retain at least as many young married people as it lost to other households. Taking in sons-in-law and daughters-in-law helped stabilize the labor supply on the farm. It also served to widen the circle in which labor or assistance might be available to a household in times of crisis.

The addition of newly married couples to the household naturally meant new offspring, whose numbers could significantly strain the carrying capacity of the farm. That situation ideally coincided with the retirement of the old parents and was the time at which the final transfer of wealth took place, as well as certain necessary adjustments in household structure. On their retirement, the old couple formally relinquished their controlling shares of landed wealth, retaining for themselves only a small garden and the contracted guarantee that the new household head would care for them in their old age. One of the young married families, usually that of the oldest son or daughter still living on the farm, would take control of the farm, along with responsiblity for the parents and for the disposition of wealth to the remaining siblings, married and unmarried. At this time, the farm was often subdivided, with the other married children acquiring the status of independent households living on subdivisions of the farm. The situation could force at least one of the young families to move elsewhere, with compensation. Under normal circumstances, the strain on resources was relieved through short-distance migration, in which families moved within a circle of farms bound together by kinship so as to equalize pressure. One farm under intense population pressure might often be balanced by another within the same kinship group with a share available for a young family. In addition, a limited amount of land clearing and reclamation was always going on in the parish, which offered possibilities for establishing new farms for families that were pushed off existing units.[51]

The key point is that there seemed to be a mechanism at work here that successfully integrated new families and population increases into the small-holding peasant economy. Through the fragmentation of existing farms by inheritance, through the careful balancing of population and resources in the form of social controls on marriage, and through the short-distance migration of families and the clearing of new lands when necessary, the peasant society of Rättvik appears to have successfully maintained a tradition by which most young adults had a reasonable expectation of acquiring the land necessary to support a family. The expectation seems to have been especially strong during the decades that followed the *storskifte*. The land reform rationalized the structure of lands to a degree that permitted the customary subdivision of farms to continue. It also encouraged the clearing and reclamation of new lands.

The decades following the *storskifte* were also relatively prosperous. Demand for the peasants' timber products increased and the region was largely free of serious agricultural failure. In other words, those who would eventually emigrate from this parish in the 1860s, 1870s, and 1880s grew up in a period when one's prospects in life looked normal. Expectations were in line with what was customary or traditional in the parish, perhaps a little brighter. No one could foresee that conditions would suddenly change in the 1860s. It would have been impossible to believe that many would be forced to travel to another continent to realize the prospects that seemed so close at hand at mid-century.

4

The Migration

Pattern and Selection, 1864–1889

"AMERICA FEVER," that highly infectious social malady, began its sweep through Sweden in the mid-1840s and reached the parish of Rättvik early in the summer of 1864. The first recorded emigrant from the parish was thirty-three-year-old Bäck Hans Ersson. Bäck Hans Ersson left his farm in the Ovanheds *fjärding* village of Gulleråsen on June 2, 1864. Accompanying him were his wife of ten years, Kerstin Andersdotter, and their four children, who ranged in age from one to nine years. His unmarried younger brother, Bäck Olof Ersson, who lived on a neighboring farm, also made the trip. They left quietly; there was little fanfare. But the repercussions of this seemingly inconsequential event soon reverberated throughout the parish. Once rooted, the idea of emigration spread rapidly and led to a series of departures, often more tumultuous than that of Bäck Hans Ersson and his party. Over the next few decades alone, the parish witnessed the departure of more than three hundred emigrant parties, nearly a thousand folk in all. America fever affected nearly everyone in the parish in some way. For many, the effect was decisive.

We may never know for certain why Bäck Hans Ersson chose to uproot his family in the early summer of 1864. No written explanation has survived. His circumstances at the time of emigration seem to have been neither dire nor especially advantageous. They were, in fact, remarkably similar to those of many others in the parish who were about his age. He was the head of a young family and the owner of a somewhat less than middling holding, to which he and his family had moved seven years earlier so that his married older brother might take over a subdivision of his father's farm. The fact that his uncle held another subdivision of the farm and that his father still retained control of the third and major subdivision had forced Bäck Hans Ersson and his family to seek a livelihood elsewhere. The new holding, which had been secured for him as a part of his inheritance, was adequate. For most of the seven years he lived there, it supported not only his own family but a "live-in" widow and her four children as well.[1] Did Bäck Hans Ersson have personal reasons to leave? We can only speculate on his possible motives. Perhaps he believed the holding was too small for his growing family; perhaps it lacked the potential to satisfy his ambition. Or was it simply restlessness that drove him, before anyone else in his village, to try something bold and new?

To ask why any of the millions of people across Sweden and Europe suddenly decided to abandon a familiar life and surroundings to journey such a long distance in search of something else is to ask the central question of migration research. This question and the myriad ancillary issues that surround it constitute the core of our curiosity about human migratory behavior. What forces at home and abroad tempted people to contemplate emigration? How were those who actually acted on that temptation "selected" from the mass of the population? To what degree were the demographic, social, and economic conditions reviewed in the previous two chapters important in determining the dimensions and character of emigration from Rättvik? What were the temporal and spatial patterns of the migration, the dynamics of its progress, its ultimate destinations?

The aim of this chapter is to place Bäck Hans Ersson's extraordinary action, and that of hundreds of others in Rättvik who followed his example, in proper context. Although it may never be possible to understand each individual's circumstantial or psychological motivation for emigrating, it is useful to try to delimit the general mechanisms of emigration at work in a place and to view the actions of individuals as best one can in light of these processes. Answers to questions such as those posed here are essential to an understanding of how the mechanism of emigration may have operated in the parish of Rättvik. At the same time, one must keep in mind that the findings all relate somehow to a larger picture. Bäck Hans Ersson's decision may have been a revolutionary event in Rättvik in the summer of 1864, but similar events had been going on all over Europe for decades and would continue for many more before the Great Atlantic Migrations finally subsided. The emigration from

Rättvik was but one small part of a very large and complex phenomenon.

Emigration from Sweden and Upper Dalarna

Collectively, the Great Atlantic Migrations constituted a massive movement of people from Europe to America that numbered in excess of fifty million souls. Sweden's total contribution to this unprecedented population movement was something over one million emigrants, a remarkable number for a small country with a population of only three and one-half million in 1850.[2] Swedish historian Sten Carlsson underscored even more forcibly the impact of the emigrations on Swedish society when he noted that somewhere between one-quarter and one-fifth of all Swedes living between 1851 and 1930 emigrated to North America.[3] There were few places in Sweden and few strata of Swedish society that escaped the experience of having people leave for America at some time or another. The idea of emigrating to America pervaded Swedish life more so than in most European countries, Ireland, Norway, and possibly Iceland excepted. By the time the exodus finally ceased, nearly every Swede could claim to know someone in America.

But the emigration was hardly a monolithic event. It was a many-sided and evolving phenomenon, intertwined with the changing demographic and socioeconomic structures of the nation, a cause and consequence of Sweden's modern history. The circumstance, composition, and experience of emigration varied substantially from place to place at different times. No simple model describes it well. More notable among the number of types were agrarian migrations motivated primarily by a hunger for land, migrations undertaken for idealistic reasons, labor migrations in search of better wages and working conditions, and seasonal migrations to alleviate temporary pressures at home. The emigration from Rättvik was in no way a microcosm of the national experience. It is best seen as a particular variation of the mass emigrations experienced by Sweden, or, by extension, Europe as a whole.

Historians and geographers customarily distinguish different types of emigration from Sweden along temporal lines. The mass emigrations may be divided into five phases.[4] The first extended from the mid-1840s to the mid-1850s. It is distinguished by relatively small numbers of emigrants (roughly 15,000), which was partly due to official restriction on emigration, and by the fact that the majority of emigrants were landed farmers and their families. They seem to have been motivated by idealism (many were religious dissenters) or economic considerations. Many emigrated in groups and most settled in the American Middle West, which was perceived at the time as a region of considerable opportunity for immigrants of means. Although many left their homeland becuse of poor agricultural conditions, few were forced from their former existence by impossible circumstances. Major recruitment areas in Sweden during this early phase were the poor upland agricultural districts of the provinces of Östergötland, Småland, and Blekinge, as well as some northern agricultural districts where feelings of religious dissent ran high, primarily in the provinces of Hälsingland, Medelpad, and parts of northern Uppland and eastern Dalarna. Economic recession in the United States during the late 1850s brought this first phase to a close and the outbreak of the American Civil War discouraged any resurgence of emigration until the latter part of the 1860s.

The second phase, which lasted only from 1868 to 1873, brought more than 100,000 emigrants across the Atlantic. This phase was instigated by the disastrous Swedish crop failures of 1867 and 1868 and by news of renewed opportunity to acquire land in America. In addition to the Homestead Act of 1862, which held out the promise of free land, immigrants were also enticed by railroad company promotions and recruitment campaigns launched by individual midwestern states. The composition of the emigrant stream resembled that of the first phase to a considerable degree. Group migration was still common, as was the emigration of landed farmers and their families, but this phase was much more broadly based. It included many more young married men and women who represented other strata of Swedish agricultural society. Sons and daughters of peasant proprietors, cotters, cottagers, farm laborers, and maid-servants were far more prevalent than they had been in the earlier phase. Like the first phase, however, the emigration of the famine years was essentially an agrarian emigration. Emigration diffused to new districts across the length and breadth of Sweden during this period. The end of this phase was marked by severe economic recession in the United States and the return of better times in Sweden.

The third and largest phase of Swedish emigration lasted from 1879 to 1893. During that period nearly 500,000 Swedes left for America. While emigration was high throughout the period, periodic fluctuations delimit three major peaks in the emigrant flow. The first was from 1879 to 1882, the second from 1886 to 1887, and the third from 1891 to 1893. As before, the fluctuations correlated with economic cycles in Sweden and America. The year 1879 was a crisis year in the Swedish timber and iron industries and the 1880s in general were disastrous years for the Swedish agricultural economy, which came under intense pressure from the introduction of cheap American and Russian grain into the Swedish market. In addition, Sweden suffered a marked industrial recession between 1891 and 1893. In America, the difficult years of the mid-1870s were followed by a period of general prosperity which, with the exception of a few years in the early 1880s, extended into the 1890s.

During this phase, Swedish emigration continued to be dominated by the agricultural sector, but workers from the industrial sector and a more substantial urban-based emigration began to intrude. The demographic character of emigration also shifted during this phase. The families and groups that had characterized the early phases were gradually replaced by the individual emigration of married or single adults. While 68 percent of the first-phase emigration was made up of family emigrants, they comprised only 29 percent of the emigrant stream by the 1890s.[5] The shifting composition of the migrant stream reflects a shift in the goals of Swedish emigrants. Whereas some form of religious or political idealism or a desire to take land in America drove the early phases, the attraction for increasing numbers by the 1880s and 1890s was the expansive American labor market, where better wages and conditions than those at home often prevailed. By the end of the third phase, the character of Swedish emigration was rapidly changing. Recruitment was still largely from agricultural districts, but the migrations were less an agricultural colonization effort and more a component of a trans-Atlantic labor market.

The last two phases of Swedish emigration took place in the early decades of the twentieth century. The first extended from 1900 to the outbreak of World War I; the second filled the decade between the Great War and the onset of the Great Depression. Nearly 300,000 emigrated during the first and something over 100,000 in the second. These phases were clearly dominated by the strong pull of the American labor market and represent a culmination of the trends that were becoming apparent in the 1879–93 phase. Emigration was increasingly urban and increasingly dominated by young single adults, especially men. Canada became an alternative destination for many who emigrated during this period. Recruitment areas remained much as before, although the characteristics of emigrants were now almost completely altered.

For Rättvik, as well as for Upper Dalarna, the most important period was a three-wave agrarian emigration that occurred during the second and third national phases (Table 4.1). Emigrant activity in Upper Dalarna during the first national phase involved relatively few participants and was highly localized. A small group who associated them-

Table 4.1 Coincidence of Major Emigrations from Sweden
and from Upper Dalarna during the Study Period

Phase I (1845–55)
Phase II (1868–73)
    1st wave in Dalarna (1868–70)
Phase III (1879–93)
    2nd wave in Dalarna (1879–82)
    3rd wave in Dalarna (1887–89)

selves with the religious visionary Erik Jansson emigrated as early as 1846, but few others left before the 1860s.[6] The first great outpouring of folk from Upper Dalarna began in the years 1861–67, peaked during the famine years of 1868–70, and declined precipitously in the early 1870s. Two subsequent waves of heavy emigration in 1879–82 and 1887–89 coincided with the first two peaks of the third national phase. Together, these three waves of emigration took just over 10,000 people from the parishes of Upper Dalarna to America. With an average population during that period of about 75,000, the region experienced an average emigration rate of 4.8 per thousand, only slightly less than the national rate of 5.0 per thousand.[7] This was the only period when Upper Dalarna's emigration rates consistently matched national averages. In all other phases, the rate of emigration from the region ranged well below the national rate.

While the Upper Dalarna emigrations may be said to represent a particular type of emigration—mainly, agrarian—differences in composition between the three regional waves become apparent with comparison. They clearly differed demographically. The first wave was largely an emigration of families, who were spurred by famine at home and attracted by news of land opportunities in America. The second wave involved an increasing number of single adults, the group that almost totally dominated the third wave. These demographic differences mirror the trend apparent in the national pattern over the same period, a progressive movement from group and family emigration to the emigration of individuals.

It was the flow of information between families and friends, however, not external economic factors, that drove the emigration of Upper Dalarna throughout the period. Migration researchers have frequently emphasized the so-called "stock effect," whereby an emigration tradition is established in a place and maintained over long periods of time by the mechanism of positive information linkages between individuals.[8]

Even in the third wave, which was associated solely with an economic boom in the United States and attracted large numbers of young unmarried adults, the vast majority of emigrants had ties with the families and family groups that had left earlier. Although they do not seem to have emigrated in order to find a secure situation for a dependent family, they did follow on the encouragement of those who had gone before, and often their first employment and abode in America were with the families that preceded them. They were still a part of the old agrarian emigration, bound at least initially by the experience, information, and aid made available by those who had left before them.

But how was the tradition first established in each settlement? The flow of information played a prime role. Just as later emigrants would be encouraged to move because of information from friends and relatives who had emigrated earlier, so, too, the first emigrants from a place must have acted on what they believed to be reliable information. Geographers have done much with information fields and the way ideas spread. The Swedish geographer Torsten Hägerstrand demonstrated the importance of social contacts in influencing the patterns of out-migration from a rural parish in southern Sweden as early as the 1940s. This study led to further work in Sweden and elsewhere on the role of information fields in the spread of ideas.[9]

The course of emigration from Upper Dalarna is a classic example of the way an innovation spreads across space and time.[10] During the formative first wave of emigration, the decision to leave spread in a series of five stages (Figure 4.1). The first infection of "America fever" appeared in southern Orsa and Våmhus parishes in the late 1850s and prompted emigration in the first few years of the 1860s. By 1863, a core area of five village settlements had accepted the idea to emigrate. The core area centered on the large Orsa village of Hansjö. The early emigration from this small area can be directly linked to the appearance of a strong religious dissenter movement there in the 1840s. A number of people in these parishes had come into contact with revival movements in Stockholm and particularly in Swedish Norrland. The result was the growth of a strong lay evangelism, which came to be known as *Orsa-läseriet*. The dissenter atmosphere made these parishes a fertile field for the Baptist movement that began to spread out from its core in Stockholm during the 1850s.

In mid-nineteenth-century Sweden, nonconformists were not viewed with favor by the state church. The Conventicle Act *(konventikelplakatet)* of 1726 forbade any private gathering for religious services, and offenders were punished by fines and prison sentences. This

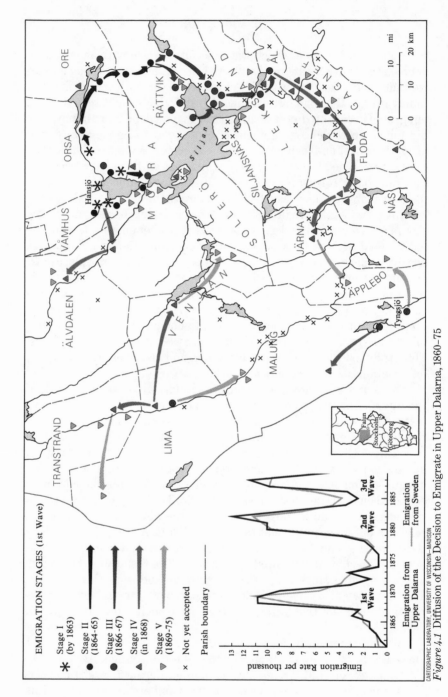

CARTOGRAPHIC LABORATORY, UNIVERSITY OF WISCONSIN–MADISON

Figure 4.1 Diffusion of the Decision to Emigrate in Upper Dalarna, 1860–75

law was abolished in 1858, and two years later a so-called "dissenter's law" was passed granting nonconformists the right to secede from state-regulated congregations if they so desired. The Baptists found the stipulations of this law onerous, however. With the exception of just one congregation in Våmhus, no Baptist congregations elected to take such action. This meant that the Baptists continued to operate outside the law and were thus subject to constant harassment by the authorities. This atmosphere of intolerance partly explains why the rate of emigration was considerably higher among Baptists, especially in the early years, than it was among the Swedish population in general.

It was probably also true that, because they were a tightly knit group, the Baptists received more encouragement and even financial aid from their compatriots who went before them than did the population at large. People who became nonconformists may also by nature have been more apt to emigrate. The psychological make-up of a person who is prepared to leave the ancestral faith may not be so different from that of a person who is ready to leave the ancestral soil. Whatever their motivations, the Baptists did emigrate in large numbers and a substantial portion of the leaders in the first-stage movement out of Upper Dalarna were Baptists from the parishes of Orsa and Våmhus.

In 1864 and 1865 (the years when the first emigrants left Rättvik), the idea began to diffuse rapidly outward from the initial core, nearly doubling the number of settlements that had accepted the idea. In this second stage, a number of the neighboring settlements in the parishes of Orsa and Våmhus began to send out emigrants in significant numbers. But the most dramatic advance was up the Ore River valley into the parish of Ore, and from there up the Ändån valley into the Ovanheds (Boda) district of Rättvik parish. The pattern is not surprising, for it follows the path of the ancient routeway around the Siljan Ring leading from Orsa to Ore, Rättvik, and Leksand. It was along this routeway that people from Orsa and Våmhus often journeyed in search of seasonal labor in southeastern Dalarna, the Bothnian coast, and Stockholm; hence it was the most likely direction for them to have personal contacts with people in other parishes. The spread of emigration southward and westward into the parish of Mora was notably more slow. Although not entirely so, the outward movement in 1864 and 1865 continued to be dominated by Baptists.

The third stage witnessed yet another doubling of affected settlements. This stage, which spanned 1866–67, is distinguished by a further rapid advance along the old Siljan Ring routeway southward through Rättvik parish and down to the lake head at Leksand. Ahead of this surge were some early acceptances in a few scattered settlements south and east of Leksand. By this time, the emigration had shed its close association with the Baptists. Its widespread acceptance in Rättvik, which harbored an insignificant number of nonconformists at the time, underscores the fact that idealism and religious intolerance no longer were the major underlying forces at work. The pull of opportunity in America was beginning to work its magic. By this time a number of shipping companies had begun actively to recruit passengers through advertisements and local agents, and a growing amount of information was circulating about settlement opportunities in the American Middle West.

In the summer of 1866, more than one hundred families from Orsa and Rättvik, as well as some of the surrounding areas, left more or less together. This was the first of the large group migrations that would typify the coming years.[11] This third stage also saw the addition of two core areas from which the idea would spread in subsequent years. One was an outlying area of Malung parish, known as Tyngsjö. The early

Plate 4.1 Emigrant party preparing to leave Rättvik's Bingsjö village. Groups of emigrants from many households often journeyed together. The day of departure was a momentous occasion with friends and relatives gathering to see the emigrants off. The two men on the right are wearing the traditional long leather coat worn in Rättvik during the winter. (Courtesy of Dalarnas Museum, 1880s)

emigration from Tyngsjö was probably stimulated by lively contacts with the settlements along the Klarälven River farther to the south in the province of Värmland. The other new core area was in the center of Lima parish on the upper Västerdalälven. Here the probable source of the outbreak of emigration was contact with Norway. The upper Västerdalälven parishes of Lima and Transtrand lay on a main routeway into Norway from Värmland and the south, and Norwegian influence can be traced even in the folk architecture of the eighteenth and nineteenth centuries in the upper part of the valley.

The serious crop failures of 1867 and 1868 had a quickening effect on the rate of emigration from Upper Dalarna; the rate more than quadrupled from 1867 to 1868. The spring was so late in 1867 that the ice on the Västerdalälven was still thick enough to drive across as late as the middle of May, when crops should have been sown. Not only was the spring extraordinarily late, but the summer was cold and rainy. There was no crop that year. Conditions were scarcely better in 1868. With food reserves dwindling, people were reduced to stripping the bark from trees, grinding it into a flour, and mixing it with small amounts of barley flour to make a foul tasting but life sustaining bread.[12] So many left in the "famine emigration" of 1868 that the year may be treated as a single stage (the fourth) in the spread of the decision to emigrate. In 1868, the number of village settlements accepting the idea to emigrate nearly doubled again. More village settlements (twenty-eight) became significant sources of emigration in that year than in any other. Four paths of movement are apparent during the fourth stage: (1) Up the Västerdalälven from its confluence with the Österdalälven, a continuation of the movement through Rättvik, Leksand, and Gagnef; (2) from the original core in Orsa and Våmhus, to the parishes of Mora and Älvdalen; (3) from Tyngsjö into the finnmark area of Malung parish; and (4) from Lima into the parishes of Transtrand and Venjan. By the end of 1868, acceptance of the idea to emigrate had reached most parts of the region. Almost every parish had at least one affected settlement.

The fifth and final stage in the diffusion process lasted from 1869 to 1875. It peaked and then rapidly declined as conditions in the region gradually improved and news of economic crisis in America began to discourage would-be emigrants. Thirty-five new settlements are counted as accepting the idea to emigrate during this stage, bringing the total to ninety-five, or just over sixty percent of all settlements.[13] By this time the frontier of emigrant activity lay largely in the west, as the idea spread up and down the river valleys from the new core areas in Lima, Transtrand, Venjan, Tyngsjö, Mora, and Älvdalen. Another

Table 4.2   Stages of Diffusion of Emigration from Upper Dalarna, 1862–89

Stage	Time of acceptance	Number of accepting settlements	Cumulative percent of all settlements accepting
First wave			
I	1862–63	5	3.2%
II	1864–65	9	9.1
III	1866–67	18	20.8
IV	1868	28	39.0
V	1869–75	35	61.7
Second wave			
VI	1876–85	24	77.3
Third wave			
VII	1886–89	8	82.5

SOURCES: Catechetical registers (husförhörslängder) and migration registers (flytt-ningslängder) for the parishes of Upper Dalarna.

thirty-two settlements would be added in the major waves that were yet to come in 1879–82 and 1886–89 (Table 4.2). These waves were the generating force behind the sixth and seventh stages in the diffusion process, but by then there is no longer a clear frontier. Instead, one sees a rather discontinuous spread of the idea within parishes; a "filling in" or secondary diffusion process. By the end of the third wave, only twenty-seven settlements still had not accepted the idea of emigration.

In sum, the emigration from Upper Dalarna between 1861 and 1889 was an agrarian emigration, primarily made up of family units bent on agricultural colonization in the American Middle West. Although the three waves of emigration from this region coincided with two of the major phases of Swedish emigration, and closely matched the annual fluctuations and demographic trends of the national pattern, they are best typified by the characteristics of the national second phase. The stock effect that built up during the formative years of the first wave drove emigration through much of the second and third waves. While the demographic composition of the later waves shifted away from family units, the later waves were in many ways complementary to the first; they completed a process of family emigration that had been cut short by changing conditions at home and abroad in the 1870s. In short, these were chain migrations in which family or relational units moved piecemeal over an extended period of time to particular destinations in America. Basic to the process was the constant flow of information between friends and relatives on both sides of the Atlantic.

Similarly, the flow of information played a key role in instigating emigration over an even wider area. The idea to emigrate was an innovation that diffused along the routes of known contacts between village settlements. The idea spread initially from parish to parish, taking root in a few villages, often the larger ones that were best situated for contacts outside the parish. A secondary diffusion process spread the idea within the parish until it was widely accepted, a sort of "filling in" process. The original infection of "America fever" came from outside the region and seems to have been associated with individuals who had outside contacts of a revolutionary nature, namely the large numbers of religious nonconformists living in Orsa and Våmhus. From this area the idea spread to other parts of the region and to other elements of the population, aided by the beginnings of organized emigrant recruitment by shipping lines and by the onset of a natural catastrophe. In general, the acceptance of the idea moved east from the original core area, folowing the old routeway around the Siljan Ring, thence down through the lower Siljan parishes of Rättvik and Leksand to the lower reaches of the Österdalälven. In later stages the idea was introduced up and down the length of the Västerdalälven and into the upper reaches of the Österdalälven.

In the end, more than 80 percent of the village settlements became significant sources of emigration. The upper Siljan parishes, especially Orsa and Våmhus; the upper valley of the Österdalälven; the upper and lower valleys of the Västerdalälven; and the parish of Gagnef at the junction of the two rivers yielded the largest numbers of emigrants. The finnmark districts, with their poor upland soils, tended to lose more of their population than the villages in the valleys. Contrasting with these areas of heavy emigration were the central valley of the Västerdalälven and the lower Siljan parishes, where emigration rates were more modest. Nonetheless, almost every parish had some settlements that experienced heavy emigration and some that experienced light emigration or none at all.

Although the parish of Rättvik accepted the idea of emigration fairly early on, it belongs to the group of lower Siljan parishes that experienced modest to low levels of emigration. One moderating factor was undoubtedly the relatively high levels of landed wealth in some of the Rättvik settlements. Another was the relative weakness of nonconformist religious activity in the parish. Compared to other parishes in the region, Rättvik's emigration was unexceptional. The parish somehow avoided the extreme experiences of areas caught in the divisive throes of idealistic religious conflict. It also escaped the debilitating depopulation suffered in areas whose resources were simply too poor and too few to support the population. Without such extreme situations to color the picture, Rättvik offers an excellent laboratory for examining the emigrant process.

The Emigration from Rättvik

As we have seen, Rättvik experienced a fairly early but modest emigration by the standards of its region. The emigration began in the summer of 1864 with the departure of Bäck Hans Ersson and his party from the Ovanheds village of Gulleråsen. Gulleråsen's location near the northern border of the parish put the village directly in the path of the spread of the idea to emigrate (Figure 4.2). Emigration had spread just the year before to Ore, the parish directly to the north of Rättvik. Of all Rättvik villages, Gulleråsen probably had the strongest contacts with Ore because a number of Ore parishioners grazed livestock in the summertime on land belonging to Gulleråsen. It comes as no surprise, therefore, that someone in that village, for whatever reasons, made the first decision to leave for America. Once the idea had been introduced it was inevitable that it would spread to other parts of the parish and that more and more people from Rättvik would join the movement.

From Gulleråsen, the idea seems to have circulated quickly through information conduits leading to neighboring villages in Ovanheds *fjärding*. Three more villages in that district sent out emigrants the following year. In 1866 and 1867, the idea seems to have exploded across the parish. By the summer of 1866, emigrant activity caught on in the core villages of Gärdsjö *fjärding* and jumped to some of the large villages near the shore of Lake Siljan in Västbygge *fjärding*, as well as to some of the poorer high villages in the southern part of Sörbygge *fjärding*. The initial penetrations of Västbygge and Sörbygge may well have been facilitated through *fäbod* contacts, for the villages involved maintained summer pasturages in the same tracts as the Gärdsjö villages that also sent out emigrants for the first time that year.[14] In 1866, the emigrants first organized themselves into "emigrant parties," essentially large groups of families that agreed to face the rigors of the journey together. By 1867, emigrant activity had spread to the interior high villages of Västbygge, especially the cluster of villages known as "Gränden," and passed southward into Leksand parish. In 1868, the first year of the famine emigrations, most of the remaining Rättvik villages joined in. Only a

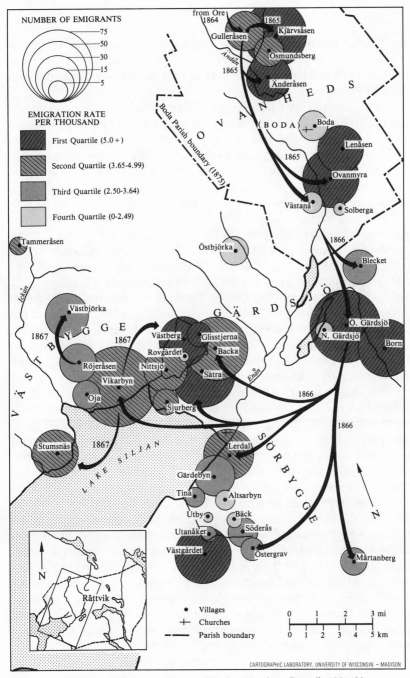

Figure 4.2 Diffusion, Volume, and Rates of Emigration from Rättvik, 1864–89

123

handful remained aloof after the first wave, the majority of them destined to be smitten in subsequent waves. By the end of the 1880s, only one village, Västergrav, can be said to have completely escaped a bout with America fever.[15]

In all, the parish surrendered 977 of its inhabitants to America between 1864 and 1889.[16] The first and largest wave of emigration began slowly in 1864 and 1865, but then rose quickly to a double-headed peak. The first of these twin high points occurred in 1866, when 97 people left for America, many of them in two large parties that left in June of that year.[17] After a slow decline in the number of departures over the next few years, the tide rose to a second high point in 1870, when 94 left. After 1870, emigration quickly fell off to virtually nothing and remained that way for nearly eight years. A total of 429 people left during the first great wave. The second wave began in 1878 and peaked quickly, reaching a high of 110 emigrants in 1880. It faltered briefly in 1881 and then finished strong with 54 and 51 departures in 1882 and 1883, respectively, before petering out in 1884. The second wave was nearly as large as the first, taking an additional 372 people out of the parish. A brief lull of two years separated the second wave from the third, which began in 1886, peaked in 1887 when 79 left for America, and then fell off rapidly over the next two years. The last of the three waves was the smallest, carrying off just 176 parishioners in all.

The close similarity between the emigration curves for Rättvik, Upper Dalarna, and Sweden suggests that emigration was driven by the same mechanisms, locally, regionally, and nationally—the classic "push and pull" factors that have been so thoroughly explored over several generations of econometric studies.[18] It is well known that changing conditions on both sides of the Atlantic often worked in harmony to produce the simultaneous fluctuations in the emigration curve all over Sweden and often over much of Europe. There is also a striking similarity between the demographic composition of the Rättvik emigration and that of emigration going on at the same time throughout Upper Dalarna. The emigration from Rättvik was predominantly a family movement (Table 4.3). This characteristic was established in the first wave, in which married adults and their dependent children accounted for 83.1 percent of all emigrants. Families were actually even more dominant than it appears, because a sizeable portion of the single adults who made up the balance of the emigrant population traveled with family units; many were adult but unmarried children, or unmarried brothers or sisters of the family head. The proportion of married adults and their children among all emigrants eroded steadily over the subsequent two

Table 4.3 Demographic Characteristics of the Emigration from Rättvik, 1864–89

Characteristics	1st wave	2nd wave	3rd wave	Total
	AGE AND CIVIL STATUS			
Married adults	167 (38.9%)	132 (35.5%)	54 (30.7%)	353 (36.1%)
Children (0–19)	187 (43.6)	148 (39.8)	27 (15.3)	362 (37.1)
Single adults	75 (17.5)	92 (24.7)	95 (54.0)	262 (26.8)
Totals	429 (100.0%)	372 (100.0%)	176 (100.0%)	977 (100.0%)
	SEX OF MARRIED ADULTS			
Males	90 (53.9%)	74 (56.1%)	42 (77.8%)	206 (54.8%)
Females	77 (46.1)	58 (43.9)	12 (22.2)	147 (41.6)
Totals	167 (100.0%)	132 (100.0%)	54 (100.0%)	353 (100.0%)
	SEX OF SINGLE ADULTS			
Males	51 (68.0%)	60 (65.2%)	66 (69.5%)	177 (67.6%)
Females	24 (32.0)	32 (34.8)	29 (30.5)	85 (32.4)
Totals	75 (100.0%)	92 (100.0%)	95 (100.0%)	262 (100.0%)

SOURCES: Catechetical registers and migration registers for Rättvik and Boda parishes.

waves, declining to less than one-half by the time the third wave subsided. But overall, families constituted nearly three-quarters of the total emigration from the parish prior to 1890.

In addition to sex and civil status, there was a clear selection process with regard to age (Table 4.4). Among adult emigrants, roughly a ten-year gap separated the average age of marrieds and singles. The average age of both married adult males and females was in the middle to late thirties throughout the period. Over half of all married adult emigrants were between the ages of thirty and forty-five. Theirs was an emigration of established families that had been in existence for five to fifteen years. Although the average age of this group declined slightly during the second wave, it rebounded in the third wave. Even though married men and women who left in the third wave may have left under somewhat different conditions and for somewhat different reasons, they continued to be selected from the same age group, which suggests that those occupying a particular stage in the life cycle remained under considerable pressure throughout the emigration years.

Single adults were also drawn heavily from a particular age group, although here the fact is less remarkable since single adults are normally concentrated within a limited age range. The average age for single adult males and females was the middle to late twenties. In all three waves, over half were between twenty and thirty-four, which was also the dominant age group in the population for all people of this status.

Table 4.4   Average Age of Emigrants from Rättvik, 1864–89

Emigrant group	1st wave	2nd wave	3rd wave	Overall average
Married adult males	38.2	35.5	36.2	36.9
Married adult females	36.7	34.9	35.3	35.9
Single adult males	26.5	24.9	24.2	25.3
Single adult females	28.3	25.0	27.4	26.6

SOURCES: Catechetical registers and migration registers for Rättvik and Boda parishes.

The average age for this group of emigrants declined slightly over the course of the three waves. These young singles, who became an increasingly important element in the emigration from Rättvik as time passed, were people approaching the major transitional stage in their lives. Most of them were near the age at which young people were expected to acquire the means necessary to support marriage and a family. That they became such an important emigrant group in the late 1880s indicates that normal expectations were breaking down.

Assessing the exact economic situation of the mass of emigrants is far more difficult than determining their demographic characteristics, mainly because detailed information on individual property and wealth is lacking between the early 1840s and the mid-1880s. This means that, at least for the first two waves, any assessment of an emigrant's economic status must be extrapolated from the economic status of his or her family in 1842, a year for which information on the landed wealth of individual farms is available in the form of a land register (jordebok). To use these data, one must assume that the inheritance process left individuals an equitable share of the ancestral farm. Such an assumption introduces a certain degree of uncertainty; yet there is reason to believe that economic mobility in the parish was not so great as to render such information unuseable. As a test, a rank correlation was done of the economic status of twenty-two families in Övre Gärdsjö village in 1842 and 1885. The result was a remarkably strong correlation coefficient of .903, which suggests that the economic order in this village, and probably in the parish as a whole, was fairly stable.[19] Furthermore, most of the adult emigrants in the first two waves were old enough to have grown up on the 1842 ancestral farms for which information exists. If nothing else, having spent one's formative years on one of these farms probably influenced one's economic expectation in life.

The 1,491 households in Rättvik in 1842 were divided into seven groups based on the tax values recorded in the land register for that year—six landed groups and a seventh comprised of landless households

Table 4.5   Economic Background of Emigrants from Rättvik, 1864–85

Economic groups in 1842	Farm value (stand. dev. from mean)[a]	Percent of all Rättvik households in 1842 (N = 1,491)	Percent of all emigrations, 1864–85 (N = 219)
I	2.0+	4.6%	12.3%
II	1.2/2.0	5.2	18.7
III	0.4/1.2	14.4	16.9
IV	-0.4/0.4	33.0	25.6
V	-1.2/0.4	36.8	24.7
VI	-1.2+	1.7	0.0
Landless	—	4.3	1.8
		100.0%	100.0%

SOURCES: Catechetical registers and 1842 land register *(jordebok)* for Rättvik parish.
[a] Based on the 1842 farm value of adult primary emigrants.

(Table 4.5).[20] In general, greater wealth seems to have been an important prerequisite for emigration. Emigrants who grew up on farms belonging to the higher economic groups were far more strongly represented than their respective shares in Rättvik's households would predict. Those in the highest two groups appear to have been the leaders in the first wave, followed closely by emigrants drawn from the third and fourth groups.[21] Emigrants drawn from the lower economic groups and the landless got off to a late start and were never important in the first two waves. The poorest landed group was never represented at all. Soldiers and the landless were only weakly represented.

Why were the wealthier economic groups so important? It may have been they were simply better able to bear the cost of emigration. Middling and relatively poor households, however, also left in significant numbers, which leads one to question the importance of cost. Another view, expressed by a number of scholars, is that the wealthier members of a society are the natural leaders in any new undertaking. Others looked up to them as more knowledgeable about the world, as innovators. Since the decision to emigrate may be seen as no more than an innovation, perhaps it is natural to expect those who are ahead to try it first, just as one might expect them to be the first to introduce a new crop or a new breed of livestock. This may be the best explanation in the case of Rättvik's emigration, for the top two economic groups seem to have included many of the leaders and innovators of Rättvik society.[22] Elected officials to the parish council and other positions of responsibility were traditionally drawn almost entirely from these economic groups.

The theory that the early emigrants were drawn from the somewhat wealthier and more purposive elements of society is borne out further by the degree of literacy among emigrants. In most Swedish parishes, parishioners were required to demonstrate their knowledge of the scriptures to members of the clergy and were rated good, fair, or poor according to their performance. This was done annually and the results were faithfully recorded in the parish catechetical registers *(husför-hörslängder)*. An analysis of the recorded literacy of all primary emigrants shows a decline over time in the importance of the better-educated among emigrants, which suggests that the earliest emigrants were more likely to have been drawn from the brighter and more literate, while the later emigrants who followed their example were more likely to rate poorly in literacy (Figure 4.3). Some caution should be exercised, however, in interpreting this material. Ratings were generally lower in the parish at the end of the period than at the beginning. While selective out-migration or even a decline in literacy may have been responsible for the lower ratings, more probably they reflect the different standards of the several clergymen who examined the parishioners over this period.

Thus, there seem to have been a number of differences between the first emigrants and those who came later. The earlier emigrants were, as a rule, older and more established. They were predominantly married landowners; most had been married long enough to have sizeable families. They belonged to the generation that had grown up in the old and relatively stable peasant society of the post-*storskifte* decades, when prospects for the future seemed relatively good. Poor harvests and growing population pressure on resources in the 1860s began to change all that. Coming in conjunction with remarkable news about landed opportunity in the American Midwest, such pressures were capable of moving individuals to momentous decisions. In contrast, many more of the emigrants of the second wave and especially the third wave were younger and less well established. They were predominantly male, and often as not unmarried. Most were born after 1850 and grew up in a time of changing conditions and declining opportunity in Rättvik. Many were landless. The titles of worker *(arbetare)*, male servant or farmhand *(dräng)*, and maidservant *(piga)*, begin to show up with some frequency in the last wave, whereas they scarcely occur in the first two waves. For these emigrants, America held out a more varied promise than for those who went before them. In addition to the ever attractive possibility of acquiring land and a farm, they were also prepared for—indeed, in many cases expected—to find not land but a job that would pay them more than they could be paid in Sweden.

While we have a good idea of the general segments of the population

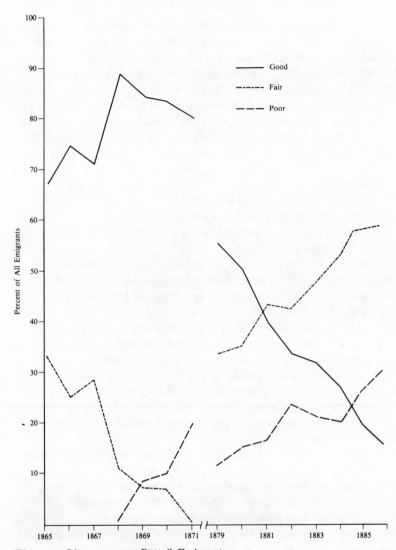

Figure 4.3 Literacy among Rättvik Emigrants

129

from which emigrants were drawn, the relative importance of emigration varied enormously, and often inexplicably, from village to village (Table 4.6). The mere existence of a population that was demographically and economically "ripe" for emigration does not necessarily predict their acceptance of the idea. Taking the average annual emigration rates for Sweden and Upper Dalarna for this period (5.0 and 4.8 per thousand) as a benchmark, it appears that about ten of the Rättvik villages experienced extraordinary levels of total emigration (more than 5.0 per thousand) over the period. Perhaps an equal number experienced what might be described as a modest level (4.0 to 5.0 per thousand). The remainder, or roughly half the settlements in the parish, were to varying degres relatively weak sources of emigration. This weakness is reflected in the average rate of emigration for the entire parish, which was 3.86 per thousand, somewhat less than the regional or national figure for the same period.

The performance of individual villages also varied considerably from one wave to the next. Villages with low or modest overall emigration rates sometimes exhibited an uncharacteristically high level of emigration in a particular wave. The village of Öja, for example, did not participate at all in the first wave, experienced only minor emigration in the second, but sent out emigrants at four times the parish average in the third. Conversely, some of the villages in which emigration was strongest failed to send any emigrants in at least one of the waves (see, for example, Västgärdet and Born). While many villages seemed to establish an emigration tradition early on that remained fairly consistent over all three waves, rather abrupt changes in behavior between waves was often the rule.

The greatest numbers of emigrants and some of the highest emigration rates occurred in the villages of Västbygge *fjärding,* especially the Gränden cluster. The core villages of Gärdsjö and a good many of the Ovanheds villages were also important. The pattern suggests some relationship between the quality of the arable resource and the pressure of population on that resource, and the level of emigration. Emigration, for example, was very light nearly everywhere in Sörbygge, which was the *fjärding* most richly endowed with arable resources. The only exception, the village of Västgärdet, paradoxically experienced one of the highest emigration rates in the parish. If one ignores deviations like Västgärdet, the variation in emigration levels between the *fjärding* districts is plausibly explained by differences in landed wealth. But at the level of village comparisons, the relationship between landed wealth and rate of emigration does not always hold. The sister villages of Nedre

Table 4.6 Emigration by Village, Rättvik Parish, 1864–89

Village	1st wave		2nd wave		3rd wave		Total	
	N	Rate	N	Rate	N	Rate	N	Rate
	SÖRBYGGE FJÄRDING							
Mårtanberg	7	6.48	0	0.00	3	5.55	10	2.85
Söderås	2	1.13	6	3.86	4	4.50	12	2.08
Östergrav	7	5.47	0	0.00	0	0.00	7	1.68
Västergrav	0	0.00	0	0.00	0	0.00	0	0.00
Utanåker	2	4.39	0	0.00	1	4.39	3	2.02
Västgärdet	22	16.87	24	21.03	0	0.00	46	10.85
Utby	0	0.00	1	0.63	0	0.00	1	0.17
Bäck	1	1.44	1	1.64	1	2.87	3	1.33
Altsarbyn	2	0.88	1	0.50	2	1.77	5	0.68
Tina	5	6.94	0	0.00	0	0.00	5	2.14
Gärdebyn	10	4.08	11	5.14	2	1.63	23	2.89
Subtotals	58	4.10	44	3.56	13	1.83	115	2.50
	VÄSTBYGGE FJÄRDING							
Stumsnäs	23	9.81	2	0.98	6	5.12	31	4.07
Öja	0	0.00	2	2.20	9	17.31	11	3.25
Tammeråsen	0	0.00	3	12.24	1	7.14	4	4.40
Röjeråsen	7	2.22	11	3.99	2	1.27	20	1.95
Västbjörka	10	4.39	9	4.51	8	7.02	27	3.64
Vikarbyn	25	3.62	26	4.30	43	12.44	94	4.18
Sjurberg	2	3.05	2	3.48	5	15.06	9	4.17
Nittsjö	11	6.46	11	7.38	1	1.17	23	4.15
Västberg	11	6.88	22	15.71	2	2.50	35	6.73
Rovgärdet	0	0.00	0	0.00	1	6.10	1	0.94
Glisstjerna	6	14.15	0	0.00	2	9.43	8	5.81
Sätra	19	16.05	45	43.44	2	3.38	66	17.15
Subtotals	114	5.20	133	6.94	82	7.48	329	4.62
	GÄRDSJÖ FJÄRDING							
Lerdal	4	1.50	21	9.01	12	9.01	37	4.27
Backa	24	6.38	12	3.65	21	11.17	57	4.66
Blecket	13	5.13	3	1.35	0	0.00	16	1.94
Born	37	18.57	10	5.74	0	0.00	47	7.26
Övre Gärdsjö	43	14.57	21	8.13	10	6.78	74	7.71
Nedre Gärdsjö	0	0.00	4	1.65	0	0.00	4	0.44
Östbjörka	5	1.80	5	2.06	1	0.72	11	1.22
Subtotals	126	6.48	76	4.46	44	4.52	246	3.89

(continued on the following page)

Table 4.6 Emigration by Village, Rättvik Parish, 1864–89 (*continued*)

Village	1st wave		2nd wave		3rd wave		Total	
	N	Rate	N	Rate	N	Rate	N	Rate
	OVANHEDS (BODA) FJÄRDING							
Västanå	6	4.81	0	0.00	0	0.00	6	1.48
Solberga	1	1.28	1	1.46	0	0.00	2	0.78
Ovanmyra	29	12.46	14	6.87	7	6.01	50	6.61
Lenåsen	21	10.67	6	3.48	5	5.08	32	5.00
Boda	0	0.00	6	1.72	6	3.01	12	0.93
Silverberg	0	0.00	8	12.03	2	5.26	10	4.05
Änderåsen	12	11.03	8	11.20	0	0.00	20	7.54
Osmundsberg	10	11.16	2	2.55	0	0.00	12	4.12
Gulleråsen	18	6.06	32	12.32	15	10.17	65	6.74
Kjärvsåsen	9	4.93	13	8.15	0	0.00	22	3.71
Subtotals	106	6.03	90	5.85	35	3.98	231	4.04
	FINNMARK							
Bingsjö	22	14.55	17	12.85	1	1.32	40	8.14
Dalstuga	0	0.00	10	12.42	1	2.17	11	3.68
Finnbacka	0	0.00	1	1.07	0	0.00	1	0.29
Dådrans bruk	3	2.66	1	1.01	0	0.00	4	1.09
Subtotals	25	5.40	29	7.16	2	0.86	56	3.72
Totals	429	5.52	372	5.47	176	4.53	977	3.87

SOURCES: Catechetical registers and migration registers for Rättvik and Boda parishes.
NOTE: Total emigration rates are calculated as the average annual rate per thousand over the entire twenty-six year period. The emigration rates for individual waves are calculated as the average annual rate per thousand for those years in which emigration reached significant levels: in the case of the first wave, 1866–73 (8 years); in the second, 1878–84 (7 years); and in the third, 1886–89 (4 years). Strictly speaking, one cannot compare directly the rates in one column with those of another.

Gärdsjö and Övre Gärdsjö are a prime example. The first experienced virtually no emigration while the second was a major source area, yet the resources and the population pressure on resources in these two villages were virtually the same. Clearly the mechanisms that caused an individual to emigrate from a particular place at a particular time were complexly and deeply intertwined with local social and economic conditions.

Kinship Networks and the Selection of Emigrants

Scholars have always looked to certain demographic and economic variables to explain the propensity for individuals to emigrate.[23] The decision to move is often seen as a function of age, family status, length of residence, and economic circumstance. As we have seen, such factors go a long way towards defining what kind of person might have emigrated from Rättvik. An additional factor is commonly assumed to play a key role in selecting which individuals among a class of potential migrants actually become one. This factor is the relative location of an individual within local kinship networks. Because the communication and reinforcement of the idea to emigrate is a necessary first step leading to the decision to emigrate, the role of personal and associative links within the community is thought to be of considerable importance. The receipt of information or encouragement from individuals who are well known and trusted is likely to have a far greater effect than information coming from more distant and impersonal sources. The process by which networks influence migration, however, is difficult to document. Most studies can only infer its operation and its relationship to other variables.

A major problem in demonstrating the influence of kinship networks is that the pattern of associations between households in any sizeable population is exceedingly difficult to unravel and define. This is especially true of historical studies. Although detailed information may exist that allows one to reconstruct kinship linkages among some households, rarely does sufficient information exist to allow a complete reconstruction of the linkages between all households. Most studies must rely on partial information or attempt to discover networks through the use of surrogates—most commonly, association by surname. More recently, the employment of reconstitution techniques and longitudinal study has helped remedy the situation. But there is yet another problem that plagues most studies: the universe is usually uncontrollable. Since kinship networks tend to spread in every direction, they quickly overflow the boundaries of any study population. A successful study of the role of kinship networks in migration depends on exceptional data and on a reasonably well-confined network system.[24]

The parish of Rättvik offers unique opportunities for the study of the relationship between kinship networks and migration. The population records, with their detailed information on marriage and residence, are exceptionally well suited to unraveling and delimiting the extent of kinship networks for any given time. Furthermore, the several subcommunities whose very existence was in part based on geographically circumscribed marriage fields offer the possibility of defining study areas that contain reasonably complete networks. With this in mind, the cluster of four villages (Övre Gärdsjö, Nedre Gärdsjö, Blecket, and Born) that constitute the core of Gärdsjö are used here as a case study. As the core of one of Rättvik's *fjärding* districts, these four villages, which will be referred to hereafter as the "Gärdsjö villages," exhibited remarkably discrete spatial patterns of marriage over much of the nineteenth century. The highly parochial nature of social contact for this area is underscored by the unique dialectal nuances in the speech of the area. The aim of the case study is first to delimit the kinship networks that operated within these four villages at the time of emigration and then to examine the pattern of emigration from the villages in the context of the delimited networks and their geographic, demographic, and economic characteristics. The expectation is that the disaggregation of the population into kinship networks will yield insights into the mechanism of migrant selection not evident from studying the population as a whole. For reasons of data limitations, the analysis is restricted to the predominantly familial emigration of the first two waves.

The delimitation of kinship networks for the four villages is based on data from the catechetical registers. It was possible to extract from the registers the material necessary to create a "life line" for each inhabitant of the four villages, spanning the period 1846–85. The life lines, which were grouped by household, depict the timing of major events in each individual's life during this period. They indicate place of domicile year by year and the dates of birth, confirmation, marriage, inheritance, migration, childbearing, remarriage, retirement, and death. In the cases of marriage and migration, the life lines and households directly affected by the event were cross-referenced so that kinship linkages between households could be systematically identified. Because emigration from these villages began in 1866, the most relevant reconstruction of kinship networks is one that delimits the networks operating at exactly that point in time. In an agricultural society, kinship networks are in large part a reflection of the efforts made by households to bolster their security through advantageous alliances. The marriages of the most recent generation to come of age are taken here as representative of the active pattern of such efforts. Accordingly, networks were established on the basis of marriages that occurred between 1846 and 1865, the two decades prior to the onset of migration.

During this period, 328 inhabitants of the Gärdsjö villages were married. Of the group, 72 percent found spouses within the confines of the four villages. The remainder married someone from elsewhere. Most of these spouses, however, came from other villages in the same *fjärding;* or, in other words, from the periphery of the larger social unit of which the Gärdsjö community was the most important and central part. No marriage links led outside the boundaries of the parish. The technique used to delimit kinship networks was simply to bind together into cells those households that had marriage links with one another. Marriage links that led outside the four Gärdsjö villages were controlled for the possibility that they might widen the networks within the four-village community. In fact, a small number of them (twelve) did establish additional links between community households by way of one or more outside households. But the small number of such instances underscores once again that the Gärdsjö community was fairly self-contained socially.

Eight networks or "cells" were delimited by this procedure (Figure 4.4). For convenience they are identified by the village name and household number that appears to be the nodal point of each cell (i.e., "ÖG 34," meaning Övre Gärdsjö 34). The eight cells comprise 122 of the 155 households in the Gärdsjö villages. The other 33 households are listed as "unattached," which means that they were either linked to only one other household or, because no household member married during the period from 1846 to 1885, they could not be associated with any of the cells. Most of the cells were quite distinct. Three of the larger ones (Övre Gärdsjö 34, Blecket 25, and Born 14) were tenuously bound to one another by a single marriage link. These cells could be viewed as one very large network, except for the fact that the larger structure clearly had three distinct clusters, hence it makes sense to ignore the tenuous link for the moment.[25]

Despite considerable variance in size, the cells are uniformly dense. A simple measure of network density, if controlled for network size, shows that each cell meets the potential for linkage more or less equally.[26] One feature of the cell networks that is not apparent in the schematic diagram is the frequency of multiple linkages. We saw earlier that the alliance of households through marriage was an important means in Rättvik for ensuring cooperation in times of distress, and that multiple marriage alliances between households were common. In the cells there are frequent examples of marriage exchanges between households in which two and, in a few cases, even three children of one household married the children of another. It seems quite apparent from the data that agricultural districts in this part of Sweden consisted of large kinship networks in which inbreeding was fairly common.

Physical distance does not seem to be a significant factor in describing the cell networks. The cells were nested, one on top of another, within the Gärdsjö community. Neighboring households were often associated with different cells. Linked households varied in their physical distance from one another; no real pattern emerges from their spatial distribution. At best, one can note that some cells were more

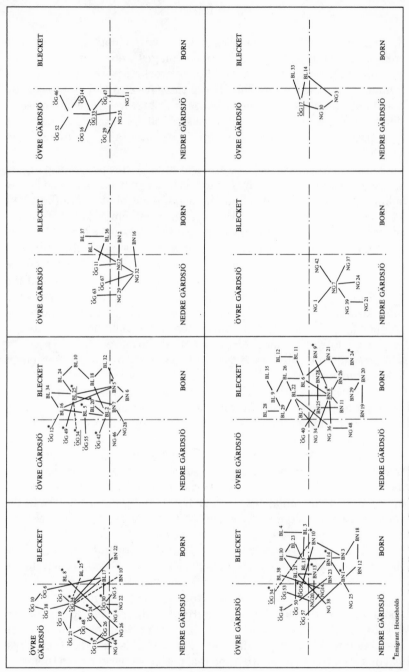

Figure 4.4 Kinship Cells in the Gärdsjö Villages, 1846–65

strongly identified with certain villages than others. What seems to be most important is the simple fact of linkage and that there apparently was an ultimate limit to the spatial dispersion of linkages, resulting in part from the apparent aversion to marriage outside the community.

In relating emigration to the operation of these kinship networks, it is important to realize that emigration was only one of several kinds of migration to which individuals might be drawn. One type of migration was normal with marriage. A new marriage necessarily moved one partner to the home farm of the other. These highly localized marriage-related moves are reflected in the kinship networks. A second type was short-distance migration, which for the most part involved movements between the Gärdsjö villages and other villages in the parish, although movements to or from more distant places in Sweden also occurred. The third type was emigration to America. It is often suggested that short-distance migration and emigration are two different manifestations of the same need to migrate and should be seen as complementary phenomena.[27]

In the Gärdsjö villages, the volume of short-distance migration was always modest and more or less constantly maintained. The rate fluctuated between two and six per thousand on an annual basis. Of a total of 205 migrants who left for local or Swedish destinations between 1846 and 1885, 115 moved no farther than a neighboring village, and 169 did not leave the parish. Roughly one-quarter of these migrants were single young adults. Those who left the parish normally belonged to this group. The remainder of the migrants moved in family groups. Much of this local migration was kinship related, moving a family from the farm of one spouse's parents to the farm of the other's parents. Such moves were commonly undertaken as an adjustment to change in the economic situation of one of the linked households. The death of a parent or adult sibling, for instance, could open up an advantageous situation on the home farm for a son or a daughter who had married into another household. Short-distance migration of this type was often a matter of back-and-forth or circular movement between two or three farms.

The pattern of emigration to America was different than short-distance migration in both timing and volume (Figure 4.5). It began abruptly in 1866 and continued at a rather high rate for the entire period of the first emigration wave. Emigration in the second wave occurred at much lower levels. The highs and lows in the emigration rate did not coincide with those in the short-distance migration rate, and the volume of emigration during the first wave was much greater. In contrast to the continuous low-volume, ebb-and-flow of short-distance migration, emi-

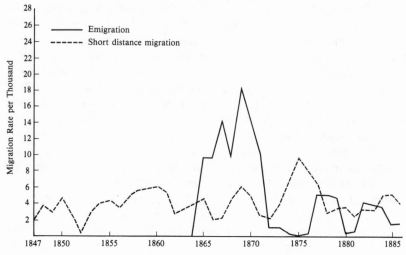

Figure 4.5 Emigration and Short-Distance Migration in the Gärdsjö Villages, 1847–86

gration was sporadic; it began suddenly, reached rather high levels, but was relatively short-lived. A total of 146 people left the Gärdsjö community for America between 1866 and 1885, mostly in family groups. The median age of the adult emigrant was thirty-one years, exactly the same as that of the short-distance migrant. This suggests that in spite of the different timing and volume of the two kinds of migration, stage of life cycle was probably an important factor in selection for both.

When participation in migration is viewed in the context of kinship cells, quite different patterns emerge for short-distance migration and emigration (Table 4.7). During the period 1866 to 1885, the participation of all kinship cells and unattached households in short-distance migration was more or less uniform, as one might expect given the normal function of this activity in household reproduction. On the other hand, only some of the cells were serious participants in the emigration to America. Eighty-seven percent of the emigration came from households in the cells designated Övre Gärdsjö 34, Blecket 25, and Born 14, each of which contained seven participating households. The remainder of the emigrants came from the Born 8 cell and from some of the unattached households. Thus, the larger and more elaborate networks generated the emigrant stream (remember that the three largest cells were tenuously linked), while the smaller cells and the unattached households were scarcely affected. In his study of migration and kinship networks in Yorkshire, R. J. Johnston postulated that more elaborate networks

Table 4.7 Kinship Cell Participation in Short-Distance Migration and Emigration, Gärdsjö Villages, 1866–85

Kinship cells	Number of short-distance migrants	Short-distance migrants as percentage of 1866 population	Number of emigrants	Emigrants as percentage of 1866 population
Ö. Gärdsjö 34	12	6.7%	44	24.6%
Blecket 25	15	8.9	52	31.0
Born 14	20	9.6	31	14.9
Born 8	15	7.9	11	5.8
N. Gärdsjö 2	10	8.7	—	—
Ö. Gärdsjö 33	5	8.8	—	—
N. Gärdsjö 7	8	13.3	—	—
Ö. Gärdsjö 17	3	8.1	—	—
Unattached Households	32	16.2	8	4.1
Totals	120	9.9	146	12.0

SOURCES: Catechetical registers and migration registers for Rättvik parish.

would be resistant to migration, while more loosely organized households would have a greater propensity to migrate because the strength of personal ties to the community would be weaker.[28] The opposite seems to be the case here, although there is an important difference between the studies in that the Yorkshire migrants were not part of an overseas chain migration. In any case, the question of why only certain cells participated remains. To answer it requires a closer examination of the circumstances of emigration in each of the cells.

Demographically and economically, the kinship cells have significantly different characteristics which may have made them more or less susceptible to the lure of emigration. A comparison of the age structure of each of the eight cells and of the unattached households in 1866, for example, reveals an array of configurations (Figure 4.6). The general pattern is one of "bulges" and "constrictions" created by the unequal relative importance of age groups. The bulges and constrictions in the age structure of each cell, which of course changed position over time as the population cohorts aged, often are not synchronized with those in other cells. Thus, at any given time, the rates of births, marriages, deaths, and quite possibly the propensity to emigrate could vary considerably between the cells.

This structural variation between cells reflects marriage patterns. When a particular age cohort in the population reached marriageable age, the product of the ensuing marriages was a kinship cell that in all probability would be relatively distinct from the cell formed by the mar-

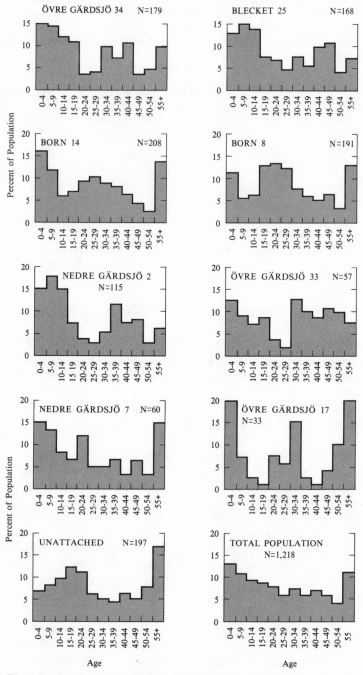

Figure 4.6 Age Structure of Kinship Cells in the Gärdsjö Villages, 1866

140

riages of the next cohort to come of age. To a large extent, the kinship cells in this study represent the marriage webs of different age cohorts, or possibly of social groups within those age cohorts. When the offspring of the generation whose marriages formed the cell reached maturity, the cycle would be repeated. If the cell were exclusive enough socially, the new generation of marriages would be endogamous to the cell. In this way the cells could be self-perpetuating.

Since half of all adult emigrants from the Gärdsjö villages ranged in age from roughly twenty-four to thirty-eight, one would logically expect that cells with high proportions of similarly aged people in 1866 would have had a high propensity to send out emigrants during the initial wave of emigration. Presumably, such cells would be highly susceptible because they would contain a surplus of young adults who were marrying, starting families, and thereby applying pressure to the limited resources of the local peasant economy. In fact, quite the opposite is the case. The active emigrant cells reached their highest rates when the number of people in this age group was smallest. The two cells that participated most strongly in the initial 1866–71 wave of emigration, Övre Gärdsjö 34 and Blecket 25, were then at low points in terms of the relative importance of this segment of the population (Figure 4.7). In both cases, the peak years for this age group had come more than a decade earlier, in the 1840s and early 1850s. The other cell that sent out a substantial number of emigrants, Born 14, experienced its last peak of young adults somewhat later and did not reach the opposite extreme in the cycle until the 1870s. The strongest emigration rates for this cell were also delayed until the 1870s. The Born 8 cell, which experienced a modest level of emigration, had an even further delayed cycle and time of emigration. For this cell, both emigration and the low point in the number of young adults occurred in the late 1870s and early 1880s. In no cases did the "moment of emigration" come when the number of eligibles was at its maximum. Instead, it came at or near the minimum. Actually, the critical time seems to have been just as the "back side" of a bulge in the age structure passed through the age bracket most representative of emigrants.

The explanation to this riddle lies in the overextension of farm households at this stage of the demographic cycle. Recall that as household heads accepted the spouses of newly married sons and daughters into the household, they parceled out resources to the new family units. This was a necessary procedure to hold newly married sons and daughters— and their labor—on the farm. These young married people, however, soon produced enough children to enlarge the size of the farm household

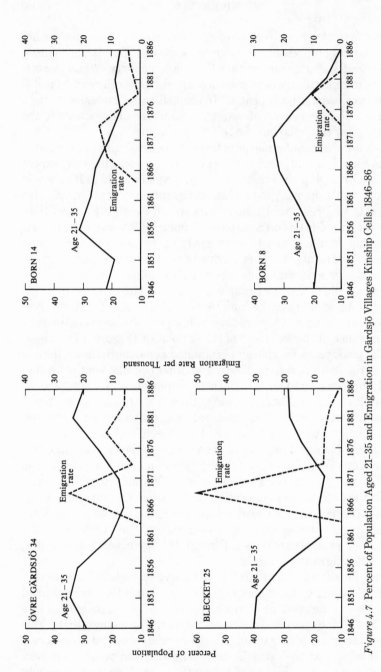

Figure 4.7 Percent of Population Aged 21–35 and Emigration in Gärdsjö Villages Kinship Cells, 1846–86

significantly and to strain the carrying capacity of the farm. This situation required that at least one of the young families find a living elsewhere.

Under normal circumstances, the strain was relieved through short-distance migration. As we have seen, however, the late 1860s was a time of extraordinarily poor agricultural conditions in Upper Dalarna, and a time flush with news of opportunity in America. In reality and by comparison, traditional opportunity in the villages looked rather bleak, all the more so when coupled with a prodigious local growth in population that stretched back over several decades to the time of the *storskifte*. In this situation the normal options were simply not enough. The number of young families facing this situation was larger in some kinship cells than in others. For many young families who weighed their prospects at that time, the best future seemed to lie in emigration to America.

Thus the point at which a population was most susceptible to emigration, given a set of push and pull factors sufficiently strong to generate migratory behavior, was when the number of young adults was on the decline, the number of young children was rising, and the number of large extended households was at its height. It was not the point in time when the new generation within a social group reached adulthood and responsibility; rather, when they had continued in such a situation for a period of time and caused a certain disequilibrium in the normal balance of things. A survey of the situation of all emigrants from this community at the time of departure lends support to this scenario (Table 4.8). Most of the emigrants were members of multiple family households. Most had been married for three to twelve years and had several children. In addition, at least one married brother or sister remained on the farm and acquired the former holdings of those who emigrated. In some cases, the emigrant was the first-married child living on the farm; in others, the emigrant was the second or third child. The sequence varied because inheritance compensation arrangements varied among households, as there was no customary arrangement that dictated the order in which offspring might eventually possess all or part of the ancestral farm. But in nearly all cases, the emigrant was established, yet forced to leave because resources were not sufficient to support everyone in the overextended household.

A prime example of the mechanism at work is the experience of the farm household known as "Ollas" in the village of Born (Born 5). In 1846 this household was headed by Ollas Hans Andersson, age 57, and his wife, Karin Jönsdotter. They had eight children ranging in age from 12 to 31. Over the next twenty years, six of their children married, one left

Table 4.8   Characteristics of Emigrants from the Gärdsjö Villages, 1866–85

Household	Year of emigration	Number of emigrants[a]	Characteristics
Born			
1	1868	2	Single adults, aged 31 and 34
2	1866	4	Family, married 11 years, second of 3 married children living on farm
8	1870	6	Family, married 9 years, first of 3 married children living on farm
9	1866	4	Family, married 6 years, first of 3 married children living on farm
10	1870	5	Family, married 9 years, first of 2 married children living on farm
13	1870	3	Family, married 8 years, second of 2 married children living on farm
14	1866	6	Family, married 13 years, first of 3 married children living on farm
24	1868	1	Single adult, age 20
Blecket			
5	1870	5	Family, household head, married 36 years, left married child on farm
8	1878	4	Family, married 8 years, first of 2 married children living on farm
20	1870	11	Family, married 9 years, third of 3 married children living on farm
25	1866	6	Family, married 10 years, only married child living on farm, left father's and uncle's families on farm
Ö. Gärdsjö			
12	1870	8	Family, household head, married 25 years, left married brothers on farm
15	1870	5	Family, married 10 years, second of 3 married children living on farm
20	1870	2	Single adults, aged 18 and 22
24	1869	10	Family, household head, married 12 years, farm liquidated
30	1885	10	Family, married 12 years, second of 2 married children living on farm
34	1868	5	Family, married 7 years, second of 2 married children living on farm
37	1883	4	Family, married 8 years, first of 3 married children living on farm
42	1882	1	Single adult, age 35
44	1868	4	Family, married 3 years, only married child living on farm
48	1868	1	Single adult, age 22

(*continued on the following page*)

Table 4.8 Characteristics of Emigrants from the Gärdsjö Villages, 1866–85 (*continued*)

Household	Year of emigration	Number of emigrants[a]	Characteristics
Ö. Gärdsjö (*Continued*)			
49	1866	7	Family, household head, married 27 years, farm liquidated
50	1866	5	Family, married 5 years, second of 2 married children living on farm
56	1866	6	Family, married 10 years, first of 2 married children living on farm
N. Gärdsjö			
18	1877	1	Single adult, age 39
19	1883	1	Single adult, age 26
44	1878	3	Family, married 10 years, second of 2 married children living on farm

SOURCES: Catechetical registers, migration registers, and population registers (*mantalslängder*) for Rättvik parish.

a Primary emigrants only; does not include later migration from the same households.

the parish, and one died. The fifth child, daughter Lisbet, was the first to marry. In 1848 she married a boy from the neighboring village of Blecket, who came to live on the Ollas farm. As the adopted son-in-law of the Ollas household, he was given a share of the farm. Before long the new couple began raising a family that would eventually include seven children. Two of Lisbet's brothers, the third and sixth children of Ollas Hans Andersson, married in 1850 and 1852; both left the farm to join brides on Blecket farms. The second and seventh children, also boys, were married in 1854 and 1855. Unlike their brothers, they remained on the home farm with their new brides, which meant that by 1856 there were four families living on the farm—a total of fifteen people. In 1856, the oldest daughter married into a household in Lerdal, one of the other villages in the *fjärding*. Two years later the fourth child left for the Bothnian coast area of Sweden, presumably to find work, and in the same year the eighth and youngest child of the original family died.

Over the next few years the size of the household continued to grow, reaching twenty-two persons by the early 1860s. At that time old Ollas Hans Andersson turned over control of the farm to the son-in-law who had married Lisbet. The old couple both had passed away by 1865, forcing a final disposition of what must have been a heavily encumbered estate. The disposition occurred at the onset of difficult times in Rättvik and undoubtedly forced the heirs of the estate to make some hard decisions. Shortly thereafter (1866) one of the two married sons decided to emigrate with his family. Most probably the other heirs agreed to compensate him for the share of the farm that he surrendered, although no record exists. The remaining two families continued on, subdividing the farm and eventually taking on two of their own married children in the late 1870s and early 1880s, thereby starting the cycle over once again.

While demographic and economic variables associated with the household life cycle were clearly important, they were not alone in prompting emigration. It required a combination of these factors and the reinforcement of an active kinship network. One would expect all kinship cells that met the appropriate conditions to participate if demographic and economic factors alone were responsible. In fact, all of the kinship cells in the Gärdsjö villages met the conditions of declining numbers of young adults, rising numbers of young children, and large extended households, at some point during the emigration years of 1866–85. Only the unattached households were never in that situation during the period. Yet it was the four largest and best developed cells that were the major participants. While the Övre Gärdsjö 34 and Nedre Gärdsjö 2 cells had very similar demographic structures, only the former sent out emigrants.

A plausible explanation of why only four kinship cells tended to channel the stress of demographic and economic pressure into emigration lies in their central, well-integrated position in the community. There is reason to believe that these cells were representative of the social core of the Gärdsjö community in the 1860s, whereas the other cells and the unattached households occupied a more peripheral position. An examination of leadership, for example, finds that the households of these four cells held all the positions of local leadership and public office in the community during the entire decade of the 1860s.[29] There is insufficient evidence to say anything with certainty about the concentration of community wealth in these cells, but if wealth were related to leadership, which in some measure it surely was, these cells were the core of the community in that sense as well.[30]

As we shall soon see, nearly all the emigrants from this community migrated to the same place in America and founded what amounted to a "daughter" or "fragment" community there. If the possibility of founding a daughter community in America was at all understood and contemplated in the Gärdsjö community during the late 1860s, it seems probable that the idea of emigration would receive widespread support within the cells that had the strongest sense of socioeconomic self-importance. Emigration to what could be thought of as a colony must have appealed to the collective conscience of a social community faced, as it was in those difficult years, with the possible dispersion of its off-spring. It was in many ways a conservative response to a difficult situation. Whereas the idea of emigrating may often be thought of as a radical or extraordinary idea, in this case it seems to have been motivated by a desire to preserve some kind of status quo. Charlotte Erickson, in her study of English and Scottish emigrants, has pointed out that an important motivation for some emigrants was a desire to preserve the social status of the family in a time of mounting uncertainty.[31] Such a desire differentiates migrants who intend to colonize from those who seek their fortune. Households that were well situated in the social network of the Gärdsjö community would have been particularly sensitive to fears of family dispersion. The smaller kinship cells and the unattached households on the social periphery may have been less concerned. This would help to explain their lack of participation in the emigration and the proportionately greater tendency for their members to migrate not to America but to randomly scattered destinations in Sweden when conditions forced them to leave their ancestral homes.

Although the foregoing offers considerable insights on the emigrant selection process operating in these villages, an important question about the method employed here remains: How permanent were these kinship cells? As these cells aged they produced new generations of marriageable people. Did marriages among the next generation perpetuate or realign the social organization of society? If they perpetuated the existing order, the explanations presented here gain considerable weight. A substantial realignment, on the other hand, would cast doubt on the significance of the kinship cell as a social influence on migratory behavior. To test this, marriage patterns were observed over the next twenty years, 1866–85, to see what effect the marriage of a new generation had on the kinship cells that were delimited on the basis of marriages between 1846 and 1865. The 219 marriages emanating from the delimited cells during this period were tabulated according to whether they linked member households with one another, with households in other cells, with unattached households, or with households located outside the community (Table 4.9).

A number of observations can be made from the results of this tabulation. First, the cells that occupied the social center of the community in 1865 proved to be the most stable over the next twenty years. This was especially true of the three cells (Övre Gärdsjö 34, Blecket 25, and Born 14) that were tenuously linked together and most strongly associated with the emigration. In each of these cells, half or more of all new mar-

Table 4.9   Marriage by Kinship Cell, Gärdsjö Villages, 1866–85

Kinship cell	Number that married	Number (percentage) that married within cell		Number (percentage) that married other cell		Number (percentage) that married into unattached households		Number (percentage) that married outside of community	
Ö. Gärdsjö 34	28	14	(50.0%)	9	(32.1%)	1	(3.6%)	4	(14.3%)
Blecket 25	33	20	(60.6)	11	(33.3)	0	(0.0)	2	(6.1)
Born 14	40	20	(50.0)	15	(37.5)	1	(2.5)	4	(10.0)
Born 8	45	18	(40.0)	18	(40.0)	4	(8.9)	5	(11.1)
N. Gärdsjö 2	32	6	(18.8)	8	(25.0)	7	(21.9)	11	(34.3)
Ö. Gärdsjö 33	11	0	(0.0)	4	(36.4)	3	(27.2)	4	(36.4)
N. Gärdsjö 7	17	0	(0.0)	6	(35.3)	4	(23.5)	7	(41.2)
Ö. Gärdsjö 17	15	0	(0.0)	7	(46.7)	6	(40.0)	2	(13.3)
Unattached Households	66	—	—	22	(33.3)	16	(24.2)	28	(42.5)
Totals	287	78	(27.2%)	100	(34.8%)	42	(14.6%)	67	(23.4%)

SOURCES: Catechetical registers and migration registers for Rättvik parish.

riages further linked households that already belonged to the cell, while approximately one-third created links with households in other cells. No internal marriages took place in the three smallest cells (Övre Gärdsjö 33, Nedre Gärdsjö 7, and Övre Gärdsjö 17). Young adults in these households married into other cells or into the unattached households. Second, marriage into unattached households appears to have been an unattractive option for young adults in the four large core cells. Only a handful of marriages linked households in these cells with unattached households. Finally, households in the core cells rarely established marriage alliances with households outside the community. Only one in ten did so, while the other cells and the unattached households did so with relative frequency.

Mixing inevitably occurred. The data suggest that some of the smaller cells were not fully developed as delimited for 1865 or were unrecognized extensions of other networks inside or outside the community. Yet the larger core cells appear to have been remarkably persistent features of the Gärdsjö community. In addition, the data suggest that the socially peripheral position of the unattached households was not a temporary condition dictated by the mechanics of the original delimitation of kinship cells. If that had been the case, the unattached households would have become well integrated once they began to marry in the 1870s and 1880s. Instead, they married among themselves, into some of the smaller kinship cells, and, to a substantial extent, with households outside the Gärdsjö community. The relative stability of the

Table 4.10   Marriage in the Four Core Cells of the Gärdsjö Villages, 1866–85

Kinship cells	Number that married	Number (percentage) that married within core cells	
Övre Gärdsjö 34	28	20	(71.4%)
Blecket 25	33	29	(87.9)
Born 14	40	33	(82.5)
Born 8	46	30	(65.2)
Totals	147	112	(76.2)

SOURCE: Catechetical registers for Rättvik parish, 1866–85.

social center is underscored when the four core cells are viewed as a single unit (Table 4.10). Viewed in this context, fully three-quarters of the young married people selected spouses within the confines of the kinship networks most central to the community. That such a social core persisted over such a long period of time lends credence to the notion that it also exerted a strong influence on who emigrated and what the goals of that emigration might have been.

Destinations

The emigration from Rättvik was a classic example of family-oriented chain migration. Its course was guided to a remarkable degree by the bonds of kinship and community. The emigration began with the out-migration of family groups during a time of economic stress brought on by somewhat unusual environmental and demographic conditions. It was perpetuated in later years through a tradition of emigration maintained within kinship networks, a tradition that gradually reunited certain families and kinship groups in America. Through emigration, certain fragments of the social community in Rättvik were transplanted into another milieu. In short, one of its major functions was colonization. Of course, not every person who left Rättvik for America between 1864 and the end of the 1880s was a part of this temporally extended transplantation process. Many left quite independently, for their own special reasons and with their own specific destinations in mind. This was increasingly true as time went on and was most evident in the third wave. Yet for the most part, the migration was distinguished by the specificity of its endpoints and the multiplicity of personal links between participants.

While Rättvik folk are known to have settled in quite a number of places across the American Middle West, two final destinations, both agricultural frontiers, stand out in particular. The first was Minnesota's Isanti County. The second destination was located much farther west, in what was then Clay County, Dakota Territory. Of the entire emigration from Rättvik prior to 1890, 454 people, 46.4 percent, appear to have settled permanently, or at least remained for a period of time, in one or both of these midwestern counties. These figures most certainly under-estimate the total. The discontinuous nature of American population records means that a good many of the emigrants from Rättvik who may have been residents of either place for a brief period of time were never recorded. It is likely that these two receiving areas were of some impor-tance to well over half, possibly even two-thirds, of Rättvik's emigrants.

Isanti County was by far the more important of the two receiving areas, accounting for 41 percent of the emigration from Rättvik. Yet the number of immigrants from Rättvik who settled in Clay County was not inconsequential and should not be ignored, although most attention in the coming sections of this book is paid to the much larger contingent that settled in the Isanti area. The remaining emigrants from Rättvik seem to have established no other major concentrations in America. Parish records indicate that many of the emigrants who did not show up in either Isanti or Clay county listed Minnesota as their destination; pre-sumably they passed through these areas without being recorded or found their way to other Swedish settlements in the state. The only other state mentioned with any frequency in the Rättvik migration records is Kansas, but even that rarely, and we know of no concentrated settlement of Rättvik emigrés there.

As one might expect, the highest proportions of emigrants to Isanti and Clay counties came out of the first and second waves. Such "closed migrations" are naturally established and maintained by the kind of family-oriented chain migration typical of the earlier waves. Only a rela-tively small proportion of the emigrants who left Rättvik in the third wave can be documented as having stayed in either of the major receiv-ing areas. Again, there is probably considerable under-reporting here, because the emigrants of the third wave were more likely to be young and single and so less likely to have remained in one place long enough to register in American population records. Nevertheless, it is this third wave that exhibits, in the Rättvik emigration registers, the greatest number of indications of planned destinations outside of Minnesota or the Dakotas. The far more diverse emigration of this period was proba-bly less sensitive to the established migration paths leading from Rätt-vik to its daughter settlements in America and more sensitive to reports of wage-labor opportunity in various places.

All of the Rättvik *fjärding* districts contributed substantially, and more or less evenly, to the emigration to Isanti County (Table 4.11). Sörbygge contributed the smallest proportion (37.4 percent) of its emigrant population to Isanti, while Gärdsjö contributed the largest (52.0 percent). But the range above and below the average for the parish as a whole was small. The only administrative division to send no emigrants to Isanti was the finnmark. Emigration to Clay County, however, was limited to people from Gärdsjö *fjärding* and the finnmark. This was a much smaller set of chain migrations than was the case with the migration to Isanti, involving no more than three or four kinship networks rather than several dozen. The participating kinship networks in Gärdsjö *fjärding* were entirely different from those that were sending emigrants to Isanti at the same time. Gärdsjö emigrants to Clay County came principally from the villages of Backa and Born, which had relatively low levels of emigration to Isanti County, and from Östbjörka, which did not participate at all in the Isanti migration. The remainder of the Clay County emigrants hailed from two of the finnmark villages; again, places with no direct links to the Isanti settlements. The selection of emigrants to each of these receiving areas appears to have been a distinctly separate process, although there is evidence that one or two emigrant parties destined for the Clay County settlement passed through the Isanti area on their way.[32]

While each of the *fjärding* districts as a whole contributed substantially to the larger and more expansive migration to Isanti, there were tremendous differences between individual villages. In a few villages the proportion of all emigrants who went to Isanti was remarkably high. In others, few or even no emigrants ended up there. In general, the rate was highest among villages that participated especially strongly in the first wave (compare Tables 4.6 and 4.11). Villages that established early and strong traditions of emigration were also villages where the kind of selection processes discussed above for the Gärdsjö community were most prevalent. They were villages where demographic and economic conditions in the late 1860s exerted considerable stress on the normal process of family formation and intergenerational transfer of landed wealth. As a consequence, emigration from these villages was especially oriented towards family groups and was especially sensitive to a larger kinship-based, group solidarity and the notion of group colonization in America. In contrast, many of the villages that sent out only a small proportion of their out-migration to specific daughter settlements in America were relative late-comers to the emigration. A prime example is the village of Vikarbyn. Although this large and relatively rich village

Table 4.11 Emigration by Village from Rättvik to Isanti and Clay Counties, 1864–89

Village	Total emigrants	Emigrants to Isanti	Percentage of all emigrants to Isanti	Emigrants to Dalesburg	Percentage of all emigrants to Dalesburg
		Sörbygge fjärding			
Mårtanberg	10	6	60.0%	0	0.0%
Söderås	12	3	33.3	0	0.0
Östergrav	7	7	100.0	0	0.0
Västergrav	0	0	0.0	0	0.0
Utanåker	3	0	0.0	0	0.0
Västgärdet	46	15	32.6	0	0.0
Utby	1	0	0.0	0	0.0
Bäck	3	0	0.0	0	0.0
Altsarbyn	5	0	0.0	0	0.0
Tina	5	0	0.0	0	0.0
Gärdebyn	23	12	52.2	0	0.0
Subtotals	115	43	37.4%	0	0.0%
		Västbygge fjärding			
Stumsnäs	31	24	77.4%	0	0.0%
Öja	11	0	0.0	0	0.0
Tammeråsen	4	0	0.0	0	0.0
Röjeråsen	20	5	25.0	0	0.0
Västbjörka	27	14	51.2	0	0.0
Vikarbyn	94	14	14.9	0	0.0
Sjurberg	9	0	0.0	0	0.0
Nittsjö	23	21	91.3	0	0.0
Västberg	35	14	40.0	0	0.0
Rovgärdet	1	0	0.0	0	0.0
Glisstjerna	8	6	75.0	0	0.0
Sätra	66	41	62.1	0	0.0
Subtotals	329	139	42.2%	0	0.0%
		Gärdsjö fjärding			
Lerdal	37	8	21.6%	0	0.0%
Backa	57	20	35.1	17	29.8
Blecket	16	15	93.8	0	0.0
Born	47	22	46.8	9	19.1
Övre Gärdsjö	74	60	81.1	0	0.0
Nedre Gärdsjö	4	3	75.0	0	0.0
Östbjörka	11	0	0.0	5	45.5
Subtotals	246	128	52.0%	31	12.6%

(*continued on the following page*)

Table 4.11 Emigration by Village from Rättvik to Isanti and Clay Counties, 1864–89
        (continued)

Village	Total emigrants	Emigrants to Isanti	Percentage of all emigrants to Isanti	Emigrants to Dalesburg	Percentage of all emigrants to Dalesburg
		OVANHEDS (BODA) FJÄRDING			
Västanå	6	0	0.0%	0	0.0%
Solberga	2	0	0.0	0	0.0
Ovanmyra	50	29	58.0	0	0.0
Lenåsen	32	20	62.5	0	0.0
Boda	12	0	0.0	0	0.0
Silverberg	10	0	0.0	0	0.0
Änderåsen	20	4	20.0	0	0.0
Osmundsberg	12	8	66.7	0	0.0
Gulleråsen	65	22	33.8	0	0.0
Kjärvsåsen	22	8	36.4	0	0.0
Subtotals	231	91	39.4%	0	0.0%
		FINNMARK			
Bingsjö	40	0	0.0%	19	47.5%
Dalstuga	11	0	0.0	3	27.3
Finnbacka	1	0	0.0	0	0.0
Dådrans bruk	4	0	0.0	0	0.0
Subtotals	56	0	0.0%	22	39.3%
Totals	977	401	41.0%	53	5.4%

SOURCES: Catechetical registers and migration registers for Rättvik and Boda parishes; federal and state manuscript censuses for Isanti and Clay counties; parish registers of Cambridge, Athens, and Dalesburg Lutheran churches.

sent out ninety-four emigrants, more than any other Rättvik village, its emigration is greatly skewed towards the second and third waves. Emigration from Vikarbyn is typified by large numbers of young single men and women, and young married men who left their wives and young families behind. Only 14.9 percent of the emigrants who left this village were ever officially recorded as residents of the Rättvik settlements in Isanti County, and nearly all of them emigrated in family units.

In a sense, the differences in emigration behavior between villages is like the differences between some of the kinship networks in the Gärdsjö community. Some were caught up in the need for large-scale relief of pressures and, because of intense social solidarity, seemed to embrace the possibilities of transplanting a fragment of themselves in another place. Others lacked either the pressures or the social solidarity necessary to spawn such enterprise, and engaged instead in a highly individualistic and desultory migrant behavior that led ultimately to the dispersal of the migrant stream. The latter type of behavior has its story, too. Those who left to make it on their own, without the comfort of a transplanted cocoon of familial, kinship, and community bonds to aid them in the new world, are an important part of the nineteenth-century emigrant experience. But this study follows across the Atlantic those who tried to transplant themselves and at least a segment of their social milieu in a new place. Did their effort, whether conscious or not, to create a familiar fabric of life in a new, distant place succeed or fail?

5

The New Land

Settlement Processes

THE MIDWESTERN AGRICULTURAL frontier that beckoned to thousands of settlers in the latter half of the 1860s was a resurgent frontier. The early 1860s had been a period of quiessence as people recuperated from a series of shocks. A major financial collapse in 1857 had shaken the confidence of the entire nation and dampened enthusiasm for frontier agricultural expansion in particular. Nearly five years of Civil War had further prevented many potential settlers from venturing to new lands, and reports of an Indian uprising in southern Minnesota in 1862 virtually depopulated many frontier zones as settlers abandoned their claims and fled eastward. By the mid-1860s, however, the economy had rebounded, the war was over, and the Indian threat had been extinguished. New settlements began to take root all along a northwest-ward pointing, vee-shaped front (Figure 5.1). Its vertex lay in the "Big Woods" zone of west central Minnesota (see Figure 1.1 on page 11), roughly one hundred miles to the northwest of the rapidly rising urban settlements of Minneapolis and St. Paul. From that point, one wing of the frontier zone stretched back to the east along the southern edge of the mixed forest zone in east central Minnesota and northern Wisconsin. The other wing reached southward across the open prairies of western Minnesota until it crossed the Iowa border. Once in Iowa, it angled sharply to the west to include two major settlement thrusts, one along the Missouri River valley into the extreme southeastern corner of

155

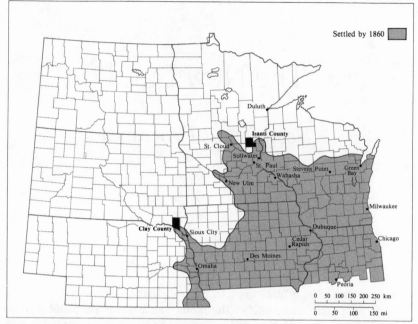

Figure 5.1 Major Receiving Areas for Immigrants from Rättvik and the 1860 Settlement Frontier in the Upper Middle West

Dakota Territory and the other along the Platte River valley into central Nebraska.

These two wings of the advancing frontier carried settlement into two radically different physical environments. The northward pushing wing drew settlers into a heavily wooded environment with a mixed deciduous and coniferous vegetation. This northern forest environment was considerably different from the less heavily wooded, mixed prairie and forest environment that had hosted much of the new settlement in previous decades, particularly in Minnesota and Wisconsin. Clearing farmland along the new northern frontier demanded more work from new settlers. The soils of the fields they cleared were generally less productive than those in older areas. Over time, it proved to be the region's slowest-moving frontier.

The westward pushing wing, on the other hand, drew settlers deeper into the vast, long-grass prairies of western Minnesota, northwestern Iowa, eastern Dakota and Nebraska. Here, for the first time, settlers were moving significant distances from the more familiar and inviting

woodland environment with its ready supply of fuel and building materials. They struggled to find ways to break the heavy prairie turf and
endured the loneliness and isolation imposed by this vast open landscape,
but they also profited from the high agricultural yields offered by its rich
prairie soils. This frontier would prove to be the richer and more rapidly
expansive of the two. Although it is not clear that new settlers recognized
the sharp differences in environment and agricultural potential that distinguished each wing of the frontier, the decision to settle on one or the
other had profound economic repercussions for them in the long run.

The mechanisms that attracted prospective settlers to the two frontiers were largely the same. During this period, all of the Upper Midwest states and territories pursued active immigration policies. Agents
representing various state immigration boards were dispatched regularly to Europe to recruit new settlers. In fact, the competition for preferred immigrant groups was quite keen. A number of states even
published immigrant guides in the languages of certain targeted
groups, extolling the virtues of settlement within their boundaries. Midwestern propaganda typically made much of the ready availability of
free government land. Many claims were also made for the quality of
soils, the remarkable capacity of rich prairies and meadowlands to support livestock for an entire winter, and the ready supply of good woodland. (While emigrant guides admitted that midwestern winters could
be severe [but not too harsh for agriculture and husbandry], few warned
of the stifling heat and humidity of the midwestern summer.) Thousands
of copies were sent overseas, often by direct mailings from lists of potential emigrants provided by friends and relatives already settled in America. Railroad companies were also beginning to pursue potential settlers
during this period, although the heydey of railroad recruitment would
come in the 1880s and 1890s. Thus a flow of "official" information about
settlement opportunities reached potential source areas of settlers in
Europe and America. Evidence shows that prospective settlers often
acquired at least a rudimentary knowledge of the region to which they
were headed and knew something of the possibility of acquiring land and
how to get along as a farmer for the first few years in a given settlement
district long before they actually decided to emigrate.[1]

Potential immigrants most eagerly sought information about land
availability and the means of acquiring land. By the time they arrived in
America, most were cognizant of a number of attractive methods by
which land could be acquired on the 1860s frontier. The best known and
the most popular was homesteading. The Homestead Act, passed by

Congress in 1862, offered land for the inconsequential cost of a filing fee, the commitment to establish a home and to work the land for five years, and a nominal charge for the land once the homestead was "proved up." This offer seemed remarkably generous to Europeans long accustomed to an agrarian economy in which the cost of land was perhaps the greatest obstacle to obtaining land or expanding one's holdings.[2] In the three years after the Homestead Act was passed, Minnesota alone registered 9,500 homestead entries, amounting to 1.25 million acres; and that was a mere drop in the bucket compared to the number of entries that would be made once the frontier fully opened up again after the Civil War.[3]

This invitation to acquire cheap land was the major impetus to the resurgence of the midwestern frontier. In many ways, it was the quintessential homestead frontier. But land companies, speculators, and railroads also had land to sell and played a significant role in the new settlement boom. They were especially adept at reaching a large, receptive audience with their various promotions, many of which were tied to state-sponsored propaganda. To the immigrant of the time, the sense of opportunity must have been dizzying; land for the taking almost everywhere. All one had to do was select a plot, put one's money down, and become a part of the new landed class in America.

Like so many rural districts in northwestern Europe, the populations of Rättvik and other Dalarna parishes were bombarded with information about opportunity in the Upper Midwest during the latter half of the 1860s. Regional newspapers carried articles on the potential of emigrating to these lands, as well as advertisements of promoters and shipping companies. Official immigrant guide books, published by the American states and territories, were passed along from household to household, their contents much discussed and argued over.[4] The role played by the dissemination of this kind of information, which in turn was supplemented and reinforced by the more trusted information sent home by some of the earliest emigrants from the district, was pivotal in directing the flow of emigration to specific destinations in America.

The decision to emigrate was a momentous one, fraught with unknown dangers and pitfalls. No one would dare take it lightly. It was absolutely essential to gather as much information and know as much about what might lie ahead as possible. People shared whatever information came their way. Those who eventually made the decision to go often agreed on common destinations and goals; safety in numbers was always a prudent strategy. As a consequence, the first emigrants from a European community commonly went to some place about which they possessed information. They in turn sent additional information home once they had reached their destination. As new emigrants followed in their footsteps, certain "axes of information and migration" developed between places on either side of the Atlantic. Once the migrant stream began moving along these axes, it became self-reinforcing, ultimately taking on all the attributes of a chain migration.[5]

Emigrants from Rättvik became caught up in two such trans-Atlantic axes of information and migration; one of which was of major importance, the other much less so. The dominant axis directed a stream of emigrants from Rättvik to the northern forest frontier of east central Minnesota. The district in which they settled was a recently organized county, with the strange-sounding name of Isanti.[6] The minor axis led emigrants from the parish to the western prairie frontier of Dakota Territory. The administrative district in which they settled was known as Clay County. Both migrant streams involved not only emigrants from Rättvik, but also emigrants from a number of other Upper Dalarna parishes. Although distinct enough on their own, the migrations from Rättvik were but one part of a broader trans-Atlantic linkage between these two American settlement districts and the entire region of Upper Dalarna. They exemplify, at an intermediate scale, a general phenomenon that occurred at a variety of scales.

This chapter is an examination of the processes by which the emigrants from Rättvik took land and established themselves in these two midwestern locations. A comparison of the settlement experience in these two places is obviously valuable, given the striking environmental differences between them, and constitutes one aim of the chapter. At the same time, however, an understanding of the process of settlement and early economic development itself, which in many ways had certain universal attributes all over the American Midwest, is the most essential ingredient here. It is best seen through a detailed treatment of the larger of the two settlement districts, Isanti County. The Clay County experience appears from time to time when it can add to the discussion of settlement processes or when it can demonstrate significant divergence from what went on in Isanti.

The Settlement Districts: Isanti and Clay Counties

The most important destination for Rättvik emigrants in America, Isanti County, had been carved from a large, roughly triangular piece of territory between the Mississippi and St. Croix rivers, an area ceded to the United States by the Chippewa Indians in 1837.[7] Many features of its early development are shared with a number of neighboring counties that also originated from this land cession. The entire region lies on the edge of the northern forests, a mixed deciduous-coniferous zone. While the soils of the region were quite varied, and often somewhat infertile, it had recognizable potential as farmland. Indeed, early pamphlets aimed at potential Scandinavian immigrants often emphasized the advantages of making farms in forested areas such as Isanti. The existence of rich pineries in many parts of the region, however, was primarily responsible for much of its early penetration and development. Situated between the major river valleys of the Upper Mississippi and the St. Croix, the region was accessible via tributary streams, such as the Rum River, and within easy reach of a rapidly expanding demand for timber at downstream sawmills.

While the Chippewa cession was initially part of the territory of Wisconsin, it became a part of Minnesota Territory at the time of Wisconsin statehood in 1849. During these early years, the district actually lay well beyond the settled ecumene. The population was sparse, principally consisting of Chippewa who remained in the area, a handful of timber cruisers and logging entrepreneurs, and the occasional squatter. In the 1850s, however, the federal land survey was completed throughout much of the region, land offices opened, and the region began to be seriously settled. The earliest settlements were located to the east and southwest of what eventually became Isanti County, along the St. Croix and Upper Mississippi valleys, but the settlement frontier soon penetrated inland to the Isanti area. During the early and middle 1850s, Isanti was part of Ramsey County, an elongated administrative district that ran north-south across the central part of the Chippewa land cession. Within Ramsey County, the Isanti area was referred to as the "Cambridge precinct." John Owens, a St. Paul newspaperman, had schemed to plat a townsite there with the intention of profiting from the sale of lots. Owens promoted the area as a prime region for settlement, emphasizing that it was relatively free of land speculation activity (his own excepted) and therefore well suited to immigrants with serious intentions of establishing themselves in farming or commerce.[8]

A growing population prompted the Minnesota territorial legislature to establish the Cambridge precinct of Ramsey County in 1857 as an independent county, with the name Isanti. The new county approximated a square four townships high and four townships wide, with a substantial bite taken out of the northeast corner where its neighbor, Chisago County, claimed two townships. The earliest settlers in Isanti County were of Old American stock, primarily New Englanders. Some

of them moved into the area to take advantage of lumbering opportunities. Others came to farm or set themselves up in business in anticipation of the district's future growth. Most of them took land under the
preemption laws or through the use of military scrip. The large-scale
influx of immigrant settlers did not begin until the 1860s.

Throughout the 1850s, however, immigrants were settling some distance to the east in the St. Croix valley counties of Chisago and Washington. Swedish immigrants had poured into those counties in astounding numbers, but when the settlement advance stalled at the
end of the decade, it had not yet reached Isanti.[9] The few Swedish families that did settle south of Cambridge in the late 1850s were, in fact,
refugees of sorts from some of these older settlements to the east. They
were Baptists who had settled in a county predominantly settled by
Swedish Lutherans. Having found their neighbors to be somewhat intolerant of their religious beliefs, they decided to move westward and take
up land in the as yet sparsely settled confines of Isanti County. These
settlers were the exception for Isanti as a whole. When settlement of the
county began in earnest in the 1860s, it was dominated by Swedish immigrants who came directly from Sweden.

By that time, the whole region between the St. Croix and Mississippi
rivers had become strongly identified as a Swedish settlement area.
During the 1860s and over subsequent periods of heavy settlement
activity, that reputation continued to attract large numbers of Swedes
to established communities and frontiers. Indeed, the region eventually
became the largest single concentration of Swedish settlement in North
America. Within the region, there was considerable segregation between immigrants who hailed from various provincial areas in Sweden. To the frontier of Isanti County in the 1860s, and again in the 1880s,
came large numbers of emigrants from a number of districts in western
and northern Sweden. Perhaps most important was the flow from
Upper Dalarna, of which the emigrants from Rättvik were a significant
part. In fact, the flow from Dalarna to this county was so strong, it
earned Isanti County the nickname, "America's Dalarna." Dalecarlians
were not the only provincial group to settle there. Large numbers also
arrived from districts in the Bothnian coast provinces of Hälsingland,
Medelpad, and Västernorrland. Smaller contingents came from the forest districts of Småland, Värmland, and Jämtland. The provincial character of this new Swedish county was markedly different from the
earlier settled counties in the St. Croix valley, where Swedish settlement had been dominated by emigrants from the south of Sweden, principally the forested districts of Småland, Blekinge, and Östergötland.

The settlement period in Isanti County lasted through the end of the 1880s. By that time most of the land had been taken by settlers and transformed into hundreds of farms; only some of the most marginal land remained unclaimed. The newly settled county was remarkably Swedish. The vast majority of the population was Swedish or of Swedish extraction. Turn-of-the-century census figures show that Swedes accounted for 89.5 percent of the county's foreign born. The minorities consisted of a small German population that had established itself in two areas, and an English-speaking population consisting chiefly of Old Americans and Irish who had moved from various states along the Great Lakes and Ohio valley. They occupied scattered locations around the county, although a sizeable concentration did exist in the extreme southwest (Figure 5.2).

Since the primary interest here is to examine the settlement experience of those who came from Rättvik and neighboring areas in Upper Dalarna, much of what follows deals with an area that is somewhat smaller than the whole of Isanti County. Most analyses are restricted to a nine-township region that more or less coincides with the settlement from Upper Dalarna. The nine townships include the central valley and big bend of the Rum River in Isanti County and will hereafter be referred to as the "Isanti study area" (Figure 5.3). Excluded are two townships in the southeast (Oxford and North Branch), which received large numbers of German settlers. The Swedish population in Oxford and North Branch came mainly from the south of Sweden and was more strongly associated with settlements of similar provincial background in neighboring Chisago County than it was with the Swedish population of the Rum valley. Also excluded are two townships in the southwest (Stanford and Spencer Brook), where English-speaking settlers dominated and where ties with places in neighboring counties to the south and west were often stronger than they were with the Swedish townships in the central and northern portions of the county.

Clay County in Dakota Territory, the other major destination for Rättvik emigrants, is located on the north side of the Missouri River, not far from the point where Minnesota, Iowa, Nebraska, and the old Dakota Territory met.[10] It was one of many counties carved out of the Yankton Sioux cession of 1858, which gave the United States jurisdiction over most of the territory between the Big Sioux and the Missouri rivers. The county is roughly rectangular, although the side fronting on the Missouri River follows the contours of the river. Early visitors to the area encountered an undulating morainic landscape clothed in lush prairie vegetation. Only the Vermillion River, winding southward

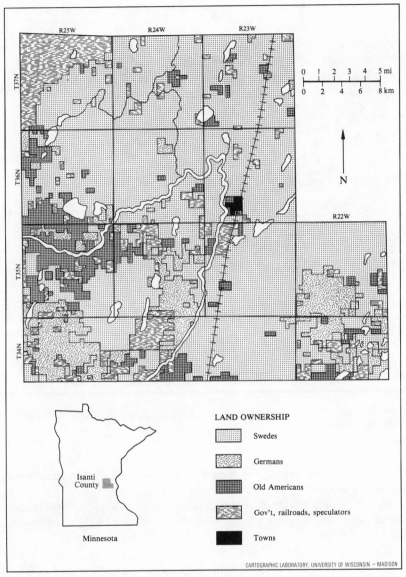

Figure 5.2 Land Ownership in Isanti County, ca. 1914

163

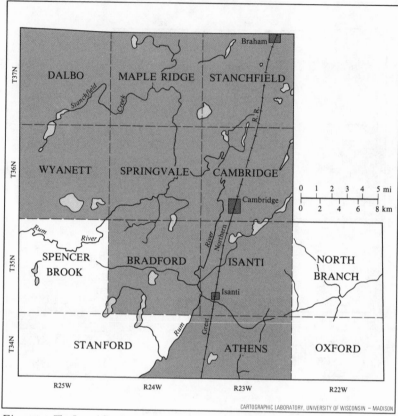

Figure 5.3 The Isanti Study Area

through the county before emptying into the Missouri, broke the monot-
ony of the prairie. Along the river and its many small tributaries were
extensive bottomlands that were subject to periodic flooding and covered with small woody vegetation and brush. The soils of the entire
region were exceptionally rich, with deep layers of humus below the
prairie turf.

Like Isanti County, Clay County saw no serious settlement prior to
the 1860s. From the late 1830s to around 1850, the area was of little interest to whites except as a source of furs. Their only presence consisted of
a small post maintained by the American Fur Company. In the 1850s,
speculators bought the site and platted the town of Vermillion, but the
panic of 1857 quashed their ambitions. Early settlement was sporadic at
best, with approximately seventy-five settlers reported in the area by

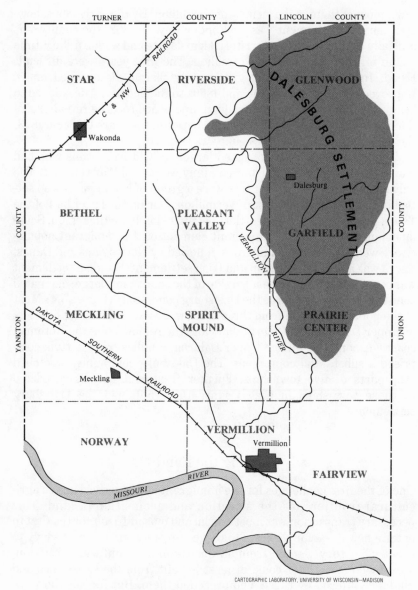

Figure 5.4 The Dalesburg Settlement of Clay County, South Dakota

165

1860, most of them in the vicinity of Vermillion. By the early 1860s, however, serious settlement was well under way. In 1862, the county was officially organized by the territorial legislature and within a short time a land office was opened in Vermillion. The first years were difficult. Flood, Indian uprising, and grasshopper plague discouraged many. Improved conditions from the mid-1860s to the end of the decade led to heavy settlement activity. Vermillion land office records reveal exceptionally high levels of land acquisition between the years 1868 and 1873, the period when much of the county was settled.

The early settlement consisted largely of Old Americans who had moved westward with the frontier. Many were Civil War veterans. The only early non-American settlers were a group of Norwegians who settled in the bottomlands west of Vermillion. During the latter half of the 1860s, however, immigrant settlers began to dominate the region. Scandinavians were the most important element of the immigrant population. Swedes were most numerous, followed by Norwegians and Danes. There was also some German and Irish settlement. Swedish settlement was concentrated on the eastern side of the county, in a large, elongated zone that became known as the Dalesburg community (Figure 5.4). Most of the population came from three areas in Sweden: the forest districts of Upper Dalarna and Östergötland and the region along the Bothnian coast.[11] Among those from Upper Dalarna, families from Rättvik comprised a substantial contingent. The Dalesburg community stretched over parts of five townships. Further treatment here is restricted to those townships in Clay County that contained the Dalesburg settlement.

Taking the Land

One of the first challenges for the immigrant newly arrived on the agricultural frontier was the selection and acquisition of land. This necessary transaction was most crucial and most difficult for the first to enter a new area, for they had to rely completely on their own savvy to exact what they wanted from an uncertain and confusing situation. Those who came later could at least benefit from the experience and guidance offered by those who preceded them. But for all who were serious about establishing themselves permanently on the land, as most immigrants from agrarian districts in Sweden were, much depended on the wisdom of this initial transaction. A bad decision could have serious consequences, and therefore was to be avoided at all costs. For most the decision was ultimately influenced by three factors. One was environmental preference. Every immigrant saw certain combinations of environmental factors, such as soil, vegetation, and proximity to water, as possessing real advantages over others. A second factor was the variety of venues through which land was available to the prospective settler. Third, most settlers were greatly influenced by the desire to settle as close to kin and countrymen as possible.

Quality land was the one thing the immigrant knew best. For these life-long farmers, appraising the potential of a parcel of land was an ingrained skill. They knew all too well that land could vary enormously in quality over relatively short distances. Proper selection depended on knowing something of the lay of the land in the new settlement district. This was especially true of the glaciated terrain that covered much of the Upper Middle West, whether forested or prairie. While one tract might be dry and fertile, a neighboring tract could be a bog or slough. One either needed the trusted advice of someone who knew the region well or one had to see it for oneself. A common spectacle at land offices across the Upper Middle West was the forming up of parties of land-seeking immigrants, who in the company of local guides would set off to tramp over parcels of land that they might return to file claim on later in the day. Not everyone viewed the land in the same way. There is evidence of cross-cultural differences in land appraisal among immigrant groups that settled the Upper Middle West.[12]

One also had to be careful how one acquired land. Land could be acquired from a variety of sources. From the moment of arrival in America, immigrants were assaulted at every place of disembarkation by small armies of "agents" who offered their services in the business of land selection and acquisition. These agents normally represented a variety of interests, including state or territorial immigration boards, railroad companies, land companies, and individual speculators. Many of them enticed immigrants with fraudulent claims, taking advantage of their overriding concern to acquire good land.[13] By the time emigrants actually reached the frontier they often had reason to be wary of business transactions of all kinds. Of course, nearly everyone had heard of free homestead land, but a surprising number of immigrant settlers did not take advantage of this inexpensive opportunity. Frequently, the best homestead lands had been picked over by the time immigrants arrived. What remained might be decidedly inferior to land for sale by railroads, land companies, and individual speculators.[14] Here again, immigrants could be hopelessly lost without the guidance of someone who knew the system and could advise them on how to get the best land at a reasonable cost.

Finally, most immigrants felt a powerful social imperative. No one wanted to be completely separated from his or her own kind in this new and strange place. New arrivals quite naturally wanted to settle in close proximity to others who spoke the same language and shared the same customs. Whenever possible, immigrants strove to settle among friends and relatives or at least folk who came from the same parish or province. In such a situation people could rely on one another in time of need. They could establish a social life that was familiar and comfortable. The social imperative caused immigrants to cluster in cohesive, culturally homogeneous groups whenever the opportunity arose. It influenced the immigrant's choice chiefly by discouraging individual selections that strayed too far afield from the collective security of the group.[15]

The nine townships of the Isanti study area presented prospective settlers with a varied physical environment (Figure 5.5). The government land survey crews and the timber cruisers who first cast an appraising eye on the landscape quickly learned that it could be divided into two distinct physical provinces.[16] The southern two-thirds were a relatively flat outwash plain, part of an extensive zone of droughty, sandy soils running across much of east central Minnesota, known as the Anoka Sand Plain. Originally the plain was covered with "oak openings and barrens," a vegetation cover consisting of scattered stands of scrub oak, aspen, birch, and white pine, interspersed with extensive brush prairies and thickets. In contrast, the northern portions of the region were morainic, with rolling hills and elongated ridges, punctuated here and there by pothole lakes, swamps, and small winding streams. Whereas the soils in the south tended to be sandy and loamy, the morainic soils in the north were predominantly a heavy, clayey material that was often difficult to work. Here the original woodland vegetation was quite dense, with none of the openings frequently found in the south. The dense forest cover was highly varied and predominantly deciduous. The most common species were oak, elm, maple, aspen, birch, basswood, and cherry, with rather large stands of white pine in the river and stream bottoms and along some of the ridges. One of the more prominent ridges sported magnificent stands of maple and came to be known locally as Maple Ridge. Many of the lower-lying, poorly drained areas were given over to dark and impenetrable tamarack and conifer bogs. A particularly large one, located in the extreme northwestern corner of the county, was so extensive and forbidding that it was never cleared or settled.

While the northern and southern portions of the region clearly differed in topography, soils, and original vegetation, the entire area was quite naturally drawn together by the drainage system. Isanti County is

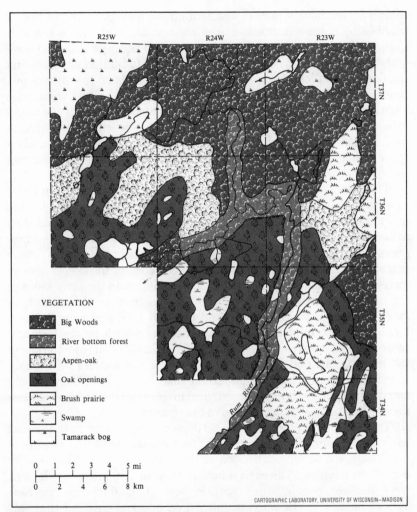

VEGETATION

- Big Woods
- River bottom forest
- Aspen-oak
- Oak openings
- Brush prairie
- Swamp
- Tamarack bog

0 1 2 3 4 5 mi
0 2 4 6 8 km

CARTOGRAPHIC LABORATORY, UNIVERSITY OF WISCONSIN—MADISON

Figure 5.5 Original Vegetation in the Isanti Study Area

drained by the Rum River, which enters the county in the west, loops to the northeast and then turns back on itself to flow southward across the Anoka Sand Plain, heading for its rendezvous with the Mississippi at a point well below the southern limits of the county. This great bend of the Rum valley is the dominant drainage feature of the county, and especially of the nine-township study area.

It was along this winding river that some of the earliest penetrations of the area were made by timber men in the 1840s. One of the first,

Joseph Stanchfield of Maine, was sent up the Rum in search of timber supplies by milling interests at the Falls of St. Anthony on the Mississippi. He reported a bountiful supply around and beyond the big bend of the river and began cutting scrub pine in the fall of that year, sending the first float of logs from the region down to mills on the Mississippi. Before long the pineries all along the Upper Rum and its tributaries were under attack, and soon thereafter portions of the hardwood forest in the northern portions of the county began to be felled. By the time the first settlers entered the region in the 1850s, the Rum was already a scene of major human activity in the winter and spring, when logging activity was most concentrated.[17]

The permanent settlement of this section of the upper Rum River valley occurred in three phases. The first phase lasted from roughly the mid-1850s to the early 1860s. A few initial settlements were established at key locations, which would become central places as settlement progressed further. Many of the settlers in this initial phase were Yankee entrepreneurs who hoped to establish themselves at the center of commercial development. The second phase, lasting from the early 1860s to the mid-1870s, brought a great wave of immigrant settlers who took large quantities of homestead and railroad land and established a number of clustered farming communities on choice locations here and there across the district. The third and final phase lasted from the end of the 1870s to the end of the 1880s. This time the settlers were again largely immigrants, but they played the role of "filling in." They consolidated established settlements and filled in the unsettled spaces between them, often taking marginal land in the process.

The first phase produced two settlements, both on or near the east bank of the Rum, which became the two principal central places in the area (Figure 5.6). One consisted of the village of Cambridge and its immediate environs. The early inhabitants of the Cambridge settlement were Yankees, people with origins in New England and upstate New York. The settlement was established on government land that was alienated through preemption claims that were paid up through the use of military land warrants or half-breed scrip. The village was platted on relatively flat land that was near to both the Rum River and the northern margins of the attractive oak openings landscape that covered much of the southern half of the district. Directly to the north of the site of Cambridge the terrain became more hilly and more heavily wooded with what the survey teams called "second rate timber." Most of the early settlers here were primarily interested in establishing themselves in commercial or investment activities. The village quickly grew to contain

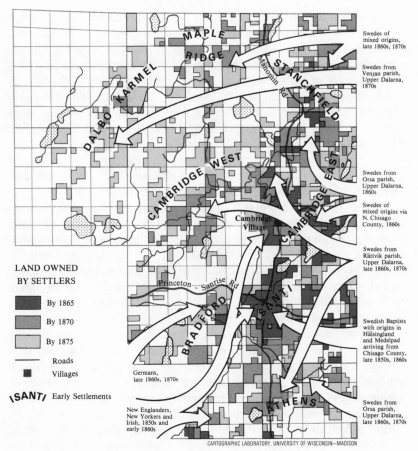

Figure 5.6 Early Settlement in the Isanti Study Area

a hotel, general store and post office, land office, sawmill, and other businesses. A location on the river and on an important trail that ran north-south across the region, proximity to good farming land on either side of the Rum, and access to the pineries along the upper reaches of the river and its tributaries gave this settlement excellent potential as the future trade center of the county.[18]

The other early settlement was located roughly five miles south and came to be known as the "Old Isanti" settlement. Most of the early inhabitants were Swedish Baptists who moved there from Chisago County around 1860. It came to be centered on a small crossroads community that arose around a general store and boarding house, established there in 1863 by a man from New York. For a period of time there was some competition between the Isanti and Cambridge settlements over which would be the county seat. Like the Cambridge settlement, the old Isanti settlement was established on land alienated from the government through the preemption laws. It occupied the northern extremities of a rather large and easily cleared brush prairie that extended southward, parallel to the Rum, for a distance of roughly seven miles and along which many of the early land claims associated with the Isanti settlement were taken. Primarily because of its location at the intersection of an old east-west trail that brought goods and set-tlers into the area and the north-south trail leading up to Cambridge and beyond, the village of Old Isanti grew and prospered for a time, although it was eventually doomed by a railroad bypass.[19]

As the pace of settlement intensified during the second phase, a number of developments intervened to complicate the picture. Two land grants to the Lake Superior and Mississippi Railroad temporarily with-drew a large portion of the unsettled land in Isanti County from the market. The railroad was to run north from St. Paul to Duluth and pass some distance east of the Isanti County line. The first land grant, from the State of Minnesota in 1857, consisted of so-called swamp land that had been allotted to the state by the federal government. The railroad was allowed to select seven sections of swamp land that lay east of the Mississippi for each mile of completed track. In addition, the railroad received a federal grant of ten sections per mile of track in 1864. As a result of the federal grant, all unalienated land in the odd-numbered sections of the Isanti area were given over to the railroad and became unavailable for settlement until the railroad chose to put them on the market, which it eventually did in 1869. In addition to controlling most of the land in the odd-numbered sections, the railroad controlled all of the land classified as swamp land in the even-numbered sections as part of its state land grant.[20]

Thus settlers entering Isanti County during most of the 1860s were barred from taking slightly more than half of the as yet unsettled land. The state still held a considerable amount of swamp land in certain sec-tions of the county. Sections 16 and 36 in every section had also been withdrawn as school lands; they would not play a role until late in the settlement period.[21] Speculators further eroded the government land base available to settlers. By the early 1860s, sizeable tracts in and around Cambridge, as well as scattered locations elsewhere, were in the hands of absentee owners or a few Yankees in Cambridge who chose to speculate in lands. The opening of the remaining federal lands in the area to homesteading in 1863 touched off a substantial boom in land claims, although such claims were restricted to even-numbered sections and, of course, only to the lands within sections that had not been previously alienated. At best, no more than a third of the land base in the Isanti study area was available to homesteading in the 1860s.

Into the mixed situation of the 1860s came the first wave of Swedish immigrants from Upper Dalarna and other parts of northern Sweden. The first to arrive were folk from the Upper Dalarna parish of Orsa, one of the first parishes of that region to send out emigrants. Emigrants from Orsa began arriving in the Isanti area as early as 1862 and continued to arrive in large numbers over much of the decade. The first to arrive passed through the Cambridge settlement and took homestead land about four or five miles to the northeast, on the southern margins of a brush prairie that covered the northeastern quarter of Cambridge township and much of the eastern half of Stanchfield township.[22] The settlement expanded rapidly as more and more people from Orsa arrived during the 1860s, eventually covering most of the even-numbered sections on the brush prairie and surrounding oak openings. The taking of odd-numbered sections of land offered for sale by the railroad between 1869 and 1873 served to consolidate this clustered settlement of Orsa folk. In 1872 and 1873 agents of the Lake Superior and Mississippi Railroad in Sweden organized a particularly large party of immigrants, many of whom were from the parish of Orsa, and successfully settled them on railroad lands.[23]

The second major group from Upper Dalarna came from Rättvik. They arrived somewhat later than the Orsa emigrants; Rättvik was farther down the path of emigration diffusion in Upper Dalarna. The first settlers from Rättvik reached Isanti County in 1864, but the first great influx of people from the parish did not arrive until 1866. The departure of the early emigrants from Rättvik was much influenced by the example and assistance of their neighbors from Orsa. Bäck Hans Ersson was from Gulleråsen village in Ovanheds *fjärding*, the part of Rättvik with the strongest ties to Orsa.

The people from Rättvik, however, did not settle among those from Orsa. The first took homestead land near that of Bäck Hans Ersson on the margins of the oak-openings due north of the old Cambridge settlement. The physical segregation of settlers from Rättvik and Orsa probably occurred because of religious differences. Many folk from Orsa were religious nonconformists who had embraced the Baptist church, while those from Rättvik steadfastly adhered to Lutheranism. The social imperative was undoubtedly at work, too. Many of the new arrivals in 1866 were from Ovanheds *fjärding* and were highly dependent on Bäck

Hans Ersson, or Hans Bäcklin as he called himself in America, for assistance once they reached Isanti. Most of them chose land in the vicinity of Bäcklin's cabin. Within a short time, a Rättvik settlement consisting primarily of folk from Ovanheds developed immediately to the north of the old Cambridge settlement.

Although they all may have been helped by Bäcklin, not all of the new arrivals from Rättvik chose to settle nearby. Many moved to new settlement areas some distance away. One of these was an aspen and oak brush prairie in west central Springvale township. The other was the southernmost extension of the Old Isanti brush prairie in Athens township. There was only a limited amount of brushy oak-openings in the area where Bäcklin settled. Heavily wooded and clayey morainic soils lay just to the north of Bäcklin's settlement. The people from Rättvik, accustomed as they were to the sandy and loamy soils of their home parish, may well have considered the morainic lands to be of inferior quality.[24] The Bäcklin settlement was also bounded to the east and northeast by the Orsa settlement and to the west by the bottomlands of the Rum valley. Therefore the movement some distance to the west and to the south by many new arrivals from Rättvik was probably precipitated in part by a shortage of preferred land in the original settlement.

This three-way subdivision of the Rättvik community is most remarkable in that each of the three settlement areas was eventually populated by people who hailed from a particular *fjärding* back in the old parish. Most of those who took land near Bäcklin's homestead were from Bäcklin's own Ovanheds *fjärding*. Those who went farther west to the aspen-oak brushlands of Springvale township were, nearly without exception, emigrants from Västbygge *fjärding*. Those who took homesteads to the south on the great brush prairie of Athens township were from Gärdsjö *fjärding*. A shortage of desirable land near the old Cambridge settlement may have prompted the search for other promising areas to settle, but cultural and social factors quite clearly influenced who would locate in a particular area.

Thus, by 1870 three distinct concentrations of Rättvik people inhabited the Isanti area, each unambiguously linked to a *fjärding* district in Sweden. Subsequent migrations in the early 1870s continued to reinforce this de facto social division by filling in and solidifying each of the three concentrations with additional settlers from the same districts. Friends, relatives, and neighbors assisted the new arrivals in selecting good land. Most newcomers sought homestead land first and then turned to the railroad land in the odd-numbered sections that was put up for sale beginning in 1869. By the time the railroad land had begun to disappear, toward the mid-1870s, the land held by Rättvik people in these three locations had come to form sizeable contiguous blocks. Although the American land survey, by its very nature, discouraged the formation of nucleated village settlements similar to those the immigrants had known in Sweden, the immigrants still did everything possible to establish themselves as close to one another as the system would allow.

There were others, of course, who settled in the Isanti area during this first phase of settlement. Tracts of land to the east of Cambridge, most of which were covered with dense stands of young aspen forest, were settled by Swedish immigrants from the provinces of Värmland and Jämtland. Unlike the Dalarna people, who for the most part arrived direct from Sweden, many of these settlers came to Isanti County after short stays elsewhere. A good many of them came by way of relatives living in older settlements in northern Chisago County. Their tracts show less cultural homogeneity than the Dalarna settlements. Renewed immigration from agricultural districts along the Bothnian coast, especially from the provinces of Hälsingland and Medelpad, brought new settlers into the Old Isanti settlement. The settlement absorbed the new influx by spreading southward over the brush prairies of Isanti township in the direction of the Rättvik settlement in Athens township. A small group of people from Upper Dalarna, principally from Orsa, also began to settle on the northern margins of the Rättvik settlement in Athens township.

Meanwhile the nuclei of several new settlements began to form. A number of Germans established a small settlement to the west of the Rum on the sandy oak barrens of southern Bradford township. In the north, Swedes of mixed origins, with people from the province of Västergötland perhaps the most numerous provincial group, somewhat hesitantly colonized the lands along the meandering brooks and streams that drained the hilly and heavily wooded expanses of Maple Ridge and western Stanchfield townships. And finally, a third parish group from Upper Dalarna began to establish itself well to the west on a rather high brushland of scrub oak and aspen. This group was from the parish of Venjan, located well into the interior of Upper Dalarna. Venjan experienced a relatively late emigration and most emigrants from this parish did not reach Isanti until the 1870s. The late arrivals found little room to establish themselves in the eastern portions of the County and, consequently, moved out to the north and west of the expanding Rättvik settlement in Springvale township. They began to take homestead land in the early 1870s near the intersection of Dalbo, Wyanett, Maple Ridge, and Springvale townships.

The third phase of settlement, which lasted from the late 1870s to the end of the 1880s, saw the establishment of no new settlements. During this period most of the remaining land with good agricultural potential was taken. Much of this land was offered by the railroads and by speculators since the previous settlement phase had greatly diminished the supply of homestead land, especially in the older settlements east of the Rum. A relatively high proportion of land in the west had fallen into the hands of land speculators early on. Now as land values began to rise and as fresh waves of immigrant settlers entered the region, speculators and land companies began to play a much larger role than they had during the early phases.[25] The Yankee names of these frontier entrepreneurs rapidly began to disappear from the county tax rolls during the 1880s as fresh waves of Swedish and German immigrants were forced to turn to them for land. By the end of the period, most arable land was in immigrant hands, with the exception of a narrow zone along the western edge of the study area, which remained in the hands of a sprinkling of New Englanders and New Yorkers. This "Yankee fringe" marked the edge of serious settlement in the region; much of the land that lay beyond to the north and west gave out to extensive tamarac swamps and was not particularly inviting to agriculturalists.

The Settlement of Athens Township

The foregoing description of settlement in the study area gives an impression of how key factors such as immigrant appraisals of the environment, the variety of sources from which land might be acquired, and the desire to cluster in culturally and socially homogeneous settlements interacted with one another to produce the settlement pattern. The interaction is, however, most effectively demonstrated at the more intimate scale of the township, where the taking of individual land parcels can be traced in detail. What follows is a case study that allows this level of analysis. It details the evolving pattern of settlement in Athens township, the southernmost of the nine townships in the Isanti study area and the location of one of the three concentrations of Rättvik settlement.

Athens is an irregularly shaped civil township (Figure 5.7). It measures only four miles from north to south, two miles short of the normal height of a survey township. The resulting loss of area, however, is com-

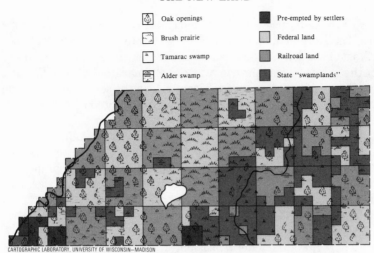

Oak openings

Brush prairie

Tamarac swamp

Alder swamp

Pre-empted by settlers

Federal land

Railroad land

State "swamplands"

CARTOGRAPHIC LABORATORY, UNIVERSITY OF WISCONSIN—MADISON

Figure 5.7 Generalized Original Vegetation and Land Holdings in Athens
Township, ca. 1865

pensated somewhat by the extension of the western boundary to the
Rum River, making the total area equal to about thirty-two square miles.
The entire township lies within the sandy outwash of the Anoka Sand
Plain. The original government surveyors judged the soils everywhere
in the township to be "less than first rate." According to the survey
plats and field notes there were four major types of pre-settlement vegetation. The central portion of the township was covered by a rather large
brush prairie, an area of low thickets, clumps of small aspen and oak
trees, and patches of open grassland. This brush prairie was a southern
extension of the one that became the site of the Old Isanti settlement
some distance to the north. To the west and east of the brush prairie
were extensive areas of oak openings, comprised of groves of burr oak
intermixed with brush prairie. Both of these vegetation zones were
mixed with smaller zones of alder and tamarack swamp.

The settlement of the township began in 1865. At that time the
largest holder of land in the township was the Lake Superior and Mississippi Railroad, which held 8,314 acres, or 39.6 percent of the total.
The land selected by the railroad was restricted to the odd-numbered
sections and was not yet on the market in 1865. The federal government
held the second largest quantity of land, 6,034 acres, or 28.7 percent of
the total. All of the federal land was available for homesteading, but was
found only in the even-numbered sections. The remainder of the land
belonged to the State of Minnesota, which had received a "swampland"

grant from the federal government, and to a handful of Yankee and Irish settlers. The state-held swamplands amounted to 5,200 acres (24.8 percent). Most of this land, which was largely concentrated to the south and east of the central brush prairie, was of only marginal use for farming and was destined to play an insignificant role in the settlement process. The 1,440 acres (6.9 percent) that had been pre-empted by settlers during the 1850s lay along the southern margin of the township.[26]

During most of the 1860s, only federal land was available to attract settlers. But even when the railroad land came on the market, its relatively high price of $2.50 per acre made it less attractive than federal land, which could be homesteaded at little cost. Immigrant settlers also preferred the brush prairie environment, primarily because it was easy to clear for planting. Therefore, the federal lands that lay on the central brush prairie of Athens township were the first to go. As early as 1867, nearly 70 percent of the federal brush prairie acreage was gone. Homesteading on the oak openings, especially on the margins of the brush prairie, proceeded rapidly as well, but somewhat later. When the railroad land began to be sold in the early 1870s, the pattern was similar. Brush prairie lands were taken first, followed by the oak openings (Figure 5.8).

In the case of the railroad lands, however, a new element was introduced—the absentee owner or speculator. Up to 1875, railroad land was sold primarily to settlers, but between 1875 and 1880 more than half of the railroad land sold went to absentee owners. In the following years, absentee owners purchased much of the state swampland as well. Thus, most settlers who took land during the third phase of settlement in the 1880s could not avail themselves of federal or railroad land, but were forced instead to turn to the land speculator. This feature of railroad land sales is often overlooked by those who argue that railroad lands played a major role in attracting new settlers.[27] In fact, the railroad sold nearly as much land to speculators as it did to bona fide settlers, much of it desirable land. To summarize, settlers first acquired land according to what was available when they arrived: federal homestead land in the 1860s, federal homestead and railroad land in the early 1870s, and mostly sale by speculators, land companies, or resident owners thereafter (Figure 5.9).

It is also true that much of the railroad land sold to settlers went to individuals who had already taken federal land, rather than to new arrivals. Between 1869 and 1874, the period during which the railroad is purported to have been most successful in luring new settlers to the district with its lands, there were twenty-one transactions between the

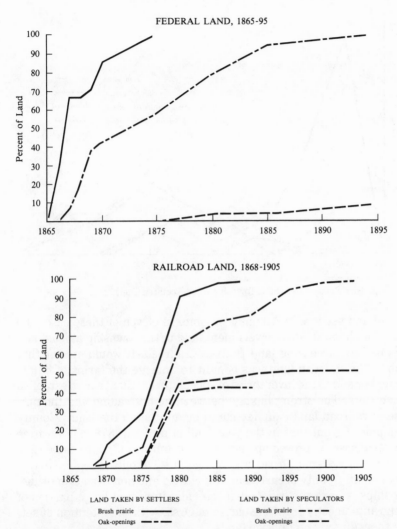

Figure 5.8 The Taking of Federal and Railroad Land by Settlers and Speculators in Athens Township, by Vegetation Type

179

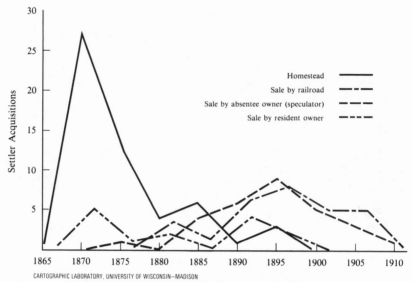

CARTOGRAPHIC LABORATORY, UNIVERSITY OF WISCONSIN–MADISON

Figure 5.9 How Settlers in Athens Township First Acquired Their Land

railroad and settlers in Athens township. In eleven of these cases the
settler had homesteaded government land in the township at least two
years before purchasing land from the railroad. It would appear that
much of the railroad land was bought to enlarge the farms of homesteaders or add to the inventories of speculators rather than to establish
new settlers. The strong linkage between homesteading and the purchase of railroad land is underscored by an item in the Isanti County
Press pointing out that in the year ending in April 1878, eighty-three
homesteads were "proved up" across the county[28] and at the same time
133 forty-acre lots of railroad land were sold.[29] The only exception to this
rule in Isanti County occurred in Stanchfield and northern Cambridge
townships, where the railroad specifically imported large parties of
immigrants, mostly from the parish of Orsa, with the intention of settling them directly on railroad lands.

The settlement of Athens township also demonstrates the process by
which social clustering occurred. This may be seen through a sequence
of maps showing land acquisition by people of specific origins in Athens
township (Figure 5.10). In 1866 just a few settlers held land. Several families from Rättvik homesteaded on the brush prairie and a few Yankee
families held military scrip or pre-emption lands in the southwestern
part of the township. Up to 1870 nearly all the land taken was government land. During this period a checkerboard pattern emerged, with

the settlers from Rättvik clustering on the brush prairie and its margins to the degree that the even-numbered distribution of government land sections allowed. Section eight became the core of the Rättvik settlement. A concentration of settlers from the parish of Orsa appeared in sections two and ten while the Yankees remained in the southwest. This pattern intensified by 1880, as settlers began to acquire the railroad lands, either directly or through speculators. By 1895, the settlement of the township was largely completed. Late arrivals from Orsa and Rättvik further filled in the clustered pattern. Areas marginal to these clusters went to people from other parts of Sweden, primarily the Ljungan valley in Medelpad and the province of Skåne. Between 1895 and 1910, there is a smattering of very late settlement on the swamp lands by people from Medelpad, which has the effect of creating a cluster from this province in the southeast.

The early predominance of homesteading on even-numbered sections is essential to the clustering process so evident here. When the first Swedish families arrived in Athens, they were forced to concentrate their homesteads in the same government section or on diagonally adjoining government sections. This provided simultaneously a core to the community and a certain degree of spacing. One of the first homestead sections usually became the core of the regional group's settlement. It often had the highest density of farmsteads and often was chosen as the site of the church that would serve the community. Section eight in Athens township is a good example of a core section. At one time it held as many as eight Rättvik farmsteads, perhaps the maximum degree of clustering possible given the U.S. land survey system and the standard homestead of 80 acres that was prevalent in this area at the time. It also contained a Lutheran church and, later, a Free Mission church, both founded by Rättvik settlers. But while a fledging community might develop a core on a government section, it was also forced to spread itself over a considerable area because only diagonally neighboring sections were available during the early years. This extended and demarcated the potential boundaries of the community at an early stage, and made the filling-in process of later years somewhat easier.

Time was also important. The clustering process was possible only if there was sufficient time to bring over friends, relatives, and neighbors and get them settled nearby before competitors encroached on the space of the community. In the Isanti area, the pace of settlement seems to have been slow enough to allow this time-consuming process to work. It took more than two decades for settlement to run its course in Athens township, time enough for parishes like Rättvik to establish and

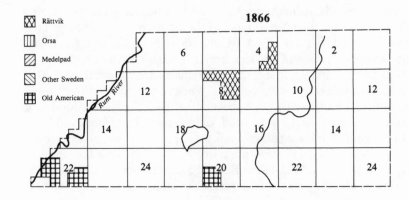

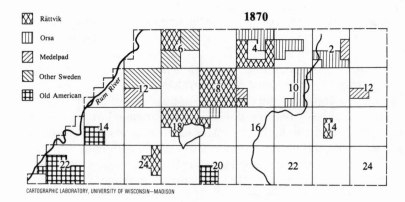

CARTOGRAPHIC LABORATORY, UNIVERSITY OF WISCONSIN–MADISON

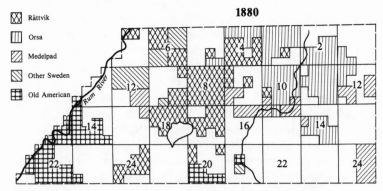

Figure 5.10 Land Ownership in Athens Township, by Culture Group

Figure 5.10 (continued)

1895

- ☒ Rättvik
- ☐ Orsa
- ☒ Medelpad
- ☒ Other Sweden
- ⊞ Old American

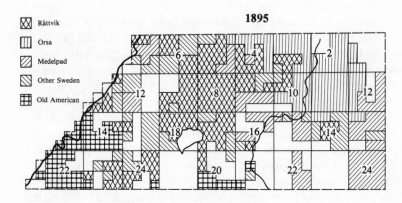

1910

- ☒ Rättvik
- ☐ Orsa
- ☒ Medelpad
- ☒ Other Sweden
- ⊞ Old American

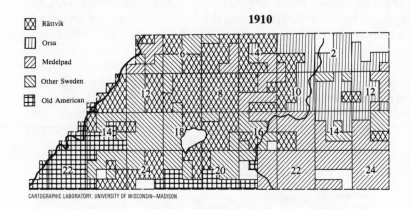

CARTOGRAPHIC LABORATORY, UNIVERSITY OF WISCONSIN—MADISON

maintain the chain migrations necessary to bring several waves of immigrants across the Atlantic. While the homestead land went quickly, ample supplies of railroad land and speculator land in the interstitial spaces became available later on, when those who would "fill in" began to arrive. Often friends and relatives in the new settlements bought adjoining lands to secure them for new arrivals. The situation was ideally suited to the slow process of community formation. Had the situation been different, had the land-taking process moved more swiftly, the degree of clustering found in Athens township as well as across much of the Isanti area would not have been possible.[30]

Under these conditions, the kinship networks that appear to have governed the first two waves of emigration from Rättvik were able to reestablish themselves on the American side. The Rättvik settlement in Athens township was primarily a community of emigrants from Gärdsjö *fjärding*, and from the village of Övre Gärdsjö in particular. Between 1866 and 1883, members of seventeen Övre Gärdsjö households left for America. All of them eventually turned up in Athens township. With few exceptions, these emigrant households were linked to one another in Övre Gärdsjö by kinship and marriage (Figure 5.11). The locations of emigrant households within the old village suggest that those not tied to other emigrant households by blood were at least neighbors.

The emigrant households of this village appear to have been clustered in five different locations. While it is remarkable that the emigrant members of these households all succeeded in moving to Athens township over a period that lasted nearly two decades, it is even more aston-

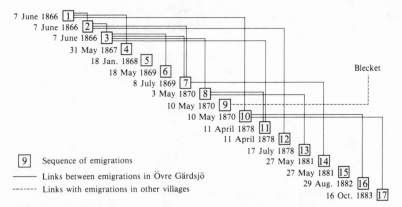

Figure 5.11 Kinship Links and the Sequence of Emigrations from Övre Gärdsjö Village, 1866–83

ishing, given the time frame, that they also succeeded in reestablishing a semblance of the old distance or nearest-neighbor relationships of residence in their new settlement. If one compares the loose groupings of neighboring emigrant households in Övre Gärdsjö with their corresponding distribution in Athens township (Figures 5.12 and 5.13), the similarities leap into view. One finds the same clusters of households in Athens township as in Övre Gärdsjö village. This accomplishment attests to the pervasive influence of kinship networks on the migration and resettlement process and to the opportunity afforded to this influence by the pace of settlement.

A similar process was at work in the other townships of Isanti County, as well as in the Dalesburg settlement out in Dakota Territory, although on the Dakota prairie the parameters were different. First, the environment was less differentiated. The quest was not to secure a piece of brush prairie, but to secure a location near a source of water. Accordingly, the spread of settlement in the Dalesburg area was governed to a high degree by the drainage pattern. Most settlers attempted to locate near a creek bed. Second, Dalesburg had no railroad land; the sequence of sources from which land might be obtained was shortened considerably and land speculation took a small role. The Dakota frontier was more of a true homestead frontier than was Isanti. And third, clustering occurred at a much broader level. The Dakota frontier moved far more rapidly than was the case in Isanti; townships filled up in the space of half a dozen years rather than a couple of decades. The absence of railroad land allowed settlement to occur in a more continuous pattern, which made clustering more difficult.

Groups did cluster in Dalesburg, but at the provincial level rather than at the level of parishes, administrative districts within parishes, or village kinship networks. Families with common provincial backgrounds tended to congregate along certain creek beds (Figure 5.14). Three major provincial groupings are apparent. People from Upper Dalarna colonized the southern portions of the settlement, taking land along Erickson Creek, Garfield Creek, and the lower and central reaches of Baptist Creek. Immigrants from the Bothnian coast concentrated heavily along the small unnamed creek that flows into the Vermillion River between low-lying areas known locally as "Cabbage Flats" and "Vermillion Bottom," while others scattered northward along the Vermillion and some of its upriver tributaries. A third group, from the province of Östergötland, occupied the area at the headwaters of Baptist Creek and for some distance to the west. The placement of these groups had as much to do with the timing of their arrival as it did with

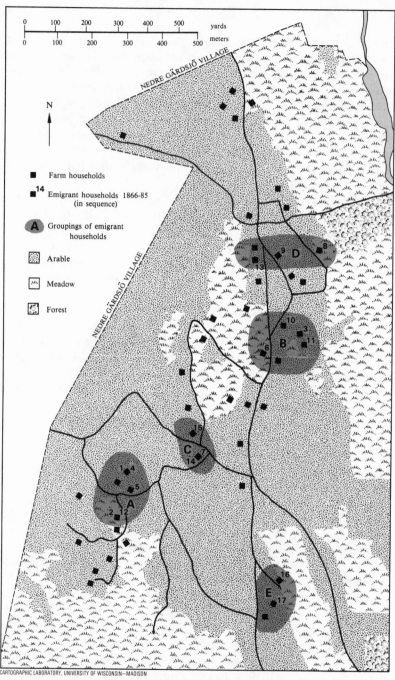

Figure 5.12 Emigrant Households in Övre Gärdsjö Village, 1866-83

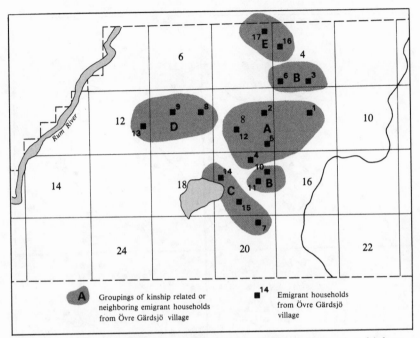

Figure 5.13 Immigrant Households from Övre Gärdsjö Village in Midsection of Athens Township, ca. 1885

cultural affinity, so rapidly did the process of land acquisition proceed.[31]

Although the Dalesburg pattern may be a reflection of broad regional or provincial loyalties among the immigrant population as well as differences in the timing and pattern of emigration from these regions, certain evidence hints at the more intimate, personal associations and loyalties to place that were so important in the Isanti settlements. For instance, the Upper Dalarna folk who settled along the lower reaches of Garfield Creek were all from the same place, the parish of Gagnef. Those who settled along Erickson Creek were largely from the parish of Svärdsjö, while residents of the neighborhood that emerged along Baptist Creek hailed largely from Rättvik. To give examples of another kind of personal association, the Bothnian coast people who located west of Baptist Creek came from widely scattered locations in Sweden, but had proceeded to Clay County by way of relatives living in Allamakee County, Iowa. Similarly, many of the Östergötland people had spent time together near Andover in Henry County, Illinois before moving to Clay County. None of these associations were as extensive, however, as those found among clusters of immigrants in Isanti County.

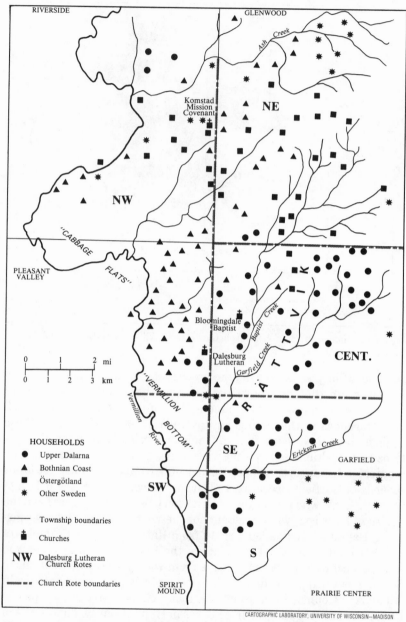

Figure 5.14 Swedish Settlement and Administrative Organization of the Dalesburg Settlement, ca. 1885

188

Time would prove the Swedish population of the Dalesburg settlement to be less particularistic and socially divided than their countrymen on the sand plains of east central Minnesota.

Farm Making on the Frontier

Any immigrant who wished to establish himself as a farmer on the frontier was embarking on a long and arduous task—a task at which many would ultimately fail. Acquiring land was only the first step. It had to be followed, often within an extremely limited amount of time, by a number of essential and difficult achievements: construction of adequate shelter, acquisition of necessary implements and minimal numbers of livestock, and breaking enough land to plant a first crop. A first crop, in turn, generated a need for fencing because frontier fields had to be protected from the ravages of both wild animals and livestock. Even then, the new farm would at best be no more than a crude establishment. Each year thereafter, perhaps for the lifetime of the immigrant farmer, would see a need for new efforts to expand production and make improvements on the physical capital of the farm.

All of this required money, time, labor, determination, and a certain amount of luck. While the initial cost of land could be small, especially if the land were homesteaded, the costs of housing, livestock, and a first crop could be considerable. Agricultural historian Merrill E. Jarchow cites an estimate by the Minnesota Commissioner of Statistics that puts the cost of opening a farm around 1860 at $795, including the costs of acquiring implements, provisions, cows, a team, and a wagon. Many undoubtedly made do with less, but no one could begin without some money or credit.[32] Timing could also be crucial. The best time to break new land was early in the summer. Many emigrants, however, left their homeland in late spring or early summer and often failed to reach the settlement frontier before late summer or early fall. This was the case with most emigrants from Rättvik, who were unable to travel until conditions permitted, usually in late May or early June. Most did not reach the Isanti area until sometime in August. By then it was far too late to break land and plant a crop. The best one could do was to acquire land and prepare shelter for the coming winter, and hope to get along until a first crop could be taken in the following year.

Getting through that first winter was often one of the most difficult hurdles settlers faced. Even by Swedish standards, winter conditions in

Plate 5.1 Logging party. Seasonal work in the pineries of east central Minnesota provided extra income for Isanti's immigrant settlers during the early years. Immigrants from forested districts, such as Dalarna, were already accustomed to winter labor in the forests. (Courtesy of Isanti County Historical Society, date unknown)

the Upper Midwest could be severe, whether on the open prairie or in the forests. Without the generosity and help of neighbors, the long winter months might have ended disastrously for many a new arrival. Accounts of numbing cold and the ferocity of winter storms were common fare in many of the early "America letters" sent to friends and relatives in the old parish. So, too, were accounts of winter conditions in the logging camps, where the menfolk frequently spent most of their winters in an effort to earn needed cash.[33] At times even seasonal work of this kind was not enough to generate necessary capital or reduce indebtedness. One Rättvik man who settled north of Cambridge in Isanti County, writing home to his brother in Ovanheds *fjärding* in the spring of 1874, complained bitterly of the small amount of money that could be realized from a winter in the logging camps once expenses for equipment, meals, and lodging had been deducted from the winter's earnings by the camp proprietors. By his reckoning, expenses could run to over four hundred dollars, leaving precious little to take home.[34]

Even though America letters often told of the hardship and the discouraging conditions associated with the winter season, they were generally filled with a cautious optimism about the prospects of good crops

Plate 5.2 Immigrant log cabin. The first crude shelter was made from logs, often using time-honored Dalecarlian woodworking skills. Posing in the foreground are the proud owners, the Johan Gustaf Krafve family, who homesteaded in section 19 of Isanti's Maple Ridge township. Three generations are present. (Courtesy of Isanti County Historical Society, 1890s)

in the coming summer and with a wondrous respect for the strange new environment. Letters were filled with serious appraisals of the land; appraisals of its potential fertility, comparisons with the land back home, assessments of the difficulties of clearing and breaking it, predictions of how much could be prepared for planting the first year. There were even cautious estimates of what a good harvest might bring, supported with reverential phrases—"God willing" or its equivalent—lest the estimator appear to forget that his prospects depended as much on divine intervention as hard work and planning. Forces that were far beyond the control of the immigrant farmer often did intervene with a vengeance. In 1866, the first crops put in by new Swedish homesteaders in Clay County were all but destroyed by grasshopper infestation. Reports of crop and livestock disease were perennial features of early editions of frontier newspapers, such as the Isanti County Press.[35] In addition to grasshopper plagues and crop or livestock disease, hail, early or late frosts, and tornadoes also took their toll from time to time.

But by and large progress was made each year, and increasingly letters home began to tell, not without pride, of the immigrant's success. One of the most frequently used measures of success, especially suited to the minds of Dalarna peasants, was an elaborate rundown of the numbers and kinds of livestock one owned. Everyone at home would be interested in the number of cows, sheep, goats, or chickens the immigrant possessed. There were also discussions of the merits of oxen, which were fairly common beasts of burden in America, as opposed to the traditional horse in Dalarna. Immigrants often demonstrated their success by describing some treasured object unavailable in Dalarna that they had acquired in America with a portion of the year's surplus proceeds. Immigrants were understandably eager to report how well they were doing to those who remained behind. At the same time, their letters drew attention to the considerable differences in economic conditions that existed between the American frontier and the old homeland.

Most immigrants set out with the intention of making good use of the many agricultural skills and techniques that had served them well in the fields and forests of Rättvik. Once in America, however, the need to adapt to new and unfamiliar conditions quickly dispossessed them of such ideals. Their relationship to the land changed markedly. The land was far more abundant, but in many ways more difficult to work than what they had known before. Labor was in short supply and prohibitively expensive. They were forced to rely on the labor that could be provided by the nuclear family, rather than on the abundant labor resources of extended families and entire kinship networks. Perhaps most important, the influence of markets was far greater in America, even during the relatively isolated and difficult early years on the frontier. Markets, rather than tradition, dictated the crops that were best grown on the land, and the crops were not those to which the peasants were accustomed. Simply put, American conditions and American agricultural practices were different and it was best to adapt as quickly as possible if one hoped to make good.

Nonetheless, to some degree the past could never be completely abandoned. Some traditional practices could be adapted to American conditions; some would actually prove to be superior. Some immigrants clung to traditions simply because they were too stubborn to give them up. The transition was never wholly completed. Even though everyone in America seemed to be producing the same things and headed in the same direction, subtle differences persisted between immigrants of different national backgrounds and sometimes even within national groups. As a consequence, the question of the immigrant's adaptation to American economic conditions can never be answered simply.[36] What follows is an examination of the degree to which the Rättvik immigrants adapted or resisted adaptation to American conditions during the *settlement period*. This was the key period, a time when relatively cheap land remained available, when markets were still relatively poor, when labor was scarce, and when immigrants of the first generation still exercised complete control over the household economies of the Rättvik settlements. At this juncture the immigrant had to meld his particular background experience to the conditions he faced in America. Adaptations made in the face of these conditions would color the future of his family and his community for generations to come.

Those from Rättvik who settled in Isanti County during the initial phase of heavy immigrant settlement (1862–1873) took land in a frontier district that was still sparsely settled and relatively isolated from the outside world. The Lake Superior and Mississippi Railroad did not complete its line between St. Paul and Duluth until August 1870, and that line ran some distance to the east of Isanti, through the western portions of Chisago County. Isanti County did not receive a rail line of its own until nearly the end of the century, much to the chagrin of Cambridge merchants, who were situated a full sixteen miles from a railhead for nearly the first four decades of the town's existence. Repeated efforts to attract a rail line to the county were made by local boosters from as early as 1875, all to little avail as project after project fell through.

Before the Lake Superior and Mississippi Railroad completed its line through western Chisago County, all contact with the outside world was made on foot via trails that led eastward from the Isanti area to the river town of Taylors Falls on the St. Croix, or southward to the town of Anoka on the Mississippi. Either trip was usually a three-day journey. Only small amounts of material could be moved over such distances on a man's or animal's back. Even after the rail line was completed, hauling harvested crops and goods over primitive roads and trails to and from the new rail towns of Harris and North Branch in Chisago County was still a time-consuming and difficult task. The constant team-drawn traffic to and from these towns provoked frequent commentary in the local newspaper. A November 1878 edition, for example, pointed up the inefficiency of the long-distance haulage, commenting on the economic cost of being without railroad access. The same message was repeated the following spring and became a standard motif after that.[37]

During the early settlement phase immigrant farmers were very much on their own and relatively free of market pressures, although the need to find a marketable cash crop must have developed quickly. Evidence shows that agricultural practices from the old world were of some importance during those years. Letters home tell of clearing forest vegetation using techniques similar to those used in Rättvik during the extensive land reclamations of the mid-1850s. Other time-honored techniques were probably important in establishing fields and fences or in sowing the first crops, although no direct evidence survives. One account of the early years, written by a man from the Upper Dalarna parish of Venjan, notes that grain was threshed in the customary manner of his home parish for at least the first five years, after which a primitive threshing machine came into use.[38] At a time when subsistence was probably the most important concern, people naturally did what was most familiar to them.

There is some evidence that barley, the principal grain crop in Rättvik, may have been one of the several grains and root crops planted during the first years. Agricultural statistics for the year 1868 list five acres of barley planted in Isanti County, a fairly substantial amount given the relatively small amount of improved land at the time. While there is no way of knowing for sure, it is quite possible that immigrants from Rättvik or other parts of Upper Dalarna were responsible for planting this early barley crop. Barley was a rare and relatively unimportant frontier crop for Americans. Also, the Isanti crop of 1868 was planted at precisely the time when large numbers of Dalecarlian immigrants were planting their first crops. Barley was not destined, however, to become a major grain crop. It continued to be grown after 1868, but was of only minor importance. Quite possibly it was planted by immigrants who brought small amounts of seed with them when they emigrated, but soon turned to American grains for which there was a market.[39]

Whatever the earliest crop mix may have been, farmers in Isanti County soon settled down to the production of three principal crops. According to the returns of the 1870 federal agricultural census (1869 harvest) the most important crop for all settlers was spring wheat, the great frontier crop of the American West. Wheat accounted for 41.2 percent of the acreage devoted to grain in that year. The second largest crop was oats (30.5 percent) and the third was corn (22.4 percent). None of these three had been of any importance in pre-migration Rättvik, although oats were grown in some of the other Upper Dalarna parishes. All three remained important throughout the settlement era. The mix of grain crops was, in fact, similar to that of surrounding counties that were at about the same stage of development, suggesting that the transition to an American practice was well under way as early as 1870. A fourth crop of some significance in Isanti was rye (6.5 percent), which was grown on small forest plots in Rättvik, but it seems to have been grown primarily by German settlers in Isanti rather than Swedes. Garden vegetables, principally potatoes, accounted for the balance of the harvest in 1869.

Farming was only a part of the early local economy. As one commentator pointed out in 1878, the county really depended on two crops: wheat and logs.[40] Every fall, throughout the 1870s and well into the 1880s, nearly all able-bodied men, older boys, and even girls made preparations to engage in the lumber trade. Participation took a variety of forms. One could go to the lumber camps in November or December to labor until the spring thaw. One could participate in the spring drives on the Rum River, or could provide hay, grain, and teams to the immense seasonal market provided by the camps. Throughout much of the settlement period, the lumber camps were perhaps the farmer's best market for both his produce and his labor. Indeed, the lure of the lumber market may have done much to retard the growth of agriculture in the county. An editorial that appeared in the Isanti County Press on the occasion of the collapse of yet another railroad project made just this point, when it suggested that the loss of the railroad was a blessing in disguise because it would "prostrate the lumbering interests." This was all to the good, concluded the editorial, because in the past too many people had depended on lumbering for a living and had not cultivated or improved their farms sufficiently. People would have to reconcile themselves to the fact that the land is good and profitable and begin serious farming.[41]

In addition, a wide variety of other economic activities occupied settlers from time to time. The forest was always a source of wealth. Trees cut from the farmer's land could be sold to the railroad, which was always in the market for ties. Or firewood could be hauled to town. Early merchants in Cambridge advertised that they would exchange goods and implements for firewood or produce. The price of a subscription to the local newspaper was a quantity of firewood. In season, there was always a ready market for locally produced maple syrup, or for freshly picked wild blueberries, raspberries, and cranberries. Many early settlers found it worthwhile to dig ginseng roots at a rate of three to four dollars a day.[42] Some found occasional markets for hay and dairy products, while others invested in small numbers of beef cattle, swine, or sheep. In short, the early economy of the Isanti area was a complex mixture of subsistence production, seasonal work off the farm, experimentation with a number of cash crops or marketable livestock, and sundry occasional activities.

The developing farm economy of the settlement era comes most clearly into focus with the aid of the 1880 federal agricultural census manuscripts.[43] By the time data for this census were collected (of the 1879 harvest), most of the first wave of immigrants had been settled on the land for eight to twelve years, long enough to have established themselves. The first of the second wave, who did not begin to arrive until 1878 and 1879, had not been there long enough to have much impact on the returns. As a result, the 1880 census provides a picture of what the first wave had achieved after approximately one decade on the land and is a good measure of conditions during the settlement era.

A substantial amount of progress had been made in the years leading up to 1880. The new settlers of the 1860s and early 1870s had managed to meet the challenges of the frontier and make the necessary adaptations to their new milieu. Nearly five hundred farms dotted the survey grid of the nine study-area townships in 1880. Yet the situation was not far removed from that of a frontier. According to the census, settlers of all backgrounds had managed to clear and cultivate an average of only twenty acres each after a decade or more on the land. Swedish settlers, especially those from Upper Dalarna, had cleared considerably less than the average. Thus, only small portions of the land held by settlers had been improved in any way. Most remained under brush or forest vegetation. In addition, plenty of land still remained unclaimed in 1880. Another full decade of settlement would take place before most of the remaining land would be settled and converted to farms. In many areas the landscape would continue to have a semi-wild appearance until as late as the 1890s.

Of the 478 farms extant in the Isanti study area in 1880, roughly four-fifths were owned by Swedish immigrants. The remainder belonged mainly to Old Americans, with a few owned by German immigrants. Among the Swedes, the largest provincial group was from Upper Dalarna (43.5 percent). The second largest group came from the Bothnian coast provinces of Hälsingland and Medelpad (19.6 percent). A number of other provincial origins were included in the balance, the most important of which was Småland (5.0 percent). Nearly all of the landowners from Upper Dalarna hailed from just three parishes: Orsa, Rättvik, and Venjan. Sixty-three farms were owned by people from the parish of Rättvik. Orsa accounted for 79 and another 15 were owned by folk from Venjan. While these numbers would change with renewed Swedish immigration throughout the decade, the pattern of provincial

Table 5.1 Farm Size, Acreage Tilled, and Acreage in Grain Crops by Culture Group, Isanti Study Area, 1880 (1879 harvest)

| Culture groups | No. of farms | Average size (acres) | Average no. of acres tilled | Acreage in grain crops as percentage of total acres tilled | | | |
				Wheat	Oats	Corn	Rye
Study area overall	478	134.8	20.0	46.4%	11.3%	11.2%	3.5%
Old American	81	158.0	24.2	35.1	9.4	14.6	6.0
German	15	148.9	28.5	49.6	9.8	18.6	9.9
Swedish	382	128.4	20.1	49.3	12.5	9.2	1.4
Bothnian provinces[a]	75	112.1	19.7	38.4	13.8	9.3	1.4
Småland	19	146.6	18.0	64.6	9.2	12.5	6.2
Upper Dalarna	166	116.1	17.2	50.5	12.9	8.7	0.9
Orsa	79	110.3	16.2	63.2	13.8	6.1	0.8
Rättvik	63	147.9	17.9	47.8	11.5	10.3	1.0
Venjan	15	115.8	16.0	45.4	10.9	8.4	1.2

SOURCE: Manuscripts of the 1880 U.S. Agricultural Census.
[a] Hälsingland and Medelpad

settlement was by and large set by 1880 and each group was present in sufficient numbers for one to be able to make at least some generalizations about differences in farming practice between cultural groups (Table 5.1).

At the most general level, there were considerable differences between national groups. Both the Old Americans and the Germans had significantly larger farms and more land cleared for cultivation than the Swedes. In part this is due to timing. The Old Americans, as a rule, had arrived earlier than the Swedes. It is also due to experience and the way land was acquired. Most Americans were well prepared for the task of farm making, often coming to Isanti from older agricultural frontiers elsewhere in the Middle West. Many arrived before land was available for homesteading and acquired their land under the pre-emption laws, which allowed claims of 160 acres. The Swedes, on the other hand, arrived late with little capital or experience. Most took up homestead land, which was limited to claims of 80 acres, and supplemented the homestead claim with a later purchase of 40 acres of railroad land. As a consequence, many Swedish farms were only 120 acres. The German settlers, unlike the Swedes, were seldom direct immigrants from Germany. Most had been in America for a considerable amount of time and had farmed elsewhere. In many ways, they could outstrip the Americans. As a group, they succeeded in placing nearly a third more of their land under cultivation by 1880 than either the Swedes or the Americans.

All three groups relied heavily on the dominant crop—wheat—but the degree of reliance varied sharply between the Old Americans and the two immigrant groups. While both Germans and Swedes devoted roughly half of their arable to wheat, the Americans devoted only slightly more than a third. The preference of immigrant farmers for larger wheat acreages has often been observed.[44] Wheat suited the needs of poor frontier farmers. Although more susceptible to failure than other grains, it was easy to grow and potentially quite profitable. For the new farmer, who had only limited capital and labor resources at his disposal and who possessed essentially free land, gambling on wheat was often the best if not the only option. If nothing else, he knew there would always be a market for wheat.

The strong inclination to grow wheat in 1880 among German and Swedish farmers is especially interesting because wheat production was becoming an increasingly risky venture at that time in much of eastern and southeastern Minnesota. Throughout these older settlement areas, land values and indebtedness were rising steadily, driving up costs. At the same time, wheat yields had begun to decline after years of continuous planting. Newly opened lands in the west began to out-produce the older lands in the east. In addition, 1878 was a disastrous year for counties throughout eastern and southern Minnesota. Poor weather conditions and a crop disease known as stem rust all but destroyed the wheat crop. The catastrophe was an added incentive to look for ways of diversifying production. Within a short time, farmers began to move away from wheat and the center of wheat production moved decidedly westward in the early 1880s to the new prairie frontier regions of western Minnesota and the Dakotas.[45]

Isanti County shared in this general development. Land prices in the county began to rise precipitously in the middle and late 1870s. In just one six-month period over the fall and winter of 1877–78, the local press reported a 15 to 25 percent rise in real estate prices. Grasshoppers and stem rust and "smut" devastated the 1878 wheat crop much as they had elsewhere in the state, carrying away as much as one-half the predicted harvest.[46] Meanwhile, reports of sensational wheat yields in the new prairie counties farther west put a damper on local spirits while also generating an intense "prairie fever" among some local residents. Large numbers of locals became involved in breaking land and assisting with the harvest in some of the prairie counties, returning with news of riches to be had on the new wheat lands.

The fever induced by these reports was widespread enough to instigate a whole series of articles and testimonials in the local press aimed at discrediting the allure of the prairie lands and redirecting interest toward possibilities overlooked or forgotten at home. One article cited a railroad agent who claimed that Isanti soils were as good as or better than soils in western counties and only half the price, adding the exhortation, "Now just ponder that you men who are crazy after the prairies."[47] Another article cited statements by no less an authority than the former State Commissioner of Statistics, who warned of the dangers of raising wheat on the prairies, the foremost of which was relying on a single crop as opposed to diversified farming combining grain and stock. The late commissioner was quoted as having said of the people of Minnesota's St. Croix, Rum, and Snake river valleys:

I found there a people more contented, more prosperous, than any similar communities on the prairies. The latter exhibit greater extremes of wealth and poverty; but in my judgement, the best average is to be found in the timber. There fuel is cheap and at the doors of farmers. Water, old and pure, is found in lakes and streams everywhere; their cattle are excellent, their butter is of finest quality and readily marketed; their winter months are not months of idleness and deprivation of income, since employment is ample for men and teams in the various pursuits of the lumberman and chopper, while a market for the productions of their farms is thus regularly and surely sustained.[48]

In fact, the wheat production in Isanti County was less competitive than in other areas, due to the lower fertility of the sandy soils. Local residents realized this despite the encouragement of testimonials. That wheat would bring declining yields in the future was clear enough. Why then, in this situation, did Swedes and Germans cling to wheat more tenaciously than their American-born neighbors? The question is difficult to answer decisively. For many Germans and Swedes, wheat was the first real cash crop they had known. Early returns from its production were substantial and made a deep impression on the immigrants. This is clear from letters home, which seem awed by the potential of wheat. Lacking their American neighbors' experience with the recurring pattern of declining yields and the growing disadvantages of aging agricultural districts in wheat production, and ignorant of the capital necessary to experiment with alternatives, immigrants may have been more prone to plant large acreages in wheat even when the potential return no longer warranted such an investment.

On the other hand, improved land was not plentiful in Isanti County, even in 1880. The acreage that Swedish settlers could devote to a grain crop was quite limited. It is not clear how much of the grain harvest was actually marketed, once a portion of the harvest was set aside for home consumption and seed. Indeed, most reports of large wheat yields and profits from wheat cited in the local press featured American farmers, not immigrants. The scale of operation may have been too small for market economics to play a great role in the mind of the immigrant farm operator. If wheat could be grown successfully and a market could always be found for any surplus—both of which conditions were part of their experience—it may not have mattered that much if the return was somewhat less than it had been in previous years. For the American farmer, the desire to maximize return was quite likely much more strongly ingrained. Unaccustomed as they were to the notion of maximizing the return of surplus production, the transplanted peasant may well have been happy with limited returns.

Yankees, Germans, and Swedes also differed from one another in their choice of secondary crops and in the livestock they kept. With the exception of rye, which was grown on relatively small acreages primarily by Germans, secondary grain crops were grown to feed livestock. The two important feed grains in Isanti County were Indian corn and oats. Since the farmer of 1880 strived to be self-sufficient in livestock feed, neither of these crops was aggressively marketed. Indian corn, of course, was a long-standing staple of midwestern farm production. It was most familiar to the Americans and Germans, who had been engaged in midwestern farming far longer than the Swedes. Conversely, oats was an important fodder crop across most of Sweden and an obvious choice for the Swedish immigrant in America. These differences in background and experience probably go a long way toward explaining the contrasting degree of reliance on these two crops by Americans and Germans on the one hand and Swedes on the other, and may well be examples of what some scholars have termed "cultural rebound."[49]

The same may be said for variation between groups in animal husbandry (Table 5.2). Here Americans and Germans stood out once again, this time as keepers of horses, cattle, and swine, while the Swedes had larger numbers of oxen and sheep. One of the most important creatures for any farming operation was the beast of burden. In 1880, Americans and Germans were more likely to use horses; Swedes were more likely to own teams of oxen. The prevalence of oxen among Swedes was undoubtedly related to the fact that they represented a smaller capital investment.[50] The newly arrived and relatively poor Swedish immigrant was quick to see the financial wisdom of investing in a relatively inexpensive

Table 5.2 Livestock Husbandry by Culture Group, Isanti Study Area, 1880

| Culture group | Average number of livestock | | | | | | Horses/ oxen | Cattle/ dairy |
	Horses	Oxen	Cattle	Dairy cattle	Sheep	Swine		
Study area overall	1.5	1.0	6.8	2.7	3.6	1.4	1.5	2.5
Old American	2.3	0.8	8.1	2.7	0.9	2.3	2.9	3.0
German	2.2	0.1	11.6	3.9	1.6	2.8	22.0	3.0
Swedish	1.4	1.0	6.0	2.6	4.8	0.8	1.4	2.3
Bothnian provinces[a]	1.1	1.5	6.7	3.0	3.7	0.9	0.7	2.2
Småland	1.7	1.0	8.1	2.6	1.6	1.0	1.7	3.1
Upper Dalarna	1.5	0.7	5.8	2.5	5.3	1.1	2.1	2.3
Orsa	1.4	1.0	5.4	2.4	6.2	1.0	1.4	2.3
Rättvik	1.6	0.6	6.4	2.6	4.4	1.2	2.7	2.5
Venjan	1.5	0.6	5.7	2.6	5.2	1.0	2.5	2.2

SOURCE: Manuscripts of the 1880 U.S. Agricultural Census.
[a] Hälsingland and Medelpad

team of oxen, even though the horse had been the primary beast of burden at home. Once established, Swedes often made the switch to the more expensive, but also more maneuverable and efficient, horse. The value of horses was underscored by the frequency of reports in the local press about runaway horses and horse stealing. Nothing was more devastating than the unexpected loss of an expensive team of horses. The only exception to the pattern of initial investment in oxen followed by a switch to horses among Swedish immigrants appears to be among immigrant farmers from Upper Dalarna, especially those from Rättvik and Orsa. These people were more inclined to have horses early on, regardless of expense, because the horse was such a deeply imbedded part of culture in Dalarna.

Swedes were also inclined to run fewer cattle than their American or German counterparts. More of the cattle they possessed were milk cows. Here again, the relative recency of the immigrant's arrival was a factor. Securing one or two milk cows was naturally a higher priority than raising cattle for meat, especially for immigrant families. Moreover, cattle were primarily used in Sweden to supply milk and cheese for home consumption. The idea of feeding and droving small herds of cattle for market would have struck Swedes as a rather novel idea. A few head of beef cattle, however, could be of real value, and most Swedes strove to enlarge their herds with non-dairy cattle over time. Nonetheless, Americans and Germans maintained the largest cattle operations. A local surplus of corn was often the precursor of feeding and droving operations in midwestern agricultural districts. This condition was met early on in Isanti by the American and German farmers, who relegated substantial acreages to corn while Swedes continued to emphasize wheat.

Among the lesser beasts, hogs were raised almost exclusively by American and German farmers. Swedish farmers raised much larger numbers of sheep. As with cattle feeding, hog production went hand in hand with large-scale production of corn, which gave both American and German farmers in Isanti County a clear advantage. There is little evidence that Swedes belatedly followed the example of their neighbors in this regard. They continued to display a clear preference for sheep raising. Swine were never of any importance in the poorer forest districts of Sweden, from which most of Isanti's immigrants came, because they required specialized fodder that was difficult to provide. Goats and sheep were much more self-reliant and could forage for themselves. The Swedish aversion to hog raising in Isanti County certainly rested in large part on past tradition in Sweden. The tendency to forego hog production among Swedish immigrant farmers in American has been noted by other scholars as well.[51]

Cultural background and, particularly, length of time in America were both key variables in explaining differences in agricultural practice. These factors also explain some of the differences between Swedish provincial groups. For example, the behavior of immigrants from the province of Småland might be expected to resemble more closely the behavior of Americans and Germans than the behavior of immigrants from Upper Dalarna or from the Bothnian provinces of Hälsingland and Medelpad. The Småland settlers came from a Swedish region that experienced very heavy emigration as early as the 1850s. They were more likely to have been in America for some time before settling in Isanti County. In fact, all of the settlers in Isanti County who were born in Småland had spent at least a few years in the Middle West and had acquired a certain familiarity with American conditions before settling in Isanti. The agricultural tradition of Småland also differed from that of Upper Dalarna and the Bothnian provinces, so culture, too, might have played a role. In any case, the acreages devoted to certain crops and the mix of livestock kept by settlers born in Småland were both distinctive from those of other Swedes and somewhat similar to those of Americans and Germans.[52]

Culture and time in America, however, provide only a partial explanation. Environmental differences also played a role. Not only were the

Småland settlers beneficiaries of a longer acquaintance with American conditions, they also occupied the same sandy oak barrens of Bradford township as did many of the German and American farmers whose operations were so similar. Many of the features that distinguished Swedish agricultural practice from American and German were most strongly associated with Swedes who settled on the brown forest soils of the morainic northern tier of townships. Among Upper Dalarna parish groups, for instance, sheep raising was most prevalent on farms owned by settlers from Venjan and Orsa, both of whom were important in settling northern townships. Sheep were far less important on Rättvik farms, most of which were located in brush prairie or oak barren environments. Rättvik farmers were also more likely to sow substantial acreages of corn and to have more catttle and swine than the Swedes in the northern part of the study area. The more rugged and heavily forested environment north and west of Cambridge was more effectively grazed by sheep than cattle, a fact that cannot be discounted as an influence on the immigrant's behavior.

One can only conclude that the reasons behind variations in farming practices were complex. A combination of factors entered into the immigrant farmer's decision to throw resources into one endeavor or another, and it is difficult to demonstrate that any one factor was overriding. The census manuscripts reveal many individuals who were doing exactly the opposite of their neighbors from the same culture group. Length of time in America had probably the strongest influence on major market decisions. If an activity offered pecuniary advantage or disadvantage, it seems to have been seized or abandoned most quickly by those who could best understand the situation. Culture seems to have had its greatest impact on activities related to basic household subsistence. Here traditional practices had no long-term pecuniary effect, no impact on any measure of success. While economic survival in a new country may have forced immigrant farmers to bow to a multitude of outside factors in deciding upon how to expend their efforts, in less economically crucial activities they could afford to let tradition play a larger role.

"Success" in America

Just a short time in America had radically changed many aspects of immigrant economic life. One of the greatest changes was their relationship with the land. Even though the average Rättvik farmer in Isanti possessed nearly the same amount of land as he possessed back in

Table 5.3 Average Farm Size among Rättvik Farmers in Isanti (1880) and All Farm Households in Rättvik (1854)

	Total acres	Acres arable	Acres meadow	Acres forest
Farms owned by Rättvik immigrants in Isanti	147.9	17.9	4.4	125.6
All farm households in Rättvik parish	147.6	3.6	14.9	128.9

SOURCES: Manuscripts of the 1880 U.S. Agricultural Census and *Beskrivning över Rättviks socken, 1854.*

the home parish (Table 5.3), a far larger portion of his land was culti-vated. Moreover, the arable in 1880 was still nowhere near its potential size. The proportion of cultivated land could be increased significantly over time with additional capital and labor. The bounds of tradition and nature that prevented the Rättvik peasant from expanding the arable in any significant way were noticeably lacking in Isanti.

Whether the land in Isanti was better than the land in Rättvik is debatable. Isanti soils were sandy and infertile in the south, clayey and difficult to work in the north. One Swedish settler in Maple Ridge town-ship is reported to have complained of the difficulty of growing crops in clayey soil that "became so dry that it cracked."[53] Certainly the marine sediments surrounding Lake Siljan were potentially richer. Similarly, natural meadowland may have been richer and certainly was more abun-dant at home. But the amount of potential arable in Isanti remained staggering to the mind of immigrant farmers from Rättvik. The pros-pect of reaching that potential propelled them further and further from the traditional heavy reliance on animal husbandry they had learned at home and from the subsistence economy they practiced during the first years in Isanti.

Clearing land was backbreaking work, but most farmers could add one or two acres to their arable a year, using just the labor of their own household. Those who were in a hurry and had exceptional means could hire the job done. Through whatever methods, breaking and grubbing new land was a perennial early summer activity on every farm. Ameri-can cash crops offered the immigrant opportunity of a sort that was simply not available at home and most pursued it enthusiastically. While most Rättvik farms in Isanti already had twice the livestock of their counterparts at home in 1880 (as measured in animal units), the relative importance of animal husbandry to growing grains was only about one-

Table 5.4 Animal Husbandry among Rättvik Farmers in Isanti (1880) and All Farm Households in Rättvik (1854)

	Average number of livestock					Average number of animal units[a]	Animal units per acre arable
	Horses	Oxen	Cattle	Sheep and goats	Swine		
Farms owned by Rättvik immigrants in Isanti	1.6	0.7	6.4	4.2	1.2	85.8	4.8
All farm households in Rättvik parish	0.8	—	2.8	7.6	0.8	59.6	16.6

SOURCES: Manuscripts of the 1880 U.S. Agricultural Census and *Beskrivning över Rättviks socken, 1854.*

[a] Animal units are derived from the old Dalarna formula used in Chapter 3 (horse or oxen = 18, cow = 6, sheep or goat = 1.5, hog = 1).

quarter as great (Table 5.4). With markets opening up and communications improving, optimism was everywhere in Isanti County at the beginning of the 1880s. Even if wheat would not sustain the optimism, one could branch off in innumerable directions. Most new settlers looked to the future with keen expectations of accumulating new wealth and a new way of life. The immigrant farmer was resolved to serve the marketplace to the best of his abilities.

A measure of this new-found sense of optimism and willingness to innovate is the speed with which immigrant farmers began to mechanize their operations in the late 1870s and early 1880s. Swedes in Isanti were as quick as anyone to embrace the plethora of new labor-saving implements coming on the market at that time.[54] The Isanti County Press, ever watchful as it was for signs of enterprise among area farmers, described the phenomenon as an absolute "mania for machinery."[55] Reapers and threshing machines were wonders of the day, perfect answers to the vexing problem of high labor costs that plagued rural districts everywhere in the Middle West. The acquisition of each new piece of machinery was a newsworthy event. Not everyone, of course, was in a position to purchase machinery. But few were forced to do without, for at the very least the machines could be hired and shared. In the summer of 1880, the Isanti County Press reported having observed a string of teams, nearly four miles in length, setting off for the railhead at North Branch to hire reapers.[56]

Once the shock of wheat competition from the western prairies began to pass, increased diversification and innovation became the order of the day. Yankee farmers led the way, but Swedes were not far behind in trying out new things. All new innovations were enthusiastically reported in the local press and with rare exception were attributed to local American farmers. A prime example was the introduction of amber sugar cane to replace declining levels of maple sugar production. American farmers in Spencer Brook township first tried the crop. The venture became successful enough in just a few years to support a number of sugar mills in that township. The practice soon spread to Swedish farmers across the county.[57] At roughly the same time, farmers began to specialize in the production of sweet potatoes and green peas.

The Isanti County Press, in its New Year's report of 1879, proudly pointed to the "progress" going on about the county. Farmers had bigger fields than ever before and had become "inundated with machinery." The only cloud on the horizon was the cost of progress, as represented by the evil of rapidly proliferating mortgage debt. With the Register of Deeds reporting record numbers of mortgages, the Press was visibly concerned about the burden of high interest on farmers.[58] Farmers, however, seemed less concerned, as they continued to increase and diversify over the next few years, building new barns and houses and purchasing new land in a wave of rising prosperity that characterized much of the 1880s.

After just over a decade in America, the old seasonal round for Rättvik farmers had been irreversibly altered by changing conditions in America. The men still spent much of the winter in the forest, but now it was in the employ of others either as a wage laborer or a supplier. Spring was still the busiest season, with fields to prepare and grain to sow, but it was also the time to break and grub new land that promised increased production in years to come. There was more opportunity for wage labor as a driver in the massive log floats on the Rum River, which often lasted well into June. Harvest time in America came at roughly the same time and with the same intensity as it had at home, but it became increasingly mechanized and less dependent on the careful marshalling of labor from family, friends, and relations. One consequence of the new machines was less need for women and children as field laborers at harvest time. Harvest became more exclusively men's work than it had been in Sweden; redefined sexual divisions of labor would be the ultimate result. Mechanization also shortened the time devoted to threshing. Most threshing was now done in the fall over a relatively short period, rather than dragging out into the winter as it had in Rättvik. This freed the immigrant family for fall plowing and other activities that were commonly deferred by the demands of threshing at home.

Plate 5.3 Haying near Stanchfield Lake in Dalbo township. Summer was an occasion to be photographed outdoors in Sunday's best clothes. Although these girls were photographed in the fields, most field work was done by men and machines by the 1890s, when this photo was taken. Note that the only person actually lifting any hay is the young man on the right. (Courtesy of Isanti County Historical Society)

The marketplace also intervened in the normal order of things by forcing farmers to be keenly aware of changes in grain prices, and to be prepared to withold grain if necessary until the market was more favorable. The farmer's economic world was more integrated with the world around him in America, even to the point of influencing where he would market his grain to take advantage of varying business practices of American buyers. Isanti grain farmers, for instance, preferred marketing their grain at the railhead in Harris rather than North Branch because the grain was not "graded as closely" there.[59] Thus, the transition from peasant to farmer was already well under way by midway through the settlement era and promised to accelerate as the decades passed.

For those who chose to settle farther west on the Dakota prairies, the differences between economic life at home and in America were even greater. The prairie environment was more radically different from Upper Dalarna's than Isanti's. It was also more rapidly broken and converted to fields. Rättvik farmers in Clay County on the average had converted one-third of their land to cropland by 1880, while their counterparts in Isanti had managed a little more than one-tenth. Clay County and its Swedish settlement at Dalesburg were also more quickly linked to markets by rail and river transport.

While crops in Clay and Isanti counties recorded in the 1880 census are not directly comparable because of the nearly total crop failure in Clay County, the high degree to which market forces drove the Dalesburg economy is rapidly apparent. Most markedly, the development of a mixed economy based on production for cash was more advanced. Driven in part by recurrent grasshopper infestation and in part by good market conditions, farmers in Clay County had moved quickly from an early reliance on wheat to a mixture of corn, hogs, and cattle. By 1880, stock farms had begun to make their appearance all across the county. Cattle feed and the production of hogs for market became a local specialty. In 1880, Rättvik immigrants in Dalesburg estimated their farms' worth at roughly one and one-half times that of their fellow parishioners in Isanti (Table 5.5). On average, they planted ten times as much corn and three times as much oats, had twice as many horses, an extra milk cow, twice as many cattle, and ten times as many swine. Rättvik farmers in Isanti were ahead only in wheat acreage, in which they led by only a small margin, and in the numbers of sheep and oxen, where differences were fairly substantial. Despite the repeated catastrophes of grasshopper infestation through much of the 1870s, the

Table 5.5   Relative Success of Rättvik Farmers in Isanti and Clay Counties, 1880

	Isanti County Average	Clay County Average
Number of farms	63	17
Farm size (acres)	147.9	184.1
Acreage tilled	17.9	51.2
Farm value (land, fences, buildings)	$822	$1,216
Acreage in wheat	8.6	6.8
Acreage in corn	1.8	18.3
Acreage in oats	2.0	5.6
Acreage in rye	0.2	0.2
Horses	1.6	3.5
Oxen	0.6	0.1
Dairy cattle	2.6	3.6
Other cattle	6.4	12.2
Sheep	4.4	1.0
Swine	1.2	11.0

SOURCE: Manuscripts of the 1880 U.S. Agricultural Census.

small number of Rättvik settlers who made their way to the Dakota prairies were clearly better off than their Isanti counterparts, and the gap would steadily widen over the next decades.

With such striking economic differences emerging between the Isanti and Dalesburg settlements, it is a wonder that more Rättvik emigrants of the second wave were not drawn off to the Dalesburg settlement in the 1880s. The answer to this paradox is simple enough. The rapid passage of the settlement era on the Dakota prairie largely precluded any secondary phase of settlement. Most available land was taken in the first few years. With its more leisurely pace of settlement, Isanti remained a place where land beckoned to fresh waves of immigrants until as late as the 1890s. In addition, the Isanti settlers had done much more to establish a social community that mimicked the one that had been left behind such a short time earlier. The sheer size of the Rättvik community in Isanti meant, quite naturally, that there was considerable pull along the axis of communication and migration that linked it with the old parish in Sweden; certainly a far greater pull than could be exerted by the much smaller number of Rättvik settlers on the Dakota prairies.

6

The Transplanted Community

The Formative Years, 1865–1889

THE EMIGRANTS who left Rättvik during the first great exodus of the late 1860s and again in the second wave of the early 1880s came from households that were often closely associated with one another in the socioeconomic structure of the old parish. As we have seen, both kinship and place exerted strong forces in bonding together the subcommunities of which the old parish was made. And in so many cases, households representing the core social networks of these subcommunities pioneered the emigration overseas. Emigrants left for both social and economic reasons. Their departure was as much an effort to preserve and reestablish a familiar social order as it was an effort to improve the economic status of a particular household or family. This was especially true for the family emigration that dominated the first two waves, less so for the more atomized migration of the third wave in the late 1880s. An integral part of the emigrant's expectations for life in America, therefore, was the reestablishment of a fragment of the social web he or she had known since childhood. It was this expectation that underlay the magnetic attraction of settlements of friends and relatives in America. It helped drive the process of community formation in hundreds of midwestern settlements that received large numbers of immigrants via particular migration axes.

While kinship ties, stretched over thousands of miles, were the key to bringing together sizable clusters of immigrants from specific European localities, the rural immigrant church is generally recognized as

the institution that played the major role in the formation and maintenance of immigrant community life.[1] There were, of course, many forces
that modulated social interaction and many possible foci for frontier
communities. Immigrants were exposed to a variety of new elements
such as open land, labor-saving machinery, trading relationships with
Yankees, new political systems, and competing religious beliefs, all of
which made social life in America more elastic. The web of new economic relationships created functional communities out of trade center
hinterlands. Townships were also communities in that they brought residents together for purposes of local self-government. But true social
communities jelled only around the old social networks maintained
through the church. Trade areas were too large and often too impervious to social and cultural boundaries to be socially meaningful. The
township also lacked social and cultural cohesion. It did not bring people
together spontaneously; rather, it imposed an outside authority that
determined the responsibilities and territory of an arbitrary social unit.[2]

Around the immigrant rural church, however, a social community
emerged largely because a group of people, who spontaneously felt a
sense of common identity and purpose, elected to band together formally. The decision to organize a congregation was usually made early in
the frontier period. The rural immigrant church served a territorial
function from almost the beginning. It defined its own territory, independent of civil administrative boundaries or trade areas, through the
spatial distribution of its membership. Aside from affiliation with a synodal parent organization, the church was self-governing. Although not
all immigrants in any given area were church-goers, the church community seemed to bind together most people living within its tributary
area, member and nonmember alike. Not only was it a place of worship,
it was also the site of picnics, socials, and meetings. It was the umbrella
organization for a myriad of social and purposive clubs and organizations. It served as a social center for a dispersed and lonely population.
Nonmembers in the area were caught up in the social network as much
as anyone and looked to the church as the community center.

Religious affiliation among new settlers in America was an important and often emotionally charged issue. In part this was due to a
heightened awareness brought on by the rise of pietism and religious
dissent in many nineteenth-century European societies. It was also due
to the American concept of the separation of church and state, which
promoted competitive denominationalism, especially among Protestants. Agricultural frontiers in the Middle West were considered fertile
missionary fields by both the established American denominations and

the new immigrant synods. Much effort was expended encouraging the establishment of frontier congregations and their association with the larger denominational and synodal groups. The result was a heavily churched landscape, especially in the strongly ethnic band of settlement that stretched across the Upper Midwest from northern Illinois and southern Wisconsin to the eastern parts of the Dakotas and Nebraska. The rate of church affiliation was very high across this band, particularly in the areas settled heavily by Germans and Scandinavians. Indeed, by the end of the century many American church leaders considered the Midwest to be "over-churched" and lamented what they clearly felt to have been overly competitive efforts to establish churches in the region.[3]

On the strength of such fervor the immigrant church was established as the center of community life. It was charged with the responsibility of upholding values and preserving continuity with the cultural past. The outside world could not be held at arm's length forever, but the church functioned as the first and in some ways the only bulwark against rapid change. It was the functional and the symbolic heart of the rural immigrant community, the center of organized resistance to social assimilation with American society, and the center of organized efforts to transplant and maintain the social order of the parent community in Europe.

The Founding and Development
of Church Communities in Isanti

The process by which immigrant church communities were founded among Swedish immigrants in Isanti County differs little from a pattern that was common across the entire Upper Middle West. Settlers from Rättvik, and other parish or provincial groups who settled in the county, moved early to establish their own congregations. While churches were seldom completely exclusive of settlers from other origins, most tended to be dominated by a particular group and most were located to serve areas colonized by certain groups. The early churches often lacked a formal clergy for a number of years, the responsibility being taken instead by laymen. Congregations also did without a permanent place of worship for a number of years. Services were simply held from time to time in parishioners' homes until conditions permitted the erection of a permanent church edifice. Another feature of the formative years was the sharing of clergy due to their chronic short supply on the frontier. Once a congregation decided to put out a call for a pastor, they often found the only option was to share a pastor with other churches in the area—a practice that created the networks of "daughter" or "sister" congregations that were so common to many areas.

Schism and interdenominational competition were also features of the midwestern religious scene in the nineteenth century. These conflicts played a role in the emerging social structure of the Isanti area as well. Most Swedes who settled in America during the latter part of the nineteenth century were members of the state church of Sweden prior to emigrating. Swedish Lutheranism in America was not plagued with bitter schismatic battles on the scale experienced among other Lutheran immigrant groups. The Norwegians, in particular, gained a reputation for their doctrinal disputes, which were often so bitterly fought as to split communities and even families.[4] Religious differences among Swedes appear to have been far less disruptive of the social fabric. Yet even they experienced a fair amount of internal strife.

Swedish Lutheranism in America owed its relative cohesion to the formation of the Augustana Lutheran Synod in 1860. This Illinois-based synod quickly became the dominant Swedish religious organization in America, claiming many hundreds of congregations in a number of states. Although in many ways a "daughter church" of Sweden's state church, the Augustana Synod was actually far more American in polity and outlook than its Swedish counterpart. Consequently, it was rather successful in accommodating itself to the cynical attitude that many Swedish emigrants held towards the state church in Sweden. The democratic form and theological flexibility of the synod in its early years made it highly adaptable to a variety of situations and pressures that might otherwise have caused it to dissolve. In fact, the synod enjoyed frosty relationships, at best, with the mother church in Sweden throughout most of the nineteenth century and has been referred to as more of a "laymen's missionary movement" than a formal church.[5]

There was always an element among Swedish immigrants, however, who found even the Augustana Synod too formal and dogmatic for their tastes. These were often emigrants of the late 1860s who had been smitten by the pietistic movements that swept parts of Sweden in the 1840s and 1850s. The great lay preacher Rosenius, was a major influence in these movements. Rosenius advised his followers to remain loyal to the old church despite their differences with it and to attempt to influence its course from within. Although many pursued such a strategy, others attracted to Rosenius's pietistic doctrine developed a great dislike for all formal church activities and the ordained ministry in particular, preferring spontaneous gatherings in homes and chapels that were led by laymen. Such activities were barely tolerated in Sweden. Their practitioners were an important element in the early emigration from Sweden and a constant source of ferment and separatist tendencies among immigrant Lutheran congregations in America.

The clergy of the Augustana Synod eventually moved to condemn any effort to establish "free churches," whether within or alongside the established church, just as their counterparts in Sweden had done earlier. Dissenters then began to form their own organizations, which were in time united under a single umbrella organization known as the Swedish Evangelical Mission Covenant Church in America. This splinter group of Swedish Lutheranism in America soon faced internal dissension as well. A group that desired an even greater break from the doctrine and formalism of traditional Lutheranism went on to separate itself from the Mission Convenant Church, establishing "Free Mission" churches in many Swedish settlement areas. Augustana Lutheran congregations in Isanti were hardly immune to this secessionary activity. They experienced the normal amount of internal strife resulting from such differences of opinion and witnessed, by the late 1880s, the formation of a fair number of Mission Covenant churches within the area, as well as the establishment of a number of Free Mission congregations in the early 1890s.

The major competitor of Swedish Lutheranism in America, however, was the Swedish Baptist Church. Although the Swedish Baptist movement in America enjoyed ties with American Baptists, its origins and strongest associations lay with the rise of the Baptist faith in Sweden during the middle and later decades of the nineteenth century. The Conventicle Act of 1726 specifically forbade religious meetings outside the state church. Swedish Baptists endured persecution and even imprisonment at the hands of the authorities until the act was finally repealed in 1858. Even then, many people who had embraced Baptist doctrines left Sweden for America to avoid the continued religious intolerance of their countrymen. In America, Baptist missionary activity found fertile ground among the Swedish immigrant population, establishing an early sphere of influence by 1860 in the many Swedish settlements of northwestern Illinois, southeastern Minnesota and east central Iowa. From there the Baptist movement diffused in subsequent decades through the newer settlements of Minnesota, Nebraska, and the Dakotas, winning many converts among the new immigrants of those settlements.[6]

The Swedish Baptists, however, were never as successful as the Augustana Synod in organizing their countrymen in America. Those who had been Baptists in Sweden constituted only a minority of all Swedish emigrants, though their numbers were disproportionately high in the early decades. In America, they won many converts through their proselytizing efforts, but to win over the great mass of Swedish immigrants who still looked to the Lutheranism of their fathers as the true faith was always an uphill battle.[7] Nonetheless, the Baptists were particularly successful in certain settlement districts and Isanti County emerged as one of their bastions. With so many immigrants from Dalarna and the Bothnian coast provinces, where the Baptist movement had been exceptionally strong, Isanti contained an uncommonly large number of Baptists who were prepared to organize and to proselytize vigorously among their neighbors. The county soon earned a reputation for being the most Baptist of any county in America dominated by Swedish settlers. The Augustana Synod and the Swedish Baptist Church were more or less on an equal footing in Isanti County. As a consequence, the competition between them was more intense than in most other places.

In fact, a Baptist church was the first Swedish church to be organized in the county. A group of Swedish Baptist settlers who had organized a congregation in Chisago County struggled under the intolerance of their predominantly Lutheran neighbors. The small Baptist congregation dissolved in the late 1850s and its membership dispersed to the Vasa community in southeastern Minnesota, where Baptists were more welcome, or to the new and as yet unprejudiced frontier in Isanti County. Those who moved to the Isanti area settled to the south of Cambridge and formed the nucleus of what eventually became the "Old Isanti" community. The congregation was formed in 1860, when a group of fourteen settlers gathered and declared themselves charter members of the Baptist Church of Cambridge, later nicknamed the "tamarack church" in reference to the building material of the first edifice. This early membership was augmented by additional Baptist settlers from the Chisago Lakes area and from the Vasa community. Most of the early members were born in the Bothnian coast provinces of Hälsingland and Medelpad or in Dalarna and had been associated with the Baptist movement in Sweden prior to emigration.[8]

The organization of the first Baptist church in Isanti County was followed closely by the founding of a Lutheran congregation just to the north. The Cambridge Evangelical Swedish Lutheran Church was organized in 1864 in the home of a Swedish settler named Edblad, originally from Jämtland, who had moved to the Isanti area from Wisconsin in 1859. The founding of this church brought together a number of early Swedish settlers of mixed provincial origins, who like Edblad had moved into the area from older settlements in Minnesota or Wisconsin. But as settlers from Rättvik streamed into the area over the next two years, the Lutheran community began to take on a progressively stronger identification with that parish. In September of 1866, the congregation was reorganized in the Edblad cabin to include formally the large number of families from Rättvik. As even more families from Rättvik continued to arrive over the next few years, the congregation became dominated by them and more or less coterminous with the developing Rättvik community in the Isanti area.[9]

A second Baptist congregation, the Stanchfield Baptist Church, was organized at roughly the same time by people from the Upper Dalarna parish of Orsa. Many had been Baptists in Sweden. Most of them, in fact, came from a single village, Hansjö, and had been members of a Baptist congregation there. One of their number, Massar Anders Persson, had even spent twenty-eight days in the provincial jail in the early 1850s for violating the Conventicle Act.[10] Even with such initial solidarity, the congregation came close to the point of dissolution in the early years as members wrangled over doctrinal differences. An outsider nearly succeeded in dissolving the original congregation and reorganizing it as a "Methodist Association," such was the fervor with which theological notions of various kinds were accepted and discarded.[11] But in the end the arrival of large numbers of new settlers from Orsa in 1869 strengthened the hand of the original founders and steadied the course of the young congregation, which went on to be the focus of one of the larger Swedish communities in the county.

Thus by the end of the 1860s, Isanti County included three major Swedish congregations—two Baptist and one Lutheran—each of which can be identified with particular culture groups and their respective settlements. There is evidence that each recognized the cultural and religious differences that distinguished it from the others and that each was conscious of its territorial bounds. One man from the Baptist community in Stanchfield, in a reminiscence written in 1954, maintained that his people were always very well aware of the fact that their neighbors in the "Isanti-Cambridge district" were not Orsa *karlar;* that "they were from other parts of Sweden and not in harmony with the Stanchfield brethern." He identified his people as belonging to a class of Swedes who were "frank and outspoken" and who "often offended other Swedes with a high degree of culture," and went on to state:

Even when I was a boy there was a spirit of rivalry between the two groups which often led to unfriendly situations. Besides both in Isanti and Cambridge several Lutherans settled, and that was something the Stanchfield Baptists didn't like. They put forth every effort to keep the Lutherans out of Stanchfield—and they succeeded remarkably well. About this, in a heated discussion, Spanner Lars Dahlman [an early leader of the Stanchfield Baptists] said: *"Vi måste göra allt hvad vi kunna för att icke gifva rum till dessa barnadöpare. Vi vill icke hafva någon fläck på vår himmel."* [We must do all that we can not to give room to any of these child-baptizers. We want no blemishes in our heaven.][12]

This kind of self-conscious affiliation with the local church was instrumental in sharply focusing the differences between settlements, thereby playing a major role in the emergence of distinctive spatial communities in the Isanti area.

Each of these early churches was active in organizing "daughter" or "sister" congregations as settlement progressed across the county. Most of these new congregations began as peripheral meeting houses or "Sunday schools" affiliated with the already established churches. They expressed the effort by the early churches to reach out to the many nascent settlement nuclei established by new settlers who might be of similar regional background or religious persuasion. These satellites were served by the clergy of the mother churches on a part-time basis until they could be incorporated into the larger congregation or established as independent congregations. The Baptist Church of Cambridge, for example, did this through the establishment of Sunday schools in the Fish Lake area of western Chisago County, the "Blomford" area of eastern Isanti township, and the village of Cambridge. Each of these satellites became an independent congregation over time. The Stanchfield Baptist Church similarly developed peripheral meeting houses in Cambridge, Springvale, and Maple Ridge townships, although only the Springvale facility ever became an independent congregation.[13]

The Cambridge Luthern Church was especially active and successful in this respect. After an early period, in which it was a "sister" congregation to the Fish Lake Lutheran Church in western Chisago County, missionary-minded pastors at the Cambridge church had a hand in organizing no fewer than five other Lutheran congregations around the county. In this way, the Venjan settlement in the northwestern part of the Isanti County received a Lutheran focus early in its development (Salem Lutheran, 1874), as did the settlement of people from Småland in Bradford township (Long Lake Lutheran, 1891) and the Swedish Lutherans of northern Stanchfield township (Rice Lake Lutheran, 1879). The Venjan congregation of Salem Lutheran went on to found a sister congregation of its own in Maple Ridge township (Siloa Lutheran, 1891).

The Cambridge Lutheran community was by far the largest of the

Isanti church communities, a fact that soon necessitated internal administrative subdivisions. This was done by instituting a system reminiscent of the subdivision of the old parish back in Sweden into *fjärding* districts. The congregation was divided into territorial units called "rotes." The early system instituted by the church consisted of four districts that reflected certain cultural and territorial divisions already extant within the community by the early 1870s. The Eastern rote took in parishioners living in the eastern portions of Cambridge township. Most of these people were of mixed provincial origins, including many of the original founding families of the church. No members who had emigrated from Rättvik were found among the Eastern rote membership (Table 6.1). There were also a Northern rote, a Western rote, and an Isanti rote. The latter three coincided with each of the three major Rättvik settlements. Those who were listed as members of the Northern rote were primarily emigrants from Rättvik's Ovanheds *fjärding* who had settled near the Bäcklin farm just north of Cambridge. Members of the Western rote were largely from Västbygge *fjärding* (especially the Gränden villages) and were residents of Isanti's Springvale township. The other unit, the Isanti rote, was physically separated from the rest of the community. It was located some distance to the south in Athens township and consisted primarily of parishioners from Rättvik's Gärdsjö *fjärding*, along with a handful of Lutheran families from the parish of Orsa. Between the Isanti rote and the main body of the Cambridge Lutheran community to the north stood the large Baptist settlement in Isanti township.[14]

Thus the spatial organization of the old Rättvik settlement, which had been transplanted to the Isanti area through the machinations of chain migration, was quickly institutionalized by the new community.

Table 6.1   Fjärding Origins of Rättvik Households in the Rotes of the Cambridge Swedish Evangelical Lutheran Church, ca. 1880

Rotes	Number of households from *fjärding* in Rättvik				
	Ovanheds	Västbygge	Gärdsjö	Sörbygge	Total
Eastern	0	0	0	0	0
Northern	20	2	1	1	24
Western	0	23	4	3	30
Isanti	1	1	32	1	35
Total	21	26	37	5	89

SOURCE: Catechetical registers of the Cambridge Swedish Evangelical Lutheran Church.

The rotes of the Cambridge Lutheran church came to serve specific administrative functions just as the *fjärding* districts had in Rättvik. Each elected deacons and trustees to the church council. These officers not only represented their respective constituencies in church matters, but were also responsible for seeing that the members of the rote met their obligations to the church. Levies for various projects, such as missions and building funds, as well as normal budgetary and maintenance requirements were customarily assigned to the respective rotes, with elected officials overseeing the mustering of resources in their respective districts. An 1872 council decision to build a parsonage, for example, was quickly followed by an order requiring each rote to requisition a certain amount of "day labor." The council also customarily asked the rotes to supply certain services, such as maintenance of the church building or cemetery upkeep, according to an annual rotation scheme. In 1880, for instance, the western rote was responsible for the upkeep of the church; in 1881 the responsibility shifted to the northern and eastern rotes, who passed it on the next year.[15] On occasion the rotes were even chastized for failure to carry their share. In 1874, three of the districts were roundly criticized at the *årsstämma*, the annual congregational meeting, for their shortcomings over the past year. The rotes almost took on personal attributes reflecting the idiosyncracies of their inhabitants, and they were often discussed or treated as some sort of "collective personality" by church administrators.[16]

The extreme extent of the Cambridge Lutheran community often made it difficult for the church to serve its far-flung membership adequately. The Isanti rote, in particular, lay far beyond the normal "team haul" distance within which travel to and from church could be accomplished easily. Parishioners of the Isanti rote were soon requesting special considerations of the parish council. As early as 1872, they petitioned for special services to be held in their district one Sunday afternoon each month to alleviate the burden of frequent long-distance travel to church. That request was quickly followed by another to build a chapel in Athens township in which special services could be held. Two years later they were demanding that communion should take place there once a year.[17] Thereafter, the council began to receive annual requests for the complete separation and independence of the Isanti rote from the Cambridge church parish. All of this eventually resulted in a council action in 1878, granting the outlying district permission to build its own church and maintain its own graveyard. However, since no pastor could be found for the new Athens Swedish Evangelical Lutheran

Plate 6.1 The "first church"—Faith Lutheran, Athens township. Most early churches were simple frame structures much like this one. This photograph, with the congregation assembled before the church, is a classic composition that was repeated countless times across the Upper Middle West. (Courtesy of Isanti County Historical Society, early 1880s)

Church, the two parishes were forced to share the same pastor, parsonage, and parish school until as late as 1892.[18]

The struggle for secession carried on by the Isanti rote for much of the 1870s is an interesting parallel to the actions taken by Ovanheds *fjärding* to establish its independence from Rättvik in the mid-nineteenth century. Both districts were physically remote from the church upon which the community focused. Both dealt with the situation by petitioning for progressively greater degrees of independence: first a chapel, then a graveyard and special services, and finally a church of their own. In short, the process and politics of the two secessions are remarkably similar. The participants had been over this ground before and were familiar with the procedure.

By the end of the 1880s, most of the Isanti area had been organized into fairly well-defined communities, based on common geographic origins in Sweden and common affiliation with a particular rural immigrant church or, in areas where denominational competition was strong, mixed affiliation with two or more competing churches. One can closely approximate the spatial structure of social interaction and cultural affinity across the region by delimiting communities on the basis of these two factors. An effort to do just that is presented here. Communities are defined spatially as areas in which at least half of all households belong to both a particular Swedish provincial or subprovincial group and at least half belong to a particular church congregation or set of competing congregations. A total of seven Swedish communities existed in the Isanti area, using this definition in conjunction with household data derived from the manuscripts of the 1885 Minnesota state census (Table 6.2 and Figure 6.1).[19]

Of the seven Swedish communities, Stanchfield was clearly the most homogeneous in both the geographic origin and religious affiliation of its population. Over 80 percent of its 159 households in 1885 hailed from the Upper Dalarna parish of Orsa and nearly 60 percent were members of the Stanchfield Baptist Church. Nearly as strong was the West Cambridge community, which consisted of the western and northern rotes of the Cambridge Lutheran congregation. Given its very large extent, it is difficult to treat the entire Cambridge Lutheran congregation as a single community, although in terms of religious affiliation it certainly was a single unit. Because of the striking cultural differences between the immigrants from Rättvik (who settled the Western and Northern rotes) and the immigrants of more diverse provincial backgrounds (who settled the Eastern rote), a division into two subcommunities seems appropriate. The West Cambridge community therefore stands by itself, with nearly 80 percent of its households hailing from Rättvik and nearly 70 percent membership in the Cambridge Lutheran Church, while the East Cambridge community is considered a related but separate entity. While this division of the Cambridge congregation may seem unjustified at first glance, its appropriateness is further borne out by subsequent analyses.

Three other communities were also exceptionally strong: the Athens community (formerly the Isanti rote of the Cambridge Lutheran Church) with its high proportion of Lutheran households from Rättvik and Orsa; the large community of Swedish Baptists from Hälsingland and Medelpad in Isanti township (the "Old Isanti" community); and the Venjan community located in the far northwest, referred to hereafter as the Dalbo-Karmel community. The Athens and Dalbo-Karmel communities were initially Lutheran, but both had experienced a fair degree of religious dissension by the end of the 1880s. The Athens congregation was split following its secession from the Cambridge church. The split

Table 6.2   Swedish Communities in the Isanti Study Area, ca. 1885

Community	Number of households	Home district		Church affiliation	
		Dominant province (parish)	Number of house- holds (%)	Congregation[a]	Number of house- holds (%)
Athens	76	Dalarna (Rättvik, Orsa)	55 (72.3%)	Athens Luth., Athens Free Mission	44 (57.9%)
Isanti	126	Hälsingland, Medelpad	90 (71.4)	Isanti Bapt.	70 (56.3)
Cambridge, East	45	Värmland, Jämtland	29 (64.4)	Cam. Luth., Eastern rote	24 (53.3)
Cambridge, West	106	Dalarna (Rättvik)	82 (77.4)	Cam. Luth., Western and Northern rotes	74 (69.8)
Stanchfield	159	Dalarna (Orsa)	134 (84.3)	Stanch. Bapt.	94 (59.1)
Maple Ridge	62	Dalsland, Värmland, Västergötland	39 (62.9)	Siloa Luth., No. Maple Ridge Cov., So. Maple Ridge Cov.	36 (58.0)
Dalbo-Karmel	127	Dalarna (Venjan)	86 (67.7)	Salem Luth., Karmel Cov., Dalbo Bapt.	69 (54.3)
Total	701		515 (73.5%)		411 (58.6%)

SOURCES: Manuscripts of the 1885 Minnesota State Census; registers of the Isanti Study Area Lutheran, Baptist and Free Mission, and Covenant churches; cemetery lists for the Isanti Study Area.

[a] Abbreviations: Bapt. = Baptist, Luth. = Lutheran, Cov. = Covenant

occurred in 1886 when a portion of the congregation broke away to found a Free Mission church. Taken together, the Athens Lutheran and Free Mission congregations comprised nearly 60 percent of the local population. The Dalbo-Karmel community was also divided. The largest number of households belonged to the Salem Lutheran Church, which was established in 1874. Large numbers of their neighbors, however, joined two competing churches in the early 1880s—the Dalbo Baptist Church (founded 1884) and the Karmel Covenant Church (founded as the

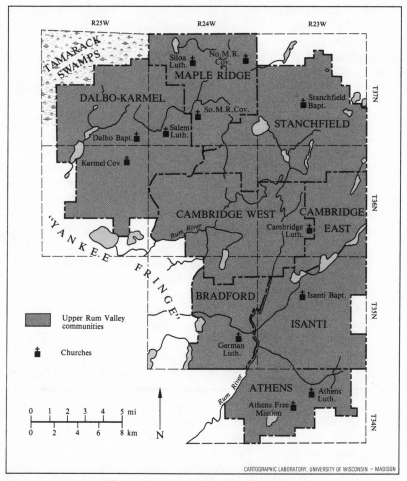

Figure 6.1 Location of Communities in the Isanti Study Area, ca. 1885

Swedish Mission Church of Wyanette in 1880). All three churches were located near one another at the center of the Dalbo-Karmel settlement and drew from the entire area, which was predominantly occupied by settlers from the Upper Dalarna parish of Venjan (67.7 percent in 1885).

Two Swedish communities were notably weaker. The Maple Ridge community had a population of somewhat mixed background whose religious allegiance was shared by three churches. The East Cambridge community, which belonged to the Cambridge Lutheran Church, was set off from the rest of that congregation because of the mixed cultural background of its population. The Maple Ridge area was first organized for religious purposes by the Salem Lutheran Church, which was actually located in the southwestern corner of Maple Ridge township. The Salem congregation reached out to include Lutherans in the central and northern portions of the township, but differences were quickly recognized between the people from Venjan, who dominated the Salem church, and the people living out in Maple Ridge township, who came predominantly from the west Swedish provinces of Värmland, Dalsland, and Västergötland. These differences led to a decision at the 1878 annual congregational meeting, directing the eastern and western parts of the congregation each to maintain a church and a burial ground, so that neither would have any reason to be bitter in the event of an eventual separation.[20] The separation was effected with the organization of Siloa Lutheran Church (1891) in northern Maple Ridge township, but not before the eastern portion of the congregation was affected by the founding of two Mission Convenant churches (North Maple Ridge Covenant Church, 1882, and South Maple Ridge Covenant Church, 1884). Although the Maple Ridge community enjoyed a certain amount of cohesion, it was easily the most divided and weakest of the seven Swedish communities.

This delimitation of Swedish communities in the late 1880s leaves some portions of the Isanti study area outside of the boundaries of any community. One such area is the eastern half of Bradford township. This area was settled by Germans, most of whom had origins in Prussia. The population was decidedly Lutheran and constituted an eighth (but non-Swedish) community centered on a German Lutheran church, St. John's, founded in 1882.[21] The delimitation also leaves out a mixed population of Old Americans strung along the western margins of the study area. By 1885, this was a remnant of the pioneering American population who first opened the area but then gave way before the massive influx of Swedish immigrants. As early as the late 1870s, in fact, the local press was reporting that the American population of the region was rapidly "thinning out"; soon "there won't be enough to tell the tale."[22] The "Yankee fringe," which remained beyond the western limits of Swedish colonization, does not seem to constitute a community in the same sense that communities have been defined for the Swedes and Germans. If anything, they belonged to the fairly dense settlement of Old Americans farther to the west in Spencer Brook township, but no obvious focus for this population, religious or otherwise, seems to have existed at the end of the 1880s.[23] The extensive, uninhabited tamarack swamps of northwestern Dalbo township also lie outside these deliberations, as do the Swedish populations of northern Stanchfield township and the extreme eastern portions of Isanti and Athens townships. Stanchfield was part of a community centered on the Rice Lake Lutheran church, left out here because it extended into townships in neighboring counties. Similarly, it is most appropriate to view the last areas as the western margins of communities located in townships just to the east of the study area.

These seven Swedish communities, taken together with the German community in Bradford township and the Yankee fringe in the west, serve as the basis for discussions of community life in this and later chapters. Although much happened in the decades following the 1880s, the spatial structure of cultural and social relationships delimited here changed very little. New settlers arrived and old settlers left, and some new churches were established around the turn of the century as the existing denominations were challenged by new forms of religious ferment. Yet the basic patterns of areal cultural homogeneity and religious affiliation that defined these communities at the end of the 1880s continued to define roughly the same local communities well into the twentieth century. These seven Swedish communities serve well as the basis for comparisons of social and economic behavior across cultural and religious lines, as well as a basis for comparison with the behavior of the non-Swedish inhabitants of Isanti, the Germans and Old Americans.

Social Organization

The processes of settlement and community formation at work in the Isanti area throughout the 1860s, 1870s, and well into the 1880s were remarkably conducive to the wholesale transplantation of social organization from the homeland. To begin with, the overwhelming "Swedishness" of the entire Isanti area, which extended into neighboring counties as well, fostered a uniquely deep sense of isolation from the host society. Americans had become a real minority in Isanti County by midway through the settlement era. Their presence was certainly felt when the immigrant farmer traveled into Cambridge village or to the railheads at Harris or Branch in Chisago County to trade. The businesses of these small trade centers were predominantly owned by Americans. There were also a good many American farms out along the fringe of settlement to the west, but few Swedish settlers were in day-to-day contact with the American population. They were in contact, for the most part, with other Swedes.

At another scale, day-to-day contact among Swedes was highly pre-scribed. The church-centered communities in which most social interaction took place were remarkably homogeneous. Not only did their respective populations largely hail from the same districts and provinces; they were also drawn together through a complex web of kinship relations. The degree to which people had known one another intimately or, at least, had shared some sort of social or economic relationship in another place, was remarkably high in all communities. These communities were, as one scholar has called them, "kinship communities." As such they saw even their countrymen in neighboring communities as removed at least one step from their own group.[24] As long as the social and culural isolation imposed by frontier conditions and their own penchant for living in exclusive communities persisted, the maintenance of a social order imported from another world can only be expected.

In his classic work on assimilation in American life, Milton Gordon suggested that social change and adaptation occur in stages, beginning with the acceptance of broad cultural values that do not directly threaten the existence of the group. This "cultural assimilation" may include participation in a host of secondary relationships, with the larger society but normally excludes primary relationships which are reserved for interaction among members of the group. Running for political office involves many secondary relationships, even when the candidate's motivation is to protect the interests of the group. For Gordon, the process of assimilation ends with "structural assimilation," in which the group's most intimate interrelationships are opened up to those outside the group. At this point the group may be willing to accept the marriage of its children with outsiders or be less concerned with the propinquity or exclusiveness of group residence patterns.[25]

Prior to 1890, the residents of Isanti's Swedish communities showed signs of broaching only the first of Gordon's stages with respect to the host American society. Assimilation with their Swedish neighbors of other origins and religious persuasion may in some ways have been even more grudging. Relations with Americans were strongly influenced, as we have seen, by eagerness to share in the opportunity and wealth offered by the American economy. Immigrants were also fascinated with everything American, and they realized that they must eventually learn to speak English and accept American ways if they were to become a part of their newly adopted country. Accordingly, some aspects of American culture, especially those with real economic utility, became part of the Swedish communities as early as the late 1870s.

The most obvious was a growing bilingualism. While few early immigrants made any serious attempt to converse with one another in English, the language crept relentlessly into their lives. American words and ideas for which there were no Swedish equivalents were rapidly incorporated into the immigrant's Swedish speech.[26] Increasingly, at least a few members of each Swedish household were acquiring the capacity to communicate with the host society in its own language. By the 1870s, most Swedish children were learning English in school. Public schools began to be organized in some of Isanti's Swedish settlement areas in the late 1860s. A total of thirty-seven schools were in operation across the county by 1880, enough to reach all settlement areas.[27] The ability to read English was also becoming more widespread among adults, as evidenced by the fact that the Isanti County Press ceased publishing a "Swede page" in every weekly edition in January 1876, substituting instead a semi-monthly special Swedish edition.

Early Swedish settlers also achieved a modest level of participation in American society through military service and politics. During the American Civil War, a number of Isanti's Swedish immigrants served in the Union Army. Most Swedes, in fact, identified readily with the northern position on slavery, for it agreed with their own moral and religious values. Such sentiments and a willingness to serve earned them a measure of solidarity with the local American population. While county politics were certainly dominated for much of the settlement era by Americans, three Swedish veterans of the Civil War—Peter Schulean (Sjölin), Matthias Smith, and Olaf Eastlund—were elected as Isanti County commissioners in the late 1860s.

The election of large numbers of immigrants to public office, however, was relatively rare until the 1880s (Table 6.3). Until that time Americans held elected office in greatly disproportionate numbers. After 1880, however, Swedish officeholders began to outnumber their American counterparts for the first time, an advantage that grew year after year thereafter. By the end of the 1880s, two out of three public offices were filled by Swedish citizens. By the 1890s, they claimed three out of four elected offices, a level they more or less maintained through the post-settlement era.

Enthusiasm for American patriotic celebrations was another early measure of the acculturation process. As early as 1870, Swedish residents of the county staged their own Fourth of July celebrations, usually out-of-doors picnics on the grounds of the church. An obviously impressed newspaper editor reported a holiday throng of three hundred Swedes picnicking on a lakeshore near the Swedish Baptist Church in

Table 6.3   Elected Officials in Isanti County, 1861–1915

	Total Number of Officials[a]	American		Swedish		German	
		Annual terms (percent of total)		Annual terms (percent of total)		Annual terms (percent of total)	
1861–65	24	24	(100.0%)	0	(0.0%)	0	(0.0%)
1866–70	48	35	(72.9)	13	(27.1)	0	(0.0)
1871–75	58	44	(75.9)	14	(24.1)	0	(0.0)
1876–80	64	38	(59.4)	26	(40.6)	0	(0.0)
1881–85	73	27	(37.0)	42	(57.5)	4	(5.5)
1886–90	75	21	(28.0)	52	(69.3)	2	(2.7)
1891–95	75	16	(21.3)	57	(76.0)	2	(2.7)
1896–1900	75	26	(34.7)	47	(62.6)	2	(2.7)
1901–5	75	17	(22.7)	58	(77.3)	0	(0.0)
1906–10	75	15	(20.0)	58	(77.3)	2	(2.7)
1911–15	75	17	(22.7)	55	(73.3)	3	(4.0)
Totals	717	280	(39.0%)	422	(58.9%)	15	(2.1%)

SOURCE: Vernon E. Bergstrom and Marilyn McGriff, *Isanti County Minnesota—An Illustrated History* (Braham, Minnesota, 1985), 299–303 (Appendix D).

[a] County Commissioner, County Attorney, County Auditor, Clerk of Court, Court Commissioner, County Coroner, Judge of Probate, Registrar of Deeds, County Sheriff, County Surveyor, and County Treasurer.

Isanti township in 1878. He particularly admired the fact that they did not seem to require "getting drunk" as a necessary ingredient to enjoying the celebration.[28] The big independence celebration in Cambridge, however, was clearly a Yankee affair. Isanti's church-centered Swedish communities continued to stage their own independence day celebrations right into the 1880s and 1890s, although participation in town-centered programs gradually became more commonplace as time went on.[29]

By and large, however, the immigrant community reestablished their traditional social calendar in Isanti. They kept alive the Christian celebrations that marked seasonal stages in the agricultural cycle. In addition to celebrating the Fourth of July, people still marked the passage of midsummer, the harvest celebrations around St. Michael's Mass, yuletide, Epiphany, and the Easter holidays, just as they had done in Sweden. The short pause between winter work and spring plowing and sowing that occurred around Easter remained the principal time for weddings and social gatherings outside of the busy Christmas season. Such occasions, peopled as they were with friends and relatives dressed in traditional costumes, eating and drinking traditional holiday fare and singing or laughing in familiar dialect, were reaffirmations in America of another place and a particular past. They were proof that the process of acculturation with the host society was still a long way from complete even after as much as two decades in America.

In all of this the role of the church as a conservative force cannot be underestimated. The church struggled from the beginning with the all-important issue of preserving the language. The Cambridge Lutheran Church, like others in the area, tried to combat the erosion of Swedish language and culture through the establishment of parochial "Swede schools," an auxiliary educational system set alongside the public schools. Children were expected to attend both. The Cambridge church, which established its parochial school as early as 1864, initially ran the school for six months a year. When the public school term was increased from five months to nine months, the church school was forced to reduce its program to three months of instruction in the summer. Instruction took place in the church vestry and periodically in the various public schools scattered about the area. When in session, classes were held seven hours a day, five days a week, with students agonizing over lessons drawn from the Swedish Bible, Swedish psalmbooks, histories and grammars, and *Hemlands Sånger* (Songs of the Homeland).[30]

The community placed tremendous importance on these schools and the effect the curriculum might have on their children. A perennial item in the official minutes of church business was the problem of obtaining qualified teachers. Graduates of Swedish universities were much sought after. One O. F. Wiotti, as a matter of fact, did quite well for himself by offering his services to a number of congregations in the Isanti area. Salem Lutheran Church of the Dalbo-Karmel community considered itself fortunate to have contracted his services in 1889, paying him the handsome salary of thirty dollars a month.[31] In later years, the parochial summer schools were a major source of employment for seminary students. As the intrusion of English became more pronounced with the rise of a new, largely American-born generation in the 1890s and early 1900s, the language question and the need for Swedish education became a heated issue that would test the cultural and educational leadership provided by the church. But for the settlement era lasting into the 1880s, it was clearly not controversial. Swedish settlers believed that their children needed to learn about their cultural past and wanted to preserve the Swedish language. They quietly set about meeting those needs through the offices of the church.

In addition to its role as conservator of the Swedish language, the church played a major role in perpetuating Swedish custom and social activity. Regular church attendance on Sundays and on the many holy days and special holidays made the church the locus of most social contact. Those who gathered there found themselves in a familiar setting, participating in familiar routines. Parishioners were called to worship by the customary practice of two bell ringings, the first to call them to the worship service and the second, called the "together ringing" *(sammanringning)*, to announce the commencement of the service. Once inside the church, the sexes were separated according to tradition, the men occupying the pews on one side of the sanctuary and the women on the other. There was also a physical separation of the more important from the common; the first pew on the men's side, known as the *gubbabänken,* was reserved for the leading men of the congregation, the deacons and elected members of the council. Segregation of the sexes was relaxed only on the Sunday following a marriage, when the newlywed couple was allowed to sit together *(ståta i kyrkan)* before returning to their respective sides for subsequent services.[32]

Worship was led, at least in the Lutheran churches, by a pastor who was attired in traditional Swedish vestments. Most wore the old Swedish *prästrock,* a black frock coat worn over a white clerical collar and bands.[33] The order of service on holy days, holidays, and special occasions was the traditional Swedish High Mass *(Högmässa)*, with Holy Communion and the singing of choral hymns from the Swedish psalmbook, while ordinary Sunday services featured the more standard or *"gudstjänst"* service. The interior of the church was decorated in familiar styles and motifs. Arching Swedish inscriptions graced the altar. Special services, such as funerals, were careful duplications of services in the Swedish parishes; black cloth draped the altar for the death of an adult, white cloth for the death of a younger person.[34] On the solemn occasion of a funeral, even the bell rang out the familiar "soul-ringing" *(själaringning)*, tolling out the age of the departed as mourners entered the chapel and again as they left.[35]

From all appearances, the frequent gatherings at the church may as well have been in Rättvik or Venjan or some other Upper Dalarna parish. In the early years, church-going parishioners even donned the old Sunday dress traditional to their home parish. C. A. Hedengran, one of the early Lutheran pastors to serve the Cambridge church, on recalling the scene of his first service at the newly erected church in Cambridge, remembered how impressed he was "to see the Dal people coming to church in festive array, with clothes cut according to the ancient style, the man dressed in the inevitable leather apron, and the woman with the short waist, red stockings and large shoes."[36] People came to church services in great numbers in all seasons. The festive services at Christmas, Easter, and midsummer often drew crowds too large to fit into the church. The social calendar of the old parish had revolved around these important holidays. Keenly anticipated and thoroughly enjoyed by all, they were fundamental to the sense of togetherness and oneness that underlay the immigrant community.

The drama and pageantry of the festive *julotta* service, in particular, did much to foster such feelings. The spectacle of the whole community arriving at the candle-lit church before the break of dawn was in itself a source of lasting wonder for many, including one small boy from Venjan who grew up in Isanti County's Dalbo-Karmel community:

> I also remember the privilege of accompanying my parents to church on an early Christmas morning. It still being very dark, each person carried a torch made out of dry pine with plenty of pitch smeared on, which burned brightly. Torches could be seen in all directions for quite a distance as the folks came toward the church. Some of the people came on skis, while others rode in sleighs drawn by horses. As each one reached the church, he stuck his light in the snow to burn as long as it lasted. This was an impressive sight in those non-electric days. Inside the church was a high arch of candles which I thought very beautiful and wonderful. There was very little of beauty or enjoyment and therefore we enjoyed anything which was a little out of the ordinary. The church had no heating plant, so although we wore home-knit stockings, home-woven clothing and sheep-lined coats, we were very cold. Before entering the church, folks would wish each other *"Glad Jul."* [37]

The immigrant church gave its parishioners color, joy, and the familiar in what was otherwise an isolated and often drab existence in the New World. It also provided a comfortable framework within which people could feel a sense of social belonging.

The immigrant church went further. It governed much in the lives of its members, as the state church had in Sweden. For the most part, its efforts followed well-established models. The Cambridge church divided its congregation administratively into culturally and socially mean-ingful territorial subdivisions (rotes), as we have seen. The practice was not isolated; most Augustana churches of any size did this. Nor was it without social purpose. The Cambridge Lutheran rotes were laid out to distinguish elements hailing from the respective *fjärding* districts of the mother parish, as well as to distinguish those who hailed from origins other than Rättvik. In Clay County's Dalesburg settlement, where no single group of emigrants dominated the Dalesburg Lutheran Church congregation, the internal territorial organization of the parish recog-nized neighborhood clusters with particularly distinctive origins in Swe-den (See Figure 5.14 on page 188).[38] The administrative organization of both the Dalesburg and the Cambridge Lutheran churches were official acknowledgments of a community social organization that was older than the communities themselves. Through its official acts, the immigrant church did much to preserve whatever social distinctions lay between these bounded areas.

The immigrant church also presided over an enduringly selective and territorial pattern of marriage, much as its counterpart had done in Sweden. In the old parish of Rättvik, the boundaries of the *fjärding* districts were remarkably impervious social barriers, across which few intervillage marriages took place. At a more intimate scale, local kinship networks seem to have played key roles in encouraging repeated marriage alliances within circumscribed social groupings. The church, which set administrative boundaries and sanctioned marriages, accepted and perhaps indirectly perpetuated these established patterns and practices. In Isanti, a strikingly similar set of marriage fields was quickly established within the first decade of settlement and persisted through the remainder of the nineteenth century.

While source materials make marriage patterns more difficult to trace in America than in Sweden, samples from church and county records reveal a remarkable acceptance of transplanted social boundaries.[39] In a sample of sixty-six marriages from the period 1871–94 that involved at least one partner from Rättvik, an overwhelming majority (83.3 percent) united couples in which both partners were members of the Cambridge church.[40] In 77.3 percent of these marriages, both partners were from Rättvik, and in 65.2 percent both partners resided in the same church rote. The social pull of the subcommunity was most notable in the case of the Isanti rote (Athens community), which was physically separated from the others and strongly dominated by people from Rättvik's Gärdsjö *fjärding*.

Transplanted kinship networks were undoubtedly a major force operating here. But the old kinship networks were necessarily redefined in America. Only fragments of the old kinship networks were present in the new American settlements. While familiar marriage alliance patterns were still possible, the high level of selectivity so common in Rättvik had to be relaxed somewhat to include households of other networks settled in the same area. The best evidence of this may be seen once again in the Isanti rote, where a total of twenty-three households hailing from Gärdsjö *fjärding* established themselves as the core of a well-defined community during the early years of settlement. In Sweden, these households belonged to four of the more central kinship cells of Rättvik's old Gärdsjö community, cells that had long-established, highly endogamous marriage patterns. Most of these immigrant households were headed by middle-aged adults with large, young families that included many Swedish-born children. The marriage behavior of this cohort of Swedish-born children is an interesting test of the strength of old patterns among the first generation to grow up in the new American settlements (Figure 6.2).

The Swedish-born children of these twenty-three Gärdsjö households grew up during the 1870s and 1880s. Most of them reached marriageable age well before the mid-1890s. Twenty-five youths, male and female, from these households married beteen 1871 and 1894. Twenty-one of them married someone from another Gärdsjö household. Three of the twenty-one had to look outside the Athens community to the western rote to locate potential spouses from their home district. The remaining four selected marriage partners from within the Isanti rote-Athens community, two who were born in other parts of Rättvik parish, one born in Orsa parish, and one from another part of Sweden.

The high level of endogamous marriage behavior displayed by these Gärdsjö-born children suggests that an uncommonly strong sense of social identification based on local origins was present throughout the settlement period. The power of individual kinship cells to influence marriage behavior, however, was diluted; most of these marriages crossed kinship cell lines. In other words, the old cells were superseded by the larger social network of the new community, just as the social network of the community core in the old Gärdsjö community in Sweden seems ultimately to have been more meaningful than the four cells of which it was composed. The community in America was by necessity somewhat larger; it admitted some to the inner circle whom the home networks would have excluded, but a minimum set of associational requirements was still necessary—if not association with the immediate kinship group, then at least association with allied groups or, at worst, origins in the same parish or a neighboring parish.

Existing social networks remained highly selective as long as the generation that emigrated and settled together retained control of their immediate households and the institutions they created. During the first decades, when this was certainly the case, it is evident that kinship groups exercised considerable social control. Not only was the pattern of marriage highly endogamous, reflecting a desire to maintain a finite boundary separating those who belonged from those who did not, society was also well-ordered from within. Those who were leaders and had status in the community, even before the migrations, maintained their position while others continued as followers. Perhaps nowhere was this

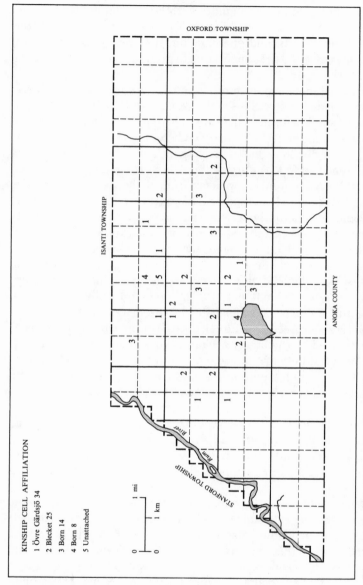

Figure 6.2 Households from the "Core" Kinship Cells of the Gärdsjö Villages in Athens Township, ca. 1885

234

more evident than in the administration of the community's central institution, the church.

Church leadership, as reflected in the election of church officials, was drawn heavily from household heads who arrived in the first wave of the 1860s and who led substantial chain migrations of kin and relatives into the community. In nearly all cases, these people had been respected leaders in their communities prior to emigration. The first three trustees of the Cambridge church to be elected by the immigrants from Rättvik were all people of well-above-average means in the old community. All three had been in direct control of productive farms before emigrating to America.[41] Two had served as local officials in the old community. All three had been among the important first contingent of emigrants to arrive in Isanti County during the summer of 1866. The records show that these individuals, along with others of similar status, were elected again and again to positions of responsibility in the church administration throughout the 1870s and 1880s. Offices of responsibility and leadership were a revolving door; the same names appeared over and over as the cycle of three-year terms for church officials at the Cambridge church moved forward.

The perpetuation of status or position, especially when it derives from another place or seems unearned, is not commonly associated with the American frontier. The notion seems to contradict Turner's characterization of the frontier as the crucible of democracy, a place where all have equal opportunity. Yet during the early decades in Isanti County, Turner's image fit only loosely. While most settlers started with similar homestead acreages and relatively meagre resources, the socioeconomic structure that quickly emerged reflected that which they had known before the emigration. As we have seen, one of the primary benefits of emigration for many well-placed Rättvik households was the chance to preserve the status quo in a time of change and uncertainty. The successful transplantation of the existing social order to the new world depended not only on the transfer of a relatively intact segment of society to a new place, but also on the perpetuation of the established social and economic structure once resettlement had been accomplished.

A phenomenon such as this can never be measured easily. Aside from elected office, the historical record leaves little information about the relative social status of individuals. But economic position, for which data do exist, is often directly related to social position. This was certainly true of Rättvik society, which clearly associated leadership with a degree of wealth, and was probably true of immigrant society in Isanti once the new community began to overcome the difficulties of frontier conditions. If that may be assumed, then one can get some notion of an immigrant's social position in Isanti County by comparing his or her pre-migration economic status with his or her later economic status in Isanti. Although the assumptions and data limitations involved make such an analysis less than conclusive, there is a positive correlation between pre-migration and post-migration economic status. Time in America is a much stronger indicator of accumulated wealth in America. Nonetheless, the fact that economic position in Sweden did have some impact is important.[42] It means that the past was not stripped away entirely, nor were socioeconomic differences completely leveled by frontier conditions.

One might conclude that the old order was transplanted to a certain extent. A farmer's position in the American community was determined largely by how long he had worked a farm in the area, but his background also played a not inconsequential role. Given the fact that the first to arrive from the old parish were often the wealthier and more influential and that their early arrival allowed them more time to accumulate wealth than those who followed, it is not surprising that the old order seems to have been transplanted to the new community and perpetuated, however unconsciously, through the early decades of the new life in America.

In America's Dalarna

One of the most recurrent themes in the immigrant letters sent home from Isanti County during the settlement era was the comfort that settlers in a raw, unfamiliar environment found in the number of relatives and neighbors living nearby and the promise of more to come. This was expected to reassure and impress those who remained at home at least as much as the breathless descriptions of the new land's potential bounty or the ease with which one could improve one's lot in America, the land of opportunity. Few wrote home without also extending greetings from some neighbor or relative living nearby. Especially revealing are accounts of festive occasions when one could scarcely tell whether the event took place in America or in the old parish.

Chain migration to America was fueled by sentiments such as these and, where conditions permitted, often resulted in the wholesale transplantation of a society and culture. By the end of the settlement era, Minnesota's Isanti County had clearly become one of these places. Peo-

Plate 6.2 "America letter" photo. This photograph accompanied a letter sent home by Olof Bergman, who was known in his home village of Osmundsberg as Marits Olof Samuelsson. The photo is carefully posed to give the best impression. It shows Olof in his potato field with his harvest, his horses and wagon, and his wife (Sjöns Lisbet), who is proudly wearing new store-bought clothing and hat. It was taken around 1890 on Bergman's farm in Cambridge township. (Courtesy of the Marits Anna Olsson family of Boda, the Cambridge Lutheran Church archive, and Dalarnas Museum)

ple began to refer to the district as "America's Dalarna" and to associate it with the many peculiar traits of the Dalarna peasantry.[43] At a more intimate scale, particular settlement districts across the county became associated with particular parishes or even neighborhood kinship circles. The major synodal organizations of the Swedish Lutheran and the Swedish Baptist churches in America quickly came to recognize the significance of regional or local culture groups in the formation of congregations. In their continual efforts to organize and promote their far-flung network of member congregations, these umbrella organizations frequently published yearbooks containing essential information about individual congregations, such as founding date, membership, buildings, and property. Most descriptions also included some indication of the Swedish origins of the parishioners, often cryptically noting that "most are from Dalarna, especially from Rättvik," "nearly all are from the Dalarna parish of Orsa," "mostly from Hälsingland," and so on.[44]

A visitor to the Isanti settlements during the early decades could not help but see evidence of a transplantation all about. Nearly everyone for miles in every direction was Swedish. Most could direct a visitor's attention to any number of homesteads nearby where in-laws, brothers and sisters, or aunts and uncles lived. Somewhere in the vicinity was a clapboard-sided church or meeting house that stood as a central symbol of the social web that was spread across the landscape. On Sunday mornings or other festive occasions, a visitor would find the building filled with the faithful, its interior laid out and decorated in a style reminiscent of a distant mother church, the congregation in its pews dressed in traditional costume and singing the old hymns and psalms, the entire proceedings sternly viewed from the *gubbebänken* by the elected elders and trustees. Outside, after services were over, there was the buzz and chatter of numerous voices engaged in excited intercourse over the news of the day, while young men and farmhands readied horses, wagons, and carts for the ride home. The scene, the sounds, could all be easily transported back to a home parish in Sweden.

Elsewhere, one would have seen other unmistakable material signs: homesteads laid out in the traditional manner, logs joined with dovetailed corners and notched to prevent shifting, in the method employed for generations.[45] In sheds and dwellings one would find tools and utensils that had been painstakingly transported in homemade chests from Sweden to America. Men worked with a variety of hand tools—axes, wooden planes, saws, chisels—that had been prized possessions in their old home and were too valuable to leave behind. Men who had been skilled carpenters and craftsmen in Sweden produced utensils and furniture of Swedish design in America. Spinning wheels, wool cards, and a host of other common utensils inside the home were unmistakably Swedish, either brought over or crafted from memory in America. Distinctive Dalarna sledges carried the wintertime hauling, while people moved about on skis.

Nor had the annual cycle of work and celebration changed signifi-

Plate 6.3 Dalecarlian woman on skis in Isanti County. Skis were one aspect of traditional material culture that remained useful in the New World. (Courtesy of Isanti County Historical Society, date unknown)

cantly. As in Rättvik, the economy and fabric of life were still organized around multifarious activities. People depended on a combination of seasonal work, either in the forests or on the railroads, crafts, cultivation of grain and garden crops, and animal husbandry to provide subsistence. Spring was still the busiest season. Although spring often arrived somewhat sooner in Minnesota, it was filled with the traditional tasks of spreading manure, harrowing fields, sowing grains, planting potatoes and garden vegetables, and reconditioning livestock after a long winter of inactivity in the barn. Even though no formal *fäbod* system was ever established in Isanti, livestock were taken out and grazed in nearby meadows in the spring and early summer.[46] After midsummer celebrations came haying and fencing, followed by grain harvesting in August and threshing, slaughter, and plowing in the autumn months.

At least during the settlement years, the traditional sexual division of labor prevailed. Women and children continued to take primary responsibility for livestock, traditional home handicrafts, berry picking, tending the garden patch, assisting with the harvest and threshing, and running the domestic household. Men did most of the heavy field work, manipulating plow, harrow, and the team of oxen or horses. They maintained tools, buildings, and fences and were often away from home in the wintertime to work in the forest. In Isanti County, the first crews began moving off to the pineries around middle or late October. Logging camps generally remained in operation until sometime in late February or early March, while floating the logs to mills could last as late as May. In the later settlement years, many men were away during the summer breaking new land on the western prairies of Minnesota or in the East River counties of Dakota Territory.

Yet, as we have seen, much had changed as the immigrants were forced to deal with the peculiar circumstances of their new surroundings. However culturally homogeneous and socially isolated the new Swedish communities may have been, their inhabitants could not escape the fact that they were new arrivals in an established society and economy. The Yankee minority in Isanti County wielded tremendous power and influence through their ability to sell land, extend credit, market the farm produce of others, and provide necessary goods. In order to survive, immigrants had to learn the Yankee's language and pay close attention to his economy and its innovations. Many were infatuated with the glamor and progressiveness of Yankee life and were hardly reluctant to adopt as much of it as they could. The Swedish immigrants to Isanti County quickly learned to grow American wheat, to purchase the new American agricultural machinery, to covet American goods, and to mimic aspects of American culture.

Thus, along with the unmistakable signs of transplantation that a visitor to Isanti County may have noted in the 1870s and 1880s, there were also signs of adaptation. While the layout of individual dwellings may have conformed to tradition, the layout of the farmstead bore little resemblance to the farmsteads of Upper Dalarna. In the open American land system, there was no longer any need to confine out-buildings to the cramped street patterns of the village.[47] Fields were enclosed and fenced, in contrast to the open fields and parcels of the old parish. Fencing was newly important (even required by American law) because livestock were present throughout the growing season, and fences were adapted to American styles. Alongside the hand tools from Sweden stood an array of essential American tools and implements: a new steel plow with a share that could be removed for sharpening; a modern "self-binder" or thresher. Quite probably the log cabin dwelling was equipped with an American back door and a cast-iron stove for heating and cooking, though there was also a Swedish-style summer kitchen attached to the house or standing nearby.[48] If the immigrant was prosperous enough, the original house could well have been enlarged with additions and porches and covered with precut wooden siding by the 1880s.

Material culture is only a reflection of things that run far deeper. It can be misleading if it magnifies the unimportant or fails to explain what makes certain artifacts significant. Material culture does not, in itself, provide incontrovertible evidence of what directions society may be taking. However, weighed with information about institutions, marriage preferences, leadership, and local economy, it can underline what has already been learned. The story that emerges here, from all kinds of evidence, tells us that by the 1880s Isanti County contained a number of distinct Swedish communities in which cultural, social, and economic patterns from parent communities in Sweden had been transplanted and perpetuated to a significant degree. It is also clear that the transplantation was never complete. In part, this was because it was never overtly planned, even though the participants may have been able to see what was going on and may have independently encouraged the process. In part, it was because the differences between Sweden and America were simply too great to allow the complete transplantation of a society with all its trappings.

The immigrant society that emerged by the late 1880s essentially occupied two worlds. On the one hand, the Swedish settlers belonged to a social community that diverged little from what they had known before emigrating to America. It revolved around the same institutions, the same kinship relationships, similar patterns of wealth and status and work roles, and was bound by common culture and language. It was a world that valued the past, a world in which one knew immediately what to do and what was expected. At the same time, the members of these tightly knit communities also belonged to a much larger economic community that was radically different from anything they had known before. This was the world of business and markets, a world of new opportunity, new inventions, new ways of doing things. It was dominated by the English-speaking host culture and was always somewhat out of reach for the first-generation immigrant, but was nonetheless a most attractive world that beckoned continuously.

Although most immigrants never gave it serious thought, the critical point in their lives was probably the place where these two worlds intersected, the place where the predictability of one world conflicted with the choices of the other. The location of this critical and shifting interface undoubtedly varied for individuals as well as for whole communities, but its movement towards one world inevitably weakened the hold of the other over the individual or the group. It is extremely difficult to judge exactly where the interface stood for the Swedish residents of Isanti County at the close of the settlement period. It is probably safe to say that, for most, the social community still dominated their lives, their relationships with one another, and the soil from which they made their living. The encroachment of the other world, however, was well under way and was destined to make significant headway in the years after 1890, which mark the onset of the post-settlement era and the rise of a new generation.

For the moment, however, the mood of the times is perhaps best summed up in a verse submitted to the Isanti County Press in 1875 by a Swedish farmer in the Stanchfield community. The verse expresses a healthy pride of accomplishment, a reverence for family and community, and a good-natured enthusiasm for the many things offered by the bustling Yankee town of Cambridge. In rough and unrhymed English translation it goes something like this:

> For quite some time now, here up in the North,
> there have been but a few poor farmers' cabins, amidst miles of
>   endless forest.
> But now great farms have begun to spring up one by one from the
>   earth,
> complete with new large houses—change is at full gallop.
>
> Now fine roads lead hither and yon, through forest and over
>   prairie, wherever one might choose to go.
> So many roads are of course necessary, never mind the cost,
> for that is the promise of the future, here in '75.
>
> For quite some time now, most farmers possessed but one poor
>   cow,
> but now there they stand in droves, tethered out in the barn.
> And out there too are a pair of fine horses, snorting in their stalls;
> Conditions here are the best I've seen, anywhere I've been.
>
> Oh, see the farmer's lovely house, standing in its garden park.
> There he lives in royal splendor, just like a king.
> And better times are coming for those who follow his example.
> Some day they too will be as great as they now are small.
>
> Neither is there strife nor want along religion's paths.
> Here one encounters churches, schools and clergy everywhere
>   about.
> How could one expect much more, after so short time?
> Could one ever find a more congenial atmosphere anywhere in
>   creation?
>
> And look at Cambridge town, which so newly has sprung up.

Look at the long lines of stores—how enticing they are.
Hotels, shops and court house, and there an apothecary,
Also residences and stables, so many I cannot list them all.

The saloons are something close to evil, they really don't belong.
But they are by chance the first stop for most that visit town.
But I shall pass them by today, and to finish off my verse,
I'll take out instead a new subscription to the "Isanti County
　　Press."[49]

7

The Maturation of Community

Land and Family in the Post-Settlement Period, 1890–1915

In his sweeping interpretation of late nineteenth- and early twentieth-century American social change, Robert Wiebe describes the breakdown of an American society of "island communities." He sees America in the late nineteenth century as a society without a core, a nation whose institutions were still oriented toward a small community life managed by the customs of a closed and personal society. The inevitable erosion of the autonomy of these communities, which may have begun as early as the 1870s, depended largely on the undermining of two conditions that were basic to the small community: its capacity to manage the lives of its members, and the illusion that the community actually had such powers.[1] Wiebe's interpretation was not aimed directly at the small immigrant communities of the agrarian Upper Middle West; he in fact was thinking more of the welter of communities found within America's towns and cities. Nonetheless, his analysis has real relevance as a starting point to understand what happened to the transplanted, inward-looking social islands of the American heartland. As the outside world impinged more and more on the comfortable order of the immigrant community, the community struggled in its effort to understand the changing conditions of its existence in terms of its own recent American experience and the pervasive trans-Atlantic antecedents of that experience. As Wiebe also observes, an ultimate failure, or at least a seminal redefinition of what the community was, emerged from its effort "to master an impersonal world through the customs of a personal society."[2]

That redefinition of community, more than anything else, describes the American outcome of the trans-Atlantic experience. It is not so much that the social and cultural side of the immigrants' dichotomous world was overwhelmed and lost to the divergent world of their surroundings. Group identity and the territorial base upon which it seemed to depend survived the changes of the post-settlement period. But there was a gradual shifting or redefinition of what the territorial community represented.[3] Although a trans-Atlantic interchange of people and ideas between the mother parish in Sweden and the daughter communities in America continued throughout the period, a thorough and complete identification with the past in another place slowly eroded and was replaced by something more symbolic, such as the observance of special celebrations or the struggle to preserve the language. The symbolic was important. It contributed mightily to the continued cohesion of the group. But primary identification shifted to an association with a new and rapidly developing local milieu. People increasingly became more aware of themselves as belonging to a "Dalbo" or "Maple Ridge" or "Athens" community, as having new and modern values based on a perception of American middle class life, and as being only vaguely aware of (although certainly not totally divorced from) their origins.

Economic Change in the Post-Settlement Period

As the immigrants took to the land, they encountered much that was unfamiliar. Some new circumstances could be handled easily with time-honored practices and techniques, while others demanded adaptations and innovations of considerable magnitude. The experience of the settlement period, as a consequence, was mixed. Subsistence as a farmer in America required the same skills, the same seasonal round, the same good fortune that had always been necessary. The greatest difference was perhaps the seemingly unlimited potential of the new land, which was keenly felt but could not be immediately realized during those early years. Progress was slow. Grubbing and breaking land dragged on for years and decades. Achievement was measured in the slow pace of improvements on the land. The region in which they settled was isolated from outside markets because of poor communications. Although wheat was produced in modest quantities as a cash crop and laboriously hauled along forest tracks to railroad towns in neighboring counties, most economic activity was directed towards local subsistence. These conditions gradually improved, but early economic life was more or less uniformly devoted to proving up the homestead, clearing additional land, and providing for the basics of life.

The post-settlement period, which began in the late 1880s and extended to World War I, was a period of profound change in economic life. Perhaps foremost among many changes was the passing of the frontier. In the 1880s and 1890s, the availability of unclaimed land declined drastically, closing off the opportunity for new settlement or the expansion of existing farm units without infringing on the property of others (compare Figures 7.1 and 7.2). During the settlement era, as many as half of the existing farms at any given time had been newly established within the previous five years. By 1890 the proportion had fallen to roughly one in six; by 1900 it had stabilized at around one in twenty. The nine-township study area as a whole reached a maximum of 1,246 farm households in 1905. The number gradually declined after 1905, as farm liquidations rose steadily in the first decade of the new century. There was also a significant rise in farm tenancy. Almost one out of every ten farms in 1900 was worked by a cash or share tenant, whereas nearly all farms in 1880 were worked by their owners. Good agricultural land became scarce and increasingly dear as the post-settlement era wore on.

This was also a time when the pace of economic activity quickened. The wheat frontier had passed this part of Minnesota. So, too, had the regular opportunity to earn supplemental income from seasonal work in nearby logging camps. Farmers were forced to clear additional land and diversify their operations in order to make a living. Agricultural census statistics for Isanti County indicate little change in the size of farms during the post-settlement period, but after 1890 the percentage of farm acreage that was improved climbs dramatically (Table 7.1). Farmers were grubbing and breaking land with renewed enthusiasm. The value of land and buildings also rose sharply after 1890. The average Isanti farm was worth twice as much in 1910 as it was in 1880.

New investment went into both grain crops and livestock as farmers experimented with a variety of mixed crop and livestock regimes. A general rise in the importance and value of livestock over the period is reflected in the declining proportion of improved land devoted to grain crops. Dairy cattle, in particular, gained importance around the turn of the century with the introduction of creameries. The overwhelming dominance of wheat as a cash crop in the early 1880s withers to almost nothing by 1890. In 1880, two-thirds of all crop land was devoted to wheat. By 1890, its proportion had dropped to just over one-tenth, although wheat did stage something of a comeback by the turn of the

Table 7.1   Agricultural Change in Isanti County, 1880–1910

	1880 (N = 868)	1890 (N = 1341)	1900 (N = 2044)	1910 (N = 1854)
Average farm acreage	108.2	109.5	108.4	115.0
Average acreage improved	30.0	28.6	41.9	52.4
Percent acreage improved	27.7%	26.1%	38.7%	45.6%
Value of lands and improvements	$884	$1020	$1728	n.a.[a]
Value of livestock	$219	$208	$288	n.a.[a]
Percent improved land in grain	54.9%	51.5%	42.6%	38.6%
Percent grain acreage:				
Wheat	66.7%	11.3%	36.6%	24.9%
Oats	13.4%	41.6%	31.9%	40.6%
Corn	14.5%	29.5%	16.1%	20.1%
Rye	5.0%	16.1%	13.6%	12.3%
Other grains (buckwheat, barley)	0.4%	1.5%	1.8%	2.1%

SOURCES: U.S. Agricultural Censuses, 1880, 1890, 1900, 1910.
[a] Not available due to changes in accounting between 1900 and 1910 agricultural censuses.

century. Farmers replaced their wheat crops with a combination of corn, rye, and oats. The spectacular rise of the latter coincided with an increased reliance on animal husbandry.

Farmers faced rising costs throughout the 1890s, as subsistence-oriented frontier homesteads were gradually transformed into market-oriented farm operations. The relatively good times of the 1880s brought a flurry of investment in land and machinery, which continued into the 1890s despite less favorable credit and market conditions. Indebtedness rose alongside. County land records reveal an avalanche of repeated mortgages on farm property, beginning in the late 1880s, which in turn prompted the first signs of agrarian unrest in the form of complaints about high interest charges. Isanti-area farmers had an active interest in the programs and grievances of the Farmer's Alliance around 1890 and persistently expressed resentment over the tyranny of uncontrollable market forces.[4] Even though farm values and productivity were on the rise, Isanti County lagged considerably behind other midwestern agricultural regions that were settled around the same time. Turn-of-the-century farm values in Clay County, for example, were nearly four times those in Isanti County.[5] The decision to settle the sandy, relatively infertile woodland soils of Isanti County instead of the richer prairie soils available at the same time in western Minnesota and the Dakotas had its cost.

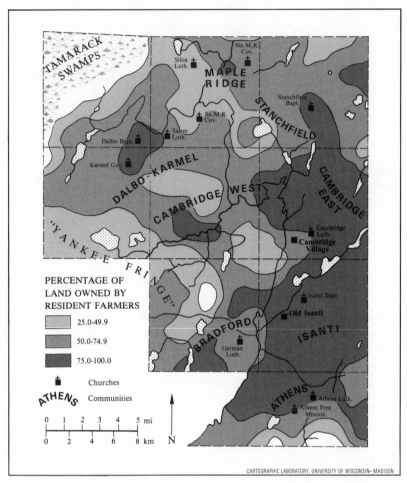

Figure 7.1 Intensity of Land Holdings and the Swedish Communities of the Isanti
Study Area, 1890

In the quest for something to replace wheat as a cash crop, farmers
tried almost everything, from ginseng to sugar cane. Most farms eventually settled on a mixture of small grains; but the ultimate winner in the
struggle to find a sound base for the local farm economy was the potato.
Ideally suited to the often droughty soils of the sand plain, potatoes
began to assume the role of a staple crop in the late 1880s. Since potatoes
were heavy and difficult to transport and the market for them was
something less than reliable, the move to potatoes was slow until around
1890, when someone hit upon the idea of producing starch from them.

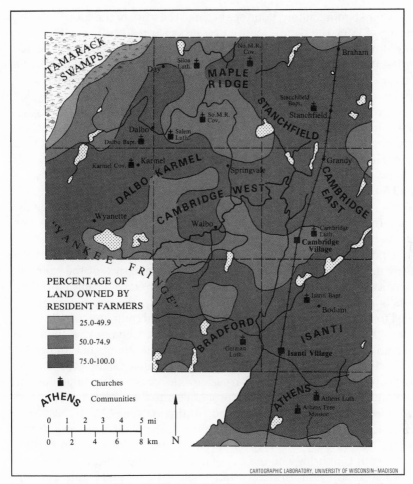

Figure 7.2 Intensity of Land Holdings and the Swedish Communities of the Isanti Study Area, 1905

The idea was actually a by-product of earlier attempts to market the potato harvest. Some Isanti area farmers had been hauling potatoes a considerable distance to a starch factory in neighboring Anoka County for some time, but they had been realizing only a small return for their efforts.[6] The obvious lesson was that if production facilities could be locally owned and operated, farmers could better control their profits. A starch factory was operating in the village of Cambridge by 1893, the product of a cooperative venture first conceived in the spring of 1890.

Almost immediately, potatoes became the wave of the future. By the spring of 1893, the Isanti County Press was earnestly offering advice to local farmers, recommending that they get in on the "profits" to be had in potatoes.[7] The response was a prodigious production that kept the factory in constant operation. Contemporary observers reported that so many wagonloads were brought in to the factory from the countryside at harvest time, the wagon queues stretched for blocks. Some townspeople even went out to offer refreshments to tired farmers waiting by their wagons in the early autumn heat.[8] By the turn of the century, additional factories were being built at Isanti, Stanchfield, and Dalbo. Isanti County was producing enormous quantities of potatoes. The better were sold for bulk shipment or for seed, while culled potatoes were consigned to the starch factories. Local boosters began to bill their district as the "potato capital of the world" and the starch factories were widely seen as "saviors" of the local farm economy.[9]

Underlying the building of starch factories and the development of a thriving regional market was the long-awaited arrival of the railroad. Bypassed in the 1870s, when the major line between St. Paul and Duluth was built through neighboring Chisago County, the Isanti area struggled for nearly three decades to entice a railroad company to build a line through the district. Speculation about various schemes was almost an annual event from the mid-1870s on, with the merchants of Cambridge, who suffered most from the lack of a railroad line, leading the charge. Early promotors despaired of arousing the local Swedish population to the cause when even translating proposals into Swedish did not stir support from the independent-minded rural populace.[10] At last, James J. Hill's Eastern Minnesota Railway built a branch line, popularly known as the "Bee Line," through Cambridge in 1899. Not only did the line finally put Cambridge on the map, but it led to the quick rise of several new market towns at Braham, Stanchfield, Grandy, and Isanti. The only real loser was the old crossroads settlement of Isanti, which was bypassed by the railroad and replaced by a new town bearing the same name a couple of miles away. The combination of potatoes and a railroad line touched off a wave of prosperity and a rapid expansion of the local service and consumer economy.

Until the 1890s, Cambridge was the only central place of any importance in the entire county. It served the needs of the county through a relatively small commercial establishment. The lack of a railroad link kept the business community small. Much potential business was lost to railroad and river towns in neighboring counties. Cambridge business in the 1880s and 1890s was largely dominated by Yankee businessmen who had established themselves early, although a number of important

Plate 7.1 Potato harvest in Isanti County. Potatoes, which did well in Isanti's sandy soils, had become the major cash crop by the 1890s. Pictured are the Johan Gustaf Krafve family of Maple Ridge township. Note the scrub oak beyond the field. (Courtesy of Isanti County Historical Society, 1890s)

establishments were owned and operated by enterprising Swedes, the best example of which was the county's largest general mercantile store, operated by two Swedes from Rättvik, Hans J. Gouldberg and D. O. Anderson. Although as many adult Swedish males resided in the town in 1880 as adult male Yankees, the Yankees were more likely to operate a business establishment. The Swedes were more likely to hold a service job, such as clerk; an equal number were artisans, such as carpenters, masons, or painters (Table 7.2). As late as the 1890s, industry in Cambridge was confined to a brickyard, a sawmill, and a flour mill, while mainstreet consisted of two or three general merchandise dealers, a pair of hotels, an implements dealer, a doctor, and the offices of two or three rather entrepreneurial attorneys who specialized in real estate and finance on the side.

Within less than a year of the railroad's arrival, however, the mainstreet business community mushroomed, boasting nearly four times the number of establishments as a decade earlier, not to mention a half

Table 7.2 Ethnic Representation in Occupational Groups, Village of Cambridge, 1880 and 1905

| | ADULT MALES | | | | | |
| | 1880 | | | 1905 | | |
Occupation	Swedes	Yankees	Others	Swedes	Yankees	Others
Business proprietors	4 (26.7%)	9 (60.0%)	2 (13.3%)	30 (50.8%)	25 (42.4%)	4 (6.8%)
Artisans	4 (100)	0 (—)	0 (—)	41 (87.2)	2 (4.3)	4 (8.5)
Service	7 (77.8)	2 (22.2)	0 (—)	43 (69.4)	17 (27.4)	2 (3.2)
Laborers	2 (22.2)	6 (66.7)	1 (11.1)	37 (92.5)	3 (7.5)	0 (—)
Total	17 (45.9%)	17 (45.9%)	3 (8.2%)	151 (72.6%)	47 (22.6%)	10 (4.8%)

| | ADULT FEMALES | | | | | |
| | 1880 | | | 1905 | | |
	Swedes	Yankees	Others	Swedes	Yankees	Others
Housewives	7 (41.2%)	8 (47.1%)	2 (11.8%)	99 (79.9%)	18 (14.5%)	7 (5.6%)
Domestics	2 (100)	0 (—)	0 (—)	32 (91.4)	0 (—)	3 (8.6)
Service	0 (—)	1 (100)	0 (—)	24 (85.7)	3 (10.7)	1 (3.6)
Total	9 (45.0%)	9 (45.0%)	2 (10.0%)	155 (82.9%)	21 (11.2%)	11 (5.9%)
Total adult population	26 (45.6%)	26 (45.6%)	5 (8.8%)	306 (77.5%)	68 (17.2%)	21 (5.3%)

SOURCES: Manuscripts of the U.S. Population Census, 1880, and manuscripts of the Minnesota State Population Census, 1905.

dozen new enterprises located along the railroad tracks. Cambridge now had a railroad district, replete with lumberyards, granaries, milling company, creamery, and potato warehouses. Judging from the proclamations of the local press, civic pride and local boosterism knew no bounds. As part of a general turn-of-the-century promotional campaign, the Isanti County Press proudly published a "bird's-eye" view of the downtown business district, featuring each of the major commercial and industrial establishments of the time and the names of their proprietors.[11] The message was clear: Cambridge was a town on the move. It was also rapidly "modernizing." The business district was electrified in 1893. The local press saw fit to comment that not only were the stores electrified but they had cash registers, too![12] Telephone service was introduced in 1900. Five years later, Cambridge boasted a telephone

Plate 7.2 Main Street Cambridge, ca. 1900. With the arrival of the railroad in 1899, the old "Yankee town" of Cambridge became the major commercial center of Isanti County. The Merchant Hotel at right claimed to be the largest between Minneapolis and Duluth. Main Street was just wide enough for team-drawn wagons to turn around. (Courtesy of Isanti County Historical Society)

exchange staffed by no fewer than eight operators. City water, the ulti-mate urban amenity, was added about the same time.

The population of the town had also grown. In 1880, it held only 136 inhabitants. By 1905, Cambridge claimed 855 residents. The majority of the expanded population was comprised of Swedes who had come in from the countryside to live in town. Swedish men now outnumbered Yankee men by more than three to one. Many were transient, working as laborers and living in boarding houses. But many others had moved to take their rightful place in the business community, which was no longer dominated by old American families. Half of all business proprietors were now of Swedish stock. In addition, a large number of young Swedes and the Isanti-born offspring of Swedish settlers had moved into town to take up a broad range of service jobs and to provide artisanal skills. The booming town of 1905 supported twenty-three individuals who listed "carpenter" as their occupation in the state census of that year. Many were quite young, but were in the company of wives and children, an indication that land was no longer the only means of achiev-ing economic responsibility. There were also many young single men and women. Among adult females residing in Cambridge, it was far more likely that a Yankee woman would be a housewife and mother than a Swedish woman, which indicates that the American population was established and stable, while many of the Swedes were young people looking for work. Nonetheless, it is clear that Cambridge was fast achieving a degree of cultural integration. The old social and economic gulf between the Yankee town and the Swedish countryside no longer seemed as wide and forbidding as it had in the past. Everyone shared in the many new opportunities offered by the rapid development of Isanti County's major commercial and administrative center.[13]

Other towns along the new rail line developed smaller but equally prosperous mainstreets and contributed to the general growth of town life in the Isanti area. Isanti emerged as the county's second town, following its move from the original site to the railroad line. Braham, located just northeast of the study area in the uppermost corner of the county, became the third. Stanchfield, which had been a small cross-roads service center before the railroad, was also moved to a more advantageous site along the tracks, while further south a small cluster of businesses known as Grandy was established coincidentally with the coming of the railroad in 1899. Each of these railroad trade centers was built around a largely Swedish owned and operated business community. They were probably more socially integrated with their hinterlands than Cambridge, which was still the county seat and the original site of Yankee political and commercial dominance in the county. Most long-distance hauling of produce to Yankee-dominated markets outside the county, such as Princeton, Anoka, and Harris, ceased around the turn of the century, and was replaced by a local system of market towns with stronger ties to the rural communities that surrounded them.

Meanwhile, out in the countryside, most rural communities came to possess some sort of small crossroads service center, typically comprised of a combination post office and general store and a blacksmith shop. The Rättvik-dominated Western rote of the Cambridge Lutheran parish, for example, became centered on the Springvale township crossroads of Walbo, which boasted a post office (founded 1892), a bank, a school, and a ferry across the Rum River. Many centers boasted a cooperative creamery. Dalbo had a bank.[14] The crossroads center, small though it was, added something new to the rural community. Where the church had been the only institutional focus or gathering place, most immigrants could now look to a more secular central place as well. The local store and post office, the school, and the town hall were alternative places where people could congregate and associate with their neighbors. The small crossroads center became the site of civic and recreational activities not directly associated with the church. Some of these places were the site of lodge and fraternal association meetings. Grange Halls were common in the 1880s, followed by lodges of the International Order of Good Templars. A number of centers sponsored baseball teams around the turn of the century. While none of this activity represented a real breakdown in the local social order, it indicated a tenuous broadening of horizons within the community.

Demographic Change: The Life Cycle of Community

The changes of the post-settlement period involved more than just improved accessibility and economic prosperity. There were also important demographic changes, which in turn were tied to the constant need to establish a favorable balance between land and family. Most important of these demographic changes was the aging of the immigrant generation. The generation that had gathered together families and friends in Sweden and transported them to a new land, where they could live in communities that transplanted the pre-migration past, was a generation that could not hold forth indefinitely. Like all generations, they were inevitably destined to age and to give way to a new generation—a cohort of young people who were either born in America or who had lived most of their lives in America. The new generation of Isanti's Rum River valley in the 1890s was a generation whose rememberance of the past and vision of the future were strongly influenced by their elders' memories and visions. It was also a generation that would begin to redefine the bounds of its existence.

Demographic historians have noted that most American frontier communities had certain demographic features in common, the most seminal being a surplus of young people just starting out. More specifically, the prominent features of American frontier populations seem to have been an excess of young adults in their twenties and thirties, an imbalance between the sexes favoring men, and an abundance of new families and households, usually with just a few children. These characteristics were the simple product of the well-known propensity for individuals to migrate at crucial stages in the life cycle. Frontier zones naturally attracted those who were young and energetic, those who could not hope to find the means to support an independent existence in long-established areas. Frontier societies, in particular, were associated with a young and highly mobile age group that was either entering or in the early stages of family and new household formations.[15]

These same processes of migratory selection lay behind the demographic structure of Isanti's Swedish communities, although the special circumstances and timing of inheritance and family formation in the immigrants' native provinces caused their American settlements to exhibit features that were somewhat different from the American frontier model. Most notable among the differences was that the Swedish immigrant population was generally older. As we have seen, the emigration from Rättvik was the emigration of a generational cohort that faced diminishing opportunity within the worlds of their particular kinship cells. A majority of the married couples that homesteaded the Isanti frontier were already in their thirties and forties, not their twenties and thirties, when they arrived; and they had more and older children with them than one normally associates with new frontier families.[16] Also, because of the efficiency of the chain migration axes, there was relatively little imbalance between the sexes. Young men who emigrated alone were quick to send home for a bride or found ample numbers of eligible young women among the many families that made up the backbone of the migration. Even though they were somewhat older and in a more advanced stage of family and household formation, the Swedish communities were very much a typical frontier population in that they were settled by people who were mostly of the same age and stage in the life cycle. As a consequence, the population can be expected to have passed through the predictable series of changes that historical demographers have documented for most American post-settlement rural populations.[17]

The expected demographic transition for American rural settlements begins with a period of high fertility and rapid population expansion. During the first two decades following settlement, the new families and households created in conjunction with frontier settlement experience very rapid growth, largely through the addition of large numbers of children. Although rural fertility rates in the United States declined steadily over the course of the nineteenth century, which makes any effort to compare rates between new and older settlement areas difficult, there is evidence that the highest rates were associated with areas that had been settled for twenty years or less. Recent study has shown that the highest rates were found in newly settled areas slightly behind the frontier, where perhaps 20 to 40 percent of the land had been improved, which was roughly the proportion that had been cleared in the Isanti study area by the 1890s (Table 7.1 on page 247).[18] As a consequence of high fertility rates among a young married population, as well as continued in-migration, the populations of new settlements tended to swell enormously during this period.

This early period of rapid growth is followed by a second phase in which population is gradually stabilized. A stabilization of the population, or even a slight decline, is brought about in large measure through a drop in fertility. Out-migration to new frontiers, towns, and cities also plays a part. Recent studies have suggested that the "escape valve" role normally assigned to out-migration may have been less of a factor than previously assumed; the major factor appears to be fertility decline.[19] The long-term decline in fertility begins roughly three decades after settlement or once land availability began to fall off sharply. Scholars have searched extensively for the cause of the decline, by and large ruling out such factors as education, variation in geographic origins of the population, mortality differentials, and the need to mobilize female and child labor in new agricultural areas. The only factor that seems to have some overall validity is the recognition of diminishing opportunity to amass capital in the form of landed wealth. Assuming that most American farmers viewed their farms as family enterprises and were anxious to establish their children in economic circumstances that were at least the equal of what they knew early in life, scholars have hypothesized that opportunity to increase one's capital was a constant concern of landowners in developing areas and that it ultimately governed the changing size of families.

In addition to long-term fertility decline, the post-settlement phase is marked by a rise in new family formation as the cohort of children born to frontier families comes of age and the parents pass beyond the age of active economic activity. The rise of a new generation is a major feature in the maturation of rural communities, although the rate of new family formation is much tempered by inheritance strategies. The proportion of eligible young women who are married is generally less than was the case during the frontier period, since declining economic opportunity has the effect of delaying marriage in addition to discouraging couples from having large numbers of children. There are also more unmarried young adults living at home despite the high rate of out-migration among unmarried men and women in their twenties. Household size is generally smaller, although the probability of a non-nuclear household increases with larger numbers of aged parents who must be supported by married children. The process of transition ends, then, with the replacement of larger, highly fertile frontier families by a second generation of smaller and less fertile families that appear to be in harmony with the carrying capacity of the local agricultural resource.

By the pre-migration standards of Rättvik parish, the immigrant Rättvik households of Isanti County's agricultural frontier were both simply composed and small in size. Just 22 percent of the 109 Rättvik households in the Isanti area at the close of the settlement period in 1885, for example, were extended to include more than a nuclear family. The comparable proportion in pre-migration Rättvik was around 60 percent. Rättvik households in Isanti averaged 5.61 members in 1885, whereas households in pre-migration Rättvik averaged 8.15 persons. The relative simplicity and smaller size of the immigrant household was, of course, a natural outcome of the migration selection process, which tended to fragment relatively young nuclear families out of complex households. These families were generally too youthful to have children old enough to marry, which eliminated one source of household extension. The abundance of new land available on the frontier probably meant that even if they did, the new couple was likely to move out and start their own household. Nor was there an abundance of older folks— parents, uncles, and aunts—to be accommodated within households headed by younger couples. Most had been left behind at the time of emigration, although increasing numbers were being brought over on prepaid tickets by the late 1880s.

Even though they were predominantly nuclear, the smaller size of the frontier immigrant household was very rapidly being redressed by an explosion in fertility. Fertility had been on the rise in Rättvik throughout the pre-migration period, and had taken a downward turn only in the 1870s in reaction to the poor harvests and difficult times that had also played a role in prompting emigration to America. Immigrant Rättvik households in Isanti staged a dramatic renewal of the rise in fertility levels that had been under way in Rättvik in the decades before 1870. As measured by standardized child–woman ratios, fertility rates among married Rättvik women in Isanti were 19.85 percent higher in 1885 than the corresponding rates in Rättvik for 1867 (Table 7.3), and an astounding 44.13 percent higher than the downturned rates in Rättvik for 1877. Some caution is necessary in interpreting these figures. The age–marital selectivity of the migrant population can affect the child–woman ratio, although standardization for age distribution and the relatively small proportion of the Rättvik population that actually emigrated work to minimize the problem.

The high fecundity of recently arrived immigrant groups is a phenomenon that has often been commented on. Hans Norman, in his study of Swedish immigrants in Wisconsin's Pepin and Burnett counties, observed a rate of reproduction among fertile Swedish immigrant women that was roughly one-third higher than in selected areas of Sweden. He also found, however, that if fertility rates are calculated only for married women of the same age, the large differential between Ameri-

Table 7.3 Number of Children Aged 0–4 per 1,000 Married Women Aged 20–49 in Pre-Migration Rättvik and among Rättvik Immigrants in the Isanti Study Area, 1885

	Pre-migration Rättvik			Isanti
Age group	1857	1867	1877	1885
20–24	916.7	933.3	625.0	1230.8
25–29	1394.7	1121.2	1153.8	1500.0
30–34	1258.1	1084.7	1034.5	1370.4
35–39	955.6	1127.3	923.1	1500.0
40–44	608.7	824.6	520.0	769.2
45–49	288.9	450.0	227.3	166.7
20–49	911.5	934.4	779.9	1096.8
20–49[a]	944.2	958.2	796.8	1148.4

SOURCES: Catechetical registers *(husförhörslängder)* for Rättvik and Boda parishes; 20 percent sample of all households, N = 260 (1857), 259 (1867), 259 (1877); and 1885 Minnesota state census manuscripts, N = 124.
[a] Standardized for the age distribution of the population.

can and Swedish rates all but disappears, suggesting that the large numbers of children in immigrant settlements is more attributable to a higher frequency of marriage than to higher marital fertility.[20] Comparisons between fertility rates in Rättvik and its daughter settlements in Isanti, however, seem to contradict Norman's findings, as do similar measures constructed by Gjerde for Norwegian immigrants in the Upper Middle West.[21] Lower ages at marriage in Isanti for both men and women, as well as substantially fewer numbers of spinsters and bachelors, certainly suggest that the frontier immigrant population enjoyed a higher frequency of marriage than had been the case in the old parish, but the differences do not appear to have been overwhelming. While the average age at marriage for women in pre-migration Rättvik had been 25.1 years, the corresponding age in Isanti during the 1865–85 settlement era was 24.5 years. The difference for men was even less: 26.9 years in Rättvik as opposed to 26.7 years in Isanti. The proportion of all women married between the ages of twenty and forty-nine was 78 percent in the Isanti settlements in 1885, not significantly more than the corresponding 1867 figure in Rättvik (73.6 percent). On the other hand, the range of marriage ages was far more narrow than it had been in Rättvik. Whereas substantial numbers of men and women in Rättvik were not married for the first time until they were in their thirties, in Isanti many more married in their twenties (Table 7.4). The higher rates of fertility observed among married Rättvik women in Isanti's frontier

Table 7.4   Percentage of Women Ever Married in Pre-Migration Rättvik and among
Rättvik Immigrants in the Isanti Study Area, 1885

	Pre-migration Rättvik			Isanti
Age group	1857	1867	1877	1885
20–29	39.7%	44.0%	38.9%	55.0%
30–39	86.4	83.2	89.9	90.4
40–49	93.8	91.5	90.0	93.6
20–49	66.2%	73.6%	66.8%	78.0%

SOURCES: Catechetical registers *(husförhörslängder)* for Rättvik and Boda parishes; 20
percent sample of all households, N = 435 (1857), 437 (1867), 457 (1877); and 1885 Minnesota state census manuscripts, N = 159.

settlements were certainly enhanced by the fact that more women were
being married in their twenties and the fact that fewer older women
were without mates, but there was also an undeniably greater frequency
of child-bearing at all ages.[22]

In any case, high rates of reproduction are to be expected in any
newly settled area. There seems to have been nothing exceptional about
the large numbers of children born into the families of Rättvik settlers.
Compared to all married women in the Isanti area, Swedish or otherwise, fertility rates for immigrant women from Rättvik were close to the
average (Table 7.5). The most fecund immigrant group in the Isanti area
in 1885 were the German settlers of Bradford township, followed by the
recently arrived Swedish settlers of the Maple Ridge area. The fairly
well-established settlements of people from the Upper Dalarna parishes
of Orsa (Stanchfield), Rättvik (Cambridge West and Athens), and Venjan (Dalbo-Karmel) also exhibited relatively high levels of reproduction,
while the longer-settled Swedish population of Isanti township and the
Old American population seem to have been more restrained in their
childbearing. The order makes sense, given the fact that the highest
rates appear to coincide with relatively new populations and the lower
rates with populations that had been in the Upper Midwest, if not in the
Isanti area, for some time, although that logic fails to explain the high
fertility among the Germans of Bradford township.[23]

As the Isanti settlements began to pass into the post-settlement era,
however, striking differences began to emerge in the degree to which
each followed the long-term American trend towards lower fertility levels in aging settlement districts. Among the most striking deviations
from the norm are the behaviors of the Rättvik settlements of Athens

Table 7.5   Number of Children Aged 0–4 per 1,000 Married Women Aged 20–49 in the Isanti Study Area, by Community, 1885–1915[a]

Community (origins)	1885 Number of children	Rank	1895 Number of children	Rank	1905 Number of children	Rank	1915 Number of children	Rank	Percent change, 1885–1915
Bradford (Germany)	1568.0	1	936.4	8	1028.3	7	981.9	7	–37.4%
Maple Ridge (mixed)	1494.3	2	1242.9	2	1158.8	3	1093.2	4	–26.8
Stanchfield (Orsa)	1235.7	3	1119.8	6	1033.1	6	985.9	6	–20.2
Cambridge East (mixed)	1231.2	4	1119.9	5	871.7	8	604.6	8	–50.9
Cambridge West (Rättvik)	1204.1	5	1024.4	7	1373.9	1	1214.8	1	+0.9
Athens (Rättvik)	1086.3	6	1338.1	1	1187.9	2	1181.5	2	+8.8
Dalbo-Karmel (Venjan)	1063.3	7	1224.4	3	1042.5	5	1116.4	3	+5.0
Old American	1038.0	8	572.1	9	716.7	9	597.6	9	–42.3
Isanti (Häls-Mdp.)	1034.0	9	1127.1	4	1142.2	4	1007.2	5	–2.6
All married women	1142.2	—	1134.0	—	1073.4	—	1043.0	—	–8.7%
All Rättvik women	1148.4	—	1120.7	—	1267.5	—	1185.6	—	+3.2%

SOURCES: Federal and state manuscript censuses, church registers, and county birth and death records. N for all married women = 615 (1885), 795 (1895), 832 (1905), 819 (1915); for Bradford, 22, 23, 33, 34; for Maple Ridge, 39, 78, 94, 99; for Stanchfield, 113, 142, 145, 137; for Cambridge East, 26, 39, 35, 33; for Cambridge West, 81, 97, 81, 83; for Athens, 43, 57, 48, 50; for Dalbo-Karmel, 97, 149, 165, 159; for Old Americans, 31, 28, 40, 42; and for Isanti, 101, 92, 95, 93.

[a] Standardized for the age distribution of the population.

and Cambridge West. While standardized fertility rates for the entire study area declined by 8.7 percent over the period 1885–1915, these two communities posted increases of 8.8 percent and 0.9 percent respectively. Fertility among all married women in households with Rättvik origins, regardless of community affiliation, increased by 3.2 percent between 1885 and 1915. The only other settlement to experience a comparable increase was the Dalbo-Karmel area, which was predominantly settled by immigrants from the Upper Dalarna parish of Venjan. All other settlements experienced declines. The Germans of Bradford township, the Old American population, and the Swedish population of mixed background in the Cambridge East community recorded the most striking declines, with fertility rates falling off by as much as one-third to one-half. Others recorded more modest, but still substantial, downward trends.

There is no clear explanation for the differences in child-bearing behavior between the various Isanti settlements. The historical record has left no statement as to why particular families, many of which were by now of the second generation, may have consciously chosen to have more or fewer children. The fact that the communities that bucked the general downward trend in fertility were all originally settled by folk from Upper Dalarna parishes suggests that cultural differences may have played a role, even though one community that experienced decline—the Orsa settlement in the Stanchfield area—was also an Upper Dalarna settlement. Religious affiliation may have been a factor, too. The Stanchfield community was Baptist, while the other Upper Dalarna communities were predominantly affiliated with the Lutheran church or with its free mission seceders.

If fertility was indeed tied to perceptions of economic opportunity and the ability to pass amassed capital on to future generations, as some have argued, then differential rates of fertility between cultural groups may be one of the better indicators of how the immigrant community's sociocultural world was related to or in conflict with the economic world that surrounded it. While some communities appear to have been well in tune with key ongoing processes of the post-settlement era that could limit their ability to provide for the future of their offspring—such as the rapid diminution of available land—others appear to have been inattentive. Or were they operating under different rules and conditions?

Land and Family in the Post-Settlement Era

One might very well argue that the key to the relationship between the two halves of the immigrant's bipolar world lies in an examination of the kinds of inheritance strategies employed by household heads during this period. Of all premeditated human activities, the intergenerational transmission of landed wealth through inheritance was one of the most crucial to the future of the agricultural immigrant community. It was affected by both the liberalizing pull of American economic life and the restraining forces of cultural and social tradition. Land on the frontier could be viewed in two ways. From the entrepreneurial angle, it was a source of speculation or quick profit. In this view material advantage easily outweighed communal and noneconomic goals. In another sense, land was the giver of life, the sacred means by which the immigrant family drew its sustenance, the symbol of familial accomplishment, independence, and identity within the community. Here the ultimate goal was its orderly inheritance in the interest of maintaining family and community continuity.[24]

The changing circumstances of the post-settlement period required by their very nature that relations between people and resources would have to be adjusted. It was during this period, as we have seen, that the number of economic units on the land reached its natural limit. The passing of the frontier in the 1890s and the declining supply of unsettled lands which followed quickly on its heels meant that the maximum number of farm households in the study area was reached shortly after the turn of the century. Only marginal lands remained unalienated or in speculators' hands. After 1905, new households could be established only through the acquisition of land parcels from already existing farms or through the outright liquidation of some existing farms.

The rate at which farms were liquidated rose steadily during the post-settlement period. In 1880, incidents of farms being bought out by another party were extremely rare; by the turn of the century, it was normal for as many as 7 or 8 percent of all farms to be on the block at any given time (see Figure 7.3), although the rate of liquidation began to abate after 1910. This sharp rise in liquidations between 1890 and 1910 occurred at precisely the same time that wholesale land transfers were being made between an aging pioneer generation and its children. The proportion of farms that were passed on to heirs roughly tripled over the period 1881–1910, followed by a slight downturn after 1910. Such processes ultimately were the cause of a gradually declining number of farm households on the land between 1905 and 1915 (Table 7.6). Indeed, the total number of farm households declined over that period by a substantial 17.5 percent. As a result of this "shake out" process, the actual size of all farms in Rum River valley communities increased gradually over the post-settlement period, from an average of just over 100 acres in 1885 to nearly 110 acres in 1915. The two trends, farm liquidation and farm ownership transfers, roughly paralleled one another and were intimately linked to generational change. Their abatement after 1910 marks the end of an era and the beginning of a new life cycle for the population of the region.

The fate of farms established during the settlement era, then, was decided in one of two ways. One was sale to an outside party. In that case, the continuity of the family's relationship with the land was lost, although the seller could realize substantial pecuniary gain in the high-

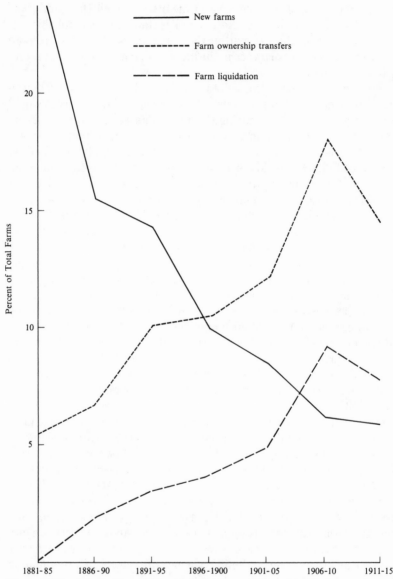

Figure 7.3 New Farms, Farm Ownership Transfers, and Farm Liquidations as a
Percentage of All Farms in the Isanti Study Area, 1881–1915

Table 7.6   Number of Farm Households in the Isanti Study Area, 1885–1915

Community	1885	1890	1895	1900	1905	1910	1915
Athens	81	83	88	89	81	73	69
Bradford	36	37	41	35	34	30	25
Cambridge East	61	62	66	54	53	48	41
Cambridge West	109	126	155	155	151	128	119
Dalbo-Karmel	129	161	200	230	231	219	215
Isanti	161	162	171	161	162	145	126
Maple Ridge	70	84	115	124	135	116	106
Stanchfield	171	197	218	218	205	187	174
Yankee fringe	58	47	49	46	46	41	36
Outside of communities	90	105	122	124	148	127	104
Total	966	1,064	1,225	1,236	1,246	1,114	1,015

SOURCE: Reconstruction of all farm households in the Isanti Study Area for the period 1885–1915 based on federal and state census manuscripts, county tax rolls, church registers, and the *1914 Atlas and Farmer's Directory* for Isanti County.

priced land market. The other was sale or inheritance within the family. In that case, continuity was maintained as some element of the family remained on the land. As farm proprietors reached retirement age and the opportunity to purchase new lands declined, there was increased incentive for some owners to sell outside their own families, usually to proprietors who needed additional lands in order to pass on sufficient landed wealth to their heirs.

The pressure to liquidate was greatest on the owners of smaller operations. Throughout the post-settlement era, the average size of liquidated farms was substantially less than the average size of inherited farms (Table 7.7). Of course, some very large farms were liquidated and some very small farms were passed on to heirs, but on the whole there seems to have been a threshold for inheritance at 80 acres. Better than two-thirds of the inherited farms were 80 acres or more in size, while approximately two-thirds of all liquidated farms were 80 acres or less.[25] In the absence of a settlement frontier, land for new farms and inheritances was taken from the estates of smaller operators.

Where farms were passed on to heirs, the inheritance procedure could vary considerably, but the basic difference was in the timing of transfer. Two systems seem to have been in use. In one system inheritance occurred before the death of the head of household. As heirs reached maturity, their parents began to transfer landed wealth to them. Sometimes the entire inheritance was passed on at once, with the parents taking on a secondary role to the son, son-in-law, or several children who took over control of the farm. In other cases, inheritances

Table 7.7 Mean Size of Liquidated and Inherited Farms, Isanti Study Area, 1881–1915

	1881–85	1886–90	1891–95	1896–1900	1901–5	1906–10	1911–15
Liquidated farms							
Number	—	18	36	48	62	107	82
Mean size (acres)	—	115.8	89.4	88.0	91.7	76.2	95.7
Inherited farms							
Number	46	60	80	78	83	102	70
Mean size (acres)	189.8	146.4	159.3	150.5	167.0	155.1	141.2

SOURCES: Federal and state manuscript censuses, Isanti County land (real property tax rolls) and probate records.

were transferred in a piecemeal fashion: heirs received parcels of land at maturity but waited until their parents' retirement before the transfer of all property was completed. In the second system inheritance occurred only after the death or departure of the household head. Inheritance was made through the instrument of a will that was enforced after death. Here, the household head tended to control property much longer, often to the frustration of heirs who faced the prospect of waiting indefinitely for the means of supporting themselves and a family. Of the two systems, the former was clearly the more efficient in affecting continuity of family ownership.

Land ownership studies also commonly distinguish between partible and impartible systems of inheritance. This appears to be a relatively meaningless distinction for the Isanti area settlements. Nearly all of the transfers were partible in the sense that something was provided for all children. Although one or two sons, or perhaps a son-in-law, may have been selected to acquire control of the parent's farm, they usually did so with the understanding that the other children would be compensated. This meant that the land was often mortgaged to provide compensatory payments to the others. In its intestacy laws, the state of Minnesota provided equal inheritance for all children. Although individual parents were free to dispose of landed wealth in any way they wished, most seemed to share this ideal.[26] The clearest measure of local differentiation in land inheritance, therefore, was in its timing.

Given the fact that there was considerable differentiation in fertility levels between the Isanti communities over the post-settlement period, and given our assumption that fertility and the expectation of providing for one's offspring are linked, it would be logical to expect variances in inheritance strategies to have occurred between these communities. Towards this end, two measures—the rate of farm liquidation and the ratio of after-death to before-death timing in the intergenerational transfer of property—were calculated for each community between 1885 and 1915 (Table 7.8).

The communities can be divided into three groups with respect to the liquidation rate. The Dalbo-Karmel, Cambridge West, and Athens communities comprise the first group. All had very low liquidation rates, with only about 30 percent of all farms liquidated over the period 1885–1915. A second group of five communities, including the Germans in Bradford township, experienced moderate liquidation rates. The Old American population and the Swedish households that lay outside community boundaries had the highest liquidation rates and constitute the third group.

If the ratio of transfer timing for households where property was passed on to heirs is placed alongside the liquidation rates for each community, the rank order and the grouping of communities remains virtually unchanged. The proportion of after-death transfers is lowest in the group with low liquidation rates, while the highest proportions of after-death transfers are associated with the most unstable commu-

Table 7.8 Farm Liquidation and Timing of Land Ownership Transfers by Community, Isanti Study Area, 1885–1915

Community	Liquidation rate[a]	Transfer after death/transfer before death[b]
Dalbo-Karmel	29.1%	0.91
Cambridge West	30.0	1.31
Athens	31.8	1.03
Stanchfield	37.5	1.63
Bradford	39.3	1.33
Maple Ridge	44.4	1.57
Cambridge East	47.4	2.17
Isanti	47.5	3.13
Yankee fringe	55.7	2.00
Swedes outside of communities	60.0	3.44
All farms	41.0%	1.63

SOURCES: Federal and state manuscript censuses, Isanti County land (real property tax rolls) and probate records.

[a] Percent of all land ownership transfers, 1885–1915, resulting in liquidation.

[b] Ratio of land ownership transfers completed after the death or departure of the household head to those completed before the death or departure of household head (includes liquidations).

nities. Landowners in some communities were better able to maintain landed wealth within their families than were landowners in other communities. The communities in which such efforts appear to have been most successful, as measured by low liquidation rates, were the same communities that exhibited high fertility rates and an apparent preference for before-death property transfers.

The experience of the immigrant Olof A. Wicklund and his family is a typical example of land inheritance strategy in one of the more stable communities (Figure 7.4). Olof A. emigrated with his wife and two children from Rättvik parish in 1867 and settled in western Springvale township (Cambridge West) in the same year. He was forty years old at the time. By the close of the settlement era in 1885, he had a well-established farm of 197 acres, valued at more than $900 according to county tax assessment figures. The fifty-nine-year-old farmer had two sons and a daughter. His oldest son was twenty-seven, the daughter was twenty-five, and his American-born son was fifteen. In 1890, his daughter Anna married and moved to a neighboring farm, taking with her a dowry of twenty-nine acres. A few years later Olof A. suffered the loss of his wife Margareta. The old man, who now headed the household by himself, purchased forty-two acres of land for his oldest son, Anders, who then married at thirty-seven years of age. When his second son, Olof, married three years later, Wiklund transferred one-half of Anders's forty-two acres to the new couple. By 1905, however, the forty-two acres had been restored to Anders and young Olof had been assisted in the purchase of forty acres of his own. By 1910, Olof A. had reached eighty-four years of age and had begun to reduce the size of his holdings, while assisting the two sons in adding to theirs. By the time he died a few years later, he had transferred the remainder of his property to his sons. Throughout his lifetime, both sons lived with their families under him in the same household; only after his death did they actually set up separate households and divide the farm into two operations.

For contrast, Hans Peterson and his family exemplify an after-death strategy in one of the less stable communities (Figure 7.5). Peterson emigrated from Torp parish in the province of Medelpad with his wife and three children at the age of thirty-five. He homesteaded in Isanti township (Isanti community). By 1885 he was fifty-four years old and operated a farm of 120 acres. Like Wicklund, he had two sons and a daughter living on the farm, all in their twenties. Over the next ten years, however, Peterson retained complete control of the farm. During this time, daughter Rachel married and his two sons reached their middle and late thirties without being married. By 1900 Peterson was sixty-

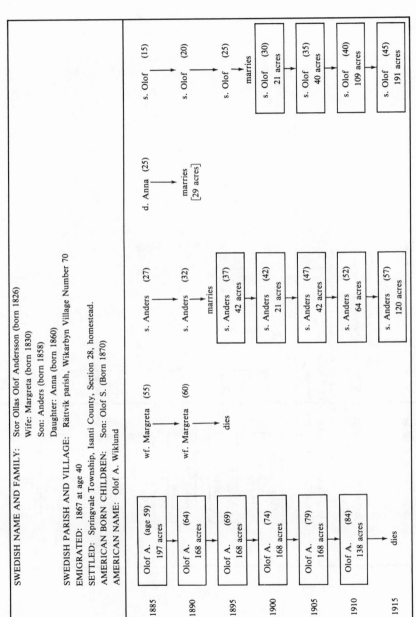

Figure 7.4 Example of a "Before-Death" Inheritance Strategy

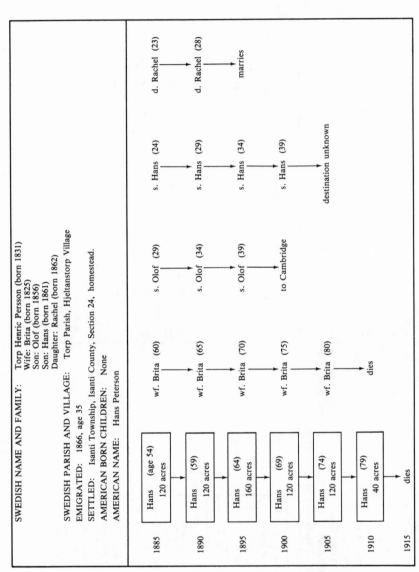

SWEDISH NAME AND FAMILY: Torp Henric Persson (born 1831)
                            Wife: Brita (born 1825)
                            Son: Olof (born 1856)
                            Son: Hans (born 1861)
                            Daughter: Rachel (born 1862)

SWEDISH PARISH AND VILLAGE: Torp Parish, Hjeltanstorp Village

EMIGRATED: 1866, age 35

SETTLED: Isanti Township, Isanti County, Section 24, homestead.

AMERICAN BORN CHILDREN: None

AMERICAN NAME: Hans Peterson

1885	Hans (age 54) 120 acres	wf. Brita (60)	s. Olof (29)	s. Hans (24)	d. Rachel (23)
1890	Hans (59) 120 acres	wf. Brita (65)	s. Olof (34)	s. Hans (29)	d. Rachel (28)
1895	Hans (64) 160 acres	wf. Brita (70)	s. Olof (39)	s. Hans (34)	marries
1900	Hans (69) 120 acres	wf. Brita (75)	to Cambridge	s. Hans (39)	
1905	Hans (74) 120 acres	wf. Brita (80)		destination unknown	
1910	Hans (79) 40 acres	dies			
1915	dies				

Figure 7.5 Example of an "After-Death" Inheritance Strategy

270

nine years old and still retained control of the land. The oldest son, Olof, now in his forties, left for Cambridge, where he worked as a laborer for a few years and then disappeared. The second son, Hans, was still on the farm and unmarried at thirty-nine years of age. Five years later, Hans, too, gave up and left the farm for an unknown destination. In the next few years Peterson's wife died and the old man, living all alone except for hired help, began to sell off parcels of land to his neighbors and a purchaser from outside the community. When he died a short time later, the remainder of the farm was liquidated.

The experience of these two families was not unusual for their respective communities. Cambridge West families on the whole were very conservative in their land transfer strategies, carefully laying out the transfer of property while the household head was still alive and active. Even their after-death transfers were more carefully planned and generally more successful than similar transfers in other communities. Most sons acquired land relatively early and were able to start families. The pressure on land that this caused was eased through the purchase of land from owners in nearby communities and through the liquidation of smaller holdings within the community that were often held by outsiders. These households tended to be more aggressive in adding to their landed wealth during the critical period of property transfer to the new generation.

In a territorial sense, the cumulative effect in Cambridge West and similar communities was to gradually expand and to sharpen the boundary of the community over time.[27] In contrast, Isanti families on the whole exhibited very mixed behavior. Retention of adult children in the community was low and the incidence of older and single land owners was relatively high. Households turned over frequently and outsiders often purchased land within the community, although a core of households did quite effectively transfer land to the new generation. Of the two examples, it seems logical that the Cambridge West community was more committed to preserving its land base and to providing the means for its children to remain within the community. Since its members had greater confidence in their ability to provide for future generations it does not seem surprising that they might also have more children.

The question that quickly arises is whether the behavior isolated here really reflects conscious strategies on the part of families and communities. Differing responses to salient economic opportunities might also be explained by noncultural restraints such as agricultural specialization, local differentiation in land values, distance from the local market town, or time of arrival. Undoubtedly these variables all had some effect, but by all available evidence the effect was slight. By the post-settlement era, agricultural specialization varied little over the region. The Germans and Old Americans were still more disposed than the Swedes to emphasize cattle production, but the difference was a matter of degree. Land values varied, but the variation was within communities, not between them. Land values were highest near the center of each community and were lowest around the peripheries, a pattern produced through the settlement process, which featured the sequential taking and improving of land in an outward direction from each community core. While this helps to explain the relative stability of core areas in the less stable communities, it says little about differences between communities. Distance to market and time of arrival certainly varied for all communties, but any correlation with land transfer practices leads to conflicting conclusions. The Dalbo-Karmel community, which was the farthest from market and the most recently settled, had the lowest liquidation rate and transfer ratio. The Cambridge West community, with exactly the opposite characteristics, had a liquidation rate and a transfer ratio similar to that of Dalbo-Karmel.

Although the precise causal mechanisms may be difficult to define, the differences seem to be cultural. The three communities that exhibited the most careful or conservative behavior were all dominated by households with origins in Upper Dalarna and were all strongly affiliated with Lutheran or Mission churches. Communities with other or mixed Swedish backgrounds and with strong Baptist affiliations, in particular, tended to be less circumspect in their land dealings. As a result, the same differences between communities show up again and again throughout the post-settlement era. For example, the rate at which households accumulated landed wealth, which may be seen as both cause and effect of inheritance practices and fertility, was significantly higher among the most conservative communities than it was for any others, with the exception of the Germans in Bradford township (Table 7.9).[28] No reference is ever made in the historical record to any form of conscious strategy on the part of families or communities to perpetuate their existence through specific inheritance practices or property accumulation designs, yet there seems to have been real effort within certain communities to achieve such ends.

In the final analysis, what happened may be no more than the unconscious perpetuation of age-old attitudes toward landed wealth. The Dalbo, Athens, and Cambridge West communities were predominantly populated by people with origins in Upper Dalarna, a provincial area known for its self-contained and self-conscious parish communities, for

Table 7.9 Mean Landed Wealth[a] per Household in the Isanti Study Area, 1885 and 1915

Community	Mean landed wealth, 1885	Mean landed wealth, 1915	Percent change, 1885–1915
Dalbo-Karmel	$176	$1,114	533%
Athens	417	2,434	484
Bradford	441	2,317	425
Cambridge West	373	1,824	389
Isanti	388	1,688	335
Maple Ridge	283	1,184	314
Stanchfield	323	1,274	294
Cambridge East	426	1,592	274
Yankee fringe	440	1,287	193
All communities	$355	$1,469	313%

SOURCES: Real property tax lists, Isanti County, Minnesota, 1885 and 1915.
a Assessed value of real property.

its population stability, and for its strong free-holding tradition. Other Swedish communities in Isanti's Rum River valley were representative of other areas of Sweden. These areas were, in many ways, less isolated from the social and economic changes under way in nineteenth-century Sweden. This was especially true of areas near the rapidly developing Bothnian Gulf coast in Hälsingland and Medelpad. Through the middle and latter part of the century, a vigorous expansion of the timber industry in this region caused dramatic changes in the social and economic system.[29] As a result, society there was more open, the population more mobile, economic opportunity more diverse, and the importance of the small freehold farm not as great as in Dalarna. Quite likely the experience with land was different and that difference was reflected in the behavior of emigrants in America.

The trans-Atlantic perpetuation of these differences may be seen by comparing the contemporaneous land transfer practices of two migration-linked source areas. One is a five-village area in Rättvik that comprised the core area of Gärdsjö *fjärding*. These five villages were strongly linked by migration, as we have seen, with Isanti's Athens community. The second area is a group of six villages in Attmar parish of Medelpad province.[30] Attmar and many nearby parishes in Medelpad's Ljungan valley experienced heavy emigration from time to time throughout the latter half of the nineteenth century. Emigrants from Attmar and other Ljungan valley parishes were the strongest element in the population of the Isanti community located just to the north of Athens. Although both source areas in Sweden were essentially agricultural districts, they differed considerably in their patterns of land tenure and social structure. The population of the Gärdsjö district was largely a small-holding peasant society. Nearly all of the 236 Gärdsjö households in 1885 owned the farms they worked. Most economic activity was traditional and tied to the land. In contrast, only about 40 percent of the 195 households in the six Attmar villages had proprietary rights over the land they worked. The remainder were *torpare,* an agricultural class that may have held some land, but largely relied on long-term contractual rights to work land on the larger free-hold farms. There was also a substantial number of landless households that depended entirely on wage labor in agriculture or the timber industry for their living.

The intergenerational land transfer practices of these two Swedish districts can be analyzed in the same manner as the Swedish-American communities to which they were linked. Over the thirty-year period between 1885 and 1915, there were 175 land transfers in the Gärdsjö villages and 149 land transfers in the Attmar villages. This was proportionately fewer than had occurred among their American counterparts. The difference is explained by the far more even age distribution of household heads in the Swedish areas, which lacked the sharply defined generational cycle of the newly settled American communities. There was, however, a clearly parallel pattern between linked communities with respect to the timing of intergenerational land transfers (Table 7.10). The Athens community, which had one of the lowest liquidation rates in the Isanti area, reflects an even lower liquidation rate among peasant households in the Gärdsjö villages, evident for the period 1885–1915. The high liquidation rate experienced by the Isanti community is not very different from the liquidation rate in the Attmar villages. Similarly, after-death transfer was low in Athens and almost nonexistent in the Gärdsjö villages from which the Athens population originated, while both the Isanti community and the Attmar villages had high proportions of after-death transfers.

There is circumstantial evidence, then, that pre-migration experience may have had an important influence on what happened in America. Peasant farmers in Rättvik and neighboring Upper Dalarna parishes regarded land as an ancestral resource. Farms and property were handed down for generations and were central to the identification of families with their past and community. In Attmar and in many districts along the Bothnian coast, the relationship between land and family was more varied. The timber milling industry, which enjoyed a heady rise along the Bothnian coast from the 1860s to the 1890s, had purchased

Table 7.10 Farm Liquidation and Timing of Land Ownership Transfers in Migration-Linked Communities, 1885–1915

Community	Liquidation rate[a]	Transfer after death/transfer before death[b]
Athens community	31.8%	1.03
Gärdsjö villages	16.4	0.34
Isanti community	47.5	3.13
Attmar villages	41.2	2.64
Freehold only	26.9	1.60

SOURCES: Federal and state manuscript censuses, Isanti County land (real property tax rolls) and probate records, population registers *(mantalslängder)*, catechetical registers *(husförhörslängder)* and tax registers *(taxeringslängder)* for Rättvik and Attmar parishes.

a Percent of all land ownership transfers, 1885–1915, resulting in liquidation.

b Ratio of land ownership transfers completed after the death or departure of the household head to those completed before the death or departure of the household head (includes liquidations).

vast tracts of land to secure access to timber, which in turn inflated the value of property and made it a speculative commodity. Industry also introduced new forms of wage earning into the economy and helped foster the early emergence of a working class. In addition, the railroads reached the area as early as the 1870s, facilitating increased contact with other parts of Sweden, greater mobility, and less reliance on traditional farm work.[31] The railroad failed to reach Rättvik until 1890, perpetuating the relative isolation of the district until near the end of the century. These differences appear to have imparted quite different responses to the question of land transfer and intergenerational change in Isanti's Rum River valley communities.

Underlying all this is the fact that land transfer traditions in the Attmar vallages were differentiated by agricultural class. If the *torpare* class is removed from the analysis of land transfer in Attmar, the liquidation rate and the transfer ratio are both reduced substantially. They are still high by Rättvik standards, but the behavior of the fully landed class in Attmar was clearly more conservative than the *torpare* class. Land ownership was always important to the crofter as a stepping stone to economic independence, but the relationship was often not as permanent as it was for the freeholder. Land could be converted to capital that would allow one to take advantage of local, nonagricultural opportunity or to leave the district altogether in search of opportunity elsewhere. A majority of the immigrants to the Isanti community came from this class; the community's overall higher rates of liquidation and after-death land transfer reflect their relatively liberal behavior towards the land. They simply had relatively little experience in the long-term management of landed wealth and a weak tradition of social ownership.

The inheritance practices employed by the aging immigrant generation from Rättvik were strategies designed to perpetuate the legacy of a trans-Atlantic past as well as to reinforce the social and cultural transplantation that had been effected during the settlement era. These strategies helped maintain a firm and unyielding front along the shifting boundary between the closed social world of the immigrant community and the intrusive economic world of the American milieu. They led to a growing population in Isanti's Rättvik-dominated communities, while population stabilized or even declined in neighboring communities. They also led to greater levels of amassed wealth among the descendents of Rättvik immigrants and the taking over of adjacent farms and neighboring areas by those descendants—in short, a stronger and more cohesive community. The Rättvik emigrants may have chosen the extraordinary alternative of group migration to America as a means of preventing the dispersal of a generation faced with difficult times. The same people, just a few decades later, seem to have taken extraordinary action again in order to insure the next generation against wholesale dispersal.

The degree to which the new generation would accept the order of things as laid down by the passing generation, however, was not clear. For the winds of change had already begun to be felt. The key bulwark against change in the immigrant community was its central institution, the church. Certain developments in the role and authority of that institution illustrate more than anything else the subtle invasion of changing social and economic attitudes that eventually pervaded the fabric of the second-generation community and precipitated its redefinition.

Church and Community

The central social role played by the immigrant church changed little from the settlement to the post-settlement decades. The church remained the heart and soul of the community; it continued on as the conservator of cultural and social values inherited from the past. Yet the influence and appeal of many of its ideals were beginning to erode in the community it served. The church, and the older immigrant generation whose ideals it so solidly represented, were forced gradually to give ground, to accommodate themselves to shifting circumstances. The retreat was grudging, concessions few. Most changes were first opposed, then agreed to in principle, and finally delayed for whatever plausible reason to another day. At the same time, many other aspects of social and institutional life in the community were not under any pressure to change at all. A solid core of relationships and mores always remained unassailable no matter how much the outside world was changing. Over these matters, the church presided comfortably, enjoying the respect and solidarity of its community. In short, the church did its best to control events and was largely successful in its efforts, though it had to give ground in a few areas. How serious were the retreats? To what degree did they cause the community to redefine itself?

Certainly one issue on which the church was eventually obliged to accept change was language. A knowledge of English and the ability to use it had always been considered an advantage from the time of first settlement. It had never seemed a threat to the community, largely because it was primarily a tool for understanding and dealing with the external world. Within the confines of the immigrant community it played a minor role, since nearly all written or spoken communication was in Swedish. Universal English education among the young posed a rather distant threat to the linguistic status quo. Most immigrants were not opposed to their children's acquisition of English language skills in the public schools, as long as there was a church-sponsored parochial school system in place to offer a counterweight of instruction in Swedish.

By the end of the century, however, a rapidly growing number among the second and third generations began to express a preference for the use of English over Swedish. The growing preference for English among the younger elements of the population went beyond business and casual usage. Many felt that English should be used in the church.[32] Although it had come up a number of times as early as the late 1880s, the matter was generally brushed aside; the congregation seemed to think it inconceivable that the word of God could be communicated in any other language than Swedish. According to an observer, the wife of one member of the church council is supposed to have exclaimed on hearing of the issue: "Can you pray in English?".[33] But in 1897, the pastor of the Cambridge Lutheran Church was served with a formal petition, with more than sixty signatures affixed, requesting that the church offer two English-language services a month.[34] After due consideration, the church council agreed to accommodate this demand by establishing

Sunday evening services in English twice a month, but to refrain from tampering with the traditional Sunday morning service, which continued to be conducted in Swedish. While this change had no immediate effect on the majority of the faithful, it does mark the beginning of a series of accommodations that gradually brought English into the institutional life of the community. An English Sunday School Department was founded in 1900 and seven of the confirmands in the pastor's catechetical class of 1900 were instructed in English.[35]

The inroads of the English language into the religious life of the community may have begun a bit earlier in the Cambridge Lutheran congregation than in some of the other Isanti communities beause of its proximity to the county seat at Cambridge, from which a sizeable new membership was being drawn around the turn of the century. Most of the Swedish religious institutions in the area, however, began to feel the pressure at roughly the same time. Nearly every congregation had begun the accommodation process by the early 1900s and experienced a quickening pace of language conversion thereafter. The real watershed came during the war years of 1917-18. This was a time when a sense of American patriotism reached a height. Ethnic communities everywhere in the United States tended to repress overt indications of their foreign background. When confirmands in the Cambridge church were given the choice of receiving English or Swedish Bibles as a gift from the congregation in 1917, ten chose English and nine chose Swedish. The following year, the English Bible recipients outnumbered the Swedish by sixteen to four. Shortly after the war, the church council finally agreed to hold one Sunday morning English service a month, relegating the Swedish service normally held at that time to the evening.[36] From then on the conversion to English proceeded quite rapidly. The church-sponsored "Swede School," which had flourished alongside the public education system for several decades, disappeared in the early 1920s. It had offered instruction in both Swedish and English during its last few years, although it is interesting to note that of the two locations at which the school was held—Cambridge Village and the rural crossroads hamlet of Walbo (Cambridge West community)—the latter continued to use Swedish until the end.[37]

It is doubtful that the transition from Swedish to English usage in business, institutional, and, eventually, every-day life, can be seen as a serious diminution of the ethnic identity of the community. It was at times an emotional issue, but it did not precipitate any great change in community loyalties or membership, with the possible exception of the inclusion of a handful of non-Swedish-speaking town folk in what had been a predominantly Swedish and rural congregation. Language was an internal matter. Acceptance and increased use of the English language was simply a part of a long-standing trend in America by which immigrant groups achieved a degree of cultural assimilation with their host societies. At worst, it emphasized the generational differences inherent in any immigrant population. The older generation spoke Swedish partly to demonstrate their allegiance to the mother country and partly because it was easier for them to communicate in their mother tongue. The younger generation replied in English or in a mixture of the two languages that was almost a language in itself. The inevitable acceptance of the English language was an outward-looking accommodation with the larger world, but for these people was never a denial of the inner world. In much the same way, the public use of the old farm-name prefix was surrendered so that people could properly identify themselves by the standards of the host society, but among friends and family the practice persisted well into the twentieth century.[38] Greater threats came from other sources. Clergy and church councils alike seemed to have been most concerned during this period with the divisive effects of interdenominational rivalries and with moral issues, where foreign and sinful influences threatened to entice the unsuspecting from the relative security and sanctity of the community fold.

The constant rivalry between competing denominations was a recurrent source of uncertainty for the established community. While ethnic historians have long emphasized the centrality of religion in ethnic life, it could also be exceptionally divisive.[39] This could be especially true when theological or doctrinal differences became combined with regional or local rivalries. Religious revivals among various elements of the population and theological debates between some of the established churches dot the history of the region throughout the 1890s and the early 1900s. Lutheran officials, in particular, worried incessantly about the lure of periodic revivals staged by the Baptists.[40] Traveling evangelists and preachers, some of whom were women, were great spectator attractions. Many were charismatic individuals, capable of generating tremendous enthusiasm. Sizable membership secessions and the establishment of competing but usually short-lived religious sects of various kinds plagued the collective conscience of most of the established church-centered communities at some time or another during this period.

One of the greatest challenges to the established order was the Seventh-Day Adventists who began prosyletizing in the Cambridge–Stanchfield area in 1889. Led by a "silver-tongued" orator from Stockholm, they were quickly able to organize a church of approximately 100 members, mostly from the Baptist communities in the area. Although most converts returned to the fold within a couple of years, the experience nearly split the Stanchfield Baptist community in two.[41] But by far the most celebrated of the great religious debates of those years, and an indication of the fervor with which such issues were followed by the local populace, was the public encounter in 1898 between pastors of the Lutheran and Baptist faiths. The great debate took place on March 29, 1898 at Fish Lake, a nearby Swedish settlement in western Chisago County. It featured a number of religious leaders from around the area, but in particular was known for the oratorical clash between the Baptist theologian, Dr. Eric Sandell, and the young, energetic pastor of the Cambridge Lutheran Church, Dr. Alfred Bergin. Attended by throngs of people from communities scattered across two counties, this debate probably did more to focus attention on local religious differences than any other religious event in the region's history.

Religious dissension was often as much a reflection of events on the other side of the Atlantic as it was a manifestation of the religious climate within the immigrant communities. While emigration from home parishes to the transplanted communities of this area had slowed enormously by the late 1880s, places on both sides of the Atlantic continued to be linked by a more or less constant flow of individuals moving back and forth along the old axes of migration and communication. Brides and laborers, aged parents, cousins and nephews continued to come over, although their presence in the American communities was often transient; and many of the old immigrants made trips home from time to time.[42] In short, there seems to have been a lively communication between mother and daughter communities long after the colonization phase was over and this link frequently served to tie together religious and social events in both places. Gossip and news, jealousies and rivalries passed freely over thousands of miles via personal couriers and government post to link social opinion and action across trans-Atlantic networks.

The best example of the efficacy of this process comes from the Athens community, which was primarily settled by emigrants from Rättvik's Gärdsjö *fjärding* during the late 1860s. Although Rättvik parish, as a whole, was slow to accept nonconformist religious activity, the old Gärdsjö district seems to have led the way with the establishment of a Mission Society in 1877.[43] Interestingly enough, the first Mission activity among Rättvik settlers in Isanti's Rum valley communities took place just a few years later in the Athens area. Members of the Athens

Lutheran Church seceded to establish a Mission Free Church just a short distance from the Lutheran church. This nonconformist "infection" that so suddenly afflicted the Athens community had come from Rättvik, quite likely via a single migrant from the Gärdsjö area—one Olof Sten, a soldier from the village of Backa. Sten had been an associate of one of the founders of the Gärdsjö Mission Society, Snis Olof Hansson, and brought with him the news of the events surrounding the establishment of the nonconformist sect in the old community. That the influence of this movement was confined in America, just as it was in Rättvik, to households associated with the old Gärdsjö community, suggests just how strongly spatial and kinship organization on both sides of the Atlantic continued to mirror one another.

Whatever the source, the community establishment fought defections and indiscretions of all kinds. Intemperance in the use of alcohol, immoral behavior among youth, the beguiling attractions of town and city, were all subjects that received ample attention from the pulpit. A Young People's Society within the Cambridge Lutheran Church, which lanquished in the mid-1890s from lack of interest, was galvanized to action in the late 1890s over the issue of temperance, going so far as to petition the State Legislature in 1898 for a law prohibiting saloons.[44] Isanti County was legally "dry" as of the late 1880s, but church leaders were vigilant in maintaining the wet/dry question as a perennial election issue. The Swedish pastor who served the Cambridge Lutheran Church in the 1880s and 1890s was known as an especially militant "dry," and Isanti County's rural Swedish population was quick to enlist in the temperance crusade led by local lodges of the Good Templars.[45]

But mostly, the leaders of the immigrant community feared the invasion of an alien and rapidly modernizing world. The Reverend Alfred Bergin, a particularly strong leader of the Cambridge Lutheran congregation, touched on this fear directly in his 1904 summation of the first forty years of the parish, when he observed:

The old pietism is not entirely gone. However, since the coming of the railroad we have been troubled by irrelevant [sic] and foreign elements. The worldly life of the large cities has invaded our community. It seems as if one is not able to differentiate between good and evil. It is more harmful for us to be thrust into the world arena, because we are not prepared to meet the dangers and temptations. We are too credulous, separated from city life as we have been for so many years.[46]

The movement of young people out of the old communities and into nearby towns and cities was an inevitable and irreversible process. It could not be completely prevented, even with careful inheritance strategies designed to keep as many young people at home as possible. There was always a waiting period before inheritances could be finalized and the uncontrollable sense of adventure that motivates youth everywhere. Those who left, however, were given ample warning of what might await them if they let down their guard. Nor were they allowed to leave without being admonished to remember from where they had come and to return home often. Where possible, colonization efforts farther west or in Canada were encouraged over random wanderings. The church took an active interest in, and even sponsored, efforts to establish daughter settlements on new frontiers. In one such colonization effort a number of households from the Athens community sought to reestablish themselves on homestead land in Alberta around 1905.[47] Just as the original emigrants from Rättvik and its neighboring Dalarna parishes may have preferred colonization in America to dispersal in Sweden, their descendants in Isanti preferred colonization schemes in Canada or Washington state to dispersal in Minnesota.

That people persisted in these communities to a greater degree than one normally expects for rural populations in the Upper Midwest is apparent from the material on inheritance strategies, as well as from periodic measures of persistence. According to persistence counts taken for the post-settlement era, the strong Lutheran communities from Dalarna exhibited by far the lowest rates of family or individual turnover of all the communities in Isanti's Upper Rum valley.[48] Within communities, persistence was highest among families that settled early and families that were formal church members. These families constituted the core of their respective communities and were the most likely to feel the bonds to place that may have been conferred by that fact. They were the ones who set out to establish a colony and so felt a special association with their chosen settlement area. They were less likely to move on than the third-wave immigrants of the late 1880s and 1890s, who often lacked the tight kinship and place identities of the core group and who found less economic opportunity waiting for them in Isanti County by virtue of their late arrival. The core families were more likely, if they did leave the area, to move as a group. Rates of persistence are often inadequate measures of the solidarity of a population, unless they are accompanied by a sense of where mobile elements of the population went.[49] Movement to a new settlement that is yet another extension of the original is in many ways no move at all.

The best way to describe what was happening to the Swedish settlements of Isanti's Upper Rum valley during the post-settlement era is to say that the communities went through a process of redefinition. This was a time of growing cultural confusion, but certainly not a time of dissolution. Leadership was passing from one generation to another with all the adjustments that such a process normally entails. Economic change was bringing the outside world within a society that had been closed to many external influences. The coming of the railroad was opening new economic oportunities and creating a market economy where only subsistence had been possible before. American middle class values and modern luxuries were increasingly visible in towns and farm-steads alike. Crude cabins and shelters were being replaced with frame houses and new barns. At the same time, however, close linkage with parent communities abroad and the strength of central institutions at home worked to keep traditional social bonds and group solidarity strong. These were ethnic communities rapidly acculturating, becoming outwardly more American with each passing decade. In language, dress, the naming of children and farms, in the furnishings of parlors never used except for the finest of company, they were becoming indis-tinguishable from the society around them. Yet inwardly they remained island communities with divergent patterns of wealth accumulation, inheritance, fertility, and mobility. It is not possible to say that they still saw themselves as an extension of Rättvik parish or as extensions of subcommunities or kinship groups within the old mother parish. Much of that was lost by the 1910s, and especially with the onset of the First World War. It would be more accurate to say that they had redefined or transferred their identity from the spatial community of their origins to the spatial community of their new existence. They were no longer tied to the small farms and villages of Gärdsjö *fjärding*, but to the farms of Athens township. The place to which they looked as home had changed, but the basic relationships between people and their institutions had in many ways changed very little.

While the built landscape is often at best a misleading indicator of human history, one could argue that the cultural confusion and the changing identity of these communities was symbolically displayed in the architecture and decoration of their central institution, the church. The Cambridge Lutheran congregation, like all rural midwestern immi-grant congregations, went through a series of construction and re-modeling phases. Most midwestern rural communities built and rebuilt their churches several times, either because fire or natural disaster destroyed the structure or because growing wealth and prosperity in the community dictated building a more imposing and stylish structure. Each reconstruction was potentially a symbolic representation of how a community may have viewed itself at the time.[50]

The Cambridge church passed through three major building phases

Plate 7.3 Success in America. With the growing affluence of the post-settlement era, log cabins were rapidly replaced with stylish frame houses, replete with specially furnished parlors. The photograph reflects the middle-class aspirations of many Isanti residents in the 1890s. (Courtesy of Isanti County Historical Society)

between its founding in 1864 and the end of the First World War.[51] The original church was a plain frame structure, lacking both bell tower and decoration. Like other early churches in the region it was spartan and functional, a reflection of the poor and struggling frontier community it served. The structure had taken nearly two years to build because of material shortages, and the finished product was something less than inspiring; the congregation's first permanent minister was reportedly depressed when he first saw it in 1872. However, within half a dozen years of its completion the community resolved to build a new and more impressive structure. The new church, completed in 1884, was a frame building of considerable size, with a tall bell tower and steeple. It fulfilled all expectations and was a source of pride for the rapidly emerging and relatively prosperous community. Further growth and rising affluence within the community, however, prompted yet a third building phase, which was essentially an effort to remodel and improve the existing structure. This phase, completed in 1892, featured a brick veneer to cover the outside of the wooden structure and modifications of the bell tower and steeple.

Plate 7.4 "Americans one and all"—mobilizing the Home Guards, Cambridge, 1918. The patriotism that surrounded the Great War did much to advance ongoing shifts in cultural identity among Isanti's immigrant population. (Courtesy of Isanti County Historical Society)

In all three buildings, relatively little about the church's external appearance was Swedish. Both the 1868 and 1884 churches were built under the direction of Jonas Norell, a local resident who was a carpenter by profession. Norell built several churches in the area, many of which were graced with unique features, but all of which were strongly influenced by contemporary church design in America. Norell may have learned his trade in Sweden, but the churches he built were far more similar in building style to other midwestern churches than they were to any Swedish prototype. Most were gothic structures of a style that diffused westward from New England during the latter half of the nineteenth century with the aid of widely disseminated published plans and particulars.[52] The exterior of the Cambridge church bore no resemblance to the mother church in Rättvik, save for the large cross with a sphere at its base that stood on top of the 1884 steeple. The cross was copied directly from the old church (compare plates 2.3 and 7.5). This throwback to the past did not last for long. It disappeared when the church was remodeled in 1892. Erected in its place was a stylish new "Trinity cross" (Plate 7.6).

While the exterior of the church always had a decidedly American appearance, the interior was highly symbolic of the congregation's cultural ties to another place. The furniture and railings were hand carved by a local craftsman. The walls and ceiling were painted and frescoed in

Plate 7.5 "New England Gothic." Of all the exterior features of the Cambridge Lutheran Church in 1884, only the "cross and ball" on the top of the spire is at all reminiscent of the old church in Rättvik. (Courtesy of Isanti County Historical Society)

the old Swedish style, replete with the carefully painted three-dimensional representations of Greek columns and arches on the flat vestry wall, a technique commonly used in Sweden to make a relatively plain interior appear ostentatious. A Swedish verse arched over the altar, and the arrangement of altar, vestry doors, and hymnboards resembled the arrangement of the old parish church in Rättvik. In the back of the church a large balcony, which housed the organ, extended outward for a considerable distance, partially blocking the first windows on either side of the building precisely as the corresponding balcony in the mother church did. Nothing could have been more carefully done to replicate the salient features of the well-remembered, ancient sanctuary on Siljan's shore. The sharp contrast between the interior and exterior decoration of the church was an apt reflection of the outlook of the post-settlement community—inwardly Swedish and outwardly American.

The interior was eventually redone, but not until 1912. A major feature of this remodeling was a rebuilding of the pulpit, which was rather oddly placed for a Lutheran church. The placement of the pulpit had

Plate 7.6 Refurbished exterior and new cross, Cambridge Lutheran Church, 1892. A brick veneer covered the church by the 1890s, reflecting the growing affluence of the community. Gone, too, was the old cross and ball, replaced by a stylish trinity cross. Horse stalls are just visible at lower left. (Courtesy of Isanti County Historical Society)

been an ongoing source of trouble. Apparently the fact that the pastor took his place in the pulpit by passing through a small door in the vestry wall behind offended many parishioners; it allowed the pastor to appear on high without having first to pass before the assembled congregation as an ordinary mortal. To a people with strong pietistic leanings, who were continually asked by their nonconformist neighbors to reevaluate their loyalty to the Lutheran church, this was too much of a reminder of the power and privilege of the clergy in the state church of Sweden. The eventual solution was to install steps leading from either side to a lowered pulpit, obligating the pastor to move about in plain view of his assembled parishioners. The incident illustrates how important the arrangement of the interior of the church was to the local population. Not only did it reflect the cultural past, but also their collective values and mores. Any change was a serious matter because of what it might imply. With this in mind, it hardly seems at all unusual that an entire meeting of the local Youth Society in the 1890s might have been devoted in all seriousness to the question: "Which is the most advantageous, to paint or tin-panel the church?"[53]

Plate 7.7 "Inwardly Swedish." The interior of the Cambridge Lutheran Church was unmistakenly Swedish. The classical columns and the arch they supported were painted on a flat wall just as they were in many Swedish churches. (Courtesy of Isanti County Historical Society, 1890s)

The interior of the church remained largely unchanged until the 1930s, when a series of remodelings lasting into the 1950s drastically altered its internal and external appearance. As happened to most midwestern country churches, an inclination to modernize everything coupled with a flagrant disregard for the past began to set in towards the middle of the twentieth century. Hand-crafted furniture and wooden altar decorations were lightly discarded or consigned to the church basement, to be replaced with factory-built interior decorations. New heating plants replaced wood-burning stoves and electric lights replaced candle chandeliers, while acoustical tiles replaced wall paintings and ceiling decorations. Such wholesale changes marked the end of a long period of ethnic community pride and stability established in rural areas of the Upper Middle West during the early decades of the post-settlement era.

8

The Society They Left Behind

*Post-Migration Adjustment and Change
in the Old Community,
1885–1915*

A COMMON FAILING of immigration studies is the tendency to regard the sending society as static. We are intensely interested in the conditions that may have contributed to emigration, but once the migrants have been selected and have made their move our interest shifts to the interaction of the migrants with the receiving society. The sending society is all but forgotten, or assumed to be unchanging. It is important to understand that emigration was only one of a myriad of interconnected changes that swept Europe and America in the nineteenth century. The conditions at home that contributed to the decision to emigrate were often complex and transitory, a momentary window through which an element of local society passed. Changing conditions often brought emigration to an abrupt end or changed its nature substantively. New opportunities intervened on both sides of the Atlantic that led people in new directions. Sometimes the new directions were parallel to one another and sometimes they diverged. A complete understanding of the migrational process requires a long view that traces developments through pre-migration, migration, and post-migration stages. This view must include simultaneous developments among both the migrant population and the population that remained behind.

The migration streams that linked places like the upper Rum River valley and the Dalesburg community with Upper Dalarna's Rättvik parish were as discrete temporally as they were spatially. The movement overseas occurred in two major waves and was largely completed in the two decades between 1865 and 1885. Although a third wave left in the late 1880s and early 1890s, it represented a different phase in the migrational experience. It lacked the specificity of the earlier period, replacing family migration with individual migration and introducing new destinations. It was also a two-way flow, with re-migration nearly balancing new emigration. The to and fro movement of the period after 1885 served more as a tenuous information linkage between two gradually diverging societies than as a net conveyor of population in either direction. How the home society was consolidated and moved in new directions in the aftermath of the mass migrations, and the degree to which these developments paralleled or diverged from developments in the American daughter community, are the subjects of this final chapter.

Economic Change in the Post-Migration Years

The emigration from Rättvik took place in an era of economic change. Beginning with the land reforms of the *storskifte* in the 1830s and 1840s, the expectations of the population had gradually been heightened. New land was brought into cultivation while a time-honored economic system was stretched to its natural limits. There was a noticeable acceleration in new family formation and new families began having more children. Some signs of modernization and change were also beginning to appear, as timber companies began acquiring the rights to peasant forest lands and a fledgling urban commercial and service economy began to develop in the center of the parish on the shores of Lake Siljan. The physical limits of the agrarian expansion, however, were soon reached. That, coupled with the natural catastrophes of the late 1860s, played a key role in making emigration an attractive economic strategy among Rättvik's peasant proprietors for more than two decades.

The catastrophic crop failures and famines that plagued the region, first in the late 1860s and again in the early 1880s, were conditions that ameliorated with the passage of time. The severity of the natural disaster in the late 1860s was extraordinary. Things were not as bad when poor weather intervened the second time in the early 1880s and no significant recurrence of bad weather and crop losses was recorded thereafter. The bad years of the emigration period were eventually a thing of the past and no longer a factor in the regional economy. In addition, the post-famine and post-migration period was a time of renewed expansion and significant modernization for the agrarian economy of Rättvik. Although the changes were at times only gradual, the agrarian economy that emerged at the turn of the century was noticeably different from that which had existed at mid-century.

One engine of change was a rapid expansion of the arable during the early post-migration years. The amount of arable recorded for the parish in 1885 was up a remarkable 46.8 percent over 1865 figures.[1] This exceptional expansion of the agricultural base was largely the result of redoubled efforts to open new lands in the 1880s. The level of arable reached during that time represents the practical maximum for the region. It has never been more than marginally improved upon since.[2] The expansion of the 1880s contributed mightily to a revitalized agricultural output in the last decades of the century. Among the new land uses made possible by the expanded arable was the planting of large crops of oats. Oats had never been important to agriculture in Rättvik in the past, but the availability of new varieties in the 1880s, along with new demands for quality fodder generated by a general upgrading of livestock breeds, prompted its speedy adoption everywhere in the parish (Table 8.1).[3] Changes in the crop base also included the introduction of new strains of potatoes from America that were less prone to blight than the old varieties, and a new interest in root crops was promoted by agricultural society propaganda in the 1890s.[4] Just as the descendants of Rättvik settlers in Minnesota grappled successfully in the 1880s and 1890s with the problem of shifting their reliance on wheat to new and diversified crops, the descendants of the friends and neighbors who remained in Rättvik succeeded in changing the structure of their crop base to become more productive and less vulnerable.

The other major revolution occurred in animal husbandry as farmers

Table 8.1 Percentage of Total Arable Devoted to Specific Crops, Rättvik Parish, 1865 and 1900

Crops	1865	1900	Gain/loss
Barley	38.0%	10.0%	−73.7%
Legumes and oats	18.0	44.0	+144.4
Rye	11.0	6.0	−45.5
Potatoes	5.0	5.0	−
Grain blends	1.0	0.7	−30.0
Flax	0.4	0.1	−75.0
Other	0.3	1.0	+233.3
Fallow	25.0	4.0	−84.0
Totals	100.0%	100.0%	−

SOURCE: Johannes Borg, "Jordbruk och boskapskötsel," in *Rättvik* II: 169 (Table 4).

began to adopt new breeds of livestock. Many of the creatures that traditionally populated the pastures and barns of the parish were small and wiry, the result of decades of meagre feed. In 1879, the regional agricultural society *(hushållningssällskap)* introduced a number of Ayrshire cattle on the *prästgård* farm, the rather large holding maintained for the support of the clergy and church. The experiment was successful and received considerable local publicity. Before long, individual proprietors from around the parish began to purchase their own Ayrshires to replace the old local breed. Hand in hand with the upgrading of the cattle herd came the rise of a commercial dairying industry. Where milk and cheese products had barely been sufficient to meet home consumption in the past, Ayrshire milk cows produced surpluses that could be collected at creameries. Three creameries were established in the parish between 1886 and 1887, two of them privately owned (in Vikarbyn and Stumsnäs) and one of them cooperative (in Söderås).[5] Additional creameries were soon established in Gärdebyn, Backa, and in Övre and Nedre Gärdsjö. By the mid-1890s, Rättvik had the largest number of creameries of any parish in Dalarna, although difficulties that emerged after the turn of the century put all but two of them out of business before 1910.

New breeds and an increasingly commercial use of livestock introduced radical changes to the way in which livestock were fed and cared for. The acquisition of new breeds raised demand for quality feed. This was responded to in part by the switch to oats as a grain crop. Farmers also met the demand for improved feed by increased cultivation of legumes. Although originally cultivated on natural meadows, legume crops came to be a major use of arable by the 1890s. The percentage of the arable put into oats and legumes increased from just 18 percent in 1865 to 44 percent by the end of the century (Table 8.1). After mid-century it remained important to gather hay from natural meadows and small leaves and branches to feed farm animals in the winter, but these old traditions were being rapidly overshadowed by the more economical and less labor intensive alternative of cultivating fodder crops on arable land. Fodder crops could be harvested with some of the new implements and machinery that began to appear in the parish around the late 1880s, greatly lessening the massive amounts of manual labor traditionally required at haying time.

The extensive nature of animal husbandry that prevailed in the parish for much of the nineteenth century began to disappear in the last decades of the century. Cattle husbandry, in particular, became a far more sedentary enterprise as more proprietors kept their cattle on the home farm year-round. With each succeeding year, fewer and fewer proprietors drove their animals to the summer meadows of the far off *fäbod*. The declining importance of the *fäbod* to the local farm economy is well illustrated in John Frödin's classic study of the *fäbod* system of the Siljan parishes between the *storskifte* years of the 1830s and 1840s and the end of the 1910s. Frödin's Rättvik data for the years 1917–1918 show that only about 35 percent of the cattle in the parish were taken to the *fäbod*, a significant decline from the 1840s, when nearly all cattle were taken there.[6] Meanwhile the numbers of sheep and goats fell off drastically (Table 8.2). These animals, which were once a mainstay of the transhumant herd, became less and less important as agriculture and animal husbandry became more sedentary and more commercial. Overall, households possessed roughly half as many animals in 1900 as they had at mid-century. The introduction of commercial fertilizers, for one thing, made a high livestock-to-arable ratio less important than it had been in the past. The only domestic creatures to increase in numbers over the latter half of the century were swine. This was not due to any specific market force. It simply became more common for households to raise a pig for purposes of home consumption towards the latter part of the century.

Many of these changes were stimulated by improved transportation linkages with the outside world (Figure 8.1). The first assault on the relative isolation of Rättvik and the other Siljan parishes was the opening of steamship traffic on Lake Siljan in 1876. Regular steamship service on the lake hastened communications with the outside world and generated a capacity for the quick transport of some bulk goods. Commercial fertilizer, for example, was brought into the parish for the first time by boat in the 1880s. A long wooden pier was built out from the shore of Siljan near the mouth of the Enån River, where a small commercial center had begun to develop early in the century. The commercial center included the lower end of Lerdal village, from which the steamboat quay

Table 8.2 Number of Animals per 100 Hectares Arable, Rättvik Parish, 1865, 1885, and 1900

	1865	1885	1900
Horses	29	28	18
Cattle	113	98	87
Sheep	154	65	53
Goats	111	88	36
Swine	11	22	18

SOURCE: Johannes Borg, "Jordbruk och boskapsskötsel," in *Rättvik* II: 170 (Table 5).

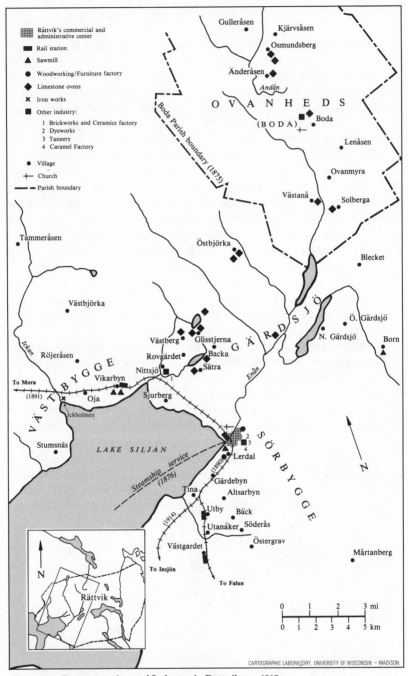

Figure 8.1 Transportation and Industry in Rättvik, ca. 1915

294

was built, as well as a growing number of commercial establishments clustered around the courthouse square *(tingshusplats)* established on the west side of the Enån in the 1820s. The church and its attendant structures were situated a bit farther to the west on a point of land jutting out into the lake. When steamboat service was initiated, the administrative and mercantile establishment was comprised of a number of official residences housing local officials and local representatives of commercial interests, a mill, a hotel and a couple of inns that were opened to serve steamboat passengers, a general store, a number of artisan workshops, and the parish's first industrial establishment—a dye works (Schwartz *färgeri,* established 1844).

Of greater significance than the introduction of steamboat service, however, was the coming of the railroad. The growing class of merchants, industrialists, and local officials who occupied the small commercial center saw much value in attracting a rail line to the parish. They began to promote railroad projects as early as the 1870s, not unlike their counterparts in Cambridge, Minnesota. In 1874, for example, there was a study of a possible line from Söderhamn on the Bothnian coast inland to Siljan via Ore parish and Rättvik's Enån valley. The idea seemed to have great potential, especially for the industrial development of the small limestone quarries and lime slaking ovens that dotted the valley. Rättvik's communal council went so far as to endorse the idea and appropriate some initial capital.[7] The project was forestalled, however, by the building of the Bergslagernes Järnväg line from Borlänge to Insjön. While this line did not reach Rättvik or any of the other upper Siljan parishes, it did connect the region with the nation's developing rail net. The next opportunity came in 1885, when a stock option for a new line connecting Rättvik to Falun came up. This time the local government was asked to raise a substantial sum, which a narrow majority of 53 percent of the voting public approved. Rättvik's commercial establishment apparently had the same difficulties as the merchants of Cambridge in drumming up popular enthusiasm in the countryside. Construction began several years later and the line reached the shore of Siljan in the center of Rättvik in August of 1890. The next year the line was extended westward to Mora. In 1914, another project connected Rättvik with the railhead at Insjön.[8]

The arrival of the railroad resulted in the consolidation and the enlargement of the administrative and commercial center of the parish. The fact that the settlement was split in two by the Enån presented some early difficulties. People were initially uncertain, for example, where to locate the railroad station. Lower Lerdal village, which

Plate 8.1 Intrusion of the outside world. The railroad reached the center of Rättvik in 1890, finally giving the parish an all-weather communication link with the outside world. The arrival of the railroad spurred the development of industry and commerce. The village of Lerdal is visible in the background. (Courtesy of Dalarnas Museum, date unknown)

already had the steamboat quay and two inns, was certainly an attraction, but they eventually decided to locate the station in front of the courthouse square, partly to make it more accessible to the church and parsonage.[9] The decision prompted the immediate construction of a new steamship pier and a new hotel and clearly shifted the center of gravity away from Lerdal. Both sites, nonetheless, were eventually engulfed in a rapidly expanding urban settlement. The area was quickly built over on a carefully laid out street plan. The main street was lighted in the early 1890s and birch trees were planted on the boulevards. By the turn of the century, the community had its first policeman. Among the new shops and commercial establishments was a doctor's office, an apothecary, a telegraph office, a bank, a bath house, a cafe, and the workshops of bakers, painters, tailors, cobblers, carpenters, and metal smiths. There were also a number of small industries, including a wagon factory, a fine woodworking factory, a caramel factory, a tannery, and a sawmill. Add a burgeoning tourist industry around the turn of the century and

Rättvik's commercial core may be said to have been every bit the equal of early twentieth-century Cambridge, Minnesota.[10]

The rapid growth of the commercial community after the arrival of the railroad is best illustrated in the multiplication of nonagricultural occupations found among resident households. In 1885, the commercial core boasted only twenty-five households, of which nearly a third were headed by individuals who held posts of various kinds within the ecclesiastical or civil administration of Rättvik *kommun*. Another third were headed by merchants or artisans and the remainder were engaged in various forms of unskilled work. By 1895, with the stimulus of a railroad connection, the number of households roughly doubled to fifty-one. Leading the expansion were the merchants and artisans, whose numbers more than tripled, and a new class of clerks and service employees, many of whom worked for the railroad. Ten years later the number of non-farm households had doubled again, to ninety-six, but by then the largest number of new households were in factory and service jobs. The commercial and industrial establishment, which was more or less in place by the turn of the century, had begun to expand through the employment of larger numbers of people in lower-level positions. This is reflected in an increasing number of "worker" households, consisting of one or two persons who had recently moved in from one of the surrounding villages to take a job as factory worker, hotel maid, or mill worker. This process continued to gain momentun over the next decade as the number of nonagricultural households doubled once again to 214. By 1915, more than a thousand people had come to depend for their livelihood on commerce and employment in Rättvik's commercial center.[11]

While it would be misleading to claim that Rättvik passed through any sort of decisive industrialization during this period, there certainly was a perceptible change and a quickening tempo to the way key resource industries employed surplus labor from the agrarian population. In general there was increased opportunity for nonagricultural day labor at certain times of the year, as well as full-time work in the industrial sector. A rising demand for wage labor had important repercussions for the local agrarian economy. Most importantly, it meant that old traditions of land tenure and inheritance would bear less pressure and perhaps even be modified as a rising proportion of young folk drifted into nonagricultural pursuits. Although far from overwhelming, a creeping proletarianization process, which was beginning to change the way households maintained themselves, was under way well before the end of the century.

Before this time, most local opportunities for wage or contract labor were derived from the demand for charcoal generated by the many small iron foundries scattered across Upper Dalarna and by the larger metallurgical industries of the nearby *Bergslagen* region. The prodigious demand for charcoal provided a ready source of seasonal labor for most peasant households. Rättvik itself had two important iron works in operation by the early years of the nineteenth century at Ickholmen and Dådran. Both drew on local labor reserves for the manufacture and hauling of charcoal and the hauling of ore and finished iron. Ickholmen, for example, is said to have employed nearly six hundred peasants in the 1830s for these purposes, mostly from the Västbygge villages of Rättvik parish and the eastern villages of neighboring Mora parish. But only twenty-four were permanently employed and living at Ickholmen. The iron works at Dådran played a similar role in the local economy of the Gärdsjö district. Like many small foundries across Sweden, both of these establishments began to decline during the latter half of the nineteenth century, creating a vacuum to be filled by new industries with different raw material and labor requirements.[12]

The most important of the new industries was the sawmilling and paper milling industry, the rise of which is often associated with industrial breakthrough in Swedish economic history. The sawmilling industry began to expand around mid-century, when steam-driven saws liberated the mills from having to rely on local water power. Nonetheless, the milling industry in Upper Dalarna developed relatively slowly in comparison to other parts of northern Sweden, mainly because the rivers were not well suited to floating timber or wood products; seasonal flows were uneven and the course of many streams was frequently broken by rapids and falls. The arrival of the railroad towards the end of the century, however, changed all of that. A thriving sawmilling industry grew up around Rättviken within just a few short years of the railroad's completion. The first two mills were established in Vikarbyn village at about the turn of the century. Both eventually became part of the large concern known as Grycksbo Papperbruk. Another mill was opened near the mouth of the Enån in 1903 and a fourth mill began operation in Born village in 1914. All four mills functioned as suppliers to the Grycksbo concern as well as to local woodworking and furniture industries. In turn, all four looked to peasant lands within the parish of Rättvik for the majority of their raw timber supplies.[13]

The milling industry employed considerable seasonal labor, just as the old iron industry had, but it also required a far larger permanent labor force, simply because the operation was less specialized and more diverse. Most mills needed a large number of hands to marshall logs, assist in the sawing operation, stack and load lumber products for delivery, and a host of other tasks that were contracted to individuals. As a result, the mills attracted a fairly large labor force to the village communities in which they were located, which was augmented further by those employed in the woodworking and wood-product finishing industries that often located near the mills. Vikarbyn village, for example, housed seventeen sawmill workers and their families in 1915 in addition to a number of men who identified themselves as "timbermen," carpenters, and woodworkers. Large numbers of young men throughout the parish were listed as "forest workers" after the turn of the century, a title that appeared only rarely before the 1880s. Among landless men with household responsibilities in the core villages of Gärdsjö *fjärding* (Nedre Gärdsjö, Övre Gärdsjö, Born, and Blecket), more than a third were listed as forest workers or woodworkers in the 1915 census rolls.

Limestone was another resource whose economic exploitation became more systematically organized and commercialized during the latter part of the nineteenth century. Surface deposits of quarry limestone were a common geologic feature of the donut-shaped Siljan Ring formation. Many of these deposits had a long history of exploitation. Building stones for pillars and portals on churches and other public buildings were quarried and shaped in the vicinity of Boda and neighboring villages from as early as the seventeenth century. But a far more common use of the resource was the production of lime *(kalkbränning)*. It originated as a peasant industry and persisted as an ancillary activity throughout the nineteenth century. Peasants burned quantities of crushed limestone in large ovens to produce lime primarily for local agricultural use. The work was done in combination with normal agricultural pursuits and spread over the year. The farmers cut and hauled wood fuel for the lime ovens during the winter and spring; broke and crushed the limestone during the lulls in summer agricultural activities; and burned the lime during the quiet months of late fall and early winter.

Later in the century, however, the burning of raw limestone to produce sulphate cakes for the paper industry became an industry of considerable scale and economic importance. The industry developed at numerous sites all up and down the Enån valley. At its peak there were perhaps eighty operations in all. Participation in the industry was especially important to the residents of several villages in Boda parish (formerly Ovanheds *fjärding*, but independent since 1875) and to the residents of the Gränden villages of Rättvik's Västbygge *fjärding*. Several of the most important production units were established early in

Plate 8.2 New industry in Rättvik. This brick factory near Boda village includes a brick-drying shed and warehouses. Boda church stands high on the horizon. (Courtesy Boda Hembygdsföreningen, photograph by Finn Lars Larsson, 1889)

Boda. The industrialist Pontus Levin erected three large ovens at a site not far from Boda village in the 1880s, where a mill and brick factory had previously been located to take advantage of a water power site. Other large ovens were located at Osmundsberg and Östbjörka. At the end of the 1890s, the peasants of the Gränden villages banded together to build a series of large ovens to provide sulphate cake for Grycksbo Paper Company. The cooperative venture was incorporated in 1898 as Kullsbergs Kalkförädlings AB. It was dominated by several unusually large families; the three principal owners together had no fewer than forty-five children.[14] Orders from the paper industry kept producers working steadily throughout the 1890s and the first decade of the next century, although the industry went into steep decline in the 1910s due to the coincidence of falling sulphate prices and rising labor costs brought on by increasing competition for labor with the local timber industry.

Revolutions within the timber and limestone industries, along with a few smaller industries that sprung up at key locations along the new railroad link—brick factories, dye works, textiles, furniture making, tourism, etc.—did much to diversify economic activity in the parish beyond agriculture. Production of all types in Rättvik was aimed less and less at local subsistence needs. The place was becoming increasingly integrated into regional and national markets both as a source of raw materials and primary industrial products and as a market for industrial goods.

With these changes came an inevitable, albeit gradual, movement away from the traditional and the customary. Even the traditional wanderings of the Dalarna folk took on a different face. The demand for migrant labor in the past had been loosely defined and seasonal, taking advantage of the well known woodworking, construction, and handicraft skills of the Dalarna peasant to meet a wide variety of extraordinary but temporally limited tasks. Demand now turned heavily in favor of a semi-permanent industrial labor force. Wanderers from the forest parishes of Dalarna were increasingly absorbed into distant jobs in the sawmilling or textile industries, which offered steady wages over longer periods of time. These employment opportunities drew migrant workers away from home for longer and often for indefinite periods of time, making it increasingly difficult to combine this kind of employment with the traditional annual cycle of work in the local agricultural economy. Economic life was becoming more specialized, with less room for the multifaceted seasonal work patterns of the past.[15]

The changing and more diversified character of the local economy is well illustrated by the declining number of landed households. Whereas nearly all households owned land at mid-century, only slightly more

Table 8.3 Landed Households in Rättvik and Boda Parishes, 1885–1915

Administrative district	Number of households (percent landed)			
	1885	1895	1905	1915
Sörbygge	424 (70.8%)	423 (61.5%)	441 (64.2%)	487 (57.5%)
Västbygge	587 (68.8)	635 (56.7)	618 (57.8)	691 (53.7)
Gärdsjö	531 (70.8)	547 (65.5)	520 (62.7)	620 (58.1)
Boda (Ovanheds)	493 (75.5)	517 (68.9)	439 (64.5)	509 (62.1)
Commercial and adm. center[a]	108 (62.0)	148 (38.5)	194 (33.0)	278 (23.0)
All households	2143 (70.9%)	2270 (61.3%)	2212 (59.4%)	2585 (53.8%)

SOURCE: Population registers *(mantalslängder)* for Rättvik and Boda parishes, 1885, 1895, 1905, and 1915.

a Includes Lerdal village and the environs surrounding the court house square *(Tingshusplatsen)*, railroad station, church, and vicarage.

than 70 percent had direct claims to agricultural land by 1885. The proportion diminished further to just over 60 percent by 1895 and fell below 60 percent for the first time in 1905 (Table 8.3). The rising number of town-dwelling nonagricultural households located in the expanding commercial center on the shore of Lake Siljan is, of course, one reason for the decline. But even if these households are set aside, there was still a substantial shift going on in the rural villages. Even up in the villages of Boda, which were most distant from the railhead, sawmills, and industries on Siljan's shore, the proportion of landed households slipped from 75.5 percent to 62.1 percent between 1885 and 1915. The increasing uncertainty about a landed future that had caused so many households to consider emigration to America in the 1860s became a reality in the latter part of the century and, in the process, forced significant changes in the economic structure of the region.

Culture and Community

Paralleling the profound economic changes of the times were a number of developments that began to alter some basic conceptions of community and place. Among these developments was the realization in 1875 of the long-sought secession of Ovanheds *fjärding* from Rättvik to form the new parish of Boda. The emergence of Boda as a separate parish redefined old notions of centrality and community for a large segment of the population, although such adjustments had actually been under way for a long period of time.[16] Reforms instituted in 1862 to separate local ecclesiastical and civil administration had even more far-reaching consequences. The new civil *kommun* administration introduced new forms of representation and responsibility to a population long accustomed to relying solely on the leadership of the clergy and a small elected council. New popular causes and concerns also intruded on the traditionally placid peasant consciousness. Low-church alternatives to the state church, which had been slow to make inroads into this parish at mid-century, became far more prevalent as the century waned. People were increasingly concerned about political issues such as the evils of alcohol and the need to redefine the electorate more broadly. New connections with the outside world served to open up Rättvik society in ways that had never been contemplated before. They generated palpable changes in old attitudes and identities that reveal the growing number of socioeconomic distinctions within the population.

Symptomatic of much of what was happening was a gradual decline in the influence of clergy and church over civil affairs. The administrative reorganization of 1862 marked the end of what could be called a wholly ecclesiastical local administration. The church retained control of its own affairs as well as the administration of schools, but many traditional functions of the old parish council *(sockenstämma)* were given over to a new representative body, the communal council *(kommunalstämma)*. The change seemed to have relatively little effect at first, for the elected leadership of the communal council differed little from that of the old parish council. The chair of the council from 1880 to 1892 was Per Pettersson, a clergyman who was known locally and nationally for his conservative values and his willingness to stubbornly defend the status quo. While growing national sentiment during this period generally advocated a liberal program of internal improvements in communication, education, and administration, the outlook of local government was often exceedingly conservative. The rise of town life and a more diversified economic structure, however, meant a growing popular interest in governance that often ran counter to that of the old order. These concerns began to have a telling effect on the leadership and administration of Rättvik by roughly the turn of the century.

Contributing to the sense of political change was the broadening of the political base that accompanied the administrative reforms of the 1860s. The right to elect representatives to the old parish council had been limited to the landed peasantry. Elections for the new civil administration enfranchised those who paid taxes on income from labor and capital as well as those who paid taxes on landed property. These changes exerted relatively little effect during the early decades, mainly because voting rights were determined on the basis of the amount of tax paid. Landowners nearly always qualified while wage earners often paid too little in taxes to meet the minimum required for enfranchisement. Furthermore, prevailing methods of computing voting rights from tax assessments tended to favor those who held property over other forms of income. The votes of property owners were given extra weight, which undermined the voting strength of wage-earning classes even in cases where they commanded larger numbers.[17]

Even had the enfranchisement rules been more equitable, there would have been little danger that political control would pass out of the hands of the landholding agrarian class before the turn of the century; their margin of control was far too formidable. Nonetheless, the proportion of voting rights claimed by the nonagricultural population began to rise steadily after 1880, especially as notions of political equality brought home by returning emigrants from the American Middle West began to take root.[18] The steady rise of a new political alignment can be seen in the declining proportion of votes cast by the landed class, from a commanding 63.7 percent in 1884 to 53.2 percent in 1896.[19] It fell to less than half for the first time in the early 1900s, after which it became increasingly difficult for the old small-holding society to deny Rättvik's growing industrial and landless agrarian classes some measure of control over local affairs. In 1910, the growing commercial town in the parish's center, from which many new economic and social demands emanated, was allowed to become an independent unit within the larger communal administration, with the right to elect its own representative council and pursue its own administration.

The fracturing of the old, homogeneous peasant society began in the 1870s. The first cracks appeared in the form of a series of religious awakenings and free church movements that began to challenge the authority of the church and clergy. Rättvik had escaped much of the religious turmoil that beset other Dalarna parishes during the middle decades of the nineteenth century. While struggles between pietistic sects tore asunder many neighboring parishes in the 1840s and 1850s, Rättvik managed to accommodate and to defuse such tendencies within its own borders. The success of such policies may be laid primarily at the feet of the parish's clerical leadership. The parson who served Rättvik between 1837 and 1874, Per Ulrik Boëthius, was a particularly strong influence. Boëthius's policy was simply to channel the pietistic movement within the bounds of the church. Rather than dogmatically resisting the pressures of the time, he met religious dissidence with openness, deftly embracing the strong social appeal of pietistic views without compromising his own position, inviting leaders of the low-church movements to speak in Rättvik's church and arranging for low-church meetings to take place in village schools. The result of this policy of open accommodation was, paradoxically, a much delayed and less strident opposition to the ministrations of the state church in this parish. The folk in Rättvik quickly earned a reputation in neighboring parishes for their steadfast loyalty to orthodox church views.[20]

The establishment of viable lay organizations within Rättvik, however, could not be fended off forever. The 1870s, in fact, turned out to be the crucial decade in this development. One factor was certainly the installation of the new parson, Per Pettersson, who established himself as a bulwark of conservatism and orthodoxy. Pettersson pursued a policy of active opposition to separatistic aspirations of all kinds and helped to fan smoldering coals into flames. In all fairness, however, it was also a far more difficult time, for at issue in the 1870s was the most sensitive of churchly prerogatives, the administration of the sacraments. The Baptists, who were the largest of the low-church movements in the region, were just emerging from a period of internecine struggle and were once again in a position to pursue new converts aggressively after a period of relative quiescence. To share the sacraments with a lesser religious authority was an accommodation the state church simply could not comtemplate for doctrinal reasons as well as in the interest of self-preservation.[21]

The Baptists were the first to establish themselves formally in Rätt-vik. The first Baptist congregation was organized in 1870 with five charter members. It drew its strength from the villages of Sörbygge *fjärding*, which seems to have been an early source of religious unrest. Although this initial congregation remained small for many years, a chapel was eventually built in the village of Altsarbyn in 1879 that has remained in continuous use ever since.

Of greater importance than the Baptists were the Mission Friends. Mission meetings were held in the vicinity of Söderås village in the mid-1870s and a mission house was built there around 1876. A second mission congregation was established in Övre Gärdsjö village roughly a year later.[22] These early free church congregations posed a slight threat to the hegemony of the state church, mainly because the initial outbreak of organized activity was limited to the districts of Sörbygge and Gärdsjö and because the congregations were far from large. The events of the 1880s, however, would offer them the kind of sustenance that would cause them to grow and spread.

Premiere among the many developments of the 1880s was a single issue that split public opinion in Rättvik and played a major role in the developing religious struggle. This was the rancorous debate over the rights of Baptists, who often established their own schools, to partici-pate in the educational system. New education regulations promulgated in the 1860s required most communes to enlarge existing school systems during the 1870s, often at considerable expense and over the protesta-tions of the landholding class, which bore the costs of such improve-ments. The experience made public education a sensitive local issue. It was exacerbated in the 1880s by a set of statutes designed to define the rights of nonconformist religions. They required that dissenters be allowed to educate only their own children. Yet it was often the case locally that non-Baptist children attended Baptist schools, or that school teachers who suddenly became Baptists found themselves in the awkward position of instructing the children of orthodox parishioners. Although the prejudicial nature of these statutes was quickly challenged in court and changed, the fact was often ignored locally, resulting in attempts to fire teachers and obstruct the rights of individuals. One such case, in which Rättvik's parson, Per Pettersson, attempted to prevent a young Baptist woman from teaching, became a celebrated example of the controversy.[23]

The increasingly inflexible positions taken by all sides was accompanied by rising numbers of adherents to Mission and Baptist congregations during the 1880s and 1890s. Established Mission congregations in the Gärdsjö and Sörbygge villages soon helped to found "mission circles" in the other districts, which eventually became congregations in their own right. The first of these circles appeared in the early 1880s amongst adherents in the Västbygge villages of Stumsnäs, Västbjörka, and Öja. Additional congregations were established in Lerdal and Bingsjö during the 1890s and in Vikarbyn around 1915. The Baptist expansion came a bit later. A new chapel was added in Vikarbyn around 1891. Baptist strength was further augmented by new congregations in Röjeråsen and in Rättvik's commercial center around the turn of the century. In addition, the decade of the 1880s saw the establishment of a new sect—the Seventh-Day Adventists. After an initial period in which the Adventists were associated with the Baptists, an Adventist congregation was founded in 1886.

Although the contest was bitter at times, the free church movement never threatened to destroy the social fabric of Rättvik. Strident religious confrontation gradually abated as the authorities became resigned to the new situation and an air of peaceful coexistence was well in place by the turn of the century. Membership in the various nonconformist congregations stabilized after 1910 at around seven or eight hundred, which constituted a significant but hardly overwhelming proportion of the faithful. The establishment and growth of nonconformist religious organizations in the latter half of the nineteenth century was, however, an early indication of emerging differences in Rättvik. The membership of these organizations was often highly restricted to certain kinship networks in certain villages or districts. Acceptance or participation occurred in a fashion similar to emigration, highlighting local social and economic distinctions. Where low-church activity happened to coincide with a strong emigration tradition, the influence of the trans-Atlantic linkage could be quite apparent. This is well demonstrated in the establishment of Rättvik's Adventist congregation, which was directly inspired by a tract sent home from America by a Rättvik woman who had emigrated a number of years earlier.[24]

There was an exceptionally strong link between the mission congregation in Övre Gärdsjö village and the Athens settlement in Isanti

County. One of the most fascinating indications of the linkage is the fact that, in the 1910s, the mission church in Övre Gärdsjö and the Lutheran church in Athens township contained nearly identical altar paintings (compare Plates 8.3 and 8.4). The duplication apparently was the result of influences moving across the Atlantic from daughter to mother community. Around 1909, the Athens church acquired an altar painting by the Norwegian-American artist, designer, and dealer in church furnishings, August Klagstad, whose work appeared in a number of Scandinavian churches across the American Middle West.[25] Someone was sufficiently impressed to take the image home to Sweden, for within a few years, the Mission Church in Övre Gärdsjö produced a nearly identical altar painting, although done by a local artist.[26] The incident is remarkable and is as clear an indication as any that there was a steady trans-Atlantic trade of ideas and cultural influences between migration-linked kinship groups that persisted well into the twentieth century.

The rise of separatist religious organizations is just one indication of emerging social differences within late-nineteenth-century Rättvik society. Another was the temperance movement. Temperance first became a national concern in Sweden during the 1830s and 1840s. Home distillation of grains and potatoes was an essential part of the local agrarian economy. A major by-product was draff, commonly used as livestock feed. Quantities of liquor were also produced and consumed, often intemperately. Concern over the high social and economic cost of alcohol consumption led to the founding of a national temperance organization *(Svenska nykterhetssällskapet)*, which boasted more than four hundred chapters by the end of the 1840s. This early temperance movement was closely allied with the church; its chapters were often led by clergymen. Rättvik's chapter was jointly run by the parson and the parish's only medical doctor, who attempted to combat intemperance primarily through educational programs.[27]

The old Swedish temperance movement, however, was radically altered in the latter half of the nineteenth century. Certain economic changes, such as the discreditation of feeding draff to livestock, the imposition of high taxes on home production of liquor, and the introduction of modern factory distilleries, led to a sharp decline in home distillation. Liquor became a relatively inexpensive and widely distributed commodity that was consumed in larger quantities than ever before. Under these conditions, temperance advocates began to view the old temperance organization as inherently weak. They mistrusted the old association with the church and sought new associations that were prepared to undertake more aggressive and political initiatives. Dif-

Plate 8.3 Altar painting, Faith Lutheran Church, Athens township. This altar painting by the Norwegian–American artist August Klagstad was acquired by the Athens congregation in 1909. (Courtesy Isanti County Historical Society)

ferences between strategies made the temperance problem a political issue. The liberal strategy advocated an unregulated but heavily taxed liquor economy in order to strengthen state finances. Restrictionist strategies sought to constrain production. New legislation in the mid-1850s sought a compromise by raising the level of taxation on the production of spirits, imposing taxes on retail liquor sales, and regulating retail sales. Regulation was eventually undertaken by communal authorities, which made the deliberations of the local council a potential battleground for temperance activists.

Plate 8.4 Altar painting, Gärdsjö Mission Church, Övre Gärdsjö village. This painting was commissioned from a local artist, Ollas Anders Hansson-Furn, just a few years after the altar painting was hung in the Athens church. The idea was quite possibly transmitted across the Atlantic by migrants passing back and forth between the communities. (Photograph by Mats Peres, 1986)

The rise of the new temperance movement appeared in Rättvik in the 1880s. It was closely tied to the rise of the free church movements and clearly influenced by developments in America. Foremost among the new temperance organizations that began to spring up everywhere was the Swedish edition of the American fraternal organization, the International Order of Good Templars. The Good Templars introduced a unique blend of religion and idealism that appealed strongly to many of the same elements that embraced religious nonconformism. As a consequence the organization expanded rapidly in Sweden after it first appeared in 1879. By 1883, Rättvik had its first lodge in Vikarbyn village. Within a few years additional lodges appeared in more than half a dozen other villages, including an especially large and successful lodge established in Rättvik's commercial center in the early 1890s.[28]

Not only did the Good Templars have a strong association with the free churches, they also had strong connections with certain socioeconomic groups. In the case of Rättvik's centrally located lodge, it was the railroad workers who were the organizing force. The broad appeal of the order and its organizational structure, which encouraged large numbers of local lodges, made it an umbrella organization for many factions. Membership could indicate certain cleavages in society wherever lodges were established. In America, religious and secular tensions within the Good Templars soon spawned an offshoot organization with stronger Christian leanings. A parallel development occurred in Sweden, resulting in the founding of the Temple Order *(Templarorden)*. By the early 1890s, Rättvik had a full complement of lodges belonging to the latter order as well.

The geographic diffusion of these temperance organizations in Rättvik was remarkably close to that of the free church movement. The villages of Sörbygge *fjärding*, in particular, were the early focus. From those villages the movement spread to the larger villages in the western portion of Rättvik and up the Enån valley, but it eventually drew most of its strength from the population of the rapidly expanding commercial town in the parish's midst. The free church and the temperance movements in Rättvik both appealed to a segment of society that harbored powerful moralistic sentiments and supported the rising national tide of liberalism. Their common preoccupation with temperance was joined in 1887 through the formation of a Rättvik temperance committee, which united the mission church, the Baptists, and the Templars in common cause. The committee proved to be a highly active and effective force in local politics, especially in the early years of the new century. Much the same development was going on in Isanti at roughly the same time.[29]

While little progress seemed possible when these organizations were established in the 1880s and 1890s, the triumph of temperance efforts became inevitable by the first decades of the new century. The difficulties of the early years stemmed from the entrenched position of the opposition. The major distribution points for spirits in the parish were a number of inns and hotels that enjoyed a long-standing right to sell spirits to travelers and guests. Although the commune had the right to suspend licenses for such establishments, it was not disposed to do so. The first victory came in 1900, when temperance forces succeeded in preventing Rättvik's tourist hotel from establishing liquor service at a new "overlook" tower constructed on the heights overlooking Siljan. At the same time, temperance forces became deeply involved in the controversy over enfranchisement as part of a general effort to win leverage over the opposition, which tied itself closely to the propertied vote. A 1909 straw vote organized by a national consortium of temperance organizations revealed a strong majority in Rättvik in favor of enforced abstinence. This led, roughly a decade later, to a series of parish-wide rallies and a campaign that ended in a binding communal "dry vote," in which

71 percent of the voting public indicated their approval of the temperance position.[30]

The political action of the temperance movement early in the twentieth century marks the beginning of a new and more diverse political era. Partly because of the homogeneity of the old landed society and partly because of the relative lateness of industrialization, Rättvik's political life was remarkably quiet throughout the nineteenth century. Local leaders and national representatives alike tended to exhibit moderately conservative philosophies. During the national customs debates of the 1880s, representatives from the region favored free trade over protectionism. Beginning in the 1890s, however, liberal representatives began to emerge, and with the reformed enfranchisement of the 1900s liberals and social democrats came to dominate. Interestingly, however, the rise of worker's movements and socialist politics was delayed until relatively late. The first socialist organization was an association of small farmers and forest workers, Dalarna's Small-holders and Forest-workers Association (*Dalarnes småbonde- och skogsarbetareförbund*), which was organized in 1907 to protect the rights of members against the wage and procurement policies of the large timber companies.[31] Sawmill workers and railroad employees also became involved later in the decade, working through the Good Templars lodge in Rättvik's commercial center. But the emergence of a strong political left in Rättvik would wait until later in the century.

Population, Land, and Family

One of the most notable changes that occurred in the years after the mass emigrations to America was demographic. Decadal increments in the Rättvik population were at their highest during the decades of the 1830s and 1840s. During those two decades the population of the parish increased by 11.3 percent and 10.8 percent, respectively. Those were optimistic times, when the agricultural economy of the parish absorbed ever-increasing numbers of new family units through the subdivision of older farms and through the colonization of new arable and meadow on the margins of the old village lands. By the late 1860s, however, declining opportunity and natural disaster had burst the bubble of prosperity. Parish society was shaken first by a series of disastrous famine years and then by the mass emigration of large numbers of young and middle-aged family units to America. Losses from disease, starvation, and out-migration, along with declining birth rates, trimmed the decadal increase in population for the 1860s to a mere 2.9 percent. Although conditions gradually improved during the 1870s, the return of hard times and the renewal of emigration at the end of that decade and through much of the 1880s caused the rate of population growth to remain relatively modest: Rättvik's population grew at a rate of roughly 5.7 percent in the 1870s and 6.5 percent in the 1880s. But those were the last decades in which any notable increase in population occurred, for after 1890 the population began to stabilize and then to decline gradually. The decade of the 1890s posted only a small increase of 1.9 percent, while the subsequent decade witnessed a decline of just under one percent.[32]

The factors that lay behind the slowing of population growth are clear. Lower population levels were in part a product of out-migration, both to America and to other parts of Sweden, and declining levels of fertility. Improvements in agricultural conditions and new transportation linkages with the outside world meant that crop failure and famine became less chronic problems and, as a consequence, the high rates of mortality that were frequently associated with such episodes disappeared. Gradual improvements in public health measures also helped produce a generally lower and certainly a more even death rate after the turn of the century. The mortality index for Dalarna as a whole during the latter half of the nineteenth century was at its highest during the famine years of the late 1860s. From that point it declined gradually over the course of the next few decades, before dropping relatively precipitously in the first decades of the new century. The mortality index for Kopparberg County between 1881 and 1901 declined by 10.9 percent. The decline for the first two decades of the twentieth century was a steeper 17.8 percent.[33]

Continued emigration to America drained the population considerably. Although the mass family emigration that occurred between the 1860s and the end of the 1880s may have had the most striking impact at home and overseas, emigrants continued to leave the parish in substantial numbers right into the twentieth century. The three waves of emigration that occurred prior to 1890 were, in fact, followed by four additional waves of emigration: the first in the early 1890s, a second in the mid-1890s, a third just after the turn of the century, and a fourth in the years prior to the onset of World War I. While emigration rates in peak years were generally somewhat lower, the twenty-five years following 1890 actually yielded about 15 percent more emigrants than the twenty-five years preceding.[34]

Other differences distinguished the turn-of-the-century emigrants from those who had gone before. The later emigrations were largely composed of landless young men, who were primarily in their late teens and early twenties and who were as yet unmarried. Nearly three-quarters of all emigrants who made up the earlier waves of emigration left in family groups. Even a large proportion of the single migrants of that period were, in fact, members of emigrant families, whose emigration either preceded or followed the main departure of other family members. The reverse was true for the turn-of-the-century emigrations. This time nearly three-quarters of all emigrants left on their own, a vast majority with only tenuous connections to family or relatives who might also have emigrated. Among adult emigrants, males outnumbered females by more than three to one (312.2 males per 100 females), a substantial difference from the earlier emigrations in which the degree of male dominance was only half as great (165.1 males per 100 females). The average turn-of-the-century emigrant was just under 26 years of age, as compared to 32 years of age several decades earlier. Few of these young men or women were listed as property-holders prior to their emigration. Most had occupational titles such as agricultural laborer, forest laborer, construction worker, carpenter, mason, servant, or maid. In many ways the turn-of-the-century emigrants were much more like the traditional short-distance or internal migrant than were their earlier counterparts.

Emigrants, in fact, had become indistinguishable from internal migrants, save for ultimate destination. Earlier in the nineteenth century, the fluctuating curves of internal migration and emigration often seemed complementary. When emigration was up, internal migration was down, and vice versa. The two kinds of out-migration served different purposes; they were responses to different sets of circumstances. But in the closing decades of the nineteenth century and the early decades of the twentieth, their respective volumes rose and fell at precisely the same times. And in most cases, the volume of emigration remained consistently one-quarter to one-third that of internal migration.[35]

Taken together, the volume of emigrants and internal migrants was considerable, equaling and often exceeding the levels experienced during the worst years of the 1860s and 1880s. Offsetting out-migration to a certain extent was a heightened volume of in-migrants, especially after 1900. Although considerable at times, the flow of in-migrants was never voluminous enough to match out-migration. Return migrants from America, who had not come in significant numbers before 1890, were a part of the in-migrant flow. They entered the parish in increasing numbers up until the turn of the century, after which their numbers dropped off rather quickly. Some of the return migrants were from the early family emigrations to daughter settlements in Minnesota and the Dakotas, but most were from the later waves of young men and women, a portion of whom usually returned after a year or two. Rättvik's return migration was never large. At its peak, it amounted to no more than 10 percent of all migration into the parish. Rättvik remained throughout the period a net exporter of manpower. Indeed, even with higher levels of in-migration in the years after 1900, net out-migration was great enough to overwhelm, any natural increase in population in no fewer than eleven out of fifteen years. This highly negative net migration was a major contributing factor in the general decline in population registered in Rättvik's *kommun* over those years.

Working hand-in-hand with the draining effect of out-migration was a generally lower level of fertility among Rättvik women. Fertility in Rättvik, as measured by child–woman ratios, was at its highest during the pre-emigration decades. Those decades saw a heightened level of new family formation and considerable population growth. Agricultural disaster and mass emigration, however, marked the onset of a different demographic profile. The difficult years of the late 1860s, the 1870s, and the early 1880s saw a sharp drop in fertility. The number of young children per 1,000 married women dropped from an all-time high of 958.2 in 1867 to fewer than 800 one decade later (Table 8.4). There it remained for more than two decades before rising slightly in the early 1890s, only to fall off once again to the mid-700s around the turn of the century. The child–woman ratio is, of course, always affected by varying levels of mortality. The decline of the famine years is, in part, a function of increased

Table 8.4 Number of Children Aged 0–4 per 1,000 Married Women Aged 20–49, Rättvik and Boda Parishes, 1867–1915 ˙

Age group	1867	1877	1885	1895	1905	1915
20–24	933.3	625.0	500.0	450.0	476.2	571.4
25–29	1121.2	1153.8	882.4	857.1	758.7	1087.5
30–34	1084.7	1034.5	1117.7	1142.9	1212.1	1053.8
35–39	1127.3	923.1	904.8	818.2	845.4	887.0
40–44	824.6	520.0	300.0	789.5	553.9	563.9
45–49	450.0	227.3	863.6	486.1	269.2	277.6
20–49	934.4	779.9	848.1	804.3	631.6	724.1
20–49[a]	958.2	796.8	797.1	808.1	750.9	790.4

SOURCES: Catechetical register *(husförhörslängder)* for Rättvik and Boda parishes, 1867 and 1877; population registers *(mantalslängder)* for Rättvik and Boda parishes, 1885, 1895, 1905, 1915. Data are based on a 20 percent sample of all households, N = 259 (1867), 259 (1877), 316 (1885), 368 (1895), 380 (1905), 398 (1915).
[a] Standardized for the age distribution of the population.

infant mortality. But levels of mortality during this period were far too low to explain the rather drastic drop in the child–woman ratio. In the late nineteenth century, declining mortality rates should have bolstered the ratio.

Women were having fewer children. They were also marrying later. The pre-migration decades witnessed a general lowering of the age at which women married as improved conditions made the earlier formation of new families possible. Declining opportunity on the land during the latter half of the century, however, made the prospects of early marriage and family less certain for young men and women alike. The percentage of women who married in their twenties dropped precipitously from highs of 44.0 and 38.9 percent in 1867 and 1877, respectively, to only 27.4 percent in 1885 (Table 8.5). As the number of landless young men multiplied in the closing decades of the century, the prospects for early marriage declined further. The percentage of women who were married in their twenties dropped to a mere 20 percent in the 1890s and reached a mere 11.3 percent in the 1910s. Even for women in their thirties, there appear to have been fewer marriage prospects. Only two-thirds of women in their thirties had found mates at the end of the century, as opposed to nearly nine-tenths of women that age two and a half decades earlier.

All of these changes are simple reflections of the fundamental reorganization of peasant society and peasant households that was being effected at the time. The onset of large-scale family emigration in the late 1860s may be seen as a conservative reaction to a growing realization that the era in which the local land base could indefinitely absorb

Table 8.5   Percentage of Women Ever Married, Rättvik and Boda Parishes, 1867–1915

	AGE					
	15–19	20–29	30–39	40–49	50–59	60+
1867	2.3%	44.0%	83.2%	91.5%	90.0%	94.8%
1877	2.4	38.9	89.8	90.0	94.8	92.1
1885	0.0	27.4	76.0	92.9	95.7	92.8
1895	0.0	20.0	75.4	86.0	93.9	94.1
1905	0.0	19.6	66.0	78.7	93.3	93.7
1915	0.0	11.3	76.6	83.3	88.7	92.4

SOURCES: Catechetical registers *(husförhörslängder)* for Rättvik and Boda parishes, 1867 and 1877; population registers *(mantalslängder)* for Rättvik and Boda parishes, 1885, 1895, 1905, and 1915. Data are based on a 20 percent sample of all households, N = 437 (1867), 457 (1877), 470 (1885), 548 (1895), 694 (1905), 802 (1915).

a growing agrarian population was drawing to a close. Faced with that reality, and perhaps spurred by the short-term consequences of repeated crop failure, many households embraced the strategy of "fragmenting away" a portion of their number to daughter colonies in America. It was a way of relieving for a time the increasingly high ratio of people to resources experienced on most peasant holdings. It helped reduce the relatively high frequency of peasant households that included more conjugal families than the land could support, and for which the course of inheritance was bound to be problematic. At the same time, it averted the difficulty of seeing sons and daughters forced off the land and out of the community. Through emigration, they could remain landed and they could remain a part of the community in the sense that American daughter settlements were an extension of the home community. Emigration, however, was not able to alleviate the problem indefinitely. The peasant household was forced to continue to free itself of responsibility for large numbers of young people who were coming of age. More and more were forced to leave at an earlier age, without the opportunity to form families or possess property. For these later migrants, there was less and less difference between migrating to other parts of Sweden in search of labor or migrating to America. They were attracted to opportunities for wage labor wherever they arose, within or without the boundaries of the home parish. Some found work in the forests or in the industries stimulated by the arrival of the railroad. Some went to America and passed through the now fully settled daughter communities, staying for a time, moving on, sometimes returning. Others moved down to the sawmills along Sweden's Bothnian coast or into the mills and factories of small towns and cities elsewhere in Sweden. The growing uncertainties of acquiring property and the heightened mobility among young people led inexorably to delayed family formation and lower levels of fertility.

These conditions also led to a more socially differentiated rural society and to more simplified household structures among Rättvik's rural population. Although the number of rural households grew steadily over the turn-of-the-century decades, the proportion of landed households declined. Peasant households were less prone to be extended at the turn of the century than they were a half century earlier. They ceased to include large numbers of married children or siblings. There was instead a sharp rise in the number of young people who appear in the population registers as new households, separate from those of their parents and quite often without land. The mean size of rural households declines steadily over the period. The average rural household at mid-century was comprised of just over eight persons, was landed, and had a better than even chance of extending to include married children, retired parents, or siblings. In contrast, the average rural household in 1895 numbered only four and one-half persons, and it had a one-in-three chance of being propertyless. Slightly more than 10 percent of households in 1895 consisted of a single adult living alone. Twenty years later the average household size had fallen to under four persons. Rural society had become almost evenly divided between households that earned their living directly from the land and households that depended on wage labor.

These developments were in sharp contrast to what was going on in the American daughter settlements. There too, finite resources were causing farm households to search for new ways of providing for one's offspring, but the situation was less pressing. Families could still move westward to new frontiers on the plains, in the Pacific Northwest, or Canada. With calculated inheritance strategies, it was still possible to place one's children on the land within existing settlement areas. Rural households in Isanti continued to grow in size long after the reverse was true in the home parish, reaching a peak mean size of nearly six persons in the 1910s (Table 8.6). While large numbers of the American-born children of Rättvik immigrants ended up as laborers, artisans, and clerks in Cambridge or other nearby urban settlements, many more still ended up on the land through inheritance of a portion of their parents' rapidly expanding holdings or through the purchase of new land with the help of their parents. Such opportunity to remain on the land was seriously lacking in Rättvik.

Table 8.6   Rural Population and Average Household Size, Rättvik and Isanti, 1885–1915

	Rättvik			Isanti Study Area		
	Population	No. of households	Avg. household size	Population	No. of households	Avg. household size
1885	9,343	2,035	4.59	4,795	966	4.96
1895	9,639	2,122	4.54	6,300	1,225	5.14
1905	9,574	2,018	4.74	7,119	1,246	5.71
1915	9,173	2,307	3.98	5,872	1,015	5.79

SOURCES: Population registers *(mantalslängder)* for Rättvik and Boda parishes, 1885, 1895, 1905, 1915; manuscripts of the Minnesota 1885, 1895, and 1905 censuses and reconstructed demographic data for Isanti County in 1915 (based on federal manuscript census reports for 1910, church records, county birth and death records, and the *Atlas and Farmer's Directory of Isanti County, Minnesota,* 1914).

What did the emigration of a fragment of a peasant household during the exodus of the 1860s or 1880s mean to those who remained behind? Did this early easing of pressure have a significant effect on the fortunes of households as they marshalled resources to face the shifting economic scene of the post-migration era? This is an important but difficult question to answer. There are so many unknown variables involved that no systematic investigation may ever be possible. However, one can glimpse what happened by following the fortunes of one household that seems typical of the many that sent out emigrants—the Perols farm of Övre Gärdsjö village.[36]

The Perols farm was a modest holding by the standards of mid-century Rättvik. The land had been subdivided for some time between the two eldest of Perols Erik Ersson's sons, Erik and Anders. A third son, whom we met in Chapter 1, Hans Ersson, had married into another farm in nearby Blecket village. The first two sons lived on the Perols farm with the widowed father. Erik was the older of the two sons and had been the first to marry, taking a bride in the late 1830s. His younger brother, Anders, was married in the early 1840s. At the time of their marriages, each received his respective portion of the farm and assumed the obligation to maintain their aging parent. The old man passed away in the summer of 1853, leaving the two brothers in complete control. Seventeen children were born to the two families by the onset of difficult times around the mid-1860s; twelve survived childhood. The eldest brother, at that time, had seven children, among whom four were over twenty years of age. The younger brother had five children, of whom two were old enough to begin thinking of land and marriage.

It was at that time that the third brother, Hans Ersson, decided to leave his home in Blecket village and emigrate to America. The older brother elected to join the emigrant party; we can only guess at the rationale behind his decision. In the spring of 1866, Perols Erik Ersson gathered his family and belongings and left for America. He was fifty years old, perhaps a bit too old to start anew, but there were a number of adult children in his immediate family as well as a good many relatives and friends in the emigrant party. They moved to Isanti's Athens township, where they amassed sufficient land and wealth to establish all members of the family on the land. Back in Rättvik, the effect of Erik Ersson's departure was immediately to reduce by nearly one-half the pressure of population on the finite resources of the Perols estate, making the remaining brother, Perols Anders Ersson, a more prosperous member of the local peasantry, although he may well have gone into debt in order to compensate his older brother for relinquishing his claims on the farm.[37]

The striking thing about the relationship between the Perols farm and its occupants over the next several decades is the relative stability of the ratio between dependents and land resources. For the next ten years, the farm supported a nuclear family of eight members. Perols Anders Ersson retained control of the land until the eldest of his children reached their late twenties, at which time a number of arrangements were made that worked to maintain the integrity of the farm and to establish the next generation on the land. One of his older sons, Hans Andersson, was married in 1876 to a woman from Blecket. The new couple took up residence on the Perols farm. One year later, another new bride was brought to the farm by a second son, although fate cruelly took her and her newborn child the following year. Within a year, however, he had remarried. Thus by 1878 a total of three nuclear families were residing on the farm. Some departures compensated for the new additions. Two more adult children were married onto other farms. A further redressing of the people–land ratio on the Perols farm was effected in 1884, when one of the two new couples then residing on the farm took their three children and moved to a new farm in neighboring Nedre Gärdsjö village, which was purchased with resources generated from the Perols estate.

Through a series of deft maneuvers, the aging couple managed to find a landed future for each of their offspring while retaining direct control of the ancestral farm. This they did not relinquish until advancing infirmity forced the issue just before the turn of the century. Now in their eighties, the old couple finally retired, passing ownership of the Perols estate into the hands of Hans Andersson, the son who married the woman from Blecket. After the old couple's death a few years later, the farm was occupied solely by Hans Andersson, his wife, and three sons.

Like his father before him, the new owner kept a tight rein on the property entrusted to him. His own three sons remained on the farm for years. The 1915 population register listed all three sons as unmarried and resident on the farm. At thirty-six, thirty-two, and twenty-seven, each of them was listed as an agricultural laborer. Their father was sixty-eight. Being in their late twenties and thirties, these young men were facing the common dilemma of all young men in the parish. They had reached the age when one normally took a bride and attempted to settle down. But unlike many other men in their situation, the land still held some promise for them. They appear to have been waiting for the chance to possess a piece of the family estate, a prospect that may not have stood before them if their grandfather's brother had not elected to relinquish his claims to the farm and emigrate to America nearly fifty years earlier.

Through the entire post-migration period, the number of people who were directly supported by the Perols estate remained relatively constant. The number ranged back and forth from a low of four to a high of eight, but not once did the burden on the land's capacities reach anything near the level that prompted the emigration of 1866. No potential heir was ever forced to forfeit his or her right to a living from the land during the fifty years that followed Perols Erik Ersson's departure. The resources of the estate were either sufficient to provide heirs with land directly, through inheritance or purchase, or to secure marriage agreements that insured a right to land. Whether such an outcome would have been possible without the emigration of one brother and his family will never be known for sure. It certainly must have improved the odds.

This is but a single example of what may have happened to households that gave up members to the great waves of family emigration. Tracing down the geneologies of all household members and the disposition of all household property over several decades is a task that can consume enormous quantities of time and energy. It requires the painstaking assembly of population and property information from population registers, tax records, probate proceedings, and similar documents on a year-to-year basis. Any systematic attempt to treat the hundreds of emigrant households in Rättvik in this way is a project that must await the energies of some future researcher. It may never be attempted, for it would likely be inconclusive; so many relevant factors and events simply cannot be documented. In a handful of instances, however, sufficient information of the right kind exists to form a general statement about what happened to the generations who remained. The Perols example is one such instance. It is drawn from a sample of twenty-eight reasonably complete reconstructions of farm households in the "Gärdsjö villages" of Blecket, Born, Övre Gärdsjö, and Nedre Gärdsjö.[38] Each of these households experienced family emigration in the 1860s or the 1880s. The experiences vary quite a bit, but the Perols case represents the most common type—a pattern discernible in nearly half of the instances. It suggests that the departure of whole families from already pressed farm households was a boost for those who remained behind. It may not have protected the beneficiaries totally from the consequences of economic changes in the parish, but it certainly provided some room for maneuver that non-emigrating households may have lacked.

In fact, most farm households in the Gärdsjö villages, from which this sample of emigrant households was taken, made steady gains in their assessed value over the period 1885–1915. The average farm's value increased by 12.4 percent over the thirty years. But the value of farms that gave up emigrants to America grew at a slightly higher rate of 13.5 percent. The difference seems small, but it is only part of the story. Another way of looking at this is to see how the relationship between farm value and the number of people dependent on that resource changed over time. The people–land ratio for all Gärdsjö village farms improved by 15.3 percent over the same period, while the amount of landed wealth per household member on emigrant farms jumped by 29.9 percent, nearly double the rate for the population as a whole (Table 8.7).

One might quickly question the significance of such statistics. For one thing, the number of people residing on a farm may vary with stage of life cycle or for reasons quite other than the departure of a family for America several decades earlier. Furthermore, since most emigrant households were among the wealthier households, it stands to reason that they might have made the most impressive gains regardless of whether they had participated in the family emigrations to America. There is little one can do to eliminate the first of these problems; the situation of these households is frequently too complex to sort out the exact cause of what happened to them. But in the case of the second, it is possible to compare the improved ratio of people to land resources in the

Table 8.7 Mean People–Land Ratios[a] among Landed Households in the Gärdsjö Villages, 1885 and 1915

	1885	1915	Percent change, 1885–1915
All households (N = 144)	172.3	198.7	+15.3%
Emigrant households between 1866 and 1885 (N = 28)	190.4	247.2	+29.9
Households with better than average people–land ratios in 1885 (N = 72)	297.2	323.7	+8.9

SOURCES: Population registers *(mantalslängder)* and tax lists *(taxeringslängder)*, 1885 and 1915.

a Equalized tax value of a farm divided by household size.

emigrant households with that of the wealthier half of society to which most of them belonged. The results suggest that some kind of difference did exist. The nearly 30 percent improvement in the situation of emigrant households contrasts sharply with the 8.9 percent improvement in the status of all households in the wealthier half of landed society in the four Gärdsjö villages. In fact, the rate of improvement among the upper half of society as a whole is less than that among the lower half. While one certainly would hesitate to make any sweeping pronouncements, it does appear that the emigration strategies of many households may have paid off over the long run.

In this context it is important to remember that family emigration was often undertaken for very conservative reasons. Many households simply sought to avoid the dispersal and complete fragmentation of long associations between land and family. Such reasoning was most common among households that possessed enough land and status to be concerned about preserving their position. The strategy worked demonstrably well in Isanti. It is somewhat more difficult to assess in the complexly changing situation of Rättvik in the post-emigration era. Nonetheless, it seems reasonable to suggest that migration-linked households on both sides of the Atlantic may have enjoyed improved positions vis-à-vis their respective milieus as reward for having engaged in such purposeful enterprise. While the respective societies to which they belonged moved in sometimes congruent and sometimes divergent ways between the end of the great family emigrations and the onset of World War I, these migration-linked households seemed to make their way through a changing world in a cadence set by their own special interests.

9

Epilogue

Looking Back on the Trans-Atlantic Experience

THE CAMBRIDGE Swedish Evangelical Lutheran Church marked its fortieth anniversary in the summer of 1904 with a large celebration. The festive occasion, which lasted for two days, was attended by throngs of people. It featured speeches and greetings by a host of visiting pastors and theologians from surrounding congregations and from Gustavus Adolphus College at St. Peter, Minnesota. The departing pastor, Dr. Alfred Bergin, commemorated the event with the publication of a congregational history. The lavish celebration included a sumptuous dinner served on the church lawn, with honored guests seated under a large tent over which a Swedish flag fluttered gently in the breeze. But it was also a very solemn occasion. There was a roll call of the aging charter members of the congregation. According to reports, there were few dry eyes among the assembled, as the elders stepped forward to answer the roll.[1] But perhaps the most emotional commemoration for all was Bergin's reading of a poem he had written for the occasion. The poem began with a wistful remembrance of the act of leaving the old parish:

> The Service is over in Rättvik's ancient temple
> that stands alone on Siljan's shore.
> But outside on the church grounds,
> most remain to visit awhile.
> Since in those long-departed times
> no newspapers could be found,

the churchyard was the place to hear
all there was to know.

The stately and taciturn men and women,
all dressed in Rättvik's native costume,
are gathered together in small groups talking.
Great curiosity is aroused.
"Have you heard that up there in Boda,
yes, down here in the parish too,
a great, great many people
have caught the "America fever."

Their homeland's beautiful valleys,
their King and Fatherland,
they soon plan to abandon
for an unknown foreign land.
The plots of ground, that for generations
their honored fathers cherished,
for them have become too small,
their homes mean nothing at all.

The graves of their dear ones, still green
around the church on Siljan's shore,
do nothing to hinder their burning desire
to journey to a new land in the West;
where a better life beckons to them,
where bark is never mixed with bread,
where everyone is his own master,
where each is his own prop and stay."

On this day for one last time,
beneath the roof of the sacred old church,
they have joined together with the great organ
to raise their voices in stirring song.
On this day for one last time,
around the sacred altar ring
they give their solemn pledge to remain
forever true to their Lord's commands.

In the morning, they will detach themselves
from everyone they love,
from all that they hold dear,
and turn to step with hope and cheer
toward the good land in the West;

where freedom and abundance
protect all from fear and troubles,
as well as scarcity and need.

In a comfortable farmer's home
deep in Isanti's Swedish community,
sat I recently one fall evening.
The day's work was finished
and in the quiet of the evening hours,
the entire farm household
was gathered together
in lively company.

At the piano, the eldest daughter,
well-versed in music's art,
played delightful melodies,
heroic Swedish songs about our ancestor's brave deeds.
The children played among themselves,
but suddenly they ceased.
The older folk stopped talking.
One could feel the heart grow tender.

Their thoughts turned back across the sea,
to the land in the distant North,
where by the shores of Siljan
good friends and neighbors still lived and worked.
Grandfather sat quietly in his chair
lost in deep and serious thought.
When in this mood, the children knew him well,
he would gladly talk of good old times.
A little blue-eyed girl approached him gently:
"Tell us, please, dear grandfather,
how it was in by-gone days!"[2]

Laden with nostalgia for the homeland and the past, the poem goes
on for many more verses, recounting the trials and tribulations of the
trans-Atlantic migration, the initial encounter with the wilds of Isanti,
the founding of church and community, the labor of farm-making on the
frontier, and the eventual spoils of hard work and faith. Dripping as it
may be with sentimentality, the poem is nonetheless a poignant reminder of the meaning of the trans-Atlantic experience in the lives of
these people. Their very identity was inextricably woven into a collective
experience that spanned both the Atlantic and the generations. It was
the record of their achievement, how they had come to possess landed

wealth and homes with comfortable parlors, replete with pianos and music lessons for the children. It was also the source of their most important human associations, kinship, family, and church.

By 1904, the primary participants of the transplantation were aged. Only five of those present at the original organizational meeting of the Cambridge Church were able to answer the roll on that bright and sunny July morning in 1904; only twenty-four who could claim to be present when the church was reorganized in 1866 answered the call.[3] Yet their achievement and their ties to another place still seem to have been unquestionably vital to the community's image of itself, even at a time when a new generation that scarcely remembered the migration and the pioneer years was taking over. The great migration and the transplantation were still the essence of what they were. Time and distance, and especially the intervention of the Great War, would work to cloud that image and eventually replace it with a more Americanized conception of cultural and social identity. They would eventually come to see themselves as an American community with peculiar cultural and social traits. There would be a gradual and inexorable redefinition, a process that was already under way by the time of the celebration in 1904. Some day, the "trans-Atlantic linkage" would provide their descendants with no more than mild satisfaction in the sense of "knowing one's roots." It would otherwise be relatively meaningless in the hubbub of modern everyday American life. But for the assembled first and second generations of Rättvik's immigrants to Isanti, the link with Sweden was still very real.

In his seminal paper of 1960, Frank Thistlethwaite admonished his audience to regard the Great Atlantic Migrations as "a complete sequence of experiences whereby the individual moves from one social identity to another."[4] This study has adopted a geographically based variant of the longitudinal approach suggested by Thistlethwaite to assess the trans-Atlantic experience of the mother and daughter communities of Rättvik and Isanti. The study has attempted to see the migration experience as the connecting tissue that temporarily bound places on both sides of the Atlantic together. We have seen that the strength of the linkage between them lies in the fact that the abundance of land and resources in Isanti made it possible to perpetuate an accustomed level of landed wealth and social status for a segment of Rättvik's peasant society that would not have been possible on the basis of resources available at home. By "sending out" immigrant families to colonize new lands in America at a time of intense difficulty at home, pre-migration economic position was maintained both at home and

Plate 9.1 Cultural confusion. The Dorcas Society of Cambridge Lutheran Church
sponsored this precursor to an ethnic festival in 1916. The costumes indicate the mixed
cultural allegiance of the Cambridge community in the early decades of the twentieth
century. Roughly half the women pictured here are wearing traditional Dalecarlian dress
while the other half are decked out in stars and stripes. (Courtesy of Isanti County
Historical Society)

abroad for certain kinship networks. In addition, the relative isolation of
the midwestern agricultural frontier and the cultural insulation provided by the proximity of large numbers of their own countrymen made
possible a virtual transplantation of traditional aspects of social life and
culture to the new American settlements. Although many adaptations
were necessary in order to conform to the new economic order in America, the old social fabric remained largely inviolate through at least the
lives of the immigrant generation.

In America, the immigrants from Rättvik seem to have been able to
realize the economic security to which they aspired at home, while also
preserving customary levels of social status vis-à-vis their peers. But life
in mother and daughter settlements could not be seen in the same
reflecting glass forever. Both old and new communities were opened to a
quickening pace of outside influences during the last decades of the
nineteenth century—a process that was accelerated by the nearly simultaneous arrival of the railroad in both places. In some ways, change at

home was more rapid and caused greater disruption of traditional relationships than was the case in America. The American settlements
seem to have maintained their isolation from the influence of the outside
world a bit longer. They did not experience any significant influx of
industry, for example, until well after the turn of the century. Swedish-
American communities in early twentieth-century Isanti County can be
viewed as more traditionally Swedish, in some respects, than the places
in Sweden from which their inhabitants came. Certainly the steadfast
dominance of the church over everyday life was stronger in the American communities. Immigrant households in Isanti perpetuated pre-
migration trends of fertility and household structure, while such things
were subjected to wholesale change in post-migration Rättvik. The
abundance of landed wealth in America may have helped preserve traditional ties to the land and the custom of partible inheritance. Even the
gradual disintegration of the axes of communication and migration
helped preserve nineteenth-century Swedish culture in the American
settlements, for it allowed that culture to fossilize. Indeed, twentieth-
century Swedish linguists in search of relatively pure nineteenth-
century forms of dialectal speech have found the daughter settlements
of the American Upper Middle West to be an exceptionally rich repository.[5]

On the other hand, much of the traditional economic life of
pre-migration Rättvik was abandoned in America. The encounter with
abundant and inexpensive land, high labor costs, American markets,
and mechanical revolutions in agricultural equipment produced a more
calculating and enterprising agriculturalist. Rättvik peasants became
American farmers, despite their overt effort to replicate the social and
cultural relationships of their Swedish past. While still confining themselves to an inward-looking, clearly defined social community, they
freely experimented in new crops, were quick to take advantage of
labor-saving equipment, and reformulated age-old patterns of labor
responsibilities between the sexes. Women became responsible for less
field work and took on increasing domestic responsibilities, including
the care of larger numbers of children. The organization of the domestic household emulated turn-of-the-century American middle-class
aspirations.[6]

To call the Rättvik-Isanti experience a "transplantation" is perhaps
too much of an exaggeration. At best it was a partial transplantation, a
brief emergence of something that resembled in certain ways the organism from which it came. It is but one type among the many associated
with the general phenomenon of European immigration and settlement

Plate 9.2 Spinning yarn in an Isanti farmhouse. Even second-generation families continued to live in a bi-polar world. The doors behind the spinning wheel are painted in the traditional Dalecarlian style, while a print of a woman in American fashions hangs nearby. (Courtesy of Isanti County Historical Society, ca. 1900)

in North America. But it is also a significant type, especially among the rural-to-rural agrarian migrations that helped populate the agricultural heartlands of America. Nineteenth-century agricultural frontiers in the Upper Middle West alone contained hundreds of similar partial transplantations involving Germans, Norwegians, Dutch, Swiss, Poles, Bohemians, Finns, even English-speaking Scots, Irish, and Welsh.

Nonetheless, the Rättvik–Isanti experience must be recognized as a somewhat exceptional example of the type, mainly because of its size. It involved numbers sufficient to form at least two substantial communities in Minnesota and to contribute a sizable subgroup to the Dalesburg community of South Dakota. Other transplantations in the Upper Middle West ranged greatly in size. While some certainly rivaled the scale of the Rättvik example, many others were smaller. Often settlements consisted of two or more subgroups from particular regions within the country of origin, a situation that could result in repeated divisions or redefinitions of the community as conflicts were resolved between them.

Irrespective of its magnitude, the Rättvik–Isanti experience contained many characteristics that can be generalized to immigrant settlements found everywhere across the Upper Middle West and other American regions. For within the experience lie the essential processes that were universal to the migration and settlement of immigrant groups in the nineteenth century. Most places in Europe were smitten at one time or another with America fever and most places underwent similar processes of migrant selection, although the local economic and social circumstances may have varied enormously over time and space. Kinship networks undoubtedly played a major role everywhere, regardless of the circumstances. All emigrants had to deal in some way with the restraints of community and pre-migration experience both at home and in America, just as there was a universal encounter with the American milieu, both physical and social. In short, the emigrants from Rättvik passed through roughly the same sequence of experiences through which most migrants were obliged to pass, and in the process fashioned for themselves a particular outcome, which was duplicated to varying degrees by many others.

Notes
Bibliography
Index

Notes

CHAPTER 1 *Introduction*

1. Hans Ersson Dahlsten was a real person. The thoughts attributed to him here are fictional, but are based on the actual events and circumstances of his life, which are well documented in the historical record. Some of the anecdotal material on the Atlantic crossing and the journey from New York to St. Paul is based on the reminiscences of Olof Olson, a Dalarna emigrant who settled in Isanti County. The manuscripts of Olson's remembrances, which were compiled by his daughter, Martha, have been published in Ann Lewis, *Eternal Heritage in Christ* (Dalbo, Minnesota, 1974): 14–26. They also appear as Olof E. Olson, "A Letter from One Generation to Another," *The Swedish Pioneer Historical Quarterly* 24 (1973): 242–58.

2. The most thorough and recent treatment of the derivation and meaning of the regional term "Middle West" is found in James R. Shortridge, "The Emergence of 'Middle West' as an American Regional Label," *Annals of the Association of American Geographers* 74 (1984): 209–20.

3. The notion that Americans were the predominant group on the "cutting edge" of the frontier and that they were followed by immigrant "fillers-in" has long been a part of American immigration and settlement history. See, for example, Marcus Lee Hansen, *The Immigrant in American History*, Arthur M. Schlesinger, ed. (Cambridge, Mass., 1940): 66–76 or Joseph Schafer, *The Social History of American Agriculture* (New York, 1936): 216.

4. The maps in Figures 1–6 are adapted from a series of maps first published in Robert C. Ostergren, "Geographic Perspectives on the History of Settlement in the Upper Middle West," *Upper Midwest History* 1 (1981): 27–39.

5. These two maps depict the configuration of settlement advance in the Upper Middle West decade by decade as it moved across the region. They are based on county census data and the standard census definition of settlement (two persons per square mile). They follow the settlement frontier to 1890, which is generally thought to be the last census year in which a continuous frontier still existed in the United States. The notion that the frontier ended in 1890 is often attributed to Robert P. Porter, the Head of the Bureau the Census, who wrote in 1890: "Up to and including 1880 the country had a frontier of settlement, but at present the unsettled area has been so broken into by isolated bodies of settlement that there can hardly be said to be a frontier line." (Department of the Interior, Census Office, *Compendium of the Eleventh Census: 1890* 1 [Washington, D.C., 1892]: xlviii). He was quite correct as far as the Upper Middle

West is concerned, because the frontier reached the line of the Missouri River around 1890 and was effectively barred from any immediate expansion further to the west by the extensive lands reserved for the Sioux on the western side of the river. The measure of two persons per square mile was used very effectively in the 1890 census, which contains a series of decadal maps depicting population densities from 1790 to 1890. John Fraser Hart has also mapped settlement advance in the Middle West on the basis of eighteen persons per square mile, resulting in a similar pattern at some lag behind the lesser density. John Fraser Hart, "The Middle West," *Annals of the Association of American Geographers* 62 (1972): 260-62.

6. Settler preference for woodland or woodland environments with small prairies and openings has received much comment and study. See, for example, Terry G. Jordan, "Between the Forest and the Prairie," *Agricultural History* 38 (1964): 205-16. In the Upper Middle West, the most preferred vegetational zone during the early decades of settlement appears to have been the prairie forest ecotone, sometimes referred to (especially in Minnesota) as the "Park Region" or the "Big Woods." John R. Borchert and Donald P. Yaeger, *Atlas of Minnesota Resources and Settlement* (St. Paul, 1968): 7. See also Anthony M. Davis, "The Prairie-Deciduous Ecotone in the Upper Middle West," *Annals of the Association of American Geographers* 67 (1977): 204-13.

7. It was possible to penetrate rather deeply into the long-grass prairie zone without moving too far from ready sources of wood because the open prairies were regularly broken by narrow strips of woody vegetation that grew along the stream beds. The prairie of northwestern Iowa and southwestern Minnesota, however, was sufficiently vast, treeless, and in some areas wet, to be avoided entirely until late in the settlement period. See, for example, Leslie Hewes and Phillip E. Frandson, "Occupying the Wet Prairie: The Role of Artificial Drainage in Story County, Iowa," *Annals of the Association of American Geographers* 42 (1952): 24-50.

8. The best treatments of the distributions of these three major immigrant groups in the Upper Middle West may be found in Hildegard B. Johnson, "The Location of German Immigrants in the Middle West," *Annals of the Association of American Geographers* 41 (1951): 1-41; Carlton C. Qualey, *Norwegian Settlement in the United States* (Northfield, Minnesota, 1938); and Helge Nelson, *The Swedes and the Swedish Settlements in North America* (Lund, Sweden, 1943).

9. The three maps, based on county-level data from the 1890 federal census, impart two pieces of information: the number of people residing in a county who were born in a particular European country (circle size) and their proportion of the total foreign-born residing in the county (circle shading). In other words, the size and the relative importance of each group may be seen at the same time. The map design is modeled after one employed by Rice in his study of ethnic settlement in Kandiyohi County, Minnesota. John G. Rice, *Patterns of Ethnicity in a Minnesota County, 1880-1905* (Umeå, Sweden, 1973): 6-9.

10. The cultural exclusiveness of many immigrant settlements in the Upper

Middle West is well known. For discussion of this tendency among Swedes, see Rice, *Patterns of Ethnicity:* 21–33 and Robert C. Ostergren, "Cultural Homogeneity and Population Stability among Swedish Immigrants in Chisago County," *Minnesota History* 43 (1973): 255–69.

11. Joseph Schafer, *Four Wisconsin Counties: Prairie and Forest* (Madison, 1927): 83–106.

12. Hansen, *The Immigrant in American History,* 69–72.

13. Kathleen Neils Conzen, "Historical Approaches to the Study of Rural Ethnic Communities," in Frederick C. Luebke, ed., *Ethnicity on the Great Plains* (Lincoln, 1980): 3–4.

14. See, for example, Merle Curti, *The Making of an American Community: A Case Study of Democracy in a Frontier County* (Stanford, 1959): 136–39.

15. Oscar Handlin, *The Uprooted: The Epic Story of the Great Migrations that Made the American People* (Boston, 1951).

16. Some seminal examples of the profusion of urban studies that have been published over the last few decades are: Stephan Thernstrom, *Poverty and Progress: Social Mobility in a Nineteenth Century City* (Cambridge, Mass., 1964); Virginia Yans-McLaughlin, *Family and Community: Italian Immigrants in Buffalo, 1880–1930* (Ithaca, 1971); Josef J. Barton, *Peasants and Strangers: Italians, Rumanians, and Slovaks in an American city, 1890–1950* (Cambridge, Mass., 1975); John Higham, *Send These to Me: Jews and Other Immigrants in Urban America* (New York, 1975); Kathleen Neils Conzen, *Immigrant Milwaukee, 1836–1860: Accommodation and Community in a Frontier City* (Cambridge, Mass., 1976); John Bodnar, *Immigration and Industrialization: Ethnicity in an American Mill Town, 1870–1940* (Pittsburgh, 1977); Caroline Golab, *Immigrant Destinations* (Philadelphia, 1977); John W. Briggs, *An Italian Passage: Immigrants to Three American cities, 1890–1930* (New Haven, 1978); John Bodnar, Roger Simon, and Michael P. Weber, *Lives of Their Own: Blacks, Italians, and Poles in Pittsburgh, 1900–1960* (Urbana, 1982); Dino Cinel, *From Italy to San Francisco: The Immigrant Experience* (Stanford, 1982); Olivier Zunz, *The Changing Face of Inequality: Urbanization, Industrial Development, and Immigrants in Detroit, 1880–1920* (Chicago, 1982); and Ewa Morawska, *For Bread with Butter: The Life-Worlds of East Central Europeans in Johnstown, Pennsylvania, 1890–1940* (Cambridge, 1985). A good summation may be found in John Bodnar, *The Transplanted: A History of Immigrants in Urban America* (Bloomington, 1985).

17. Conzen, "Historical Approaches." See also Robert P. Sweirenga, "Towards the New Rural History: A Review Essay," *Historical Methods Newsletter* 6 (1973): 111–22 and idem, "The New Rural History," *Great Plains Quarterly* 1 (1981): 211–23.

18. Recent exceptions include: Jon Gjerde, *From Peasants to Farmers: The Migration from Balestrand, Norway, to the Upper Middle West* (Cambridge, 1985); Walter D. Kamphoefner, "Transplanted Westfalians: Persistence and Transformation of Socioeconomic and Cultural Patterns in the Northwest Ger-

man Migration to Missouri" (Ph.D. diss., University of Missouri, Columbia, 1978); Ann Marie Legreid, "The Exodus, Transplanting, and Religious Reorganization of a Group of Norwegian Lutheran Immigrants in Western Wisconsin, 1836-1900" (Ph.D. diss., University of Wisconsin-Madison, 1985); and Yda Saueressig, "Emigration, Settlement and Assimilation of Dutch Catholic Immigrants in Wisconsin, 1850-1905" (Ph.D. diss., University of Wisconsin-Madison, 1982). A pioneering study is Hans Norman, *Från Bergslagen till Nordamerika: Studier i migrationsmönster, social rörlighet och demografisk struktur med utgångspunkt från Örebro län 1851-1915* (Uppsala, 1974).

19. Thomas Bender, *Community and Social Change in America* (New Brunswick, N.J., 1978): 28-58.

20. Robert H. Wiebe, *The Search for Order, 1877-1920* (New York, 1967). For a critique of the historiographic theme of community disintegration in colonial history, see James A. Henretta, "The Morphology of New England Society in the Colonial Period," *Journal of Interdisciplinary History* 2 (1971): 379-98.

21. Robert V. Hine, *Community on the American Frontier: Separate But Not Alone* (Norman, 1980): 199.

22. James T. Lemon, *The Best Poor Man's Country: A Geographical Study of Early Southeastern Pennsylvania* (Baltimore, 1972): 1-41. See also idem, "The Weakness of Place and Community in Early Pennsylvania," in James R. Gibson, ed., *European Settlement in North America: Essays on Geographical Change in Honour and Memory of Andrew Hill Clark* (Toronto, 1978): 190-207; and idem, "Early Americans and Their Social Environment," *Journal of Historical Geography* 6 (1980): 115-31.

23. R. Cole Harris, "The Simplification of Europe Overseas," *Annals of the Association of American Geographers* 67 (1977): 469-83.

24. R. Cole Harris, "The Historical Geography of North American Regions," *American Behavioral Scientist* 22 (1978): 123.

25. James A. Henretta, "Families and Farms: Mentalité in Pre-Industrial America," *William and Mary Quarterly* 35 (1978): 4-5.

26. For an appreciation of the range of work done on this issue in Scandinavia alone, see Sune Åkerman, Hans Christian Johansen, and David Gaunt, eds., *Chance and Change: Social and Economic Studies in Historical Demography in the Baltic Area* (Odense, 1978).

27. Bender, *Community and Social Change:* 33.

28. Historical geography's long tradition of research on the subject of European settlement and development in North America is inexorably intertwined and complementary to the work of historians. Some recent examples of scholarly interchange between historical geographers and historians are: John Jakle, "Time, Space and the Geographic Past: A Prospectus for Historical Geography," *American Historical Review* 76 (1971): 1084-1103; Alan Kulikoff, "Historical Geographers and Social History: A Review Essay, *Historical Methods Newsletter* 6 (1973): 122-28; David Ward, "The Debate on Alternative Ap-

proaches in Historical Geography, *Historical Methods Newsletter* 8 (1975): 82-87; Donald W. Meinig, "The Continuous Shaping of America: A Prospectus for Geographers and Historians," *American Historical Review* 83 (1978): 1186-1217; and Edward M. Cook, Jr., "Geography and History: Spatial Approaches to Early American History," *Historical Methods* (1980): 19-28.

29. There are, of course, many examples of historian's work that seem to transcend the line between history and historical geography. See, for example, Conzen, *Immigrant Milwaukee;* Zunz, *The Changing Face of Inequality;* or Gjerde, *From Peasants to Farmers.*

30. Frank Thistlethwaite, "Migration from Europe Overseas in the Nineteenth and Twentieth Centuries," *XIe. Congrès International des Sciences Historiques, Rapports, V: Histoire Contemporaine* (Stockholm, 1960): 32-60.

31. The range and quality of Swedish historical records is discussed in many places. An excellent account with special relevance to emigration studies may be found in Lars-Göran Tedebrand, "Sources for the History of Swedish Emigration," in Harald Runblom and Hans Norman, eds., *From Sweden to America: A History of the Migration* (Minneapolis and Uppsala, 1976): 76-93.

32. Most of the work of the Uppsala Group has appeared in the form of monographs, but is summed up nicely in Runblom and Norman, *From Sweden to America.* For a concise treatment of the organization and aims of the research group, see Harald Runblom, "A Brief History of a Research Project," ibid.: 11-18. See also Robert C. Ostergren, "Swedish Migration to North America in Transatlantic Perspective," in Ira Glazier and Luigi De Rosa, eds., *Migration Across Time and Nations: Population Mobility in Historical Contexts* (New York, 1986): 125-47.

33. This is the largest area of contiguous Swedish settlement in North America. A good description of settlement in the region may be found in Nelson, *Swedes and Swedish Settlements:* 190-202.

34. Excellent local histories for both sending and receiving areas have been indispensable aids to this study. A remarkably comprehensive history of Rättvik parish may be found in *Rättvik,* 4 vols. (Västerås, 1966.) A book-length history of Isanti County has just recently been published: Vernon E. Bergstrom and Marilyn McGriff, *Isanti County, Minnesota—An Illustrated History* (Braham, Minnesota, 1985). And a very good history of Clay County exists in Herbert S. Schell, *History of Clay County, South Dakota* (Vermillion, S.D., 1976).

35. The Swedish population registers *(mantalslängder)* date from 1628 and are usually quite reliable from roughly the middle of the eighteenth century onwards. The catechetical registers stem from the Church Law of 1686, which established a system of uniform church registration in Sweden. Most Swedish parishes have well-kept and uninterrupted registers dating well back into the eighteenth century.

36. Swedish-American church records have been microfilmed and placed in two repositories, the Emigrant institute in Växjö, Sweden and the Swenson

Swedish Immigration Research Center on the campus of Augustana College in Rock Island, Illinois.

CHAPTER 2 The Old Community

1. Nils Wohlin, "Den jordbruksidkande befolkningen i Sverige 1751–1900. Statistisk-demografisk studie på grundval af de svenska yrkesräkningarna," in *Emigrationsutredningen*, no. 9 of 20 vols. (Stockholm, 1909–13): 4–5.

2. Dorothy Swaine Thomas, *Social and Economic Aspects of Swedish Population Movements, 1750–1933* (New York, 1941): 20.

3. Sune Åkerman, "Internal Migration and Its Relation to Emigration," in Nils Hasselmo, ed., *Perspectives on Swedish Immigration: Proceedings of the International Conference on the Swedish Heritage in the Upper Midwest* Chicago, 1978): 36–76.

4. This term is the Scandinavian counterpart of the French *pays* or the German *Landschaft*. For a thorough discussion of the concept, see Gerd Enequist, "Bygd som geografisk term," *Svensk Geografisk Årsbok* 17 (1941): 7–21 and idem, *Region, bygd, landskap* (Uppsala, 1955).

5. A good overview of eighteenth-century Swedish land policy may be found in John S. Lindberg, *The Background of Swedish Emigration to the United States: An Economic and Sociological Study in the Dynamics of Migration* (Minneapolis, 1930): 89–94.

6. Lennart Jörberg, "Structural Change and Economic Growth: Sweden in the Nineteenth Century," *Economy and History* 8 (1965): 4.

7. Undoubtedly one of the most thorough treatments of the politics that surrounded the liberalization of Swedish agricultural policy is found in Nils Wohlin, *Den svenska jordstyckningspolitiken i de 18de och 19de århundradena.* (Stockholm, 1912).

8. Thomas, *Social and Economic Aspects,* 52–53.

9. Wohlin, "Den jordbruksidkande befolkningen," 127.

10. Ibid.

11. This point has been made by a number of Scandinavian scholars. See, for example, Orvar Löfgren, "The Potato People: Household Economy and Family Patterns among the Rural Proletariat in Nineteenth Century Sweden," in Sune Åkerman, Hans Christian Johansen, and David Gaunt, eds., *Chance and Change: Social and Economic Studies in Historical Demography in the Baltic Area* (Odense, 1978): 95–106; Sune Åkerman, "Människor och miljöer," *Scandia* 44 (1978): 114–44; and David Gaunt, "Människans villkor: replik till Sune Åkerman om ett ekologiskt synsätt," *Scandia* 45 (1979): 133–46.

12. To describe the province in these terms is extremely common. See, for example, Gustaf Näsström, *Dalarna som svenskt ideal* (Stockholm, 1937) or H. S. Nyberg, "Dalarna," in Olle Veirulf, ed., *Dalarna: Ett vida berömt landskap* (Stockholm, 1951): 9.

13. For an excellent geographic description of the province, see Helge Nelson, *Studier över svenskt näringsliv, säsongarbete och befolkningsrörelser under 1800- och 1900-talen* (Lund, Sweden, 1963): 304–14. See also Nyberg, "Dalarna," 9–17.

14. The classic linguistic work on the province is Lars Levander, *Dalmålet*, 2 vols. (Uppsala, 1925 and 1928).

15. Sam Rönnegård, "Kyrkolivet," in Veirulf, *Dalarna*, 175.

16. These figures are taken from Wohlin, "Den jordbruksidkande befolkningen": 196–323 and Gustav Sundbärg, "Ekonomisk-statistisk beskrifning öfver Sveriges olika landsdelar," in *Emigrationsutredningen* 5: 339–41.

17. Nelson, "Studier över svenskt näringsliv," 335–36.

18. Wohlin, "Den jordbruksidkande befolkningen," 256–57.

19. Nelson, "Studier över svenskt näringsliv," 346.

20. Like many Dalarna parishes, Rättvik has an excellent history. See *Rättvik*, 4 vols. (Västerås, 1966).

21. For good treatments of finnmark settlement in Dalarna, see Sigvard Montelius, "Finnmarksbebyggelsen," in Veirulf, *Dalarna:* 135–46 or idem, "Finn Settlement in Central Sweden," *Geografiska Annaler* 42 (1960): 285–93. The history of Rättvik's finnmark is recounted in Erik Sandbäck, "Finnarna och finnmarken," in *Rättvik* I,2: 31–55.

22. Gerda Boëthius, *Dalarna. Skildringar av natur, folk och kultur* (Stockholm, 1929): 71.

23. Olle Veirulf, "Byar i äldre tid," in *Rättvik* I,1: 59.

24. Rönnegård, "Kyrkolivet": 175.

25. Erik M. Berg, Den kommunala utvecklingen," in *Rättvik*, I,1: 238–39.

26. Selim A. Åberg and Georg Landberg, "Folkrörelser. Ideella och ekonomiska föreningar," in *Rättvik* III: 280–81.

27. Veirulf, "Byar i äldre tid," 60–62.

28. This figure is from a simple count of all marriages recorded in the pages of the 1858–67 catechetical registers. Maps of these marriage patterns are found in Robert C. Ostergren, "Rättvik to Isanti: A Community Transplanted" (Ph.D. diss., University of Minnesota, 1976), 20–21.

29. Stig Björklund, "Rättviks huvuddrag," in *Rättvik* III: 9–14.

30. In 1640, certain individuals in Ore parish and Ovanheds *fjärding* actually entered into secret negotiations over a proposed union. See Georg Landberg, "Ovanheds frihetskamp och Bodas tillblivelse," in *Rättvik* I,2: 61.

31. Ironically, Boda has been reunited with Rättvik under Sweden's modern *kommun* organization.

32. Landberg, "Ovanheds frihetskamp," 81.

33. Georg Landberg, "Samhällets uppkomst," in *Rättvik* I,1: 205–17.

34. Farmstead layouts and buildings styles for all of Upper Dalarna are described in Lars Levander, *Övre Dalarnes bondekultur*, no. 3 of 4 vols. (Lund, 1947): 5–156.

35. There is a growing literature on the topic of "social control" in historic times. See, for example, Jan Sundin, ed., *Kontroll och kontrollerade: Formell och informell kontroll i ett historiskt perspektiv* (Umeå, Sweden, 1982).

36. Any attempt to generalize about household size and extension in historical populations involves methodological problems. See, for example, the criticism of Peter Laslett and Richard Wall, eds., *Household and Family in Past*

Time (Cambridge, 1972) raised in Lutz K. Berkner, "The Stem Family and the Development Cycle of the Peasant Household: An Eighteenth-Century Austrian Example," *American Historical Review* 77 (1972): 398–418. For a discussion with special relevance to Sweden, see David Gaunt, "Household Typology: Problems, Methods, Results," in Åkerman, Johansen, and Gaunt, *Chance and Change:* 69–83.

37. Through inheritance one could acquire "shares" in the ancestral farm, which meant that a single farm could have as many as three or four owners without necessarily infringing on its self-sufficiency. For a complete treatment of the special characteristics of the ancestral farm in Dalarna, see Britta Pallin, "The 'Bytomt' (Village Tofts)—Its Significance and Function," *Geografiska Annaler* 50B (1968): 52–61. On the retirement of aged couples in Scandinavian peasant societies, see Hans Christian Johansen, "The Position of the Old in the Rural Household in a Traditional Society," *Scandinavian Economic History Review* 24 (1976): 129–42.

38. Georg Landberg, "Personregister," in *Rättvik* I,2: 329.

39. Harry Ståhl, "Om gårdsnamnen," in *Rättvik* III: 73–85.

40. Selim Åberg, "Fattigvården," in *Rättvik* I,2: 281.

41. For an excellent description of soldier life in Rättvik, see Alf Åberg, "Soldaterna," in *Rättvik* I,2: 264–78.

42. Midsummer was a time for courting in most Dalarna parishes. See Erik Lindholm, "Året runt på 1800-talets bondgård," in *Gagnef och Mockfjärd—en Hembygdsbok* (Falun, 1952): 195.

43. For an overview of household relationships in Scandinavian peasant society, see Orvar Löfgren, "Family and Household among Scandinavian Peasants: An Exploratory Essay," *Ethnologica Scandinavica* (1974): 17–52.

44. Selma Lagerlöf, *Jerusalem*, Velma Swanston Howard, trans. (Garden City, 1915): 8–9.

45. Robert C. Ostergren, "Kinship Networks and Migration: A Nineteenth Century Swedish Example," *Social Science History* 6 (1982): 292–320.

46. See, for example, John G. Rice, "Studying the Modernization Process," in Jan Sundin and Erik Söderlund, eds., *Time, Space and Man: Essays in Microdemography* (Umeå, Sweden, 1979): 97–99.

47. Jon Gjerde, *From Farmers to Peasants: The Immigration from Balestrand, Norway, to the Upper Middle West* (Cambridge, 1985): 99.

48. This measure is particularly useful in showing change over time because it only uses children under five, which gives a closer approximation of current fertility than measures that use children under ten. The category of married women, aged 20–49, covers most child-bearing activity among Rättvik women, since there were few teen-age marriages. It also eliminates the effects of temporal changes in the frequency of marriage by counting only married women as opposed to all women. The method, which parallels one proposed by Hareven and Viniskovis, is also standardized for the age distribution of the population to make the results comparable with other studies. See Tamara K. Hareven and

Maris A. Viniskovis, "Patterns of Childbearing in Late Nineteenth-Century America: The Determinants of Marital Fertility in Five Massachusetts Towns in 1880," in idem, eds., *Family and Population in Nineteenth-Century America* (Princeton, 1978): 88-94.

49. This is true for most of Sweden. A detailed overview of historic Swedish population trends is Erland Hofsten and Hans Lundström, *Swedish Population History: Main Trends from 1750 to 1970* (Stockholm, 1976).

CHAPTER 3 *The Land They Left*

1. A thorough survey of agricultural change in Dalarna is Sigurd Örjangård, *Jordbruket i Dalarna under 100 år: 1850-1950* (Falun, 1951).

2. Helge Nelson, *Studier över svenskt näringsliv, säsongarbete och befolkningsrörelser under 1800- och 1900-talen* (Lund, Sweden, 1963): 304-6.

3. Ibid. 342-64.

4. Hans Aldskogius, "Changing Land Use and Settlement Development in the Sijan Region," *Geografiska Annaler* 42 (1960): 257.

5. Orvar Löfgren, "Peasant Ecotypes: Problems in the Comparative Study of Ecological Adaptation," *Ethnologica Scandinavica* (1976): 100-115. See also David Gaunt, "Pre-Industrial Economy and Population Structure: The Elements of Variance in Early Modern Sweden," *Scandinavian Journal of History* 2 (1977): 182-210.

6. See the classic definition in A. V. Chayanov, *The Theory of Peasant Economy,* Daniel Thorner, Basile Kerbley, and R. E. F. Smith, eds. (Homewood, Ill., 1966).

7. Ester Boserup, *The Conditions of Agricultural Growth: The Economics of Agrarian Change under Population Pressure* (Chicago, 1965). For a recent discussion of Boserup's theories in a Swedish context, see Carl-Johan Gadd, *Järn och potatis. Jordbruk, teknik och social omvandling i Skaraborgs län 1750-1860* (Gothenburg, 1983).

8. For a description of the parish's geology and soils, see Per Thorslund, "Rättvikstraktens geologiska historia," in *Rättvik* II (Västerås, 1961): 9-32.

9. The *storskifte* redistribution of land was carried out in Rättvik during the years 1828-39. A good account of the workings of the *storskifte* in Dalarna may be found in Werner Nordenstedt, "Skiftes- och avvitringsväsendet i Dalarna," in *Svenska lantmäteriet 1628-1928,* 2 vols. (Stockholm, 1928).

10. Johannes Borg, "Jordbruk och boskapsskötsel," in *Rättvik* II: 127.

11. Anders Vikar, "Allmogens levnadssätt i äldre tid," in *Rättvik* II: 265-67.

12. An 1854 description of the parish containing statistics of population, land, crops and livestock may be found in the archives of *Lantmäteriet* in Stockholm. The data make possible a mid-nineteenth-century analysis of landed wealth and economic activity.

13. The reclamation of wetlands was especially significant during this period, primarily because the state encouraged it through subsidy and loan programs. Borg, "Jordbruk och boskapsskötsel," 128-29.

14. Ibid., 146.

15. Simon Ahlman, "Rättviks skogsbruk," in *Rättvik* II: 223.

16. Selim A. Åberg, "Fattigvården," in *Rättvik* I,2: 280–81.

17. Vikar, "Allmogens levnadssätt": 271–72. The classic work on transhumant settlement in the Sijan region is John Frödin, *Siljansområdets fäbodbygd* (Lund, 1925).

18. Borg, "Jordbruk och boskapsskötsel," 149.

19. A detailed listing and description of Rättvik's *fäbod* system, based on the written codification introduced by the *storskifte*, "Fäbode Reglerings Werk för Rättviks socken af År 1834," may be found in Vikar, "Allmogens levnadssätt," 274–77.

20. For a most informative treatment of *svedjebruk* in Dalarna, see Sigvard Montelius, "The Burning of Forest Land for the Cultivation of Crops— 'Svedjebruk' in Central Sweden," *Geografiska Annaler* 35 (1953): 41–54.

21. Borg, "Jordbruk och boskapsskötsel," 123.

22. Ahlman, "Rättviks skogsbruk," 218–21.

23. Rättvik's production of charcoal in 1837 was listed as 13,700 *stigar.* See Göran Rosander, *Herrarbete. Dalfolkets säsongvisa arbetsvandringar i jämförande belysning* (Uppsala, 1967): 406–7.

24. Åhlman, "Rättviks skogsbruk," 224.

25. Ibid., 229–30. For a useful description of the early period of forest exploitation by the timber companies in Upper Dalarna, see Lars Levander, *Våmhusfjärdingen* (Stockholm, 1944): 210–34.

26. See Gösta Berg, "Dalfolk på herrabete," in Olle Veirulf, ed., *Dalarna: Ett vida berömt landskap* (Stockholm, 1951): 100–8; Bertil Boëthius, "Dalfolkets herrarbete," *Rig* 16 (1933): 1–28; Sigurd Erixon, "Bidrag till dalkarlsvandringarnas historia," *Dalarnas hembygdsbok* (1934): 80–85; Einar Lindberg, "Seasonal Migration of Labour from the Siljan Area and Its Economic Background," *Geografiska Annaler* 42 (1960): 262–66; Nelson, *Studier över svenskt näringsliv:* 342–76; and Rosander, *Herrarbete.*

27. Nelson, "Studier över svenskt näringsliv," 342–64.

28. Rosander, *Herrarbete,* 163.

29. Borg, "Jordbruk och boskapsskötsel," 135.

30. The following description is based on a variety of sources, both general and specific. Because there were often remarkable differences in the way things were done, even between neighboring Dalarna parishes, general works can be only the first step. An especially useful guide, nonetheless, is Lars Levander's comprehensive ethnographic discussion of Upper Dalarna peasant life and material culture, *Övre Dalarnes bondekultur,* 4 vols. (Uppsala, 1943–1953). At the other extreme, special mention should be made of Olof Montelius's extremely detailed description of the seasonal round in his home village of Möje in Gagnef parish, *Möje. Arbetslivet i en Gagnefsby kring sekelskiftet* (1962). In many ways, Montelius's work served as an organizational model, with allowances made for the many ways in which practice differed in Rättvik. Much information was gleaned from permanent exhibits housed in Rättvik's public library

and local farmstead museums. Historical exhibits and materials in Leksand's public library were also of great interest.

31. Levander, *Övre Dalarnes bondekultur* I: 396.

32. Ibid., 395.

33. Borg, "Jordbruk och boskapsskötsel," 138.

34. Ibid., 139.

35. Vikar, "Allmogens levnadssätt," 265.

36. Borg, "Jordbruk och boskapsskötsel," 141.

37. Levander, *Övre Dalarnes bondekultur* I: 325.

38. Borg, Jordbruk och boskapsskötsel," 142.

39. For some, the difficulty of frequent travel to and from the *fäbod* was eased somewhat because they could cover some of the distance by boat. This was especially true for those who traveled to the summer pastures around Lake Ljugaren. The boats they maintained for this purpose were housed in a cluster of boat houses that stood on the beach of Lake Ljugaren near the village of Born.

40. Borg, "Jordbruk och boskapsskötsel," 152.

41. Levander, *Övre Dalarnes bondekultur* I: 342.

42. Ibid.: 414–15.

43. Borg, "Jordbruk och boskapsskötsel," 159.

44. Ibid., 159–60.

45. Ibid., 130.

46. Ibid.

47. Ibid. 133.

48. The actual figure was 1,100 *reducerade bandland*. The areal measure, *"bandland,"* was a medieval standard that dates from the early Middle Ages, but remained in use in Upper Dalarna as late as the nineteenth century. It was a subdivision of a *"spannland,"* the rough equivalent of a day's work in the fields (1 *spannland* = 216 *bandland* = 2,808 square meters). The term *reducerad,* or "reduced," indicates that the figure has been weighted according to the *storskifte* grading system. Meadowland was normally given one-half the weight of arable land. Britta Pallin, "The 'Bytomt' (Village Tofts)—Its Significance and Function," *Geografiska Annaler* 50B (1968): 54.

49. Aldskogius. "Changing Land Use and Settlement," 257.

50. See the discussion in Pallin, "The 'Bytomt' (Village Toft)," 52–55.

51. For a detailed discussion of these processes in Rättvik, see Robert C. Ostergren, "Kinship Networks and Migration: A Nineteenth Century Swedish Example," *Social Science History* 6 (1982): 293–320.

CHAPTER 4   *The Migration*

1. With the sale of the holding and the departure of Bäck Hans Ersson and his family, the widow and her children also left the parish, moving down to Söderhamn on the Bothnian coast.

2. A lively scholarly interest in the Great Atlantic Migrations of the nineteenth and early twentieth centuries has generated a large and rather far-flung

literature on the subject. Of a great many general books on the subject, the following are standard reference works: Marcus Lee Hansen, *The Atlantic Migration, 1607–1860: A History of the Continuing Settlement of the United States*, edited by Arthur M. Schlesinger (Cambridge, Mass., 1940); Maldwyn Allen Jones, *American Immigration* (Chicago, 1960); and Phillip Taylor, *The Distant Magnet: European Emigration to the U.S.A.* (New York, 1971). General works on Swedish emigration to America include: John S. Lindberg, *The Background of Swedish Emigration to the United States: An Economic and Sociological Study in the Dynamics of Migration* (Minneapolis, 1930); Florence Janson, *The Background of Swedish Immigration, 1840–1930* (Chicago, 1931); and Lars Ljungmark, *Den stora utvandringen: Svensk emigration till USA 1840–1925.* (Stockholm, 1965).

3. Sten Carlsson, "Chronology and Composition of Swedish Emigration to America," in Harald Runblom and Hans Norman, eds., *From Sweden to America: A History of the Migration* (Minneapolis and Uppsala, 1976): 129.

4. This is done best in Ibid., 114–48.

5. Sten Carlsson, "Från familjeutvandring till ensamutvandring. En utvecklingslinje i den svenska emigrations historia," in *Emigrationer. En bok till Vilhelm Moberg*, edited by M. von Platen. (Stockholm, 1968): 110. Such figures are always somewhat difficult due to the large number of young adults and even children who migrated without their families, but eventually joined them in America. Such accounting difficulties, however, hardly deny the general trend.

6. Official emigration statistics for the province are not available until 1851. The departure of the Janssonists, however, is documented in the press. See Björn Hallerdt, "Emigration från Dalarna till Nordamerika" in idem, ed., *Emigration från Dalarna* (Falun, 1968): 5.

7. John G. Rice and Robert C. Ostergren, "The Decision to Emigrate: A Study in Diffusion," *Geografiska Annaler* 60B (1978): 6–7. According to official statistics, a total of 20,761 people emigrated from the region between 1851 and 1925, over half of them during the three decades between 1860 and 1890.

8. See, for example, Carlsson, "Chronology and Composition," 138–40 and Sune Åkerman, Bo Kronberg, and Thomas Nilsson, "Emigration, Family and Kinship," *American Studies in Scandinavia* 9 (1977): 105–22.

9. Torsten Hägerstrand, "En landsbygdsbefolknings flyttningsrörelser. Studier över migrationen på grundval av Asby sockens flyttningsrörelser 1840–1944," *Svensk Geografisk Årsbok* 23 (1947): 114–42. See also idem, *Innovation Diffusion as a Spatial Process* (Lund, 1967); Julian Wolpert, "Behavioral Aspects of the Decision to Migrate: The Decision Process in a Spatial Context," *Papers and Proceedings of the Regional Science Assocation* 15 (1965): 159–69; and Holger Wester, *Innovationer i befolkningsrörligheten. En studie av spridningsförlopp i befolkningsrörligheten utgående från Pentalax socken i Österbotten* (Uppsala, 1977).

10. Much of the material that follows on the diffusion of the decision to emigrate in Upper Dalarna, including the map in Figure 4.1, is based on findings in

Rice and Ostergren, "The Decision to Emigrate," 1-15. The map shows how the idea to emigrate spread from village to village in a series of stages. It is based on the assumption that the best definition of when a place has accepted the idea to emigrate is when emigration from a settlement reaches a certain intensity—in this case, when the rate of emigration from a settlement first matches the rate for the region as a whole. Although such a working definition is not without problems, it seems better than any of the alternatives, such as when the first emigrant leaves a settlement or when emigration from a settlement peaks. The difficulty with the former lies in cases where the first emigration is an isolated case. The difficulty with the latter lies in cases where emigration is especially heavy and doesn't peak until long after a significant rate is reached. One problem with the method used here is that it may be affected by the small base populations of some villages. Another is the effect of erratic fluctuations that may occur in the emigration rate for a settlement. The effects of both problems were reduced by grouping small villages into larger settlements and smoothing emigration rates with five-year moving averages.

11. Hallerdt, "Emigrationen från Dalarna," 12.

12. Erik Montelius, "Svåra tider," in *Gagnef och Mockfjärd—en hembygdsbok* (Falun, 1952): 301-302.

13. The total number of settlements in the region was 154.

14. Anders Vikar, "Allmogens levnadssätt i äldre tid," in *Rättvik*, 4 vols. (Västerås, 1961), II: 275-77.

15. There were a fair number of Rättvik villages, however, that suffered only minor losses to emigration.

16. The emigration figures were derived from information contained in the catechetical registers *(husförhörslängder)* and the migration registers *(flyttningslängder)*. Of the two sources, the former is the more reliable. The margin of error in reporting emigration was 2 percent for the catechetical registers and 6 percent for the migration registers.

17. Two large parties left the parish within ten days of one another in June of 1866, one on the sixth and the other on the sixteenth.

18. The classic works are: Harry Jerome, *Migration and the Business Cycle* (New York, 1927): Dorothy Swaine Thomas, *Social and Economic Aspects of Swedish Population Movements, 1750-1933* (New York, 1941); and Brinley Thomas, *Migration and Economic Growth: A Study of Great Britain and the Atlantic Economy* (Cambridge, 1954). See Charlotte Erickson, "Explanatory Models in Immigration and Migration Research," in Ingrid Semmingsen and Per Seyersted, eds., *Scando-Americana: Papers on Emigration to the United States* (Oslo, 1972): 7-26 for a good summary with respect to Scandinavian emigration. Recent scholarship on the Swedish migrations that has looked into the role of push and pull factors has come up with somewhat contradictory conclusions. See, for example, Björn Rondahl, *Emigration, folkomflyttning och säsongarbete i ett sågverksdistrikt i södra Hälsingland 1865-1910: Söderala Kommun med särskild hänsyn till Ljusne industrisamhälle* (Uppsala, 1972): 66-68;

Lars–Göran Tedebrand, *Västernorrland och Nordamerika 1875–1913: Utvandring och återinvandring* (Uppsala, 1972): 181–82; and Fred Nilsson, *Emigrationen från Stockholm till Nordamerika 1880–1893. En studie i urban utvandring* (Uppsala, 1970): 253–60.

19. Robert C. Ostergren, "Rättvik to Isanti: A Community Transplanted" (Ph.D. diss., University of Minnesota, 1976): 48–50.

20. Although economic groups can easily be delimited in this way, it is important to keep in mind that the economic differences between these groups were not great. In many ways it is difficult to distinguish between rich and poor in a small-holding peasant economy where the range in landed wealth amounted to only a few acres of arable.

21. When viewed over time, the relative importance of the wealthier groups declines vis-à-vis the groups with more modest landed wealth; see Ostergren, "Rättvik to Isanti," 51–52.

22. This point is made in Sune Åkerman, "From Stockholm to San Francisco: The Development of the Historical Studies of External Migrations," *Annales Academiae Regiae Scientiarum Upsaliensis* 19 (1975): 44. Similar findings for Gagnef parish may be found in Rice and Ostergren, "The Decision to Emigrate," 8–9.

23. Parts of this section were previously published in Robert C. Ostergren, "Kinship Networks and Migration: A Nineteenth-Century Swedish Example," *Social Science History* 6 (1982): 293–320.

24. Lacking such prerequisites, many studies have attempted to examine the role of kinship networks in migration by simply establishing the existence or lack of kinship linkages in migrant populations. In the former cases they conclude that networks must have been instrumental in promoting migration; in the latter, that their absence inhibited migration. However, such findings are not based on a clear picture of the pattern of kinship network in the population at risk, only in the population that migrated. See Hägerstrand, "En landsbygdsbefolknings flyttningsrörelser"; James S. Brown, Harvey K. Schwarzweller, and Joseph J. Mangalam, "Kentucky Mountain Migration and the Stem-Family: An American Variation on a Theme by LePlay," *Rural Sociology* 28 (1963): 48–69; R. J. Johnston, "Resistance to Migration and the Mover/Stayer Dichotomy: Aspects of Kinship and Population Stability in an English Rural Area," *Geografiska Annaler* 53B (1971): 16–27; Åkerman, Kronberg, and Nilsson, "Emigration, Family and Kinship"; Irene W. D. Hecht, "Kinship and Migration: The Making of an Oregon Isolate Community," *Journal of Interdisciplinary History* 28 (1977): 45–67; Rosemary E. Omner, "Highland Scots Migration to Southwestern Newfoundland: A Study of Kinship," in John J. Mannion, ed., *The Peopling of Newfoundland: Essays in Historical Geography* (St. John's, Newfoundland, 1977): 212–33; John W. Adams and Alice B. Kasakoff, "Migration and the Family in Colonial New England; The View from Geneologies," *Journal of Family History* 9 (1984): 24–43; and Yda Saueressig-Schreuder, "Dutch Catholic Immigrant Settlement in Wisconsin," in Robert P.

Swierenga, ed., *The Dutch in America: Immigration, Settlement, and Cultural Change* (New Brunswick, N.J., 1985): 105-24.

In order to evaluate the role of kinship in the migration process, studies must define the kinship networks extant in the population at risk and then relate patterns of migration to them. Observed linkages in the migrant population alone are difficult to evaluate, especially when the migrants are from a community in which most members are linked to one another by kinship. The challenge is to find the mechanism by which kinship is relevant to the selection of migrants.

25. Nevertheless, the two marriages that link these clusters emanated from the same household (Övre Gärdsjö 34) and that household was the central household of its own cluster. It is useful, therefore, to keep in mind the fact that these three cells were connected to one another, however tenuously.

26. The measure of network density applied to these kinship network cells was based on a technique in Darrett B. Rutman, "Community Study," *Historical Methods* 13 (1980): 29-41. When the results are adjusted to compensate for variation in cell size, which seems a necessary adjustment, the percentage of potential links that are actually active is roughly the same for all cells: Övre Gärdsjö 34 = 9.2 percent; Blecket 25 = 10.1 percent; Born 14 = 9.7 percent; Born 8 = 9.0 percent; Nedre Gärdsjö 2 = 8.8 percent; Övre Gärdsjö 33 = 8.0 percent; and Övre Gärdsjö 7 = 8.0 percent.

27. Åkerman, "From Stockholm to San Francisco," 24-26 and idem, "Internal Migration and Its Relationship to Emigration," in Nils Hasselmo, ed., *Perspectives on Swedish Immigration: Proceedings of the International Conference on the Swedish Heritage in the Upper Midwest* (Chicago, 1978): 36-76. See also Sivert Langholm, "Short-Distance Migration, Circles and Flows: Movement to and from Ullensaker According to the Population Census Lists of 1865," *Scandinavian Economic History Review* 23 (1975): 36-62.

28. Johnston, "Resistance to Migration," 20-23. Similar conclusions were reached in Bieder's study of migration in Michigan; see Robert E. Bieder, "Kinship as a Factor in Migration," *Journal of Marriage and the Family* 35 (1973): 437-38.

29. Lists of the holders of public office may be found in parish records. These offices include members of the parish council *(ledamöter i sockenstämma)*, members of the tax assessment committee *(ledamöter i taxeringskommitté)*, village school inspector *(skolinspektor)*, members of the Church and school committee *(ledamöter i Kyrko-och skolrådet)*, and district supervisor *(fjärdingsman)*. During the decade of the 1860s, members of eleven households in the Gärdsjö villages held these positions, all of them from the four largest kinship cells.

30. A survey of office holders in Rättvik during the 1840s found them to have been drawn overwhelmingly from the wealthier households. See Ostergren, "Rättvik to Isanti," 51-53.

31. Charlotte Erickson, *Invisible Immigrants: The Adaptation of English and*

Scottish Immigrants in 19th Century America (Leicester, 1972), 25–31. See also Jon Gjerde, *From Peasants to Farmers: The Migration from Balestrand, Norway, to the Upper Middle West* (Cambridge, 1985), 114–15.

32. Many immigrant parties moved step-wise across the American Middle West, stopping in various settlements before finally settling somewhere on the frontier. Most immigrants from Dalarna in the 1860s, however, were among the first to venture to America from their province; knowing of no one to visit in America, they generally proceeded directly to the frontier. Robert C. Ostergren, "Prairie Bound: Migration Patterns to a Swedish Settlement on the Dakota Frontier," in Frederick C. Luebke, ed., *Ethnicity on the Great Plains* (Lincoln, 1980): 80–84. For an excellent demonstration of the step-wise migration of immigrant groups to the Dakotas, see John C. Hudson, "Migration to an American Frontier," *Annals of the Association of American Geographers* 66 (1976): 242–65.

CHAPTER 5 *The New Land*

1. The classic treatment of immigrant recruitment efforts is Theodore C. Blegen, "The Competition of the Northwestern States for Immigrants," *Wisconsin Magazine of History* 3 (1919): 1–29. For an excellent review of Minnesota's immigration recruitment policies, with special relevance to Scandinavian immigration, see Lars Ljungmark, *For Sale—Minnesota: Organized Promotion of Scandinavian Immigration, 1866–1873* (Chicago, 1971). For the Dakotas, see Herbert S. Schell, "Official Immigration Activities of Dakota Territory," *North Dakota Historical Quarterly* 7 (1932): 5–24 and Kenneth M. Hammer, "Come to God's Country: Promotional Efforts in Dakota Territory, 1861–1889," *South Dakota History* 10 (1980): 291–309.

2. F. Dovring, "European Reaction to the Homestead Act," *Journal of Economic History* 22 (1962): 461–72.

3. Theodore C. Blegen, *Minnesota: A History of the State* (Minneapolis, 1963): 253.

4. See Ljungmark, *For Sale—Minnesota,* 17–69.

5. The term "axes of migration," which has become fairly common in the literature, was first used in Sune Åkerman, "From Stockholm to San Francisco: The Development of the Historical Study of External Migrations," *Annales Academiae Regiae Scientarium Upsaliensis* 19 (1975): 19.

6. "Isanti" derives from the name of a division of the Dakota or Sioux Indians that once occupied the region in which the county is located. Warren Upham, *Minnesota Geographical Names: Their Origin and Historic Significance* (St. Paul, 1969): 249.

7. A small portion was derived from a Sioux land cession of the same year.

8. Vernon E. Bergstrom and Marilyn McGriff, *Isanti County, Minnesota—An Illustrated History* (Braham, Minnesota, 1985): 49.

9. The most comprehensive treatment of Swedish settlement in the St. Croix valley may be found in Helge Nelson, *The Swedes and the Swedish Settlements*

in North America (Lund, Sweden, 1943): 190–96. See also Robert C. Ostergren, "Cultural Homogeneity and Population Stability among Swedish Immigrants in Chisago County," *Minnesota History* 43 (1973): 255–69.

10. For a comprehensive history of Clay County, see Herbert S. Schell, *History of Clay County, South Dakota* (Vermillion, S.D., 1976.)

11. E. G. Trotzig, "Early Swedish Settlements in the Dakota Territory," *Swedish Pioneer Historical Quarterly* 28 (1977): 106–17. See also August Peterson, *History of the Swedes Who Settled in Clay County, South Dakota and Their Biographies* (Vermillion, S.D., 1947). For an overview of settlement processes in the Dakotas, see Robert C. Ostergren, "Settlement and Ethnicity Patterns on the Agricultural Frontiers of South Dakota," *South Dakota History* 13 (1983): 49–82 and John C. Hudson, "Two Dakota Homestead Frontiers," *Annals of the Association of American Geographers* 63 (1973): 442–62.

12. This is an old theme in the history of agricultural settlement in the Upper Middle West. The classic example is found in Joseph Schafer, *Four Wisconsin Counties: Prairie and Forest* (Madison, 1927): 83–139 *passim.*

13. Ljungmark, *For Sale—Minnesota*, 22–25.

14. John G. Rice, "The Effect of Land Alienation on Settlement," *Annals of the Association of American Geographers* 68 (1978): 61–72.

15. For a discussion of these processes among Swedish immigrants in the Upper Middle West, see John G. Rice, *Patterns of Ethnicity in a Minnesota County, 1880–1905* (Umeå, Sweden, 1973): 21–32 and Ostergren, "Cultural Homogeneity and Population Stability."

16. A detailed picture of the soils and early vegetation cover of the region may be gleaned from the survey plats and field notes prepared for the original government land survey.

17. Bergstrom and McGriff, *Isanti County,* 36–39. See also Blegen, *Minnesota: A History of the State,* 320–21.

18. An excellent history of Cambridge exists in Jeanne Johnson, *On the Banks of the Rum* (Cambridge, Minnesota, 1966).

19. Bergstrom and McGriff, *Isanti County,* 82–87.

20. The land grant of the Lake Superior and Mississippi Railroad is treated extensively in Ljungmark, *For Sale—Minnesota,* 155–262.

21. The first sale of school land in Isanti County did not occur until 1879.

22. The civil township of Stanchfield was created from the eastern part of Maple Ridge township in 1874.

23. Ljungmark, *For Sale—Minnesota,* 246-55.

24. There are many indications that early appraisals of the northern morainic lands were somewhat negative, such as newspaper references to the fact that crops were not as good in the "timber country" around Maple Ridge. *Isanti County Press,* August 21, 1879.

25. The role of land speculators in American settlement is a long-standing historiographic theme. For a good review of the literature, see Robert P.

Swierenga, "Land Speculation and Its Impact on American Economic Growth and Welfare: A Historiographic Review," *Western Historical Quarterly* 8 (1977): 283–302.

26. These figures are derived from copies of the original land alienation records housed in the Department of Natural Resources, St. Paul, Minnesota. Records of the land transactions of the Lake Superior and Mississippi Railroad are kept in the archives of the Minnesota State Historical Society.

27. See Ljungmark, *For Sale—Minnesota,* 255–62.

28. Homestead claims had to be occupied and improved by a settler for five years before final patent could be awarded, a process known as "proving up."

29. *Isanti County Press,* May 7, 1878.

30. Similar conclusions about the importance of a relatively slow pace of settlement as a prerequisite to clustering are found in Rice, "The Effect of Land Alienation on Settlement," 71.

31. The settlement and clustering of Swedish provincial and parish groups in the Dalesburg settlement is treated in greater detail in Robert C. Ostergren, "Prairie Bound: Migration Patterns to a Swedish Settlement on the Dakota Frontier," in Frederick C. Luebke, ed., *Ethnicity on the Great Plains* (Lincoln, 1980): 73–91.

32. Merrill E. Jarchow, *The Earth Brought Fourth: A History of Minnesota Agriculture to 1885* (St. Paul, 1949): 6.

33. John C. Hudson has demonstrated a circular migration pattern that was in constant operation between the pineries and the agricultural frontiers of the Upper Middle West. See John C. Hudson, "Migration to an American Frontier," *Annals of the Association of American Geographers* 66 (1976): 260–61.

34. Björn Hallerdt, ed., *Emigration från Dalarna* (Falun, 1968): 44–45. Dalarnas Museum in Falun, Sweden has an extensive collection of "America letters" written by Dalarna emigrants, some of which are excerpted in Hallerdt's book. Another useful repository of letters and reminisences is the archive of the Isanti County Historical Society in Cambridge, Minnesota. See also *Emigranternas spår. Om utflyttningen från Dalarna till Amerika,* Dalarnas Museum—Historieverkstaden 3 (Falun, 1983) and H. Arnold Barton, *Letters from the Promised Land: Swedes in America, 1840–1914* (Minneapolis, 1975).

35. Reports of wheat rust and "black leg" disease appear nearly every year in the *Isanti County Press* between 1874 and 1880.

36. Allan G. Bogue, *From Prairie to Cornbelt: Farming on the Illinois and Iowa Prairies in the Nineteenth Century* (Chicago, 1963): 237.

37. *Isanti County Press,* November 14, 1878 and May 7, 1879.

38. Reminisences of Olof E. Olson in Ann Lewis, *Eternal Heritage in Christ* (Dalbo, Minnesota, 1974): 25.

39. *Minnesota Executive Documents,* 1868. Only a very small amount of barley was harvested in Isanti County in 1869 according to the 1870 federal agricultural census.

40. *Isanti County Press,* April 11, 1878.

41. Ibid., August 15, 1878.

42. Ibid., August 27, 1875.

43. The manuscripts of the 1880 federal agricultural census have been widely employed by researchers despite certain drawbacks. The major drawback is that the census records each farmer's own appraisal of his operation. This raises questions as to how well he knew the extent and value of his efforts, how different his perceptions might have been from his neighbor's, and to what extent he tried to camouflage his worth for tax reasons or privacy. These problems are acknowledged by the census itself. United States Bureau of the Census, *Tenth Census. Statistics of Agriculture* (Washington, D.C., 1880): vii–xxvi. See also Hildegard Binder Johnson, "King Wheat in Southeastern Minnesota: A Case Study of Pioneer Agriculture," *Annals of the Association of America Geographers* 47 (1957): 355–57.

44. See, for example, Jon Gjerde, *From Peasants to Farmers: The Migration from Balestrand, Norway, to the Upper Middle West* (Cambridge, 1985): 180–83, and John G. Rice, "The Role of Culture and Community in Frontier Prairie Farming," *Journal of Historical Geography* 3 (1977): 165.

45. Jarchow, *The Earth Brought Forth*, 183–87.

46. *Isanti County Press,* August 15, 1878.

47. Ibid., June 6, 1878.

48. Ibid.

49. This notion suggests that traditional crop and livestock preferences were often never completely lost to the lure of American cash crops. Rather, they were temporarily overwhelmed by the early need to participate in the American market system. Once the difficult years of adjustment were over and some measure of prosperity or stability was achieved, traditional practices tended to reemerge in the form of secondary crops or specialized livestock husbandry. See Terry G. Jordan, *German Seed in Texas Soil* (Austin, 1966): 199, and Bradley H. Baltensperger, "Agricultural Change among Nebraska Immigrants, 1880–1920," in Luebke, ed., *Ethnicity on the Great Plains,* 186–88.

50. Bogue, *From Prairie to Cornbelt*, 119–20.

51. Rice, "Culture and Community," 167; Eva M. Hamberg, *Studier i internationell migration* (Stockholm, 1976): 59–92.

52. Rice, "Culture and Community," 163–64.

53. Bergstrom and McGriff, *Isanti County,* 6.

54. The classic treatment of agricultural mechanization in Minnesota is Jarchow, *The Earth Brought Forth*, 148–64.

55. *Isanti County Press,* July 18, 1878.

56. Ibid., July 1, 1880. Terms of hire could be a problem. Farmers in Stanchfield and Maple Ridge townships reportedly suffered severe losses when they rebelled against the unreasonable terms demanded by owners of threshing machines, idem, October 10, 1878.

57. Ibid., April 4, 1878; January 30, 1879; September 16, 1880.

58. Ibid., January 2, 1879.

59. Ibid., November 14, 1878.

CHAPTER 6 *The Transplanted Community*

1. The role of the immigrant country church as a unifying force among newly arrived immigrants is a major conclusion in George M. Stephenson, *The Religious Aspects of Swedish Immigration: A Study of Immigrant Churches* (Minneapolis, 1932): 407-8. Rural sociologists writing in the 1920s to the 1940s also emphasized the importance of the immigrant church as a focal institution in community life. See, for example, Vernon Davies, "Neighborhoods, Townships, and Communities in Wright County, Minnesota," *Rural Sociology* 8 (1943): 51-61; Louis Bultena, "Rural Churches and Community Integration," *Rural Sociology* 9 (1944): 257-64. Recent studies that have also underlined the special role of the church are Robert C. Ostergren, "Cultural Homogeneity and Population Stability among Swedish Immigrants in Chisago County," *Minnesota History* 43 (1973): 255-69; John G. Rice, *Patterns of Ethnicity in a Minnesota County, 1880-1905* (Umeå, Sweden, 1973): 39-48; Jon Gjerde, "The Effect of Community on Migration: Three Minnesota Townships, 1885-1905," *Journal of Historical Geography* 5 (1979): 403-22; Terry G. Jordan, "A Religious Geography of the Hill Country Germans of Texas," in Frederick C. Luebke, ed., *Ethnicity on the Great Plains* (Lincoln, 1980): 114-16; Robert C. Ostergren, "The Immigrant Church as a Symbol of Community and Place on the Landscape of the American Upper Midwest," *Great Plains Quarterly* 1 (1981): 224-38; and Jon Gjerde, "Conflict and Community: A Case Study of the Immigrant Church in the United States," *Journal of Social History* 19 (1986): 681-97. Also of relevance are the arguments found in: Martin Marty, "The Skeleton of Religion in America," *Church History* 41 (1972): 5-21; Timothy L. Smith, "Religion and Ethnicity in America," *American Historical Review* 83 (1978): 1155-85; and Robert M. Kingdon, "Protestant Parishes in the Old World and the New: The Cases of Geneva and Boston," *Church History* 48 (1979): 290-304.

2. The only other possibilities were farmers' associations, cooperatives, and fraternal organizations, but these were generally not frontier institutions. They came much later.

3. See the map of "churched population" in the Upper Middle West, ca. 1890, published in Ostergren, "The Immigrant Church," 228. The problem of "overchurching" was a major concern of the so-called rural church movement of the early twentieth century, which sought to combat a decline in the vitality of the rural church. See, for example, March Rich, *The Rural Church Movement* (Columbia, Missouri, 1957). On the competition for adherents between American protestant denominations, see Sidney E. Mead, "Denominationalism: The Shape of Protestantism in America," *Church History* 23 (1954): 291-320; L. A. Loetscher, "The Problem of Christian Unity in Early Nineteenth Century America," *Church History* 32 (1963): 3-16; and T. Scott Miyakawa, *Protestants and Pioneers: Individualism and Conformity on the American Frontier* (Chicago, 1964).

4. See, for example, Peter A. Munch, "Authority and Freedom: Controversy in Norwegian-American Congregations," *Norwegian-American Studies and Records* 28 (1980): 3–34; Ann M. Legreid and David Ward, "Religious Schism and the Development of Rural Immigrant Communities: Norwegian Lutherans in Western Wisconsin," *Upper Midwest History* 2 (1982): 13–29; Gjerde, "Conflict and Community"; and Hans Robert Haug, "The Predestination Controversy in the Lutheran Church in America," (Ph.D. diss., Temple University, 1968).

5. Stephenson, *The Religious Aspects of Swedish Immigration*, 265.

6. Three sources are particularly useful for comparing the geographic distribution, size, and regional organization of Swedish Baptist and Swedish Lutheran congregations in Minnesota and the eastern Dakotas: P. Rydén, *Svenska Baptisternas i Minnesota Historia* (Minneapolis, 1918); Minnesota Conference of the Augustana Synod, *The Beginnings and Progress of Minnesota Conference of the Lutheran Augustana Synod of America* (Minneapolis, 1929); and Emil Lund, *Minnesota konferensens och dess församlingars historia* (Rock Island, 1923).

7. Stephenson, *The Religious Aspects of Swedish Immigration*, 246–47.

8. There are many accounts of the early organization and history of this congregation, the most recent and comprehensive of which is Wilbur W. Bloom and Jonathon L. Larson, *North Isanti Baptist Church: Cambridge, Minnesota 1860–1985* (n.p., 1985).

9. An excellent history of the Cambridge church exists in Jeanne Johnson, *The Lighted Spire: The Story of the First 100 Years of the Cambridge Lutheran Church and the Community in Whose Midst It Has Thrived Throughout those Years* (Cambridge, Minnesota, 1964). The early members and their origins are listed in the original ministerial books.

10. The timing of Persson's arrival in Isanti and his role in organizing the Stanchfield church are matters of some dispute. See the 1954 letter from Rev. Charles A. Nelson to Professor Adolph Olson of St. Paul, Minnesota, which is held in the archive of Stanchfield Baptist Church. For a history of the Stanchfield Baptist congregation, see *Stanchfield Baptist Church Centennial History* (n.p., 1966).

11. The outsider's name was Schorling. A "memorial sketch" published by the church in 1916 gives accounts of his brief but disruptive influence. The original manuscripts can be found in the church archive.

12. Letter from Nelson to Olson, 1954.

13. A good overview of all religious organizations in Isanti County can be found in Vernon E. Bergstrom and Marilyn McGriff, *Isanti County Minnesota–An Illustrated History* (Braham, Minnesota, 1985), 97–121. On the development of "satellite facilities," see especially 102–6.

14. Additional administrative districts were added later for parishioners living in Cambridge village and Bradford township. The names of the rotes were

also changed later to honor the names of important families who lived there; i.e., "Findell's rote" (west), "Forslund's rote" (north), "Stake's rote" (east).

15. Minutes *(Protokoll)* of the Church Council, Cambridge Swedish Evangelical Lutheran Church, November 18, 1872; January 11, 1874; November 6, 1874; December 31, 1879; and December 31, 1880.

16. Ibid., December 31, 1874.

17. Ibid., November 18, 1872; January 1, 1873; and December 31, 1875.

18. All members of the Athens church were listed in the Cambridge church records until 1892. For a complete history of Athens Swedish Evangelical Lutheran Church (Faith Lutheran), see Faith Lutheran Church, *Faith of Our Fathers* (Isanti, Minnesota, 1977).

19. The community boundaries were drawn to include all households in the Isanti study area known to be from a particular area of origin or members of a particular church or churches. The delimitation was based on information gleaned from numerous sources, but especially the manuscripts of the Minnesota 1885 census, Isanti County land records, and membership registers or cemetery lists for the area churches. Since the origins and church affiliation of every household in the area cannot be accounted for, the figures in Table 6.2 are imperfect. In actuality, the proportion of households in each community hailing from specific origins or belonging to specific churches was probably somewhat higher. This is especially true of membership in the Baptist and Mission churches, where the frequent absence of membership registers makes it necessary to rely heavily on cemetery lists. A similar delimitation of communities for the Isanti area appears in Robert C. Ostergren, "Land and Family in Rural Immigrant Communities," *Annals of the Association of American Geographers* 71 (1981): 400-11.

20. Johnson, *The Lighted Spire,* 66.

21. There was a German congregational church in the Bradford community for a short period around the turn of the century.

22. *Isanti County Press,* November 14, 1878.

23. A Methodist church was organized in Spencer Brook township in 1898.

24. Helge Nelson, *The Swedes and the Swedish Settlements in North America* (Lund, Sweden, 1943): 64.

25. Milton M. Gordon, *Assimilation in American Life: The Role of Race, Religion and National Origins* (New York, 1964): 68-83. There is a voluminous literature on the processes by which immigrants have been assimilated into the mainstream of American society, in which Gordon's model plays a central role. See also John Higham, "Integrating America: The Problem of Assimilation in the Nineteenth Century," *Journal of American Ethnic History* 1 (1981): 7-25.

26. The authoritative sources on Swedish-American speech are Nils Hasselmo, *Amerikasvenska. En bok om språkutvecklingen i Svensk-Amerika* (Lund, Sweden, 1974) and Folke Hedblom, "Swedish Dialects in the Midwest: Notes from Field Research," *Svenska landsmål och svenskt folkliv* (1981): 7-26.

27. Bergstrom and McGriff, *Isanti County,* 212-19.

28. *Isanti County Press,* July 11, 1878.

29. Ibid., June 21, 1888 and September 19, 1889.

30. Johnson, *The Lighted Spire,* 138.

31. Ann Lewis, *Eternal Heritage in Christ* (Dalbo, Minnesota, 1974): 55.

32. Johnson, *The Lighted Spire,* 135.

33. At the Cambridge church, however, there is no indication that pastors ever wore the *prästkappa,* a long flowing cape that hung from the shoulders onto the floor. Ibid., 137-38.

34. Ibid., 135.

35. Lewis, *Eternal Heritage in Christ,* 37.

36. Quoted in Johnson, *The Lighted Spire,* 47.

37. Lewis, *Eternal Heritage in Christ,* 22-23.

38. Robert C. Ostergren, "Prairie Bound: Migration Patterns to a Swedish Settlement on the Dakota Frontier," in Luebke, *Ethnicity on the Great Plains,* 84-90.

39. Others have dealt with ethnic marriage patterns in the upper Middle West. See, for example, Hildegard Binder Johnson, "Intermarriages Between German Pioneers and Other Nationalities in Minnesota in 1860 and 1870," *American Journal of Sociology* 51 (1946): 331-39; Lowry Nelson, "Intermarriages among Nationality Groups in a Rural Area of Minnesota," *American Journal of Sociology* 49 (1944): 582-92; and John G. Rice, "Marriage Behavior and the Persistence of Swedish Communities in Minnesota," in Nils Hasselmo, ed., *Perspectives on Swedish Immigration: Proceedings of the International Conference on the Swedish Heritage in the Upper Midwest* (Chicago, 1978): 136-50. Only Rice has worked on marriage patterns within ethnic groups.

40. Information on marriages was drawn from the first two volumes of Isanti County marriage records (1871-84, 1883-94) and from the ministerial records of the Cambridge and Athens Lutheran churches.

41. The names, villages, and farm value (standard deviation from the mean) of each of these men in Rättvik were: Helsing A. Andersson, Glissterna, +1.99; A. P. Granholm, Övre Gärdsjö, +.30; and Marits O. Samuelsson, Omundsberg, +.40.

42. The only extant source from which an indication of pre-migration economic status in Rättvik may be drawn is an 1842 *jordebok,* or land register, which lists the assessed tax value of all landholdings in the parish. While this register precedes the emigration years by nearly two decades, it offers a reasonably good approximation of the relative value of farms left behind by the emigrants of the 1860s, given the slow pace of economic mobility known to have existed in the parish during the period. County tax assessments for real property are a comparable measure of landed wealth on the American side. For the purposes of comparing pre-migration and post-migration landed wealth, the assessments for 1890 are used here.

To what degree was economic position in 1890 among Rättvik farm households in Isanti County directly related to previous position in the pre-migration society? Some indication is obtained by a simple correlation between landed wealth in Isanti and landed wealth in Rättvik for the fifty-five migrant households who were clearly propertied in both situations (R12). The resulting coefficient is moderately positive (+.255), suggesting that economic position in Rättvik had some influence, but clearly was not the only factor. Another variable, long recognized by scholars as perhaps the greatest influence on accumulated wealth in an American farming population, is the length of time a settler had been in the area. The correlation of landed wealth in Isanti with adult years in America (R13) yields a significantly higher coefficient (+.508), substantiating the notion that length of occupance profoundly influences economic status. A multiple correlation (R123) was run to see how well the combination of the two predictors, farm value in Rättvik and adult years in America, explains the dependent variable, farm value in Isanti. The resulting coefficient was slightly higher (+.521) than that produced in the second simple correlation, which means that together the two variables contributed somewhat more to the 1890 economic order in Isanti than did time in America alone and substantially more than previous economic position alone.

The same correlations were also run with a larger population in a similar analysis that appears in Robert C. Ostergren, "A Community Transplanted: The Formative Experience of a Swedish Immigrant Community in the Upper Midwest," *Journal of Historical Geography* 5 (1979): 207-8.

43. Alfred Bergin, "I Americas Dalarne: eller Svenskarne i och omkring Cambridge, Minnesota," *Prärieblomman* 3 (1900): 117-36.

44. See, for example, Lund, *Minnesota konferensens* and Ryden, *Svenska Baptisternas.*

45. Lena A:son-Palmqvist, *Building Traditions among Swedish Settlers in Rural Minnesota: Material Culture—Reflecting Persistence or Decline of Traditions* (Stockholm, 1983). See also Ruben L. Parson, *Ever the Land: A Homestead Chronicle* (Staples, Minnesota, 1978): 123.

46. There is some evidence that local farmers went together to purchase small lots of twenty acres or less in some of the outlying marshy areas for purposes of summer grazing and haying. See Robert C. Ostergren, "Rättvik to Isanti: A Community Transplanted" (Ph.D. diss., University of Minnesota, 1976): 87-88.

47. A:son-Palmqvist, *Building Traditions among Swedish Settlers,* 33-34.

48. Ibid., 36-47.

49. Freely translated by the author from the *Isanti County Press,* January 28, 1875.

CHAPTER 7 *The Maturation of Community*

1. Robert H. Wiebe, *The Search for Order, 1877-1920* (New York, 1967): xiii.

2. Ibid., 12.

3. For an insightful review of the relationship between territory and ethnic

identity see D. Aidan McQuillan, "Territory and Ethnic Identity: Some New Measures of an Old Theme in the Cultural Geography of the United States," in James R. Gibson, ed., *European Settlement and Development in North America: Essays on Geographical Change in Honour and Memory of Andrew Hill Clark* (Toronto, 1978): 136-69.

4. *Isanti County Press,* February 20, 1890; February 27, 1890; March 20, 1890; March 27, 1890; April 10, 1890; and November 9, 1891.

5. The 1900 federal agricultural census valued the average Isanti farm at $1,728 and its counterpart in Clay County at $6,542.

6. *Isanti County Press,* April 18, 1889.

7. Ibid., March 16, 1893.

8. *The Isanti County Traveler* 1 (1986): 4.

9. Vernon E. Bergstrom and Marilyn McGriff, *Isanti County, Minnesota—An Illustrated History* (Braham, Minnesota, 1985): 127-29.

10. *Isanti County Press,* December 8, 1876 and December 22, 1876.

11. Ibid., March 15, 1900.

12. Ibid., January 5, 1893.

13. The resolution of cultural differences between small towns and the hinterland they served is a well-studied issue in American history. See, for example, Don H. Doyle, *The Social Order of a Frontier Community: Jacksonville, Illinois 1825-1870* (Urbana, 1978). For a good overview, see Robert V. Hine, *Community on the American Frontier: Separate But Not Alone* (Norman, 1980): 127-52.

14. The development of Isanti County's crossroad settlements is reviewed in Bergstrom and McGriff, *Isanti County,* 77-92.

15. John C. Hudson, "The Study of Western Frontier Populations," in Jerome O. Steffen, ed., *The American West: New Perspectives, New Dimensions* (Norman, 1979): 35-60. See also Jack E. Eblen, "An Analysis of Nineteenth-Century Frontier Populations," *Demography* 2 (1965): 399-413.

16. These differences were actually slight. Compare with data presented in Richard A. Easterlin, George Alter, and Gretchen Condren, "Farms and Farm Families in Old and New Areas: The Northern States in 1860," in Tamara Hareven and Maris Viniskovis, eds., *Family and Population in Nineteenth-Century America* (Princeton, 1978): 22-84.

17. Richard E. Easterlin, "Population Change and Farm Settlement in the Northern United States," *Journal of Economic History* 31 (1976): 45-75. See also Don R. Leet, "Human Fertility and Agricultural Opportunities in Ohio Counties: From Frontier to Maturity, 1810-1860," in David C. Klingaman and Richard K. Vedder, eds., *Essays in Nineteenth Century Economic History: The Old Northwest* (Athens, Ohio, 1975): 138-57.

18. Easterlin, Alter, and Condren, "Farms and Farm Families," 61.

19. Easterlin, "Population Change and Farm Settlement," 46.

20. Hans Norman, *Från Bergslagen till Nordamerika: Studier i migra-*

tionsmönster, social rörlighet och demografisk struktur med utgångspunkt från Örebro län 1851-1915 (Uppsala, 1974): 276–86.

21. Jon Gjerde, *From Peasants to Farmers: The Migration from Balestrand, Norway, to the Upper Middle West* (Cambridge, 1985): 209–11. The differences in standardized fertility rates between Balestrand, Norway and its daughter settlements in America are even higher than the differences between Rättvik and its daughter settlements in Isanti County.

22. Except for women in their late forties.

23. The relationship between fertility and ethnicity is explored in Douglas G. Marshall, "The Decline in Farm Family Fertility and Its Relationship to Nationality and Religious Background," *Rural Sociology* 15 (1960): 42–49. The extraordinary fertility rates of the Germans demonstrated here may be just a function of small numbers.

24. Studies of colonial society have shown the relationship between land and family to be a key variable in community development. See, for example, John Demos, *A Little Commonwealth: Family Life in Plymouth Colony* (New York, 1970); Philip J. Greven, *Four Generations: Population, Land, and Family in Colonial Andover, Massachusetts* (Ithaca, 1970); and Kenneth A. Lockridge, *A New England Town: The First Hundred Years, Dedham, Massachusetts, 1636–1736* (New York, 1970).

A rather voluminous literature exists on the subject of culture, community, and inheritance strategies in the nineteenth and twentieth centuries, of which some relevant examples are: James D. Tarver, "Intra-Family Farm Succession Practices," *Rural Sociology* 17 (1952): 266–71; Marian Deininger and Douglas G. Marshall, "A Study of Land Ownership by Ethnic Groups from Frontier Times to the Present in a Marginal Farming Area in Minnesota," *Land Economics* 35 (1955): 351–60; David Gagan, "Historical Demography and Canadian Social History: Families and Land in Peel County, Ontario," *Canadian Historical Review* 54 (1973): 27–47; Ingolf Vogeler, "Ethnicity, Religion, and Farm Land Transfers in Western Wisconsin," *Ecumene* 7 (1975): 6–13; David Gagan, "The Indivisibility of Land: A Microanalysis of the System of Land Inheritance in Nineteenth Century Ontario," *Journal of Economic History* 36 (1976): 126–41; Sonya Salamon, "Ethnic Differences in Family Farm Land Transfers," *Rural Sociology* 45 (1980): 290–308; Herbert J. Mays, "A Place to Stand: Families, Land and Permanence in Toronto Gore Township, 1820–1890," *Canadian Historical Papers, 1980* (Toronto, 1981): 185–211; and Mark W. Friedberger, "The Farm Family and the Inheritance Process: Evidence from the Corn Belt, 1870–1950," *Agricultural History* 57 (1983): 62–81.

Portions of the material presented here on land transfer practices in the Isanti study area also appeared in Robert C. Ostergren, "Land and Family in Rural Immigrant Communities," *Annals of the Association of American Geographers* 71 (1981): 400–411.

25. A total of 872 farm transfers of farm ownership occurred over the period 1885–1915; 353 were liquidations and 519 were inheritances or in-family sales.

26. Conzen came to similar conclusions in her study of German settlers in Minnesota: Kathleen N. Conzen, "Farm and Family: A German Settlement on the Minnesota Frontier," (Paper presented at the American Historical Association annual meeting, Washington, D.C., December, 1976).

27. Munch has suggested that the change in the ecological structure of immigrant communities is a reflection of the "open" or "closed" nature of society. In both the Athens and Cambridge West communities there was a noticeable consolidation of land-holdings. In the Dalbo-Karmel community, the land held by community members was compactly distributed from the beginning. See Peter A. Munch, "Segregation and Assimilation of Norwegian Settlements in Wisconsin," *Norwegian-American Studies and Records* 18 (1954): 102-40.

28. The Germans of the Bradford community took more care in planning inheritance strategies. Even though the community had a fairly high liquidation rate and the number of German households declined steadily, remaining households accumulated a fairly high level of wealth.

29. The classic work on economic development in this area is Filip Hjulström, Gunnar Arpi, and Esse Lövgren, *Sundsvall-distriktet, 1850-1950* (Uppsala, 1955). See also Lennart Schön, Västernorrland in the Middle of the Nineteenth Century: A Study in the Transition from Small-Scale to Capitalistic Production," *Economy and History* 15 (1972): 83-111 and Anders Norberg, *Sågarnas ö. Alnö och industrialisering 1860-1910* (Uppsala, 1980). On emigration and industrialization in this region, see Björn Rondahl, *Emigration, folkomflyttning och säsongarbete i ett sågverksdistrikt i södra Hälsingland 1865-1910. Söderala kommun med särskild hänsyn till Ljusne industrisamhälle* (Uppsala, 1972) and Lars-Göran Tedebrand, *Västernorrland och Nordamerika 1875-1913. Utvandring och återinvandring* (Uppsala, 1972).

30. The six Attmar villages are Attmarby, Fjölsta, Söderlindsjö, Skedvik, Hamre, and Harv.

31. A recent and very good description of economic and social change in an area similar to Attmar is Mats Rolén, *Skogsbygd i omvandling. Studier kring folkningsutveckling, omflyttning och social rörlighet i Revsunds tingslag 1820-1977* (Uppsala, 1979).

32. Helge Nelson presents an array of interesting data on the status of English in the Swedish Lutheran congregations of neighboring Chisago County around the mid-1920s. Helge Nelson, *The Swedes and the Swedish Settlements in North America* (Lund, Sweden, 1943): 194-96.

33. Esther Starr Desmond, "The Bridge Between Two Bridges," (unpublished manuscript, archives of the Isanti County Historical Society, 1947).

34. Not all signatories were Swedish members of the congregation; a substantial number were English-speaking residents of Cambridge village. Jeanne Johnson, *The Lighted Spire: The Story of the First 100 Years of the Cambridge Lutheran Church and the Community in Whose Midst It Has Thrived Throughout those Years* (Cambridge, Minnesota, 1964): 104.

35. Ibid., 105-6.

360 NOTES TO PAGES 278-282

36. Ibid., 154. In the congregational minutes of the Athens Lutheran Church, the first use of English was a report from the Luther League written in 1918. See Faith Lutheran Church, *Faith of Our Fathers* (Isanti, Minnesota, 1977).

37. Johnson, *The Lighted Spire*, 157.

38. Hardly a trace of the old Dalarna "farm name" exists in the public records of Isanti County. By the turn of the century, however, there is a fair incidence of American-style farm names, such as "Sunnyside Farm" or "Fair Oaks Farm." See the listings in *Farmer's Atlas and Directory of Isanti County* (1914). The rare public use of farm names among Swedish immigrants in America is confirmed in Folke Hedblom, "Place Names in Immigrant Communities: Concerning the Giving of Swedish Place Names in America," *The Swedish Pioneer Historical Quarterly* 23 (1972): 253-56.

39. Timothy L. Smith, "Religion and Ethnicity in America," *American Historical Review* 83 (1978): 1155-85.

40. Stanchfield Baptist alone had evangelical revivals in 1888, 1889, 1892, 1893 and 1915. See *Stanchfield Baptist Church Centennial History, 1866-1966* (n.p., 1966): 13.

41. Letter from Rev. Charles A. Nelson to Professor Adolph Olson of St. Paul, Minnesota (Archive of the Stanchfield Baptist Church, 1954).

42. Official statistics put the rate of remigration among Swedish immigrants from the United States between 1875 and 1930 at 18.2 percent. Information about remigration from the Isanti settlements is too elusive to estimate the remigration rate with any degree of certainty, but it appears to have been somewhat less than 10 percent of the population at risk, judging from the evidence available in the church record and newspapers (1875-1900). That figure is significant, but well below the average. The discrepancy may be due to poor data, in which case the trans-Atlantic traffic between Isanti and Rättvik is underestimated here. Or the figure may reflect the fact that the older family emigrations may have been less prone to return than the more atomized later waves. On the other hand, Lars-Göran Tedebrand has demonstrated that agricultural districts with an established emigration tradition were as likely to receive return migrants as industrial or urban districts. See Lars-Göran Tedebrand, "Remigration from America to Sweden," in Harald Runblom and Hans Norman, *From Sweden to America: A History of the Migration*, (Minneapolis and Uppsala, 1976): 201-27.

43. For a history of the Gärdsjö Mission Church, see *Minnesskrift utgiven av Gärdsjö Missionsförsamling till dess 55-årsjubileum* (Falun, 1932).

44. Johnson, *The Lighted Spire*, 103.

45. Bergstrom and McGriff, *Isanti County*, 127.

46. Quoted in Johnson, *The Lighted Spire*, 120-21.

47. These settlements were founded around Ambrose and Czar, Alberta. See Faith Lutheran Church, *Faith of Our Fathers*.

48. Persistence studies ordinarily measure rates of total population turnover between censuses. The pioneering efforts to measure persistence (or turnover)

in midwestern farm populations are found in James C. Malin, "The Turnover of Farm Population in Kansas," *Kansas Historical Quarterly* 4 (1935): 339-72 and Merle Curti, *The Making of an American Community: A Case Study of Democracy in a Frontier County* (Stanford, 1959). See also Robert C. Ostergren, "Cultural Homogeneity and Population Stability among Swedish Immigrants in Chisago County," *Minnesota History* 43 (1973): 255-69 and John G. Rice, *Patterns of Ethnicity in a Minnesota County, 1880-1905* (Umeå, Sweden, 1973). A study that has looked closely at the relationship between community solidarity and rates of out-migration with a high degree of sophistication is Jon Gjerde, "The Effect of Community on Migration: Three Minnesota Townships, 1885-1905," *Journal of Historical Geography* 5 (1979): 403-22. A more detailed treatment of persistence in the Isanti area may be found in Robert C. Ostergren, "Rättvik to Isanti: A Community Transplanted" (Ph.D. diss., University of Minnesota, 1976): 102-6.

49. As Hudson has noted, this is nearly always lacking in conventional persistence counts between two censuses. John C. Hudson, "Migration to an American Frontier," *Annals of the Association of American Geographers* 66 (1976): 243.

50. See Robert C. Ostergren, "The Immigrant Church as a Symbol of Community and Place on the Landscape of the American Upper Midwest," *Great Plains Quarterly* 1 (1981): 224-37.

51. The Cambridge church possesses a very useful architectural history in Alan Bergman, *A History of the Cambridge Lutheran Church Building* (Cambridge, Minnesota, 1968). The comments of Mr. Randolph Johnson of Cambridge, Minnesota on various aspects of the church's architectural past are gratefully acknowledged.

52. See, for example, *Upjohn's Rural Architecture: Designs, Working Drawings and Specifications for a Wooden Church and Other Rural Structures* (New York, 1852); or George E. Woodward, *Rural Church Architecture: A Series of Designs for Churches, Exemplified in Plans, Elevations, Sections and Details.* (New York, 1876).

53. Johnson, *The Lighted Spire*, 84.

CHAPTER 8 *The Society They Left Behind*

1. Based on statistics recorded in Johannes Borg, "Jordbruk och boskapsskötsel," in *Rättvik*, 4 vols. (Västerås, 1966), II: 128. The size of the increase may be overstated somewhat, because the author believes the figures for 1865 to be somewhat low.

2. Some increases occurred during the early 1900s.

3. Swedish statistics do not distinguish between oats and legumes, as both were fodder crops. Their joint increase is nevertheless a fair measure of the increase for each.

4. Borg, "Jordbruk och boskapsskötsel," 139-43.

5. There is some evidence that this may have been the first cooperative in

Sweden, although credit is usually given to another creamery that was organized in Skåne in 1890. Ibid., 155–56.

6. John Frödin, *Siljansområdets fäbodbygd* (Lund, Sweden, 1925), 170.

7. After the administrative reorganization of 1862, Rättvik was governed by a communal council.

8. Erik M. Berg, "Den kommunala utvecklingen," in *Rättvik* I,1: 286–89.

9. Georg Landberg, "Samhällets uppkomst," in *Rättvik* I,1: 220. Way-stations were also established at Utby, Västgärdet, Vikarbyn, and Stumsnäs villages.

10. Georg Landberg, "Turismen och dess bakgrund i äldre gästgiveriorganisation," in *Rättvik* II: 323–34.

11. These figures were derived from the manuscript population registers *(mantalslängder)*.

12. P. H. Rosenström, "Bruk och industrier," in *Rättvik* II: 239–52.

13. Ibid., 254–58.

14. Björn Hallerdt, "Bergsbruk i Rättvik," in *Rättvik* II: 202.

15. Einar Lindberg, "Arbetsvandringar förr och nu," in *Rättvik* II: 178.

16. The history of the secession of Ovanheds *fjärding* from Rättvik to become the parish of Boda is found in Georg Landberg, "Ovanheds frihetskamp och Bodas tillblivelse," in *Rättvik* I,2: 57–84.

17. Berg, "Den kommunala utvecklingen," 239–45.

18. Liberals and Social Democrats in Sweden advocated reforms as early as the 1880s. A major influence was the writing of Isidor Kjellberg, a reformist editor who had spent time in the American Middle West.

19. Berg, "Den kommunala utrecklingen," 243–44.

20. Selim A. Åberg and Georg Landberg, "Folkrörelser. Ideella och ekonomiska föreningar," in *Rättvik* III: 281.

21. For a concise treatment of the development of the Baptist movement in Sweden, as well as most other nonconformist sects, see George M. Stephenson, *The Religious Aspects of Swedish Immigration: A Study of Immigrant Churches* (Minneapolis, 1932). A thorough discussion of the Baptist movement may be found in N. Nordström, *Svenska Baptistsamfundets historia,* 2 vols. (Stockholm, 1923).

22. Åberg and Landberg, "Folkröelser," 287–99.

23. Ibid., 285–86.

24. Ibid., 299.

25. A catalogue of church furnishings—"pulpits, lecturns, hymnboards, baptismal fonts, altar railings, chairs, statues, etc."—was published by the Klagstad Studios of Minneapolis, Minnesota around the turn of the century (Wisconsin State Historical Society Pamphlet Collections). Artful detective work on the acquisition of the Klagstad painting by the Athens Lutheran congregation was done for the author by Ms. Marilyn McGriff of the Isanti County Historical Society.

26. The Gärdsjö Mission Church painting was done by Ollas Anders Hans-

son–Furn. *Minnesskrift utgiven av Gärdsjö Missionsförsamling till dess 55-årsjubileum* (Falun, 1932), 15.

27. Åberg and Landberg, "Folkrörelser," 303–6.

28. Ibid., 307.

29. Ibid., 310–11.

30. Ibid., 314–15 and Berg, "Den kommunala utvecklingen," 326–27.

31. Georg Landberg, "Politiska och fackliga organisationer," in *Rättvik* III: 351.

32. The population of Rättvik's *kommun* (Rättvik and Boda parishes) peaked early in the first decade of the new century at just under 11,000 inhabitants. By 1915 it had fallen to just a little more than 10,000.

33. Erland Hofsten and Hans Lundström, *Swedish Population History: Main Trends from 1750 to 1970* (Stockholm, 1976), 119–25.

34. Nine hundred seventy-seven emigrants left Rättvik for America during the twenty-five years leading up to 1890; 1,125 emigrants left in the twenty-five years following.

35. See, for example, the graphs of out-migration and emigration compiled for Boda parish in Pär Ivarsson, "Emigrationen från Boda socken i Dalarna 1863–1930," (unpublished paper, Department of History, University of Uppsala, 1984).

36. This is, in fact, the very farm on which Hans Ersson Dahlsten, the immigrant farmer in Athens township with whom this book began, was born and raised.

37. Exactly what arrangements were agreed to is not known.

38. This is the same sample that was used to delimit emigrant characteristics in Chapter 4.

CHAPTER 9 *Epilogue*

1. Reported in Jeanne Johnson, *The Lighted Spire: The Story of the First 100 Years of the Cambridge Lutheran Church and the Community in whose Midst It Has Thrived Throughout Those Years* (Cambridge, Minnesota, 1964), 123–24.

2. Freely translated by the author from Dr. Alfred Bergin, *Minneskrift från fyrtioårs-festen i Cambridge, Minnesota. Den 3 Och 4 juli, 1904* (Cambridge, Minnesota, 1904), with passages omitted. This poem has also been translated and published in its entirety in Johnson, *The Lighted Spire*, 35–39.

3. Johnson, *The Lighted Spire*, 122–24.

4. Frank Thistlethwaite, "Migration from Europe Overseas in the Nineteenth and Twentieth Centuries," *XIe Congrès International des Sciences Historiques, Stockholm, 1960, Rapports V: Histoire Contemporaine* (Stockholm, 1960), 37.

5. See, for example, Folke Hedblom, "Swedish Dialects in the Midwest: Notes from Field Research," *Svenska landsmål och svenskt folkliv* (1981): 7–26.

6. Many of these themes are well documented in Jon Gjerde's study of Norwegian immigrant farm households in the Upper Middle West. Jon Gjerde,

From Peasants to Farmers: The Migration from Balestrand, Norway, to the Upper Middle West (Cambridge, 1985). For an overview of the Swedish-American population and its accommodation to America in the post-World War I era, see Sture Lindmark, *Swedish America, 1914–1932. Studies in Ethnicity with Emphasis on Illinois and Minnesota* (Uppsala, 1971).

Bibliography

Åberg, Alf. "Soldaterna." In *Rättvik* I, 2. Västerås, Sweden: Rättvik parish, 1967: 264–78.

Åberg, Selim A. "Fattigvården." In *Rättvik* I, 2. Västerås, Sweden: Rättvik parish, 1967: 279–92.

Åberg, Selim A. and Landberg, Georg. "Folkrörelser. Ideella och ekonomiska föreningar." In *Rättvik* III. Västerås, Sweden: Rättvik parish, 1959: 280–348.

Adams, John W. and Alice B. Kasakoff. "Migration and the Family in Colonial New England: The View from Geneologies." *Journal of Family History* 9 (1984): 24–43.

Åhlman, Simon. "Rättviks skogsbruk." In *Rättvik* II. Västerås, Sweden: Rättvik parish, 1961: 216–37.

Åkerman, Sune. "The Psychology of Migration." *American Studies in Scandinavia* 8 (1972): 46–52.

Åkerman, Sune. "From Stockholm to San Francisco: The Development of the Historical Study of External Migrations." *Annales Academaie Regiae Scientiarum Upsaliensis* 19 (1975): 18–46.

Åkerman, Sune. "Internal Migration, Industrialization and Urbanization (1895–1930): A Summary of the Västmanland Study." *Scandinavian Economic History Review* 23 (1975): 149–158.

Åkerman, Sune. "Swedish Social Development from 1840–1970 as Reflected in Emigration." In *Sweden's Development from Poverty to Affluence, 1750–1970*, edited by Steven Koblik. Minneapolis: University of Minnesota Press, 1975: 167–79.

Åkerman, Sune. "Theories and Methods of Migration Research." *In From Sweden to America: A History of the Migration*, edited by Harold Runblom and Hans Norman. Minneapolis and Uppsala: University of Minnesota Press and Acta Universitatis Upsaliensis, 1976: 19–75.

Åkerman, Sune. "An Evaluation of the Family Reconstitution Method." *Scandinavian Economic History Review* 25 (1977): 160–70.

Åkerman, Sune. "Swedish Migration and Social Mobility: The Tale of Three Cities." *Social Science History* 1 (1977): 178–209.

Åkerman, Sune. "Internal Migration and Its Relationship to Emigration." In *Perspectives on Swedish Immigration: Proceedings of the International Conference on the Swedish Heritage in the Upper Midwest*, edited by Nils Hasselmo. Chicago: The Swedish Pioneer Historical Society, 1978: 36–76.

365

Åkerman, Sune. "Människor och miljöer." *Scandia* 44 (1978): 114–44.

Åkerman, Sune. "Towards an Understanding of Emigrational Processes." *Scandinavian Journal of History* 3 (1978): 131–54.

Åkerman, Sune, Per G. Cassel, and Egil Johansson. "Background Variables of Population Mobility: An Attempt at Automatic Interaction Detector Analysis," *Scandinavian Economic History Review* 22 (1974): 32–60.

Åkerman, Sune, Hans Christian Johansen, and David Gaunt, editors. *Chance and Change: Social and Economic Studies in Historical Demography in the Baltic Area*. Odense: Odense University Press, 1978.

Åkerman, Sune, Bo Kronberg, and Thomas Nilsson. "Emigration, Family and Kinship," *American Studies in Scandinavia* 9 (1977): 105–22.

Aldskogius, Hans. "Changing Land Use and Settlement Development in the Siljan Region." *Geografiska Annaler* 42 (1960): 250–261.

Allen, J. P. "Migration Fields of French Canadian Immigrants to Southern Maine," *Geographical Review* 62 (1972): 366–83.

Anderson, Michael. *Family Structure in Nineteenth Century Lancashire*. Cambridge: Cambridge University Press, 1972.

Arensberg, Conrad M. and Solon T. Kimball. *Culture and Community*. New York: Harcourt, Brace & World, 1965.

A:son-Palmqvist, Lena. *Building Traditions among Swedish Settlers in Rural Minnesota: Material Culture—Reflecting Persistence or Decline of Traditions*. Stockholm and Växjö: The Nordiska Museet and The Emigrant Institute, 1983.

Baines, Dudley. *Migration in a Mature Economy: Emigration and Internal Migration in England and Wales 1861–1900*. Cambridge: Cambridge University Press, 1985.

Baltensperger, Bradley H. "Agricultural Change among Nebraska Immigrants, 1880–1920." In *Ethnicity on the Great Plains*, edited by Frederick C. Luebke. Lincoln: University of Nebraska Press, 1980: 170–89.

Barton, H. Arnold. *Letters from the Promised Land: Swedes in America, 1840–1914*. Minneapolis: The Swedish Pioneer Historical Society, 1975.

Barton, H. Arnold. "Scandinavian Immigrant Women's Encounter with America." *Swedish Pioneer Historical Quarterly* 25 (1974): 37–42.

Barton, Josef J. *Peasants and Strangers: Italians, Rumanians, and Slovaks in an American City, 1890–1950*. Cambridge, Mass.: Harvard University Press, 1975.

Beider, Robert E. "Kinship as a Factor in Migration." *Journal of Marriage and the Family* 35 (1973): 429–39.

Beijbom, Ulf. *Swedes in Chicago: A Demographic and Social Study of the 1846–1880 Immigration*. Studia Historica Upsaliensia 38. Stockholm: Scandinavian University Books, 1971.

Beijbom, Ulf. *Utvandrarna och svensk-Amerika*. Stockholm: LTs förlag, 1986.

Bender, Thomas. *Community and Social Change in America*. New Brunswick, N.J.: Rutgers University Press, 1978.

Berg, Erik M. "Den kommunala utvecklingen." In *Rättvik* I, 1. Västerås, Sweden: Rättvik parish, 1966: 229–351.

Berg, Gösta. "Dalfolk på herrarbete." In *Dalarna: Ett vida berömt landskap,* edited by Olle Veirulf. Stockholm, Svensk Litteratur, 1951: 100–8.

Bergin, Alfred. *Minneskrift från fyrtioårs-festen i Cambridge, Minnesota. Den 3 och 4 juli, 1904.* Cambridge, Minnesota: Cambridge Lutheran Church, 1904.

Bergin, Alfred. "I Amerikas Dalarne: eller Svenskarne i och omkring Cambridge, Minnesota." *Präireblomman* 3 (1900): 117–36.

Bergman, Alan. *A History of the Cambridge Lutheran Church Building.* Cambridge, Minnesota: Archives Committee of the Cambridge Lutheran Church, 1968.

Bergstrom, Vernon E. and Marilyn McGriff. *Isanti County Minnesota—An Illustrated History.* Braham, Minnesota: Bergstrom & McGriff, 1985.

Berkhofer, Robert F., Jr. "Space, Time, Culture and the New Frontier." *Agricultural History* 38 (1964): 21–30.

Berkner, Lutz K. "Rural Family Organization in Europe: A Problem in Comparative History." *Peasant Studies Newsletter* 1 (1972): 149–56.

Berkner, Lutz K. "The Stem Family and the Developmental Cycle of the Peasant Household: An Eighteenth-Century Austrian Example." *American Historical Review* 77 (1972): 398–418.

Bernard, Jessie. *The Sociology of Community* Glenview, Illinois: Scott, Foresman & Company, 1973.

Berthoff, Roland. "The American Social Order: A Conservative Hypothesis." *American Historical Review* 65 (1960): 495–514.

Bjorklund, Elaine M. "Ideology and Culture Exemplified in Southwestern Michigan." *Annals of the Association of American Geographers* 54 (1964): 227–41.

Björklund, Stig. "Rättviks huvuddrag." In *Rättvik* III. Västerås, Sweden: Rättvik parish, 1959: 9–41.

Blegen, Theodore C. *Norwegian Migration to America, 1825–1860.* Northfield, Minnesota: Norwegian–American Historical Association, 1931.

Blegen, Theodore C. *Norwegian Migration to America: The American Transition.* Northfield, Minnesota: Norwegian–American Historical Association, 1940.

Blegen, Theodore C. *Land of Their Choice.* Minneapolis: University of Minnesota Press, 1955.

Blegen, Theodore C. *Minnesota: A History of the State.* Minneapolis: University of Minnesota Press, 1963.

Blegen, Theodore C. "The Competition of the Northwestern States for Immigrants." *Wisconsin Magazine of History* 3 (1919): 1–29.

Blomberg, Susan E., Mary F. Fox, Robert M. Warner, and Sam Bass Warner, Jr. "A Census Probe into Nineteenth Century Family History: Southern Michigan, 1850–1880." *Journal of Social History* 5 (1971): 26–45.

Bloom, Wilbur W. and Jonathon L. Larson. *North Isanti Baptist Church: Cambridge, Minnesota 1860-1985.* N.P.: North Isanti Historical Committee, 1985.

Bodnar, John E. *Immigration and Industrialization: Ethnicity in an American Mill Town, 1870-1940.* Pittsburgh: University of Pittsburgh Press, 1977.

Bodnar, John E. *The Transplanted: A History of Immigrants in Urban America.* Bloomington: Indiana University Press, 1985.

Bodnar, John E. Roger Simon, and Michael P. Weber. *Lives of Their Own: Blacks, Italians, and Poles in Pittsburgh, 1900-1960.* Urbana: University of Illinois Press, 1982.

Boëthius, Bertil. "Dalfolkets herrarbete." *Rig* 16 (1933): 1-28.

Boëthius, Gerda. *Dalarna. Skildringar av natur, folk och kultur.* Stockholm, 1929.

Bogue, Allan G. *From Prairie to Cornbelt: Farming on the Illinois and Iowa Prairies in the Nineteenth Century.* Chicago: University of Chicago Press, 1963.

Bogue, Allan G. "Social Theory and the Pioneer." *Agricultural History* 34 (1960): 21-34.

Borchert, John R. and Donald P. Yaeger. *Atlas of Minnesota Resources and Settlement.* St. Paul: Minnesota State Planning Agency, 1968.

Borg, Johannes. "Jordbruk och boskapsskötsel." In *Rättvik* II. Västerås, Sweden: Rättvik parish, 1961: 122-72.

Boserup, Ester. *The Conditions of Agricultural Growth: The Economics of Agrarian Change under Population Pressure.* Chicago: Aldine Press, 1965.

Boserup, Ester. *Population and Technology.* Chicago: Chicago University Press, 1981.

Bowers, William L. "Crawford Township, 1850-1870: A Population Study of a Pioneer Community." *Iowa Journal of History* 58 (1960): 1-29.

Brattne, Berit. *Bröderna Larsson. En studie i svensk emigrantagentverksamhet under 1800-talet.* Studia Historica Upsaliensia 50. Uppsala: Acta Universitatis Upsaliensis, 1973.

Breen, T. H. "Persistent Localism: English Social Change and the Shaping of New England Institutions." *William and Mary Quarterly* 32 (1975): 3-28.

Breen, and Stephen Foster. "Moving to the New World: The Character of Early Massachusetts Immigration." *William and Mary Quarterly* 30 (1973): 189-222.

Briggs, John W. *An Italian Passage: Immigrants to Three American Cities, 1890-1930.* New Haven: Yale University Press, 1978.

Brown, James S., Harvey K. Schwarzweller, and Joseph J. Mangalam. "Kentucky Mountain Migration and the Stem-Family: An American Variation on a Theme by LePlay." *Rural Sociology* 28 (1963): 48-69.

Brown, Ralph H. *Historical Geography of the United States.* New York: Harcourt, Brace & World, 1948.

Brunger, Alan G. "Geographical Propinquity among Pre-Famine Catholic Irish

Settlers in Upper Canada." *Journal of Historical Geography* 8 (1982): 265–82.

Bultena, Louis. "Rural Churches and Community Integration." *Rural Sociology* 9 (1944): 257–264.

Cahnman, Werner J. "Toennies in America." *History and Theory* 15 (1976): 147–67.

Carlsson, Sten. "Från familjeutvandring till ensamutvandring. En utvecklingslinje i den svenska emigrations historia." In *Emigrationer. En bok till Vilhelm Moberg*, edited by M. von Platen. Stockholm, 1968: 101–22.

Carlsson, Sten. "From Mid-Sweden to the Midwest." *Swedish Pioneer Historical Quarterly* 25 (1974): 193–207.

Carlsson, Sten. "Chronology and Composition of Swedish Emigration to America." In *From Sweden to America: A History of the Migration*, edited by Harald Runblom and Hans Norman. Minneapolis and Uppsala: University of Minnesota Press and Acta Universitatis Upsaliensis, 1976: 114–48.

Chayanov, A. V. *The Theory of the Peasant Economy*, edited by Daniel Thorner, Basile Kerbley, and R. E. F. Smith. Homewood, Illinois: Irwin, 1966.

Cinel, Dino. *From Italy to San Francisco: The Immigrant Experience.* Stanford: Stanford University Press, 1982.

Clark, Andrew Hill. "Old World Origins and Religious Adherence in Nova Scotia." *Geographical Review* 50 (1960): 317–44.

Cogswell, Seddie. *Tenure, Nativity and Age as Factors in Iowa Agriculture, 1850–1880.* Ames: Iowa State University Press, 1975.

Cole, John W. and Eric R. Wolf. *The Hidden Frontier: Ecology and Ethnicity in an Alpine Valley.* New York: Academic Press, 1974.

Commager, Henry S., ed. *Immigration and American History: Essays in Honor of Theodore C. Blegen.* Minneapolis: University of Minnesota Press, 1961.

Conzen, Kathleen Neils. *Immigrant Milwaukee, 1836–1860: Accommodation and Community in a Frontier City.* Cambridge, Mass.: Harvard University Press, 1976.

Conzen, Kathleen Neils. "Farm and Family: A German Settlement on the Minnesota Frontier." Paper presented at the American Historical Association annual meeting, Washington, D.C., December, 1976.

Conzen, Kathleen Neils. "Immigrants, Immigrant Neighborhoods, and Ethnic Identity: Historical Issues." *Journal of American History* 66 (1979): 603–15.

Conzen, Kathleen Neils. "Historical Approaches to the Study of Rural Ethnic Communities." In *Ethnicity on the Great Plains*, edited by Frederick C. Luebke. Lincoln: University of Nebraska Press, 1980: 1–18.

Conzen, Michael P. *Frontier Farming in an Urban Shadow: The Influence of Madison's Proximity on the Agricultural Development of Blooming Grove, Wisconsin.* Madison: The State Historical Society of Wisconsin, 1971.

Conzen, Michael P. "Spatial Data from Nineteenth Century Manuscript Censuses: A Technique for Rural Settlement and Land Use Analysis." *Professional Geographer* 21 (1969): 337–43.

Conzen, Michael P. "Local Migration Systems in Nineteenth Century Iowa," *Geographical Review* 64 (1974): 339–61.

Cook, Edward M., Jr. "Geography and History: Spatial Approaches to Early American History." *Historical Methods* (1980): 19–28.

Curti, Merle. *The Making of an American Community: A Case Study of Democracy in a Frontier County.* Stanford: Stanford University Press, 1959.

Danhof, Clarence H. *Change in Agriculture: The Northern United States, 1820–1870.* Cambridge, Mass.: Harvard University Press, 1969.

Dannfeldt, H. Juhlin. *Dalarnes lantbruk.* Stockholm, 1929.

Davies, Vernon. "Neighborhoods, Townships, and Communities in Wright County, Minnesota." *Rural Sociology* 8 (1943): 51–61.

Davis, Anthony M. "The Prairie-Deciduous Ecotone in the Upper Middle West." *Annals of the Association of American Geographers* 67 (1977): 204–213.

De Geer, Eric. *Migration och influensfält. Studier av emigration och intern migration i Finland och Sverige 1816–1972.* Studia Historica Upsaliensia 97. Uppsala: Acta Universitatis Upsaliensis, 1977.

De Geer, Eric. "Emigrationen i Västsverige i slutet av 1800-talet." *Ymer* (1959): 194–223.

Deininger, Marian and Douglas G. Marshall, "A Study of Land Ownership by Ethnic Groups from Frontier Times to the Present in a Marginal Farming Area in Minnesota." *Land Economics* 35 (1955): 351–360.

Demos, John. *A Little Commonwealth: Family Life in Plymouth Colony.* New York: Oxford University Press, 1970.

Desmond, Esther Starr. "The Bridge Between Two Bridges." Unpublished manuscript in the archives of the Isanti County Historical Society, 1947.

Dinnerstein, Leonard and David M. Reimers. *Ethnic Americans: A History of Immigration and Assimilation.* New York: Harper & Row, 1975.

Dovring, F. "European Reaction to the Homestead Act." *Journal of Economic History* 22 (1962): 461–72.

Dowie, J. Iverne and Ernest M. Espelie, eds. *The Swedish Immigrant Community in Transition: Essays in Honor of Dr. Conrad Bergendoff.* Rock Island, Illinois: Augustana Historical Society, 1963.

Doyle, Don H. *The Social Order of a Frontier Community: Jacksonville, Illinois 1825–1870.* Urbana: University of Illinois Press, 1978.

Doyle, Don H. "Social Theory and New Communities in Nineteenth-Century America." *Western Historical Quarterly* 8 (1977): 151–65.

Dunlevy, James A. "Nineteenth Century European Immigration to the United States: Intended versus Lifetime Settlement Patterns." *Economic Development and Cultural Change* 29 (1980): 77–90.

Dunlevy, James A. and Henry A. Gemery. "Some Additional Evidence on Settlement Patterns of Scandinavian Migrants to the United States: Dynamics and the Role of Family and Friends." *Scandinavian Economic History Review* 24 (1976): 143-52.

Easterlin, Richard A. "Population Change and Farm Settlement in the Northern United States." *Journal of Economic History* 31 (1976): 45-75.

Easterlin, Richard A., George Alter, and Gretchen Condren. "Farms and Farm Families in Old and New Areas: The Northern States in 1860." In *Family and Population in Nineteenth-Century America*, edited by Tamara Hareven and Maris Viniskovis. Princeton: Princeton University Press, 1978: 22-84.

Eblen, Jack E. "An Analysis of Nineteenth-Century Frontier Populations." *Demography* 2 (1965): 399-413.

Ellemers, J. E. "The Determinants of Emigration: An Analysis of Dutch Studies in Migration." *Sociologica Neerlandica* 2 (1964): 41-58.

Emigranternas spår. Om utflyttningen från Dalarna till Amerika. Dalarnas Museum—Historieverkstaden 3. Falun, Sweden, 1983.

Emigrationsutredningen. Betänkande och bilagor. 20 vols. Stockholm: P. A. Nordstedt & Söner, 1909-13.

Enequist, Gerd. *Region, bygd, landskap.* Uppsala, 1955.

Enequist, Gerd. *Geographical Changes of Rural Settlement in Northwestern Sweden since 1523.* Meddelanden från Uppsala universitets geografiska institutionen, Ser. A, 143. Uppsala: Acta Universitatis Upsaliensis, 1959.

Enequist, Gerd. "Bygd som geografisk term." *Svensk Geografisk Årsbok* 17 (1941): 7-21.

Enequist, Gerd. "Advance and Retreat of Rural Settlement in Northern Sweden." *Geografiska Annaler* 42 (1960): 211-20.

Erickson, Charlotte. *Invisible Immigrants: The Adaptation of English and Scottish Immigrants in 19th Century America.* Leicester: Leicester University Press for the London School of Economics, 1972.

Erickson, Charlotte. *Emigration from Europe, 1815-1914: Select Documents.* London: A. and C. Black, 1976.

Erickson, Charlotte. "Explanatory Models in Immigration and Migration Research." In *Scando-Americana: Papers on Emigration to the United States*, edited by Ingrid Semmingsen and Per Seyersted. Olso: The American Institute, 1972: 7-26.

Eriksson, Ingrid and John Rogers. *Rural Labour and Population Change. Social and Demographic Developments in East-Central Sweden during the Nineteenth Century.* Studia Historica Upsaliensis 100. Uppsala: Acta Universitatis Upsaliensis, 1978.

Erixon, Sigurd. "Bidrag till dalkarlsvandringarnas historia." *Dalarnas hembygdsbok* (1934): 80-85.

Faith of Our Fathers. Isanti, Minnesota: Faith Lutheran Church, 1977.

Fite, Gilbert C. *The Farmer's Frontier, 1865-1900.* New York: Holt, Rinehart & Winston, 1966.

Fjellström, Phebe. *Swedish-American Colonization in the San Joaquin Valley in California: A Study of the Acculturation and the Assimilation of an Immigrant Group.* Studia Ethnographica Upsaliensia 33. Uppsala: Acta Universitatis Upsaliensis, 1970.

Friedberger, Mark W. "The Farm Family and the Inheritance Process: Evidence from the Corn Belt, 1870-1950." *Agricultural History* 57 (1983): 62-81.

Friedberger, Mark W. "Handing Down the Home Place: Farm Inheritance Strategies in Iowa, 1870-1945." *Annals of Iowa* 47 (1984): 518-36.

Frimannslund, Rigmor. "The Old Norwegian Peasant Community: Farm Community and Neighborhood Community," *Scandinavian Economic History Review* 4 (1956): 62-81.

Frödin, John. *Siljansområdets fäbodbygd.* Skrifter utgivna av Vetenskapssocieteten i Lund 5. Lund, Sweden: Gleerup, 1925.

Gadd, Carl-Johan. *Järn och potatis. Jordbruk, teknik och social omvandling i Skaraborgs län 1750-1860.* Meddelanden från ekonomisk-historiska institutionen vid Göteborgs universitet 53. Gothenburg: Institute of Economic History, 1983.

Gagan, David. "Historical Demography and Canadian Social History: Families and Land in Peel County, Ontario." *Canadian Historical Review* 54 (1973): 27-47.

Gagan, David. "Geographic and Social Mobility in Nineteenth Century Ontario: A Microstudy." *Canadian Review of Sociology and Anthropology* 13 (1976): 126-41.

Gagan, David. "The Indivisibility of Land: A Microanalysis of the System of Land Inheritance in Nineteenth Century Ontario." *Journal of Economic History* 36 (1976): 126-41.

Gagan, David. "Land, Population and Social Change: The Critical Years in Canada West." *Canadian Historical Review* 59 (1978): 299-306.

Gagan, David and Herbert Mays. "Historical Demography and Canadian Social History: Families and Land in Peel County, Ontario." *Canadian Historical Review* 54 (1973): 35-57.

Gagnef och Mockfjärd—en hembygdsbok. Falun: Falu Nya Boktryckeri, 1952.

Gates, Paul W. *Landlords and Tenants on the Prairie Frontier: Studies in American Land Policy.* Ithaca: Cornell University Press, 1973.

Gaunt, David. "Pre-Industrial Economy and Population Structure: The Elements of Variance in Early Modern Sweden." *Scandinavian Journal of History* 2 (1977): 183-210.

Gaunt, David. "Household Typology: Problems, Methods, Results." In *Chance and Change: Social and Economic Studies in Historical Demography in the Baltic Area,* edited by Sune Åkerman, Hans Christian Johansen, and David Gaunt. Odense: Odense University Press, 1978: 69-83.

Gaunt, David. "Människans villkor: replik till Sune Åkerman om ett ekologiskt synsätt." *Scandia* 45 (1979): 133-46.

Gissel, Svend. ""Agricultural Decline in Scandinavia." *Scandinavian Journal of History* 1 (1976): 43–54.

Gjerde, Jon. *From Peasants to Farmers: The Migration from Balestrand, Norway, to the Upper Middle West.* Cambridge: Cambridge University Press, 1985.

Gjerde, Jon. "The Effect of Community on Migration: Three Minnesota Townships, 1885–1905." *Journal of Historical Geography* 5 (1979): 403–22.

Gjerde, Jon. "Conflict and Community: A Case Study of the Immigrant Church in the United States." *Journal of Social History* 19 (1986): 681–97.

Glazier, Ira and Luigi De Rosa, eds. *Migration Across Time and Nations: Population Mobility in Historical Contexts.* New York: Holmes & Meier, 1986.

Golab, Caroline. *Immigrant Destinations.* Philadelphia: Temple University Press, 1977.

Gordon, Milton M. *Assimilation in American Life: The Role of Race, Religion, and National Origins.* New York: Oxford University Press, 1964.

Gould, J. D. "European Inter-Continental Emigration 1815–1914: Patterns and Causes." *Journal of European Economic History* 8 (1979): 593–679.

Gould, J. D. "European Inter-Continental Emigration: The Role of Diffusion and Feedback." *Journal of European Economic History* 9 (1980): 267–315.

Greven, Philip J. *Four Generations: Population, Land, and Family in Colonial Andover, Massachusetts.* Ithaca: Cornell University Press, 1970.

Gullberg, Bo and Birgitta Odén. "AID Analysis and Migration History." *Scandinavian Economic History Review* 24 (1976): 1–32.

Habakkuk, H. J. "Family Structure and Economic Change in Nineteenth Century Europe," *Journal of Economic History* 15 (1955): 1–12.

Hägerstrand, Torsten. *Innovation Diffusion as a Spatial Process.* Lund, Sweden, 1967.

Hägerstrand, Torsten. "En landsbygdsbefolknings flyttningsrörelser. Studier över migrationen på grundval av Asby sockens flyttningsrörelser 1840–1944." *Svensk Geografisk Årsbok* 23 (1947): 114–42.

Hallerdt, Björn. ed. *Emigration från Dalarna.* Falun: Dalarnas fornminnes och hembygdsförbund, 1968.

Hallerdt, Björn. "Bergsbruk i Rättvik." In *Rättvik* II. Västerås, Sweden: Rättvik parish, 1961: 193–215.

Hamberg, Eva M. *Studier i internationell migration.* Stockholm Studies in Economic History 2. Stockholm: Acta Universitatis Stockholmiensis, 1976.

Hammer, Kenneth M. "Come to God's Country: Promotional Efforts in Dakota Territory, 1861–1889." *South Dakota History* 10 (1980): 291–309.

Handcock, W. Gordon. "English Migration to Newfoundland." In *The Peopling of Newfoundland: Essays in Historical Geography,* edited by John J. Mannion. St. John's, Newfoundland: Memorial University of Newfoundland, 1977: 15–48.

Handlin, Oscar. *The Uprooted: The Epic Story of the Great Migrations that Made the American People.* Boston: Little, Brown & Co., 1951.

Hansen, Marcus Lee. *The Atlantic Migration, 1607-1860: A History of the Continuing Settlement of the United States.* Arthur M. Schlesinger, ed. Cambridge, Mass.: Harvard University Press, 1940.

Hansen, Marcus Lee. *The Immigrant in American History,* Arthur M. Schlesinger, ed. Cambridge, Mass.: Harvard University Press, 1940.

Hansen, Borje. "Common Folk and Gentlefolk." *Ethnologia Scandinavica* (1973): 67-100.

Hareven, Tamara K. and Maris A. Viniskovis. "Patterns of Childbearing in Late Nineteenth-Century America: The Determinants of Marital Fertility in Five Massachusetts Towns in 1880." In *Family and Population in Nineteenth-Century America,* edited by Tamara K. Hareven and Maris A. Viniskovis. Princeton: Princeton University Press, 1978: 85-125.

Hareven, Tamara K. and Maris A. Viniskovis, eds. *Family and Population in Nineteenth-Century America.* Princeton: Princeton University Press, 1978.

Harris, R. Cole. "The Simplification of Europe Overseas." *Annals of the Association of American Geographers* 67 (1977): 469-83.

Harris, R. Cole. "The Historical Geography of North American Regions." *American Behavioral Scientist* 22 (1978): 115-30.

Hart, John Fraser. "The Middle West." *Annals of the Association of American Geographers* 62 (1972): 258-82.

Hartz, Louis. *The Founding of New Societies: Studies in the History of the United States, Latin America, South Africa, Canada, and Australia.* New York: Harcourt, Brace & World, 1964.

Hasselmo, Nils. *Amerikasvenska. En bok om språkutvecklingen i Svensk-Amerika.* Skrifter utgivna av Svenska språknämden 51. Lund, Sweden: Esselte Studium, 1974.

Hasselmo, Nils. ed. *Perspectives on Swedish Immigration: Proceedings of the International Conference on the Swedish Heritage in the Upper Midwest.* Chicago: Swedish Pioneer Historical Society, 1978.

Haug, Hans Robert. "The Predestination Controversy in the Lutheran Church in America." Ph.D. dissertation, Temple University, 1968.

Hecht, Irene W. D. "Kinship and Migration: The Making of an Oregon Isolate Community." *Journal of Interdisciplinary History* 28 (1977): 45-67.

Heckscher, Eli F. *An Economic History of Sweden.* Translated by Göran Ohlin. Harvard Economic Studies 95. Cambridge, Mass.: Harvard University Press, 1954.

Hedblom, Folke. "Place Names in Immigrant Communities: Concerning the Giving of Swedish Place Names in America." *The Swedish Pioneer Historical Quarterly* 23 (1972): 253-56.

Hedblom, Folke. "Swedish Dialects in the Midwest: Notes from Field Research." *Svenska landsmål och svenskt folkliv* (1981): 7-26.

Hedblom, Margaretha and Gunnar Ternhag, eds. *Emigranternas spår. Om utflyttningen från Dalarna till Amerika.* Dalarnas Museum, Historiverkstaden 3. Falun: Dalarnas Museum, 1983.

Henretta, James A. "The Morphology of New England Society in the Colonial Period." *Journal of Interdisciplinary History* 2 (1971): 379–98.

Henretta, James A. "Families and Farms: Mentalité in Pre-Industrial America." *William and Mary Quarterly* 35 (1978): 3–32.

Hewes, Leslie. "Some Features of Early Woodland and Prairie Settlement in a Central Iowa County." *Annals of the Association of American Geographers* 40 (1950): 40–57.

Hewes, Leslie and Phillip E. Frandson. "Occupying the Wet Prairie: The Role of Artificial Drainage in Story County, Iowa." *Annals of the Association of American Geographers* 42 (1952): 24–50.

Higham, John. *Send These to Me: Jews and Other Immigrants in Urban America.* New York: Atheneum, 1975.

Higham, John. "Integrating America: The Problem of Assimilation in the Nineteenth Century." *Journal of American Ethnic History* 1 (1981): 7–25.

Hill, George W. "The Use of the Culture-Area Concept in Social Research." *American Journal of Sociology* 47 (1941): 39–47.

Hill, George W. and Tarver, James D. "Indigenous Fertility in the Farm Population of Wisconsin, 1848–1948." *Rural Sociology* 16 (1951): 359–62.

Hine, Robert V. *Community on the American Frontier: Separate But Not Alone.* Norman: University of Oklahoma Press, 1980.

Hjulström, Filip, Gunnar Arpi, and Esse Lövgren. *Sundsvall-sdistriktet, 1850–1950.* Skrifter från Uppsala universitets geografiska institution 26. Uppsala: Almqvist & Wiksell, 1955.

Hoffman, Oscar F. "Cultural Change in a Rural Wisconsin Ethnic Island." *Rural Sociology* 14 (1949): 39–50.

Hofsten, Erland and Hans Lundström. *Swedish Population History: Main Trends from 1750 to 1970.* Urval 8. Stockholm: National Central Bureau of Statistics, 1976.

Hollingshead, A. B. "The Life Cycle of Nebraska Rural Churches." *Rural Sociology* 2 (1937): 180–91.

Hollingshead, A. B. "Changes in Land Ownership as an Index of Succession in Rural Communities." *Journal of Sociology* 43 (1938): 764–77.

Hovde, Brynjolf J. "Notes of the Effect of Emigration upon Scandinavia." *Journal of Modern History* 6 (1934): 253–79.

Hudson, John C. "Two Dakota Homestead Frontiers." *Annals of the Association of American Geographers* 63 (1973): 442–62.

Hudson, John C. "Migration to an American Frontier." *Annals of the Association of American Geographers* 66 (1976): 242–65.

Hudson, John C. "The Study of Western Frontier Populations." In *The American West: New Perspectives, New Dimensions,* edited by Jerome O. Steffen. Norman: University of Oklahoma Press, 1979: 35–60.

Hvidt, Kristian. *Flight to America: The Social Background of 300,000 Danish Emigrants.* New York: Academic Press, 1975.

Ivarsson, Pär. "Emigrationen från Boda socken i Dalarna 1863–1930." Unpublished paper, Department of History, University of Uppsala, 1984.

Jakle, John. "Time, Space and the Geographic Past: A Prospectus for Historical Geography." *American Historical Review* 76 (1971): 1084–1103.

Janson, Florence. *The Background of Swedish Immigration, 1840–1930.* Chicago: University of Chicago Press, 1931.

Jarchow, Merrill E. *The Earth Brought Forth: A History of Minnesota Agriculture to 1885.* St. Paul: Minnesota Historical Society, 1949.

Jerome, Harry. *Migration and the Business Cycle.* New York: National Bureau of Economic Research, 1927.

Johannes, Per. *Siljansbygden.* Stockholm: P. A. Nordstedt & Söners, 1948.

Johansen, Hans Christian. "The Position of the Old in the Rural Household in a Traditional Society." *Scandinavian Economic History Review* 24 (1976): 129–42.

Johnson, Emeroy. *God Gave the Growth.* Minneapolis: T. S. Denison & Co., 1958.

Johnson, Hildegard Binder. "The Distribution of the German Pioneer Population in Minnesota." *Rural Sociology* 51 (1941): 16–34.

Johnson, Hildegard Binder. "Factors Influencing the Distribution of the German Pioneer Population in Minnesota." *Agricultural History* 19 (1945): 39–57.

Johnson, Hildegard Bender. "Intermarriages Between German Pioneers and Other Nationalities in Minnesota in 1860 and 1870." *American Journal of Sociology* 51 (1946): 331–39.

Johnson, Hildegard Binder. "The Location of German Immigrants in the Middle West." *Annals of the Association of American Geographers* 41 (1951): 1–41.

Johnson, Hildegard Binder. "King Wheat in Southeastern Minnesota: A Case Study of Pioneer Agriculture." *Annals of the Association of American Geographers* 47 (1957): 350–62.

Johnson, Jeanne. *The Lighted Spire: The Story of the First 100 Years of the Cambridge Lutheran Church and the Community in Whose Midst It Has Thrived Throughout those Years.* Cambridge, Minnesota: Cambridge Evangelical Lutheran Church, 1964.

Johnson, Jeanne. *On the Banks of the Rum.* Cambridge, Minnesota: Cambridge Centennial, Inc., 1966.

Johnson, Randolph E. "Rural 'Swede Schools' of Isanti County, Minnesota." *Swedish Pioneer Historical Quarterly* 23 (1972): 109–13.

Johnston, R. J. "Resistance to Migration and the Mover/Stayer Dichotomy: Aspects of Kinship and Population Stability in an English Rural Area." *Geografiska Annaler* 53B (1971): 16–27.

Jones, Maldwyn Allen. *American Immigration.* Chicago: University of Chicago Press, 1960.

Jörberg, Lennart. "Structural Change and Economic Growth: Sweden in the Nineteenth Century." *Economy and History* 8 (1965): 3-46.

Jordan, Terry G. *German Seed in Texas Soil.* Austin: University of Texas Press, 1966.

Jordan, Terry G. "Between the Forest and the Prairie." *Agricultural History* 38 (1964): 205-216.

Jordan, Terry G. "A Religious Geography of the Hill Country Germans of Texas." In *Ethnicity on the Great Plains,* edited by Frederick C. Luebke. Lincoln: University of Nebraska Press, 1980: 109-28.

Kälvemark, Ann-Sofie. *Reaktionen mot utvandringen. Emigrationsfrågan i svensk debatt och politik 1901-1904.* Studia Historica Upsaliensia 41. Uppsala: Acta Universitatis Upsaliensis, 1972.

Kälvemark, Ann-Sofie, ed. *Utvandring: Den svenska emigrationen till Amerika i historiskt perspektiv.* Stockholm: Wahlström & Widstrand, 1973.

Kälvemark, Ann-Sofie. "The Country that Kept Track of Its Population: Methodological Aspects of Swedish Population Records." *Scandinavian Journal of History* 2 (1977): 211-30.

Kamphoefner, Walter D. *Transplanted Westfalians: Chain Migration from Germany to a Rural Midwestern Community.* Princeton: Princeton University Press, 1987.

Kamphoefner, Walter D. "Transplanted Westfalians: Persistence and Transformation of Socioeconomic and Cultural Patterns in the Northwest German Migration to Missouri." Ph.D. dissertation, University of Missouri, Columbia, 1978.

Katz, Michael B. *The People of Hamilton, Canada West: Family and Class in a Mid-Nineteenth Century City.* Cambridge, Mass.: Harvard University Press, 1975.

Kelly, Kenneth. "Wheat Farming in Simcoe County in the Mid-Nineteenth Century." *Canadian Geographer* 2 (1971): 95-112.

Kero, Reino. *Migration from Finland to North America in the Years Between the United States Civil War and the First World War.* Turku, Finland: Turun Yliopisto, 1974.

Kero, Reino. "The Character and Significance of Migration Traditions from Finland to North America." *American Studies in Scandinavia* 9 (1977): 95-104.

Kingdon, Robert M. "Protestant Parishes in the Old World and the New: The Cases of Geneva and Boston." *Church History* 48 (1979): 290-304.

Kirk, Gordon W. and Carolyn T. Kirk. *The Promise of American Life: Social Mobility in a Nineteenth Century Immigrant Community, Holland, Michigan, 1847-1894.* Philadelphia: American Philosophical Society, 1978.

Kirk, Gordon W. and Carolyn T. Kirk. "Migration, Mobility and the Transformation of the Occupational Structure in an Immigrant Community: Holland, Michigan, 1850-80." *Journal of Social History* 7 (1974): 142-64.

Koblik, Steven, ed. *Sweden's Development from Poverty to Affluence, 1750–1970.* Minneapolis: University of Minnesota Press, 1975.

Kronberg, Bo and Thomas Nilsson. *Stadsflyttare. Industrialisering, migration och social mobilitet med utgångspunkt från Halmstad, 1870–1910.* Studia Historica Upsaliensia 65. Uppsala: Acta Universitatis Upsaliensis, 1975.

Krontoft, Torben. "Factors in Assimilation: A Comparative Study." *Norwegian-American Studies* 26 (1974): 184–205.

Kulikoff, Alan. "Historical Geographers and Social History: A Review Essay." *Historical Methods Newsletter* 6 (1973): 122–28.

Lagerlöf, Selma. *Jerusalem.* Translated by Velma Swanston Howard. Garden City: Doubleday, Page & Co., 1915.

Landberg, Georg. "Politiska och fackliga organisationer." In *Rättvik* III. Västerås, Sweden: Rättvik parish, 1959: 349–70.

Landberg, Georg. "Turismen och dess bakgrund i äldre gästgiveriorganisation." In *Rättvik* II. Västerås, Sweden: Rättvik parish, 1961: 301–41.

Landberg, Georg. "Personregister." In *Rättvik* I, 2. Västerås, Sweden: Rättvik parish, 1967: 310–29.

Landberg, Georg. "Samhällets uppkomst." In *Rättvik* I: 1. Västerås, Sweden: Rättvik parish, 1966: 205–28.

Landberg, Georg. "Ovanheds frihetskamp och Bodas tillblivelse." In *Rättvik* I: 2. Västerås, Sweden: Rättvik parish, 1967: 57–84.

Landelius, Otto Robert. *Swedish Place Names in North America.* Karin Franzén, trans., Raymond Jarvi, ed. Carbondale and Edwardsville, Illinois: Southern Illinois University Press, published for the Swedish-American Historical Society, 1985.

Langholm, Sivert. "Short-Distance Migration, Circles and Flows: Movement to and from Ullensaker According to the Population Census Lists of 1865." *Scandinavian Economic History Review* 23 (1975): 36–62.

Langholm, Sivert. "On the Scope of Micro-History." *Scandinavian Journal of History* 1 (1976): 3–24.

Larsen, Ulla Margrethe. "A Quantitative Study of Emigration from Denmark to the United States, 1870–1913." *Scandinavian Economic History Review* 30 (1982): 101–28.

Laslett, Peter and Richard Wall, eds. *Household and Family in Past Time.* Cambridge: Cambridge University Press, 1972.

Lee, Everett S. "A Theory of Migration." *Demography* 3 (1966): 47–57.

Leet, Don R. "Human Fertility and Agricultural Opportunities in Ohio Counties: From Frontier to Maturity, 1810–1860." In *Essays in Nineteenth Century Economic History: The Old Northwest,* edited by David C. Klingaman and Richard K. Vedder. Athens, Ohio: Ohio University Press, 1975: 138–57.

Legreid, Ann Marie. "The Exodus, Transplanting, and Religious Reorganization of a Group of Norwegian Lutheran Immigrants in Western Wisconsin, 1836–1900." Ph.D. dissertation, University of Wisconsin-Madison, 1985.

Legreid, Ann Marie. and David Ward. "Religious Schism and the Development of Rural Immigrant Communities: Norwegian Lutherans in Western Wisconsin, 1880-1905." *Upper Midwest History* 2 (1982): 13-29.

Lemon, James T. *The Best Poor Man's Country: A Geographical Study of Early Southeastern Pennsylvania.* Baltimore: Johns Hopkins University Press, 1972.

Lemon, James T. "The Weakness of Place and Community in Early Pennsylvania." In *European Settlement in North America: Essays on Geographical Change in Honour and Memory of Andrew Hill Clark,* edited by James R. Gibson. Toronto: University of Toronto Press, 1978: 190-207.

Lemon, James T. "Early Americans and Their Social Environment." *Journal of Historical Geography* 6 (1980): 115-31.

Le Play Society. *Sweden: Dalarna Studies.* London: The Le Play Society, 1939.

Levander, Lars. *Dalmålet.* 2 vols. Uppsala, 1925 and 1928.

Levander, Lars. *Övre Dalarnes bondekultur.* 4 vols. Lund, Sweden, Carl Bloms Boktryckeri, 1943-53.

Levander, Lars. *Våmhusfjärdingen.* Stockholm, 1944.

Lewis, Ann. *Eternal Heritage in Christ.* Dalbo, Minnesota: Salem Lutheran Church Centennial Committee, 1974.

Lindberg, Einar. "Seasonal Migration of Labour from the Siljan Area and Its Economic Background." *Geografiska Annaler* 42 (1960): 262-66.

Lindberg, Einar. "Arbetsvandringar förr och nu." In *Rättvik* II. Västerås, Sweden: Rättvik parish, 1961: 173-92.

Lindberg, John S. *The Background of Swedish Emigration to the United States: An Economic and Sociological Study in the Dynamics of Migration.* Minneapolis: University of Minnesota Press, 1930.

Lindholm, Erik. "Året runt på 1800-talets bondgård." In *Gagnef och Mockfjärd—en Hembygdsbok.* Falum, 1952: 191-203.

Lindmark, Sture. *Swedish America, 1914-1932. Studies in Ethnicity with Emphasis on Illinois and Minnesota.* Studia Historica Upsaliensia 37. Uppsala: Acta Universitatis Upsaliensis, 1971.

Lindmark, Sture. "The Language Question and Its Resolution." *Swedish Pioneer Historical Quarterly* 23 (1972): 71-98.

Ljungmark, Lars. *Den stora utvandringen: Svensk emigration till USA 1840-1925.* Stockholm: Sveriges Radio, 1965.

Ljungmark, Lars. *For Sale—Minnesota: Organized Promotion of Scandinavian Immigration, 1866-1873.* Chicago: Swedish Pioneer Historical Society, 1971.

Ljungmark, Lars. "Canada's Campaign for Scandinavian Immigration, 1873-1876." *Swedish-American Historical Quarterly* (1982): 21-42.

Ljungmark, Lars. "Canada: An Alternative for the Swedish Emigration to the New World, 1873-1875." *Swedish-American Historical Quarterly* (1984): 253-66.

Lockridge, Kenneth A. *A New England Town: The First Hundred Years, Dedham, Massachusetts, 1636–1736.* New York: W. W. Norton & Co., 1970.

Loetscher, L. A. "The Problem of Christian Unity in Early Nineteenth Century America." *Church History* 32 (1963): 3–16.

Löfgren, Orvar. "Family and Household among Scandinavian Peasants: An Exploratory Essay." *Ethnologica Scandinavica* (1974): 17–52.

Löfgren, Orvar. "Peasant Ecotypes: Problems in the Comparative Study of Ecological Adaptation." *Ethnologica Scandinavica* (1976): 100–115.

Löfgren, Orvar. "The Potato People: Household Economy and Family Patterns among the Rural Proletariat in Nineteenth Century Sweden." In *Chance and Change: Social and Economic Studies in Historical Demography in the Baltic Area,* edited by Sune Åkerman, Hans Christian Johansen, and David Gaunt. Odense: Odense University Press, 1978: 95–108.

Löfgren, Orvar. "Historical Perspectives on Scandinavian Peasantries." *Annual Review of Anthropology* 9 (1980): 187–215.

Lovoll, Odd S. *Cultural Pluralism vs. Assimilation.* Northfield, Minnesota: Norwegian–American Historical Association, 1977.

Lowell, Briant Lindsay, *Scandinavian Exodus: Demography and Social Development of 19th-Century Rural Communities* (Boulder, Co.: Westview Press, 1987).

Luebke, Frederick C. *Immigrants and Politics: The Germans of Nebraska, 1880–1900.* Lincoln, University of Nebraska Press, 1969.

Luebke, Frederick C., ed. *Ethnicity on the Great Plains.* Lincoln: University of Nebraska Press, 1980.

Luebke, Frederick C. "The Immigrant Condition as a Factor Contributing to the Conservatism of the Lutheran Church." *Concordia Historical Institute Quarterly* 38 (1965): 19–28.

Luebke, Frederick C. "Ethnic Group Settlement on the Great Plains." *Western Historical Quarterly* 8 (1977): 405–30.

Lund, Emil. *Minnesota konferensens och dess församlingars historia.* 2 vols. Rock Island: Augustana Book Concern, 1923.

Lunden, Kare. "Some Causes of Change in a Peasant Economy." *Scandinavian Economic History Review* 21 (1974): 117–35.

MacDonald, John S. and Leatrice D. MacDonald. "Chain Migration, Ethnic Neighborhood Formation and Social Networks." *Milbank Memorial Fund Quarterly* 42 (1964): 82–97.

Malin, James C. "The Turnover of Farm Population in Kansas." *Kansas Historical Quarterly* 4 (1935): 339–72.

Mannion, John J. *Irish Settlements in Eastern Canada: A Study of Cultural Transfer and Adaptation.* Toronto: University of Toronto Press, 1974.

Mannion, John J. *The Peopling of New Foundland: Essays in Historical Geography.* St. John's, Newfoundland: Memorial University of Newfoundland, 1977.

Marshall, Douglas G. "The Decline in Farm Family Fertility and Its Relationship to Nationality and Religious Background." *Rural Sociology* 15 (1960): 42–49.

Marty, Martin. "The Skeleton of Religion in America." *Church History* 41 (1972): 5–21.

Mays, Herbert J. "A Place to Stand: Families, Land and Permanence in Toronto Gore Township, 1820–1890." *Canadian Historical Papers* (1980): 185–211.

McManis, Douglas. *The Initial Evaluation and Utilization of the Illinois Prairies, 1815–1840.* University of Chicago, Department of Geography Research Paper 94. Chicago: University of Chicago, Department of Geography, 1963.

McQuillan, D. Aidan. "Farm Size and Work Ethic: Measuring the Success of Immigrant Farmers on the American Grasslands, 1875–1925." *Journal of Historical Geography* 4 (1978): 57–76.

McQuillan, D. Aidan. "Territory and Ethnic Identity: Some New Measures of an Old Theme in the Cultural Geography of the United States." In *European Settlement and Development in North America: Essays on Geographical Change in Honour and Memory of Andrew Hill Clark*, edited by James R. Gibson. Toronto: University of Toronto Press, (1978): 136–69.

McQuillan, D. Aidan. "The Mobility of Immigrants and Americans: A Comparison of Farmers on the Kansas Frontier." *Agricultural History* 53 (1979): 576–96.

Mead, Sidney E. "Denominationalism: The Shape of Protestantism in America," *Church History* 23 (1954): 291–320.

Medick, Hans. "The Proto-Industrial Family Economy: The Structural Function of the Household during the Transition from Peasant Society to Industrial Capitalism." *Social History* 3 (1976): 291–315.

Meinig, Donald W. "The Continuous Shaping of America: A Prospectus for Geographers and Historians." *American Historical Review* 83 (1978): 1186–1217.

Mendels, Franklin F. "Proto-Industrialization: The First Phase of the Industrialization Process." *Journal of Economic History* 32 (1972): 241–61.

Meyer, Carl S. "Lutheran Immigrant Churches Face the Problems of the Frontier." *Church History* 29 (1960): 440–62.

Meyer, Judith W. "Ethnicity, Theology and Immigrant Church Expansion." *Geographical Review* 65 (1975): 180–97.

Mills, Dennis R. "The Residential Propinquity of Kin in a Cambridgeshire Village." *Journal of Historical Geography* 4 (1978): 265–76.

Mills, Dennis R. "The Nineteenth-Century Peasantry of Melbourn, Cambridgeshire." In *Land, Kinship and Life-cycle*, edited by Richard M. Smith. Cambridge: Cambridge University Press, 1985: 481–518.

Minnesskrift utgiven av Gärdsjö Missionsförsamling till dess 55-årsjubileum. Falun, Sweden, 1932.

Minnesota Conference of the Augustana Synod. *The Beginnings and Progress of Minnesota Conference of the Lutheran Augustana Synod of America.* Minneapolis: Lund Press, 1929.

Mitchell, Robert D. *Commercialism and Frontier: Perspectives on the Early Shenandoah Valley.* Charlottesville: University Press of Virginia, 1977.

Miyakawa, T. Scott. *Protestants and Pioneers: Individualism and Conformity on the American Frontier.* Chicago: University of Chicago Press, 1964.

Modell, John. "Family and Fertility on the Indiana Frontier, 1820." *American Quarterly* 23 (1971): 615–34.

Montelius, Erik. "Svåra tider." In *Gagnef och Mockfjärd—en hembygdsbok.* Falun, Sweden: Falu Nya boktryckeri, 1952: 295–305.

Montelius, Olof. *Möje. Arbetslivet i en Gagnefsby kring sekelskiftet.* Gagnef, Sweden, 1962.

Montelius, Sigvard. "Finnmarksbebyggelsen." In *Dalarna. Ett vida berömt landskap,* edited by Olle Veirulf. Stockholm: Svensk Litteratur, 1951: 135–46.

Montelius, Sigvard. "The Burning of Forest Land for the Cultivation of Crops—'Svedjebruk' in Central Sweden." *Geografiska Annaler* 35 (1953): 41–54.

Montelius, Sigvard. "Finn Settlement in Central Sweden." *Geografiska Annaler* 42 (1960): 285–93.

Morawska, Eva. *For Bread with Butter: The Life-Worlds of East Central Europeans in Johnstown, Pennsylvania, 1890-1940.* Cambridge: Cambridge University Press, 1985.

Morell, Mats. "On the Stratification of the Swedish Peasant Class." *Scandinavian Economic History Review* 28 (1980): 15–32.

Morrill, Richard L. and Pitts, Forrest R. "Marriage, Migration and the Mean Information Field: A Study in Uniqueness and Generality." *Annals of the Association of American Geographers* 57 (1967): 401–22.

Munch, Peter A. "Social Adjustment Among Wisconsin Norwegians." *American Sociological Review* 14 (1949): 780–87.

Munch, Peter A. "Segregation and Assimilation of Norwegian Settlements in Wisconsin." *Norwegian-American Studies and Records* 18 (1954): 102–40.

Munch, Peter A. "Authority and Freedom: Controversy in Norwegian-American Congregations." *Norwegian-American Studies and Records* 28 (1980): 3–34.

Näsström, Gustaf. *Dalarna som svenskt ideal.* Stockholm, Wahlström & Widstrand, 1937.

Nelson, Helge. *The Swedes and the Swedish Settlements in North America.* Skrifter utgivna av Kungl. Humanistiska vetenskapssamfundet i Lund 37. Lund, Sweden: Acta Regiae Societatis Humaniorum Litterarum Lundensis, 1943.

Nelson, Helge. *Studier över svenskt näringsliv, säsongarbete och befolkningsrörelser under 1800- och 1900-talen.* Lund, Sweden: Acta Regiae Societas Humaniorum Litterarum Lundensis, 1963.

Nelson, Helge. "Dalarna: näringsliv och arbetsvandringar 1800-1950. Ett bidrag och preliminärt meddelande." *Svensk Geografisk Årsbok* 34 (1958): 91–120.

Nelson, Lowry. "Intermarriages among Nationality Groups in a Rural Area of Minnesota." *American Journal of Sociology* 49 (1944): 582–92.

Nilsson, Fred. *Emigrationen från Stockholm till Nordamerika 1880–1893. En studie i urban utvandring.* Studia Historica Upsaliensia 31. Uppsala: Acta Universitatis Upsaliensis, 1970.

Nisbet, Robert A. *The Quest for Community.* New York: Oxford University Press, 1953.

Norberg, Anders. *Sågarnas ö. Alnö och industrialisering 1860–1910.* Studia Historica Upsaliensia 116. Uppsala: Acta Universitatis Upsaliensis, 1980.

Nordenstedt, Werner. "Skiftes- och avvitringsväsendet i Dalarna." In *Svenska lantmäteriet 1628–1928.* 2 vols. Stockholm, 1928.

Nordenström, N. *Svenska Baptistsamfundets historia.* 2 vols. Stockholm, 1923.

Norelius, Eric. *De svenska lutherska församlingarnas och svenskarnas historia i Amerika.* 2 vols. Rock Island, Augustana Book Concern, 1916.

Norman, Hans. *Från Bergslagen till Nordamerika: Studier i migrationsmönster, social rörlighet och demografisk struktur med utgångspunkt från Örebro län 1851–1915.* Studia Historica Upsaliensia 62. Uppsala, Acta Universitatis Upsaliensis, 1974.

Nyberg, H. S. "Dalarna." In *Dalarna: Ett vida berömt landskap,* edited by Olle Veirulf. Stockholm: Svensk Litteratur, 1951: 9–17.

O'Brien, Michael J. *Grassland, Forest, and Historical Settlement: An Analysis of Dynamics in Northeast Missouri.* Lincoln: University of Nebraska Press, 1984.

Odén, Birgitta. "Emigrationen från Norden till Nordamerika." *Historisk Tidskrift* 83 (1963): 261–77.

Olson, Olof E. "A Letter from One Generation to Another." *The Swedish Pioneer Historical Quarterly* 24 (1973): 242–58.

Olsson, Gunnar. "Utflyttningar från centrala Värmland under 1880-talet." *Meddelanden från Uppsala Universitets Geografiska Institution,* Series A, 178. Uppsala, 1962.

Omner, Rosemary E. "Highland Scots Migration to Southwestern Newfoundland: A Study of Kinship." In *The Peopling of Newfoundland: Essays in Historical Geography,* edited by John J. Mannion. St. John's, Newfoundland: Memorial University of Newfoundland, 1977: 212–33.

Omner, Rosemary E. "Primitive Accumulation and the Scottish Clan in the Old World and the New." *Journal of Historical Geography* 12 (1986): 121–41.

Örjangård, Sigurd. *Jordbruket i Dalarna under 100 år: 1850–1950.* Falun, Sweden, 1951.

Ostergren, Robert C. "Cultural Homogeneity and Population Stability among Swedish Immigrants in Chisago County." *Minnesota History* 43 (1973): 255–69.

Ostergren, Robert C. "Rättvik to Isanti: A Community Transplanted." Ph.D. dissertation, University of Minnesota, 1976.

Ostergren, Robert C. "A Community Transplanted: The Formative Experience of a Swedish Immigrant Community in the Upper Midwest." *Journal of Historical Geography* 5 (1979): 189–212.

Ostergren, Robert C. "Prairie Bound: Migration Patterns to a Swedish Settlement on the Dakota Frontier." In *Ethnicity on the Great Plains*, edited by Frederick C. Luebke. Lincoln: University of Nebraska Press, 1980: 73–91.

Ostergren, Robert C. "Land and Family in Rural Immigrant Communities." *Annals of the Association of American Geographers* 71 (1981): 400–11.

Ostergren, Robert C. "The Immigrant Church as a Symbol of Community and Place on the Landscape of the American Upper Midwest." *Great Plains Quarterly* 1 (1981): 224–38.

Ostergren, Robert C. "Geographic Perspectives on the History of Settlement in the Upper Middle West." *Upper Midwest History* 1 (1981): 27–39.

Ostergren, Robert C. "Kinship Networks and Migration: A Nineteenth Century Swedish Example." *Social Science History* 6 (1982): 292–320.

Ostergren, Robert C. "Settlement and Ethnicity Patterns on the Agricultural Frontiers of South Dakota." *South Dakota History* 13 (1983): 49–82.

Ostergren, Robert C. "Swedish Migration to North America in Transatlantic Perspective." In *Migration Across Time and Nations: Population Mobility in Historical Contexts*, edited by Ira Glazier and Luigi De Rosa. New York: Holmes & Meier, 1986: 125–47.

Ostergren, Robert C. "The Transplanted Swedish Rural Community in the Upper Middle West." In *Scandinavia Overseas: Patterns of Cultural Transformation in North America and Australia*, edited by Harold Runblom and Dag Blanck. Uppsala Multiethnic Papers 7. Uppsala: Center for Multiethnic Research, 1986: 18–39.

Østerud, OIivind. "The Transformation of Scandinavian Agrarianism: A Comparative Study of Political Change around 1870." *Scandinavian Journal of History* 1 (1976): 201–13.

Pallin, Britta. "The 'Bytomt' (Village Tofts)—Its Significance and Function." *Geografiska Annaler* 50B (1968): 52–61.

Parkerson, Donald. "How Mobile Were Nineteenth Century Americans?" *Historical Methods* 15 (1982): 99–109.

Parson, Ruben L. *Ever the Land: A Homestead Chronicle.* Staples, Minnesota: Adventure Publications, 1978.

Peterson, August. *History of the Swedes Who Settled in Clay County, South Dakota and Their Biographies.* Vermillion, South Dakota: The Swedish Pioneer Historical Society of Clay County, South Dakota, 1947.

Pierson, George M. "The M Factor in American History." *American Quarterly* 14 (1962): 275–89.

Powell, Sumner C. *Puritan Village.* Middletown, Connecticut: Wesleyan University Press, 1963.

Power, Richard L. *Planting Corn Belt Culture: The Impress of the Upland Southerner and Yankee in the Old Northwest.* Indianapolis: Indiana Historical Society, 1953.

Price, Charles A. *Southern Europeans in Australia*. Melbourne: Oxford University Press, 1963.

Qualey, Carlton C. *Norwegian Settlement in the United States*. Northfield, Minnesota: Norwegian-American Historical Association, 1938.

Quigley, John M. "An Economic Model of Swedish Emigration." *Quarterly Journal of Economics* 86 (1972): 111-26.

Raitz, Karl B. "Ethnic Maps in North America." *Geographical Review* 68 (1978): 335-50.

Rättvik. 4 vols. Västerås, Sweden: Rättvik parish, 1959-1967.

Remiggi, Frank W. "Ethnic Diversity and Settler Location on the Eastern Lower North Shore of Quebec." In *The Peopling of Newfoundland: Essays in Historical Geography*, edited by John J. Mannion. St. John's, Newfoundland: Memorial University of Newfoundland, 1977: 185-211.

Rice, John G. *Patterns of Ethnicity in a Minnesota County, 1880-1905*. Geographical Reports 4. Umeå, Sweden: Department of Geography, University of Umeå, 1973.

Rice, John G. "The Role of Culture and Community in Frontier Prairie Farming." *Journal of Historical Geography* 3 (1977): 155-75.

Rice, John G. "The Effect of Land Alienation on Settlement." *Annals of the Association of American Geographers* 68 (1978): 61-72.

Rice, John G. "Indicators of Social Change in Rural Sweden in the Late Nineteenth Century." *Journal of Historical Geography* 4 (1978): 23-34.

Rice, John G. "Marriage Behavior and the Persistence of Swedish Communities in Minnesota." In *Perspectives on Swedish Immigration: Proceedings of the International Conference on the Swedish Heritage in the Upper Midwest*, edited by Nils Hasselmo. Chicago, Swedish Pioneer Historical Society, 1978: 136-50.

Rice, John G. "Studying the Modernization Process." In *Time, Space and Man: Essays in Microdemography*, edited by Jan Sundin and Erik Söderlund. Umeå, Sweden: Almqvist & Wiksell International, 1979.

Rice, John G. and Robert C. Ostergren. "The Decision to Emigrate: A Study in Diffusion." *Geografiska Annaler* 60B (1978): 1-15.

Rich, March. *The Rural Church Movement*. Columbia, Missouri: Juniper Knoll Press, 1957.

Robinson, Edward Van Dyke. *Early Conditions and the Development of Agriculture in Minnesota*. Minneapolis, 1915.

Rogers, Susan C. and Sonya Salamon. "Inheritance and Social Organization among Family Farmers." *American Ethnologist* 10 (1983): 529-50.

Rolén, Mats. *Skogsbygd i omvandling. Studier Kring folkningsutveckling, omflyttning och social rörlighet i Revsunds tingslag 1820-1977*. Studia Historica Upsaliensia 107. Uppsala: Acta Universitatis Upsaliensis, 1979.

Rondahl, Björn. *Emigration, folkomflyttning och säsongarbete i ett sågverksdistrikt i södra Hälsingland 1865-1910: Söderala kommun med särskild hänsyn till Ljusne industrisamhälle.* Studia Historica Upsaliensia 40. Uppsala: Acta Universitatis Upsaliensis, 1972.

Rönnegård, Sam. "Kyrkolivet." In *Dalarna: Ett vida berömt landskap,* edited by Olle Veirulf. Stockholm: Svensk Litteratur, 1951: 171–83.

Rosander, Göran. *Herrarbete: Dalfolkets säsongvisa arbetsvandringar i jämförande belysning.* Skrifter utgivna genom Landsmåls- och folkminnesarkivet i Uppsala, Ser. B, 13. Uppsala: Lundequistska Bokhandeln, 1967.

Rosenström, P. H. "Bruk och industrier." In *Rättvik* II. Västerås, Sweden: Rättvik parish, 1961: 239–52.

Runblom, Harald and Dag Blanck. *Scandinavia Overseas: Patterns of Cultural Transformation in North America and Australia.* Uppsala Multiethnic Papers 7. Uppsala: Center for Multiethnic Research, Uppsala University, 1986.

Runblom, Harald and Lars-Göran Tedebrand. "Future Research in Swedish–American History: Some Perspectives." *Swedish Pioneer Historical Quarterly* 30 (1979): 129–40.

Runblom, Harald and Hans Norman, eds. *From Sweden to America: A History of the Migration.* Minneapolis and Uppsala: University of Minnesota Press and Acta Universitatis Upsaliensis, 1976.

Runeby, Nils. *Den nya världen och den gamla. Amerikabild och emigrationsuppfattning i Sverige, 1820–1860.* Stockholm: Läromedelsförlaget, 1969.

Russo, David. *Families and Communities: A New View of American History.* Nashville: American Association of State and Local History, 1974.

Rutman, Darrett B. "Community Study." *Historical Methods* 13 (1980): 29–41.

Rydén, P. *Svenska Baptisternas i Minnesota Historia.* Minneapolis: Nygren Printing Co., 1918.

Salamon, Sonya. "Ethnic Differences in Family Farm Land Transfers." *Rural Sociology* 45 (1980): 290–308.

Salamon, Sonya and Ann Mackey Keim. "Land Ownership and Women's Power in a Midwestern Farming Community." *Journal of Marriage and the Family* 41 (1979): 109–19.

Salamon, Sonya and Shirley O'Reilly. "Family Land and Development Cycles among Illinois Farmers." *Rural Sociology* 44 (1979): 525–54.

Sandaker, Arvid. "Emigration from Land Parish to America, 1866–1875." *Norwegian–American Studies and Records* 26 (1974): 49–74.

Sandbäck, Erik. "Finnarna och finnmarken." In *Rättvik* I: 2. Västerås, Sweden: Rättvik parish, 1967: 31–55.

Sanderson, Dwight. "The Rural Community in the United States as an Elementary Group." *Rural Sociology* 1 (1936): 142–150.

Saueressig, Yda. "Emigration, Settlement, and Assimilation of Dutch Catholic Immigrants in Wisconsin, 1850–1905." Ph.D. dissertation, University of Wisconsin-Madison, 1982.

Saueressig-Schreuder, Yda. "Dutch Catholic Emigration in the Mid-Nineteenth Century Noord Brabant, 1847-1871." *Journal of Historical Geography* 11 (1985): 48-69.

Saueressig-Schreuder, Yda. "Dutch Catholic Settlement in Wisconsin." In *The Dutch in America: Immigration, Settlement, and Cultural Change*, edited by Robert P. Swierenga. New Brunswick, New Jersey: Rutgers University Press, 1985: 105-24.

Schafer, Joseph. *Four Wisconsin Counties: Prairie and Forest*. Madison: State Historical Society of Wisconsin, 1927.

Schafer, Joseph. *The Social History of American Agriculture*. New York: Macmillan, 1936.

Schafer, Joseph. "The Yankee and the Teuton in Wisconsin," *Wisconsin Magazine of History* 6 (1922): 125-28.

Schell, Herbert S. *History of Clay County, South Dakota*. Vermillion, South Dakota: Clay County Historical Society, 1976.

Schell, Herbert S. "Official Immigration Activities of Dakota Territory." *North Dakota Historical Quarterly* 7 (1932): 5-24.

Schön, Lennart. "Västernorrland in the Middle of the Nineteenth Century: A Study in the Transition from Small-Scale to Capitalistic Production." *Economy and History* 15 (1972): 83-111.

Scott, Franklin D. "The Study of the Effects of Emigration." *Scandinavian Economic History Review* 8 (1960): 161-74.

Semmingsen, Ingrid. *Norway to America: A History of the Migration*. Minneapolis: University of Minnesota Press, 1978.

Semmingsen, Ingrid. "Family Emigration from Bergen, 1874-92." *Americana Norvegica* 3 (1971): 38-63.

Semmingsen, Ingrid. "Nordic Research into Migration." *Scandinavian Journal of History* 3 (1978): 107-29.

Semmingsen, Ingrid and Per Seyersted. *Scando-Americana: Papers on Emigration to the United States*. Olso: American Institute, University of Oslo, 1972.

Shannon, Fred A. *The Farmer's Last Frontier*. New York: Holt, Rinehart & Winston, 1945.

Shortridge, James R. "Patterns of Religion in the United States." *Geographical Review* 66 (1976): 420-34.

Shortridge, James R. "The Emergence of 'Middle West' as an American Regional Label." *Annals of the Association of American Geographers* 74 (1984): 209-20.

Skårdal, Dorothy Burton. *The Divided Heart: Scandinavian Immigrant Experience through Literary Sources*. Lincoln: University of Nebraska Press, 1974.

Smith, Richard M., ed. *Land, Kinship and Life Cycle*. Cambridge: Cambridge University Press, 1985.

Smith, Timothy L. "Religious Denominations as Ethnic Communities: A Regional Case Study." *Church History* 35 (1966): 207-26.

Smith, Timothy L. "Religion and Ethnicity in America." *American Historical Review* 83 (1978): 1155-85.

Söderberg, Kjell. *Den första massutvandringen. En studie av befolkningsrörlighet och emigration utgående från Alfta socken i Hälsingland 1846-1895.* Umeå Studies in the Humanities 39. Umeå, Sweden: Acta Universitatis Umensis, 1981.

Söderberg, Kjell. "Personal Characteristics and Selective Migration." *American Studies in Scandinavia* 9 (1977): 127-154.

Sogner, Sølvi. "Freeholder and Cottar: Property Relationships and the Social Structure in the Peasant Community in Norway during the 18th Century." *Scandinavian Journal of History* 1 (1976): 181-99.

Spear, Allan H. "Marcus Lee Hansen and the Historiography of Immigration." *Wisconsin Magazine of History* 64 (1961): 258-68.

Spiegel, H. W. "The Altenteil: German Farmer's Old Age Security." *Rural Sociology* 3 (1939): 203-18.

Ståhl, Harry. "Om gårdsnamnen." In *Rättvik III.* Västerås, Sweden: Rättvik parish, 1959: 73-85.

Stanchfield Baptist Church Centennial History, 1866-1966. N.P., 1966.

Steffen, Jerome O., ed. *The American West: New Perspectives, New Dimensions.* Norman: University of Oklahoma Press, 1979.

Stephenson, George M. *The Religious Aspects of Swedish Immigration: A Study of Immigrant Churches.* Minneapolis: University of Minnesota Press, 1932.

Sundbärg, Gustav. "Ekonomisk-statistisk beskrifning öfver Sveriges olika landsdelar." In *Emigrationsutredningen* 5. Stockholm: P. A. Nordstedt & Söner, 1910.

Sundin, Jan, ed. *Kontroll och kontrollerade: Formell och informell kontroll i ett historiskt perspektiv.* Forskningsrapporter från Historiska institutionen i Umeå 1. Umeå, Sweden: Historiska institutionen vid Umeå Universitet, 1982.

Sundin, Jan and Eric Söderlund, eds. *Time, Space and Man: Essays in Microdemography.* Stockholm: Almqvist & Wiksell International, 1979.

Svalestuen, Andres A. "Five Local Studies of Nordic Emigration and Migration." *American Studies in Scandinavia* 9 (1977): 17-63.

Swierenga, Robert P. *Pioneers and Profits: Land Speculators on the Iowa Frontier.* Ames: Iowa State University Press, 1968.

Swierenga, Robert P. *Acres for Cents: Delinquent Tax Auctions in Frontier Iowa.* Westport: Greenwood Press, 1976.

Swierenga, Robert P., ed. *The Dutch in America: Immigration, Settlement and Cultural Change.* New Brunswick, New Jersey: Rutgers University Press, 1985.

Swierenga, Robert P. "Towards the New Rural History: A Review Essay." *Historical Methods Newsletter* 6 (1973): 111-22.

Swierenga, Robert P. "Land Speculation and Its Impact on American Economic Growth and Welfare: A Historiographic Review." *Western Historical Quarterly* 8 (1977): 283–302.

Swierenga, Robert P. "Dutch Immigrant Demography." *Journal of Family History* 5 (1980): 390–405.

Swierenga, Robert P. "Ethnicity and American Agriculture." *Ohio History* 89 (1980): 323–44.

Swierenga, Robert P. "Dutch International Migration Statistics, 1820–1880: An Analysis of Linked Multinational Nominal Files." *International Migration Review* 15 (1981): 445–70.

Swierenga, Robert P. "The New Rural History." *Great Plains Quarterly* 1 (1981): 211–23.

Swierenga, Robert P. and Yda Saueressig-Schreuder. "Catholic and Protestant Emigration from the Netherlands in the 19th Century: A Comparative Social Structural Analysis." *Tijdschrift voor economische en sociale geografie* 24 (1983): 25–40.

Tarver, James D. "Intra-Family Farm Succession Practices." *Rural Sociology* 17 (1952): 266–71.

Taylor, Philip. *The Distant Magnet: European Emigration to the U.S.A.* New York: Harper & Row, 1971.

Tedebrand, Lars-Göran. *Västernorrland och Nordamerika 1875–1913: Utvandring och återinvandring.* Studia Historica Upsaliensia 42. Uppsala: Acta Universitatis Upsaliensis, 1972.

Tedebrand, Lars Göran. "Remigration from America to Sweden." In *From Sweden to America: A History of the Migration,* edited by Harald Runblom and Hans Norman. Minneapolis and Uppsala: University of Minnesota Press and Acta Universitatis Upsaliensis, 1976: 201–27.

Tedebrand, Lars-Göran. "Sources for the History of Swedish Emigration." In *From Sweden to America: A History of the Migration,* edited by Harald Runblom and Hans Norman. Minneapolis and Uppsala: University of Minnesota Press and Acta Universitatis Upsaliensis, 1976: 76–93.

Thernstrom, Stephan. *Poverty and Progress: Social Mobility in a Nineteenth Century City.* Cambridge, Mass.: Harvard University Press, 1964.

Thernstrom, Stephan. *The Other Bostonians: Poverty and Progress in the American Metropolis, 1880–1970.* Cambridge, Mass.: Harvard University Press, 1973.

Thistlethwaite, Frank. "Migration from Europe Overseas in the Nineteenth and Twentieth Centuries." *XIe. Congrès International des Sciences Historiques. Rapports V: Histoire Contemporaine.* Stockholm, 1960: 32–60.

Thomas, Brinley. *Migration and Economic Growth: A Study of Great Britain and the Atlantic Economy.* Cambridge: Cambridge University Press, 1954.

Thomas, Dorothy Swaine. *Social and Economic Aspects of Swedish Population Movements, 1750–1933.* New York: Macmillan Co., 1941.

Thomas, William I. and Florian Znaniecki. *Polish Peasants in Europe and America.* 2 vols. New York: Alfred A. Knopf, 1927.

Thorslund, Per. "Rättvikstraktens geologiska historia." In *Rättvik* II. Västerås, Sweden: Rättvik parish, 1961: 9–32.

Throne, Mildred. "Southern Iowa Agriculture, 1833–1890: The Progress from Subsistence to Commercial Corn-Belt Farming." *Agricultural History* 23 (1949): 124–30.

Tilly, Charles and C. Harold Brown. "On Uprooting, Kinship and the Auspices of Migration." *International Journal of Comparative Sociology* 8 (1967): 139–64.

Trotzig, E. G. "Early Swedish Settlements in the Dakota Territory." *Swedish Pioneer Historical Quarterly* 28 (1977): 106–17.

Unseem, John and Ruth Hill. "Minority Group Pattern in Prairie Society." *American Journal of Sociology* 50 (1945): 377–85.

Upham, Warren. *Minnesota Geographical Names: Their Origin and Historic Significance.* St. Paul: Minnesota Historical Society, 1969.

Upjohn's Rural Architecture: Designs, Working Drawings and Specifications for a Wooden Church and Other Rural Structures. New York, 1852.

Vangdrup, Arne. "Demographic and Migrational Conditions in Torslev Parish, 1870–1901." *American Studies in Scandinavia* 9 (1977): 65–86.

Vecoli, Rudolph J. "Contadini in Chicago: A Critique of *The Uprooted.*" *Journal of American History* 51 (1964): 404–17.

Veirulf, Olle. "Byar i äldre tid." In *Rättvik* I:1. Västerås, Sweden: Rättvik parish, 1966: 58–83.

Veirulf, Olle, ed. *Dalarna: ett vida berömt landskap.* Stockholm: Svensk Litteratur, 1951.

Vikar, Anders. "Allmogens levnadssätt i äldre tid." In *Rättvik* II. Västerås, Sweden: Rättvik parish, 1961: 264–300.

Vogeler, Ingolf. "Ethnicity, Religion, and Farm Land Transfers in Western Wisconsin." *Ecumene* 7 (1975): 6–13.

Ward, David. *Cities and Immigrants: A Geography of Change in Nineteenth Century America.* New York: Oxford University Press, 1971.

Ward, David. "The Debate on Alternative Approaches in Historical Geography." *Historical Methods Newsletter* 8 (1975): 82–87.

Wehrwein, George S. "The Problem of Inheritance in American Land Tenure." *Journal of Farm Economics* 9 (1927): 163–75.

Wehrwein, George S. "The Post-Ownership Steps on the 'Agricultural Ladder' in a Low Tenancy Region." *Journal of Land and Public Utility Economics* 7 (1931): 65–73.

Wester, Holger. *Innovationer i befolkningsrörligheten. En studie av spridningsförlopp i befolkningsrörligheten utgående från Pentalax socken i Österbotten.* Studia Historica Upsaliensia 93. Uppsala: Acta Universitatis Upsaliensis, 1977.

Wheeler, Wayne. *An Analysis of Social Change in a Swedish Immigrant Community: The Case of Lindsborg, Kansas.* New York: AMS Press, 1986.

Wiebe, Robert H. *The Search for Order, 1877-1920.* New York: Hill & Wang, 1967.

Wilkinson, Maurice. "Evidences of Long Swings in the Growth of Swedish Population and Related Variables, 1860-1965." *Journal of Economic History* 27 (1967): 17-39.

Wilkinson, Maurice. "European Migration to the United States: An Econometric Analysis of Aggregate Supply and Demand." *Review of Economics and Statistics* 52 (1970): 272-79.

Winberg, Christer. *Folkökning och proletarisering. Kring den sociala strukturomvandling på Sveriges landsbygd under den agrara revolutionen.* Meddelanden från historiska institutionen i Göteborg 10. Gothenburg: Gothenburg University, Historical Institute, 1975.

Winberg, Christer. "Familj och jord i tre Västgötasocknar. Generationskiften bland självägande bönder ca. 1810-1870." *Historisk Tidskrift* (1981): 278-310.

Winters, Donald L. *Farmers Without Farms: Agricultural Tenancy in Nineteenth Century Iowa.* Westport: Greenwood Press, 1978.

Wirén, Agnes. *Uppbrott från örtagård: Utvandring från Blekinge under begynneleskedet till och med år 1870.* Bibliotheca Historica Lundensis 34. Lund: CWK Gleerup, 1975.

Wohlin, Nils. *Dens svenska jordstyckningspolitiken i de 18de och 19de århundradena.* Stockholm, 1912.

Wohlin, Nils. "Den jordbruksidkande befolkningen i Sverige 1751-1900. Statistisk-demografisk studie på grundval af den svenska yrkesräkningarna." In *Emigrationsutredningen.* No. 9 of 20 vols. Stockholm: P. A. Nordstedt & Söner, 1909: 1-159.

Wolpert, Julian. "Behavioral Aspects of the Decision to Migrate: The Decision Process in a Spatial Context." *Papers and Proceedings of the Regional Science Association* 15 (1965): 159-69.

Woodward, George E. *Rural Church Architecture: A Series of Designs for Churches, Exemplified in Plans, Elevations, Sections and Details.* New York: 1876.

Yans-McLaughlin, Virginia. *Family and Community: Italian Immigrants in Buffalo, 1880-1930.* Ithaca: Cornell University Press, 1971.

Zunz, Olivier. *The Changing Face of Inequality: Urbanization, Industrial Development, and Immigrants in Detroit, 1880-1920.* Chicago: University of Chicago Press, 1982.

Index

Acculturation. *See* assimilation

Agriculture, American: pioneer conditions in the Upper Midwest, 189–93; in Clay County, 207–09

—in Isanti: immigrant adaptations, 192–93; early lack of markets, 193–94; use of traditional techniques, 194, 238–39; crops cultivated, 194–15, 198–200, 246; animal husbandry, 200–202, 205, 246; land clearance, 204, 246; mechanization, 205, 240, 247; diversification, 205–6, 246, 248; seasonal round, 206, 239, 245; marketing of grain, 207

Agriculture, Swedish: crop failures 112, 119, 290

—in Rättvik: land colonization, 75, 102, 291; animal husbandry, 81, 83, 88, 91–93, 205, 291–93; seasonal round, 87–102; cooperation, 88, 100; field systems, 89; spring planting, 89; rotation systems, 89–91; crops cultivated, 89–91, 291, 292; haymaking, 94–95; harvesting, 95–96; threshing, 96–97; slaughter, 97, 99; creameries, 292

Ål parish: property subdivision in, 103

Allamakee County, 187

Altsarbyn village: Baptists in, 305

Älvdalen parish: emigration from, 119

"America fever": in Rättvik, 5, 109; in Sweden, 109; in Upper Dalarna, 115, 121

America letters: content of, 190–192, 236

American Fur Company, 164

Americans, Old: as early settlers, 14; in Isanti, 160–61, 162, 170, 176, 196, 224; agricultural preferences of, 197–203, 272; as agricultural innovators, 200, 206; political influence of, 227; eco-nomic influence of, 240; and land inheritance, 267, 272

Amungen, lake, 46

Ancylus, lake, 70, 72–73

Anderson, D. O., 251

Andersson, Ollas Hans, 143, 145–46

Andersson, Stor Ollas Olof. *See* Wicklund, Olof A.

Anoka, Minnesota, 193, 254

Anoka Sand Plain, 168, 169, 177

Arvika, Sweden, 6

Assimilation: stages of, 226; in Isanti, 226–28, 241–42, 279

Athens Free (Mission) Church: mentioned, 182, 221–22; trans-Atlantic connections of, 280–81, 306–7

Athens Lutheran Church: founding of, 9; mentioned, 182

secession from Cambridge Lutheran, 219–20, 221; altar painting of, 307

Athens township: settlement of, 8, 174, 175, 177–80; original soils and vegetation of, 177; land alienation in, 178; land speculation in, 178; railroad lands in, 178, 189; social clustering in, 180–83; marriage patterns and kinship networks in, 232–33

Attmar parish: inheritance practices in, 273–76

Augustana Lutheran Synod, 213–14

Bäck village: soils of, 75

Backa village: emigration from, 151; creamery in, 292

Bäcklin, Hans Ersson: mentioned, 7; emigration of, 109, 122; assistance to other immigrants, 173–74

Backstugusittare. See Cottagers

Baptist Church of Cambridge: founding of,